Measures of Spirituality/Religiosity (2018)

Measures of Spirituality/Religiosity (2018)

Special Issue Editor
Arndt Büssing

MDPI • Basel • Beijing • Wuhan • Barcelona • Belgrade

Special Issue Editor
Arndt Büssing
Witten/Herdecke University
Germany

Editorial Office
MDPI
St. Alban-Anlage 66
4052 Basel, Switzerland

This is a reprint of articles from the Special Issue published online in the open access journal *Religions* (ISSN 2077-1444) from 2017 to 2019 (available at: https://www.mdpi.com/journal/religions/special_issues/Measure)

For citation purposes, cite each article independently as indicated on the article page online and as indicated below:

LastName, A.A.; LastName, B.B.; LastName, C.C. Article Title. *Journal Name* **Year**, *Article Number*, Page Range.

ISBN 978-3-03897-932-6 (Pbk)
ISBN 978-3-03897-933-3 (PDF)

Cover image courtesy of pexels.com user Colin Smitt.

© 2019 by the authors. Articles in this book are Open Access and distributed under the Creative Commons Attribution (CC BY) license, which allows users to download, copy and build upon published articles, as long as the author and publisher are properly credited, which ensures maximum dissemination and a wider impact of our publications.

The book as a whole is distributed by MDPI under the terms and conditions of the Creative Commons license CC BY-NC-ND.

Contents

About the Special Issue Editor vii

Arndt Büssing
Introduction of the Special Issue "Measures of Spirituality/Religiosity (2018)"
Reprinted from: *Religions* **2019**, *10*, 214, doi:10.3390/rel10030214 1

Philip Austin, Jessica Macdonald and Roderick MacLeod
Measuring Spirituality and Religiosity in Clinical Settings: A Scoping Review of Available Instruments
Reprinted from: *Religions* **2018**, *9*, 70, doi:10.3390/rel9030070 2

Arndt Büssing, Daniela Rodrigues Recchia, Harold Koenig, Klaus Baumann and Eckhard Frick
Factor Structure of the Spiritual Needs Questionnaire (SpNQ) in Persons with Chronic Diseases, Elderly and Healthy Individuals
Reprinted from: *Religions* **2018**, *9*, 13, doi:10.3390/rel9010013 16

Aisha Kashif and Zaira Kanwal
Translation, Cultural Adaptation of Spiritual Needs Questionnaire in Pakistan
Reprinted from: *Religions* **2018**, *9*, 163, doi:10.3390/rel9050163 27

Tânia Cristina de Oliveira Valente, Ana Paula Rodrigues Cavalcanti, Arndt Büssing, Clóvis Pereira da Costa Junior and Rogerio Neves Motta
Transcultural Adaptation and Psychometric Properties of Portuguese Version of the Spiritual Needs Questionnaire (SpNQ) Among HIV Positive Patients in Brazil
Reprinted from: *Religions* **2018**, *9*, 135, doi:10.3390/rel9040135 35

Seyma N. Saritoprak, Julie J. Exline and Nick Stauner
Spiritual Jihad among U.S. Muslims: Preliminary Measurement and Associations with Well-Being and Growth
Reprinted from: *Religions* **2018**, *9*, 158, doi:10.3390/rel9050158 45

Olga Riklikiene, Snieguole Kaseliene and John Fisher
Translation and Validation of Spiritual Well-Being Questionnaire SHALOM in Lithuanian Language, Culture and Health Care Practice
Reprinted from: *Religions* **2018**, *9*, 156, doi:10.3390/rel9050156 67

Hartmut August, Mary Rute G. Esperandio and Fabiana Thiele Escudero
Brazilian Validation of the Attachment to God Inventory (IAD-Br)
Reprinted from: *Religions* **2018**, *9*, 103, doi:10.3390/rel9040103 81

Rito Baring, Philip Joseph Sarmiento, Nestor Sibug, Paolo Lumanlan, Benita Bonus, Cristina Samia and Stephen Reysen
Filipino College Students' Attitudes towards Religion: An Analysis of the Underlying Factors
Reprinted from: *Religions* **2018**, *9*, 85, doi:10.3390/rel9030085 102

Arndt Büssing, Daniela R. Recchia, Mareike Gerundt, Markus Warode and Thomas Dienberg
Validation of the SpREUK—Religious Practices Questionnaire as a Measure of Christian Religious Practices in a General Population and in Religious Persons
Reprinted from: *Religions* **2017**, *8*, 269, doi:10.3390/rel8120269 116

Arndt Büssing, Markus Warode, Mareike Gerundt and Thomas Dienberg
Validation of a Novel Instrument to Measure Elements of Franciscan-Inspired Spirituality in a General Population and in Religious Persons
Reprinted from: *Religions* **2017**, *8*, 197, doi:10.3390/rel8090197 . . . . **132**

Arndt Büssing, Daniela R. Recchia and Klaus Baumann
Validation of the Gratitude/Awe Questionnaire and Its Association with Disposition of Gratefulness
Reprinted from: *Religions* **2018**, *9*, 117, doi:10.3390/rel9040117 . . . . **146**

Harold G. Koenig
Measuring Symptoms of Moral Injury in Veterans and Active Duty Military with PTSD
Reprinted from: *Religions* **2018**, *9*, 86, doi:10.3390/rel9030086 . . . . **157**

About the Special Issue Editor

Arndt Büssing (*1962) is a medical doctor and full professor for "Quality of Life, Spirituality and Coping" at the Witten/Herdecke University (Germany) since 2010. His research interests are (1) empirical studies on quality of life, spirituality and coping (i.e., spirituality as a resource to cope; spiritual needs; spiritual dryness), (2) non-pharmacological integrative medicine interventions to treat patients with chronic diseases (i.e., meditation, yoga), and (3) questionnaire development specifically in the field of spirituality and coping.

Editorial

Introduction of the Special Issue "Measures of Spirituality/Religiosity (2018)"

Arndt Büssing

Professorship Quality of Life, Spirituality and Coping, Faculty of Health, Witten/Herdecke University, Gerhard-Kienle-Weg 4, 58313 Herdecke, Germany; Arndt.Buessing@uni-wh.de

Received: 15 March 2019; Accepted: 18 March 2019; Published: 21 March 2019

The interest in the topic of spirituality as a more or less independent dimension of quality of life is continuously growing. Furthermore, the research questions in this topic have started to change because also the fields of religiosity are changing, becoming more diverse and pluralistic. To address the new topics in health research, one may rely on standardized questionnaires. Several of these new questions cannot be easily answered with the instruments designed for previous questions and thus, new instruments need to be constantly developed. There is a growing number of instruments intended to measure specific aspects of spirituality and they are difficult to value particularly the new ones.

This special issue intends to focus on some of the already established instruments (and to update the knowledge or adaptation to different languages and cultures) and describe the features and intentions of newly developed instruments, which may be potentially used in larger studies to obtain knowledge that is relevant to spiritual care and practice. Some of these are rather 'inclusive' (also embracing secular concepts of spirituality and may thus be less specific) and others are rather 'exclusive' (or specific for circumscribed religious groups and thus, not suited for varying denominations or non-religious persons). This issue should become a resource of relevant instruments in the wide range of organized religiosity, the individual experience of the divine and the open approach in the search for meaning and purpose in life.

Conflicts of Interest: The author declares no conflict of interest.

 © 2019 by the author. Licensee MDPI, Basel, Switzerland. This article is an open access article distributed under the terms and conditions of the Creative Commons Attribution (CC BY) license (http://creativecommons.org/licenses/by/4.0/).

Review

Measuring Spirituality and Religiosity in Clinical Settings: A Scoping Review of Available Instruments

Philip Austin [1,*], Jessica Macdonald [2] and Roderick MacLeod [2,3]

[1] Department of Pain Management, HammondCare, Greenwich 2065, Australia
[2] Department of Palliative Care, HammondCare, Greenwich 2065, Australia; jessica.macdonald84@gmail.com
[3] Medical School-Northern, The University of Sydney, St Leonard's 2065, Australia; rmacleod@hammond.com.au
* Correspondence: paustin@hammond.com.au

Received: 22 February 2018; Accepted: 28 February 2018; Published: 4 March 2018

Abstract: Aims: Numerous measures exist that assess dimensions of spirituality and religiosity in health, theological and social settings. In this review, we aim to identify and evaluate measures assessing factors relating to spirituality and religiosity in clinical settings. Methods: A systematic literature search was conducted using PubMed, EMBASE and PsycINFO databases with search terms relating to spirituality, religiosity that also included well-being, needs, distress and beliefs used in self-reporting and clinician-administered measures. Only articles relating to the validation and subsequent administration of measures used in clinical settings were eligible for review. Results: Of 75 measures selected for initial screening, 25 had been validated and used in clinical settings and were reviewed for this study. Most measures were validated in oncological and palliative care settings where the Functional Assessment of Chronic Illness Therapy Spiritual Well-being (FACIT-Sp12) and the World Health Organization Quality of Life Spiritual, Religious and Personal Beliefs (WHOQOL-SRPB) were most validated and frequently used. Only six measures were found that assessed spiritual distress and/or the needs of which only two had been investigated more than twice. Two measures assessing spirituality and religious beliefs in healthcare staff were also reviewed. Conclusions: This review provides a current summary of measures evaluating several dimensions of spirituality and religiosity used in clinical settings. Currently there is a lack of reliable measures evaluating spiritual needs and distress.

Keywords: spirituality; spiritual well-being; religiosity; religious beliefs; clinical setting; evaluation; measurement; scoping review

1. Introduction

Recently, associations between spirituality, religion, health and quality of life have been investigated in many areas of healthcare including general medicine, psychology and nursing. Spirituality and religiosity are intricate constructs that describe peoples' fundamental beliefs about existence that form attitudes and behavior across many different cultures (Baumsteiger and Chenneville 2015). Generally, studies show that people with higher levels of spirituality and religiosity have lower levels of depression and anxiety, improved quality of life, a higher pain tolerance and a lower prevalence of chronic disease (Lucchetti et al. 2013; Koenig 2009; Koenig 2012). Additionally, spiritual and religious people show strong humanitarian attitudes while also interacting in large social networks (Becker and Dhingra 2001). Although spirituality and religion are closely related, definitions differ and as such for the purposes of measurement can be considered as two separate constructs. Religiosity is often defined as the adherence to beliefs, doctrines, ethics, rituals, texts and practices associated with a higher power either alone or among organized groups (Hood and Spilka 2003). Alternatively, spirituality is defined as a set of inner experiences and feelings through which a person inwardly seeks meaning and purpose as well as relationships to self, family, others, society, nature and the significant or sacred (Baumsteiger and Chenneville 2015; Austin et al. 2017). Although there is some overlap in definitions where many believe spirituality to encompass religious practices, studies investigating opinion suggest both religious leaders and laypeople consider religion as beliefs based on rules associated with organized practice whereas spirituality is more personal, internal and independent of communal relationships (Hyman and Handal 2006; Zimmer et al. 2016).

Given these definitions, it is not surprising that religion and spirituality have been identified as important coping resources for patients during times of chronic and terminal illness. Here, patients often think about their life, its meaning and the experience of the disease process especially in times of anxiety, pain, loneliness and deprivation, all which challenge ideals and beliefs (Austin et al. 2017). Recent studies show differences in self-reported spirituality and religiosity towards these negative emotional experiences. For example, MacLeod and colleagues show that strong religious beliefs are associated with high levels of anxiety in people thinking about their own death compared to those with strong spiritual beliefs who show significantly lower levels of anxiety about their own death (MacLeod et al. 2017). Cotton and coworkers also show differences in the meaning of religion and spirituality when characterizing these belief systems in a large and diverse sample of HIV/AIDS patients. Here they found that those patients used their religion/spirituality to cope with difficult situations such as guilt, shame and bereavement associated with the disease that in turn were associated with improvements in life satisfaction and self-rated health (Cotton et al. 2006). Given these findings, it is important to be aware the effect of potentially life-threatening diagnoses can have on a person's ability to cope with religious and spiritual issues during clinical meetings. Thus, health professionals must have the emotional, social and spiritual resources to both evaluate and carry out their work both individually and as part of a multi-disciplinary team.

However, to offer spiritual and religious interventions, evidence-based, valid assessments or measures must be available in clinical settings. Additionally, definitions of religion and more-so spirituality in the context of healthcare vary greatly where in simplistic terms they describe spirituality as good and religion as bad. Such definitions overlook the potentially helpful and harmful effects of religious and spiritual interventions (Hill and Pargament 2003). Moreover, it is also unknown if and what measures are applicable in clinical settings to assess levels of religious and/or spiritual distress and thus appropriate intervention (Puchalski et al. 2009). Although several authors have reviewed the concepts and implications of religion and spirituality in clinical and healthcare research settings (Monod et al. 2011), none have addressed the range, classification or the validity of available measures to reliably assess these constructs. In a systematic review, Monod and colleagues identified 35 measures evaluating general spirituality, spiritual well-being and spiritual coping. However, 35% of selected measures had only been studied within clinical settings with the remaining being investigated in social, theological and psychiatric settings. Thus, the purpose of this study is to provide a scoping review of measures currently used to identify and evaluate levels of spirituality, spiritual well-being, spiritual distress and religion in clinical settings.

2. Methods

Our scoping review was conducted using a framework defined by Colquhoun and colleagues as "a form of knowledge synthesis that addresses an exploratory research question aimed at mapping key concepts, types of evidence and gaps in research related to a defined area or field by systematically searching, selecting and synthesizing existing knowledge (Colquhoun et al. 2014). The research question for this review is "Do current instruments identify and evaluate levels of spirituality, religiosity spiritual needs and distress in clinical settings?" PubMed, EMBASE and PsycINFO databases were searched in December 2017 (Table 1). Eligibility criteria required publications to (a) relate to instrument development and validation and use thereafter; (b) that instruments were applicable to clinical settings and (c) Acceptance of English and non-English articles. Due to the volume of articles describing the use of self-reporting measures relating to our specific areas of interest, and the time-scale allowed for searching and evaluating located articles, as recommended by Mateen and colleagues we screened for keywords in titles of publications (Mateen et al. 2013). Once measures were selected, we modified our search protocols to search both titles and abstract using the name of the measure to locate and verify the number of investigations within clinical settings.

Table 1. Keywords used in the location of articles investigating the use of measures evaluating spirituality, Spiritual well-being, spiritual distress, religiosity and religious beliefs.

PubMed	EMBASE	PsycINFO
Keywords limits • Advanced search—"Title" • Boolean search—"AND"	**Keywords limits** • Multifield search—"Title" • Boolean search—"AND" • Exclude Medline journals	**Keyword limits** • Multifield search—"Title" • Boolean search—"AND" • Peer-review only
AND		
Keywords Spirituality Spiritual well-being Spiritual distress Spiritual needs Religiosity Religious beliefs		**Keywords** Scale Measure Instrument Index Inventory Questionnaire

3. Results

Using the above search protocols, we located 386 articles relating to the use and validation of measures evaluating spirituality and religiosity/religious beliefs in a variety of settings. We then selected articles for initial screening that related to the development, validation and subsequent use of self-reporting measures specific to spirituality, spiritual well-being, spiritual distress, spiritual needs, religiosity and religious beliefs (n-156). After removing all duplicates, 121 articles were selected for further evaluation. Of remaining articles, 72 investigated spirituality and religiosity in clinical settings, 16 in psychiatric clinical settings and 33 in social settings (Figure 1). Overall, we identified 25 measures used in a variety of clinical settings and 30 measures used in psychiatric, theological and social settings. For the purposes of this study, we shall briefly review measure of spirituality, spiritual well-being, religiosity, religious beliefs, spiritual distress and spiritual needs used in clinical settings (Tables 2 and 3).

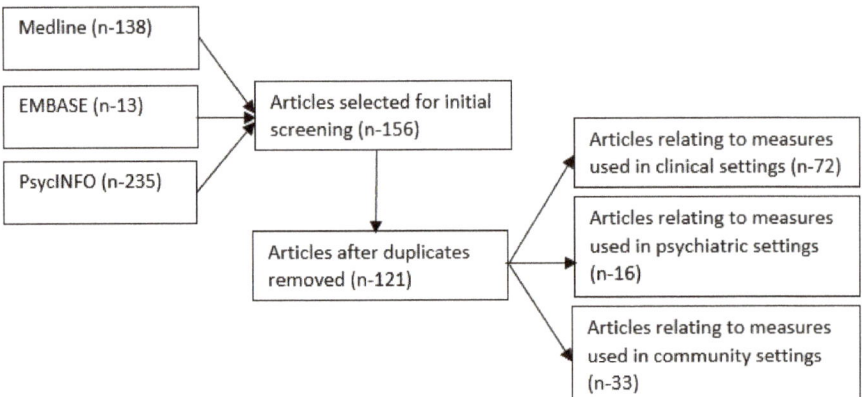

Figure 1. Search flow chart showing total numbers of articles located and screen for review.

Table 2. Spirituality, spiritual well-being, religiosity and religious beliefs measures used in clinical settings.

Authors	Instrument Name	Sample Size	Type of Study	Findings
Daaleman and Frey 2004	The Spirituality Index of Well-Being (SIWB)	523 outpatients from family practice	Factor analysis/test–retest reliability	Correlations with quality of life, health status and depression
Kaczorowski 1989	The Spiritual Well-Being Scale	114 cancer patients	Cross-sectional	Inverse correlations between low levels of spiritual well-being and high levels of anxiety
Peterman et al. 2014	The Functional Assessment of Chronic Illness Therapy—Spiritual Well-Being (FACIT-Sp)	2923 cancer and HIV patients	Factor analysis and Observational	Strong internal consistency and moderate to strong correlations between FACIT-Sp and quality of life, especially meaning and peace
De Camargos et al. 2015	WHOQOL-SRPB	525 oncology patients / 525 health professionals	Cross-sectional	Daily use of spiritual and religious resources positively effects patient perceptions of QOL
Bussing and Koenig 2008	BENEFIT Scale	229 chronic pain patients	Reliability and validation	The BENEFIT scale correlates uniquely with spiritual and religious attitudes in clinical studies
Vivat et al. 2017	EORTIC QLC-SWB32	451 palliative care patients from 14 countries	Validation	The EORTIC QLC-SWB32 measures distinct aspects of QOL
Bussing et al. 2016	SpREUK	275 cancer patients	Factor analysis and reliability	A valid measure of important aspects of spirituality and religious attitudes
Kreitzer et al. 2009	Brief Serenity Scale	87 post solid organ transplant patients	Factor analysis and reliability	The Brief Serenity Scale captures dimensions of spirituality, a state of acceptance, inner haven and trust that is distinct from other spirituality instruments
Delaney 2005	The Spirituality Scale	226 patients with chronic illness	Reliability and validation	The Spirituality Scale provides a 3-factor framework (self-discovery, relationships and eco-awareness) that help with nursing care
Ironson et al. 2002	The Ironson–Woods Spirituality/Religiosity Index	279 HIV positive patients and long-term AIDS survivors	Reliability and validation	Long-term survival related to frequency of positive prayer and non-judgmental attitudes
Johnstone et al. 2016	The Brief Multidimensional Measure of Religiousness/Spirituality (BMMRS)	109 traumatic brain injury patients	Factor analysis	The BMMRS is a valid measure of emotional connectedness with higher power and social support among different spiritual and religious variables
Hatch et al. 1998	The Spiritual Involvement and Beliefs Scale	50 primary care patients and 23 family practice educators	Factor analysis	The SIBS shows that included terms avoid cultural and religious bias in both beliefs and actions
McBride et al. 1998b	The Brief Pictorial Instrument for Assessing Spirituality	442 family practice patients	Reliability and validation	The pictorial instrument provides a quick assessment of intrinsic spirituality correlating with other spirituality measures
VandeCreek et al. 1995	The Index of Core Spiritual Experience (INSPIRIT)	371 medical and surgical outpatients	Reliability and validation	INSPIRIT assessment reflects intrinsic religiosity and spirituality
Kimura et al. 2012	The Daily Spiritual Experience Scale DSES)	179 surgical patients	Cultural adaptation and validation	The DSES shows evidence of reliability and validity in assessing spiritual experiences among hospitalized patients
Gherghina et al. 2014	The Spiritual Distress Assessment Tool (SDAT)	72 elderly erioperative patients	Validation	The SDAT appears to be a reliable and valid instrument to assess spiritual distress in elderly hospitalized patients
Chiang et al. 2017	The Religious Belief Scale	619 clinical nurses	Factor analysis	A reliable and valid scale for measuring religious beliefs of nurses
McSherry et al. 2002	The Spirituality and Spiritual Care Rating Scale	549 ward-based nurses	Factor analysis	Factors identified: spirituality, spiritual care, religiosity and personal care
Kouloulias et al. 2017	The QRFPC-25	156 cancer patients undergoing radiotherapy	Reliability and validation	A reliable and valid gauge for assessment of religiosity in cancer patients

Table 3. Spiritual needs and spiritual distress measures used in clinical settings.

Bussing et al. 2018	Spiritual Needs Questionnaire	627 chronic disease patients 940 elderly ill patients 1468 healthy adults	Factor analysis and reliability	This large study provides evidence for a cultural and religious sensitive measure that evaluates peoples spiritual needs
Ku et al. 2010	The Spiritual Distress Scale (SDS)	85 cancer patients	Factor analysis	The SDS is both reliable and valid in assessing patients in oncological settings and aids nurses in the assessment of spiritual distress
Astrow et al. 2015	The Spiritual Needs Assessment for Patients (SNAP)	727 haematology and cancer patients	Observational and validation	SNAP is reliable and valid in measuring spiritual needs in patients from different cultural and religious backgrounds
Buck and McMillan 2012	The Spiritual Needs Inventory (SNI)	410 cancer patient caregivers	Reliability and Validity	Use of the SNI in hospice caregivers can aid nurses in the identification of patients' spiritual needs
Monod et al. 2010	The Spiritual Needs Assessment Tool (SDAT)	203 Geriatric rehabilitation patients	Reliability and Validity	The SDAT shows adequate reliability and validity in assessing levels of spiritual distress
Fischbeck et al. 2013	The Advanced Cancer Patients' Distress Scale	168 advanced cancer patients	Factor analysis	Initially shown to be reliable in identifying patients spiritual needs

4. Self-Reporting Measures (Spiritual and Religious Well-Being)

Nearly all measures were validated in oncological and palliative care settings. The instrument validated in the largest clinical population was the FACIT-Sp12. This 12-item measure consists of three factors, those being meaning, peace and faith and has been designed to be used specifically in healthcare settings in people with chronic and life-threatening conditions. The FACIT-Sp12 was initially validated in a population of 1617 cancer patients to determine structure and initial validity of the questionnaire and second in 131 cancer patients to establish reliability (Peterman et al. 2002). More recently, in a larger study, the FACIT-Sp12 has also been used to examine spiritual well-being in nearly 9000 cancer survivors across the United States (Munoz et al. 201). Overall, the FACIT-Sp12 one of the most commonly used is shown to be a brief, reliable and probably the most valid measure of spirituality in quality of life in both religious and nonreligious people.

Although the WHOQOL-SRPB has been well-validated in social settings across 18 different countries (WHOQOL SRPB Group 2006), it has only recently been validated and used regularly within clinical settings. Here we found one study where Rusa and colleagues evaluated both the WHOQOL-SRPB and its short-form version; the WHOQOL-SRPB BREF in 110 chronic kidney disease patients undergoing hemodialysis (Rusa et al. 2014). The authors found that most participants showed high spirituality, religion and personal belief scores, especially in those where their disease was well-controlled. Patients whose disease hemodialysis was not well controlled showed lower scores and, thus less able to cope with chronic kidney failure.

The Spiritual Well-Being Scale (SWBS) was initially validated among social (Genia 2001) and psychiatric settings (Fernander et al. 2004). However, this measure is now being used within clinical settings and has been translated into several different languages such as Persian and Thai. Recently, for example, Ghodsbin and coworkers used the SWBS to show improvements in spiritual well-being in 90 coronary artery disease patients during a positive thinking training compared to a control group (Ghodsbin et al. 2015).

The Spirituality Index of Well-Being (SIWB) is also considered one of the more valid measures for the assessment of patients' current spiritual state (Monod et al. 2011). This measure is a 20-item instrument consists of two subscales relating to religious and existential well-being (Daaleman and Frey 2004). However, although this measure was initially validated in 509 adult outpatients at 10 city primary care clinics, it is not widely used. The SIWB shows associations in health and well-being constructs across primary care and geriatric outpatient settings (Daaleman et al. 2002) and has recently been translated into Chinese (Wu et al. 2017).

The 26-item Spiritual Involvement and Beliefs Scale (SIBS) was initially validated in primary care settings to assess levels of spiritual beliefs and practice (Hatch et al. 1998). However, the SIBS has been mostly been used in palliative care settings. Here, for example in the same cohort of 82 cancer patients, Mystakidou and colleagues produced four studies investigating relationships between spirituality and mood disorders (Mystakidou et al. 2007), predictors of spirituality in advanced cancer (Mystakidou et al. 2006, 2008a) and at the end of life (Mystakidou et al. 2008b).

5. Self-Reporting Measures (Spiritual Needs and Distress)

Our search protocols show The Spiritual Needs Questionnaire (SpNQ) to be the most widely used measure assessing patients' spiritual needs. Büssing and colleagues developed this measure in a heterogeneous sample of 210 German patients with chronic pain conditions and cancer (Büssing et al. 2010). However, at the time of writing our review, Büssing and colleagues further published an article increasing the validity of this measure by examining the structure of the SpNQ in a large sample of ill and healthy younger and elderly adults (n-2095) (Büssing et al. 2018). The SpNQ has also been translated into several languages including Chinese (Bussing et al. 2013a) and Persian (Moeini et al. 2018).

The Spiritual Distress Scale was the only self-reporting measure we located evaluating levels of spiritual distress in clinical settings. Originally developed in Chinese by Ku and colleagues in 2010 (Ku et al. 2010), it has since been translated and validated into Portuguese (Simao et al. 2016). Although only two studies have used this questionnaire, both sets of authors suggest that an internationally validated self-reporting measure assessing spiritual distress is needed, especially in the recognition of this phenomenon in clinical practice.

The Spiritual Needs Assessment for Patients (SNAP) is a 23-item instrument with domains assessing psychosocial, spiritual and religious needs. Here Sharma and colleagues initially validated SNAP in 47 ambulatory cancer patients from many different religious and cultural backgrounds and shown to be a valid measure of spiritual needs diverse patient populations (Sharma et al. 2012). Recently, SNAP has been translated into Chinese (Astrow et al. 2012) and Portuguese (De Araujo Toloi et al. 2016a, 2016b).

Several other spirituality/spiritual well-being/spiritual needs/spiritual distress measures have also been used within clinical setting, but only on three or less occasions. These include:

- The BENEFIT Through spirituality/religiosity scale (chronic diseases and spinal cord injury) (Bussing and Koenig 2008; Xue et al. 2016),
- The Brief Pictorial Instrument for Assessing Spirituality (primary care patients) (McBride et al. 1998b),
- The Spirituality Scale (cardiovascular disease and chronic disease patients) (Delaney 2005; Delaney et al. 2011),
- The Index of Core Spiritual Experience (primary care and hospital outpatients) (McBride et al. 1998a; VandeCreek et al. 1995),
- The Ironson–Wood Spirituality/Religiosity Index (HIV and chronic heart failure patients) (Bekelman et al. 2010; Ironson et al. 2002; Mistretta et al. 2017)
- The Brief Multidimensional Measure of Religion and Spirituality (hospital inpatients) (Curcio et al. 2015; Johnstone et al. 2009)
- The Daily Spiritual Experience Scale (surgical, hospice care and HIV patients) (Kimura et al. 2012; Oji et al. 2017; Steinhauser et al. 2008)
- The Brief Serenity Scale (post-transplant patients (Kreitzer et al. 2009)
- The Spiritual Needs Inventory (Hermann 2006; Buck and McMillan 2012)
- The Spiritual Distress Assessment Tool (SDAT) (Monod et al. 2010, 2012a)

- The Advance Cancer Patients' Distress Scale (Fischbeck et al. 2013)
- The Spiritual Care Competence Scale (Van Leeuwen et al. 2009)

Very recently, just before the application of our search protocols, two spirituality/religiosity measures gained validation, both in cancer care. First the QRFPC25, a measure of religiosity and spirituality was validated and shown to be reliable in 156 people with neoplastic disease (Kouloulias et al. 2017). In a larger study, the European Organization for Research and Treatment of Cancer Quality of Life Group Spiritual Well-being-32 (EORTC QLQ-SWB32) was validated in 451 palliative care patients from 14 countries (Vivat et al. 2017).

6. Clinician-Administered Measures

Monod and colleagues developed an a spiritual distress assessment tool (SDAT) designed to evaluate spiritual distress in hospitalized older patients using the hypothesis that the greater the degree to which spiritual needs are not met, the greater the level of spiritual distress (Monod et al. 2012b). This measure has four factors, those being meaning (orientation in life), transcendence (relationships with an external foundation), values (determination of goodness and trueness) and psycho-social identity (patient's environment). This clinician administered measure has so far showed to be reliable and valid in both hospital rehabilitation and perioperative hospital settings (Monod et al. 2012b; Gherghina et al. 2014).

7. Self-Reporting Tools Assessing Healthcare Staff Understanding of Spirituality and Spiritual Care

We located two measures that establish how people working in health care perceive spiritualty and spiritual care. The Spirituality and Spiritual Care Rating Scale (SSCRS) was developed by McSherry and colleagues to evaluate how nurses perceive spirituality and spiritual care (McSherry et al. 2002). However, this measure has now been translated into several languages (Fallahi Khoshknab et al. 2010; Wu and Lin 2011) and has also been evaluated amongst clinicians, physiotherapists and ancillary workers who have regular contact with patients (Austin et al. 2017). The second measure was validated at the time of writing up this review. Here, the Religious Belief Scale was developed to assess religious beliefs of nurses in order to determine their competence in providing spiritual care to patients. Exploratory factor analysis showed a 17-item scale with four factors: religious effects, divine, religious query and religious stress and was provisionally reliable and valid in measuring religious beliefs in Taiwanese nurses (Chiang et al. 2017).

8. Discussion

This scoping review identified 25 measures used to evaluate levels of spirituality, spiritual well-being, spiritual distress, spiritual needs, religiosity and religious beliefs in clinical settings. This review aimed to continue the earlier work of Monod and colleagues (Monod et al. 2011) in identifying more recently validated measures, while also refining the location of measures to those specifically validated and used in clinical settings. The latter aim of this review is relevant as many more (n-30) spiritual and religious measures were located but were validated and applied in psychiatric, theological and social settings and thus it is not known if they are reliable or valid in clinical settings.

Nearly all measures assess patients' current spiritual state or current levels of religiosity, the most widely utilized being the FACIT-Sp 12, the WHOQOL-SRPB, the SIWB and more recently, the EORTC QLQ-SWB32. However, from our results, of the 25 accepted measures, only six assess spiritual needs or distress, where only two have been applied in clinical studies twice or more, those being the Spiritual Needs Questionnaire (Büssing et al. 2010) and the Spiritual Distress Scale (Ku et al. 2010). These findings raise important questions as to the relevance of measures assessing current levels of spirituality/religiosity and the relevance of outcomes determined as a result. Puchalski partially answers these questions in her paper describing the role of spirituality in health care (Puchalski 2001). Here, she describes how spirituality is shown to reduce mortality, aids in the ability to cope with illness, pain and life stresses, while also helping to boost recovery from illness and surgery. However, probably the most important statement from her article relates to the importance of understanding patients' spirituality in relation to whole patient care and subsequent health care decisions.

Although, these observations help to gain insight toward correlations between levels of spiritual and religious well-being and the ability to cope and understand their illness from a spiritual/religious perspective, most measures do not assess spiritual needs and levels of spiritual distress. Our observations are similar to Monod and colleagues who rightly suggest that an absence of spiritual well-being is unlikely to equate to a state of spiritual distress (Monod et al. 2011). Furthermore, we found no clinician-administered measures evaluating behaviors associated with spiritual distress. This is also an important finding as although several measure exist evaluating healthcare professionals' understanding of spirituality and spiritual care (Chiang et al. 2017; McSherry et al. 2002), none contain items describing behavior associated with spiritual needs and distress. This deficit was highlighted by Highfield and Carson who found that nurses recognized only five of 31 behaviors, where four of the five contained direct references to God. More recently, Austin and colleagues in a study investigating the ability of clinical and non-clinical staff to recognize patients' spiritual needs showed that although participants were able to recognize written examples of spiritual needs, the majority felt unable to neither recognize nor deal with such needs (Austin et al. 2016, 2017). Such findings suggest that although acquiring information on different areas of spirituality and religiousness in clinical settings is useful, the practical application of this information remains unclear. Thus, as suggested by several authors, in order to make best use of these data concerning effective patient care, spiritual care training is required for both health care staff who administer such measures and staff who have regular contact with patients (Cetinkaya et al. 2013; Balboni et al. 2013; Rasinski et al. 2011).

Interestingly, several measures have recently been developed that examine more specific forms of spiritual distress that may be beneficial for application in clinical settings. Here, constructs such as "spiritual struggle" developed by Exline and colleagues (Exline et al. 2014), a form of inner crisis known as "spiritual dryness" conceived and developed by Büssing and colleagues (Büssing et al. 2013b) and Koenig's "moral injury" (Koenig et al. 2017) have been validated in a number of social setting but may also have relevance in clinical settings when attempting to more accurately identify specific forms of spiritual distress such as burnout and inner peace needs.

Our review, like that of Monod and colleagues in 2011 shows that although there is an abundance of available spiritual and religious measures, there is inadequate data on the psychometric properties for most. This is due mainly to the lack of test–retest reliability and subsequently, predictive validity due to the seldom use of many questionnaires. Additionally, sample size in many validation and factor analysis studies were small, thus lowering the statistical power and the true outcome of these measures. Moreover, most measures evaluate a combination of both spiritual and religious factors while only one measure uniquely assessed religiosity (Chiang et al. 2017). Given the differences in definition and significant differences in attitudes between people who are spiritual compared to those who are religious, we suggest the development of novel religious measures or the validation of those previously used in psychiatric, theological and social settings in clinical settings are required.

Our scoping review had two limitations. First, our search protocols were limited to multiple field searching of keywords in titles only using three databases. Before committing to these search methods, we validated our approach by following the work of Mateen and colleagues who show a titles-only approach to be an efficient method for screening articles in a systematic review (Mateen et al. 2013). However, we, like Mateen and colleagues found that although there was lower search precision, the number of measures located were acceptable. Second, we searched databases associated with clinical and medical research data and thus missed relevant journals whose main focus are religion and spirituality. Here, for example we located two studies investigating the use of the BENEFIT scale and SpNQ, however, several further articles (Büssing and Recchia 2016; Büssing and Koenig 2010; Büssing et al. 2013c) were published in journals not cited by PubMed, EMBASE and PsycINFO. Additionally, several measures although not used in clinical settings were evaluated in samples such as stressed soldiers, mothers of sick children and elderly people in care homes whose data would have benefited our review (Büssing and Recchia 2016; Erichsen and Büssing 2013; Büssing et al. 2017). Our scoping review also had several strengths. First, our literature search was focused only on those measures used in clinical settings and thus useful for physicians when trying to determine which instruments to use during clinical assessment. Although, measures validated and applied in psychiatric, social and theological settings may be useful in clinical settings, they were excluded from this review. Second, once measures were accepted, we expanded our protocols to search the name of each measure using "titles and abstracts" to identify and given an indication of validity and reliability, the number of translations to different languages and the number times applied within clinical settings.

9. Conclusions

This scoping review provides a current summary on self-reporting and clinician-administered measures used in clinical settings. These measures evaluate several dimensions of spirituality and religiosity that include well-being, beliefs, needs and distress. Importantly, we show a current lack of reliable measures evaluating spiritual needs and distress where outcomes will assist in the spiritual care of patients. Here, our findings suggest that studies are required to develop (a) clinician-administered measures evaluating spiritual needs and distress and (b) further develop self-reporting measures evaluating spiritual needs and distress.

Author Contributions: Philip Austin and Roderick MacLeod conceived and designed the scoping review; Philip Austin and Jessica Macdonald performed the scoping review; Philip Austin and Jessica Macdonald analyzed the data; Philip Austin wrote the paper.

Conflicts of Interest: The authors declare no conflict of interest.

References

Astrow, Alan B., Rashmi K. Sharma, Yiwu Huang, Yiquing Xu, and Daniel P. Sulmasy. 2012. A Chinese version of the Spiritual Needs Assessment for patients survey instrument. *Journal of Palliative Medicine* 15: 1297–315. [CrossRef] [PubMed]

Astrow, Alan B., Gary Kwok, Rashmi K. Sharma, and Daniel Sulmasy. 2015. Spiritual needs and patient satisfaction in multi-cultural patient population. *Journal of Clinical Oncology* 33: e20589.

Austin, Philip D., Roderick Macleod, Philip J. Siddall, Wilf McSherry, and Richard Egan. 2016. The Ability of Hospital Staff to Recognize and Meet Patients' Spiritual Needs: A Pilot Study. *Journal for the Study of Spirituality* 6: 20–37. [CrossRef]

Austin, Philip, Roderick Macleod, Philip Siddall, Wilf McSherry, and Richard Egan. 2017. Spiritual care training is needed for clinical and non-clinical staff to manage patients' spiritual needs. *Journal for the Study of Spirituality* 7: 50–63. [CrossRef]

Balboni, Michael J., Adam Sullivan, Adaugo Amobi, Andrea C. Phelps, Daniel P. Gorman, Angelika Zollfrank, John R. Peteet, Holly G. Prigerson, Tyler J. VanderWeele, and Tracy A. Balboni. 2013. Why is spiritual care infrequent at the end of life? Spiritual care perceptions among patients, nurses, and physicians and the role of training. *Journal of Clinical Oncology* 31: 461–67. [CrossRef]

Baumsteiger, Rachel, and Tiffany Chenneville. 2015. Challenges to the Conceptualization and Measurement of Religiosity and Spirituality in Mental Health Research. *Journal of Religion and Health* 54: 2344–54. [CrossRef] [PubMed]

Becker, Penny Edgell, and Pawan H. Dhingra. 2001. Religious involvement and volunteering: Implications for civil society. *Sociology of Religion* 62: 315–35. [CrossRef]

Bekelman, David B., Carla Parry, Farr A. Curlin, Traci E. Yamashita, Diane L. Fairclough, and Frederick S. Wamboldt. 2010. A comparison of two spirituality instruments and their relationship with depression and quality of life in chronic heart failure. *Journal of Pain and Symptom Management* 39: 515–26. [CrossRef] [PubMed]

Buck, Harleah G., and Susan C. McMillan. 2012. A psychometric analysis of the spiritual needs inventory in informal caregivers of patients with cancer in hospice home care. *Oncology Nursing Forum* 39: E332-9. [CrossRef] [PubMed]

Bussing, Arndt, and Harold G. Koenig. 2008. The BENEFIT through spirituality/religiosity scale—A 6-item measure for use in health outcome studies. *The International Journal of Psychiatry in Medicine* 38: 493–506.

Büssing, Arndt, and Harold G. Koenig. 2010. Spiritual Needs of Patients with Chronic Diseases. *Religions* 1: 18. [CrossRef]

Büssing, Arndt, and Daniela Rodrigues Recchia. 2016. Spiritual and Non-spiritual Needs Among German Soldiers and Their Relation to Stress Perception, PTDS Symptoms, and Life Satisfaction: Results from a Structural Equation Modeling Approach. *Journal of Religion and Health* 55: 747–64. [CrossRef] [PubMed]

Büssing, Arndt, Hans J. Balzat, and Peter Heusser. 2010. Spiritual needs of patients with chronic pain diseases and cancer—validation of the spiritual needs questionnaire. *European Journal of Medical Research* 15: 266–73. [CrossRef]

Bussing, A., Xiao F. Zhai, Wen B. Peng, and Chang Q. Ling. 2013. Psychosocial and spiritual needs of patients with chronic diseases: Validation of the Chinese version of the Spiritual Needs Questionnaire. *Journal of Integrative Medicine* 11: 106–15. [CrossRef] [PubMed]

Büssing, Arndt, Andreas Günther, Klaus Baumann, Eckhard Frick, and Christoph Jacobs. 2013. Spiritual Dryness as a Measure of a Specific Spiritual Crisis in Catholic Priests: Associations with Symptoms of Burnout and Distress. *Evidence-Based Complementary and Alternative Medicine* 2013: 10. [CrossRef] [PubMed]

Büssing, Arndt, Annina Janko, Klaus Baumann, Niels Christian Hvidt, and Andreas Kopf. 2013. Spiritual Needs among Patients with Chronic Pain Diseases and Cancer Living in a Secular Society. *Pain Medicine* 14: 1362–73. [CrossRef] [PubMed]

Büssing, Arndt, Undine Waßermann, Niels Christian Hvidt, Alfred Laengler, and Michael Thiel. 2017. Spiritual needs of mothers with sick new born or premature infants—A cross sectional survey among German mothers. *Women and Birth: Journal of the Australian College of Midwives*. [CrossRef]

Büssing, Arndt, Daniela R. Recchia, Harold Koenig, Klaus Baumann, and Ecjhard Frick. 2018. Factor Structure of the Spiritual Needs Questionnaire (SpNQ) in Persons with Chronic Diseases, Elderly and Healthy Individuals. *Religions* 9: 13. [CrossRef]

Cetinkaya, Bengü, Sebahat Dundar, and Arife Azak. 2013. Nurses' perceptions of spirituality and spiritual care. *Australian Journal of Advanced Nursing* 31: 5–10.

Chiang, Yi-chien, Hsiang-chun Lee, Tsung-lan Chu, Chin-yen Han, and Ya-chu Hsiao. 2017. Psychometric Testing of a Religious Belief Scale. *The Journal of Nursing Research: JNR* 25: 419–28. [CrossRef] [PubMed]

Colquhoun, Heather L., Danielle Levac, Kelly K. O'Brien, Sharon Straus, Andrea C. Tricco, Laure Perrier, Monika Kastner, and David Moher. 2014. Scoping reviews: Time for clarity in definition, methods, and reporting. *Journal of Clinical Epidemiology* 67: 1291–94. [CrossRef] [PubMed]

Cotton, Sian, Christina M. Puchalski, Susan N. Sherman, Joseph M. Mrus, Amy H. Peterman, Judith Feinberg, Kenneth I. Pargament, Amy C. Justice, Anthony C. Leonard, and Joel Tsevat. 2006. Spirituality and Religion in Patients with HIV/AIDS. *Journal of General Internal Medicine* 21: S5–S13. [CrossRef] [PubMed]

Curcio, Cristiane S., Giancarlo Lucchetti, and Alexander Moreira-Almeida. 2015. Validation of the Portuguese version of the Brief Multidimensional Measure of Religiousness/Spirituality (BMMRS-P) in clinical and non-clinical samples. *Journal of Religion and Health* 54: 435–48. [CrossRef]

Daaleman, Timothy P., and Bruce B. Frey. 2004. The Spirituality Index of Well-Being: A New Instrument for Health-Related Quality-of-Life Research. *Annals of Family Medicine* 2: 499–503. [CrossRef] [PubMed]

Daaleman, Timothy P., Bruce B. Frey, Dennise Wallace, and Stephanie A. Studenski. 2002. Spirituality Index of Well-Being Scale: Development and testing of a new measure. *The Journal of Family Practice* 51: 952. [PubMed]

De Araujo Toloi, Diego, Deise Uema, Felipe Matsushita, Paulo Antonio da Silva Andrade, Tiago Pugliese Branco, Fabiana Tomie Becker de Carvalho Chino, Raquel Bezerra Guerra, Túlio Eduardo Flesch Pfiffer, Toshio Chiba, Rodrigo Santa Cruz Guindalini, and et al. 2016. Validation of questionnaire on the Spiritual Needs Assessment for Patients (SNAP) questionnaire in Brazilian Portuguese. *Ecancermedicalscience [Internet]* 10: 1–694. [CrossRef] [PubMed]

De Araujo Toloi, Diego, Deise Uema, Felipe Matsushita, Paulo Antonio da Silva Andrade, Tiago Pugliese Branco, Fabiana Tomie Becker de Carvalho Chino, Raquel Bezerra Guerra, Túlio Eduardo Flesch Pfiffer, Toshio Chiba, Rodrigo Santa Cruz Guindalini, and et al. 2016b. Validation of questionnaire on the Spiritual Needs

Assessment for Patients (SNAP) questionnaire in Brazilian Portuguese. *Ecancermedicalscience* 10: 694. [CrossRef] [PubMed]

Delaney, Colleen. 2005. The Spirituality Scale: Development and psychometric testing of a holistic instrument to assess the human spiritual dimension. *Journal of Holistic Nursing* 23: 145–67, discussion 68–71. [CrossRef]

Delaney, Colleen, Cynthia Barrere, and Mary Helming. 2011. The influence of a spirituality-based intervention on quality of life, depression, and anxiety in community-dwelling adults with cardiovascular disease: A pilot study. *Journal of Holistic Nursing: Official Journal of the American Holistic Nurses' Association* 29: 21–32. [CrossRef] [PubMed]

Erichsen, Nora-Beata, and Arndt Büssing. 2013. Spiritual Needs of Elderly Living in Residential/Nursing Homes. *Evidence-Based Complementary and Alternative Medicine* 2013: 10. [CrossRef] [PubMed]

Exline, Julie J., Kenneth I. Pargament, Joshua B. Grubbs, and Ann Marie Yali. 2014. The Religious and Spiritual Struggles Scale: Development and initial validation. *Psychology of Religion and Spirituality* 6: 208–22. [CrossRef]

Fallahi Khoshknab, Masoud, Monir Mazaheri, Sadat S.B. Maddah, and Mehdi Rahgozar. 2010. Validation and reliability test of Persian version of The Spirituality and Spiritual Care Rating Scale (SSCRS). *Journal of Clinical Nursing* 19: 2939–41. [CrossRef] [PubMed]

Fernander, Anita, John F. Wilson, Michele Staton, and Carl Leukefeld. 2004. An exploratory examination of the Spiritual Well-Being Scale among incarcerated black and white male drug users. *International Journal of Offender Therapy and Comparative Criminology* 48: 403–13. [CrossRef] [PubMed]

Fischbeck, Sabine, Bernd O. Maier, Ulrike Reinholz, Cornelia Nehring, Rainer Schwab, and Manfred E. Beutel. 2013. Assessing somatic, psychosocial, and spiritual distress of patients with advanced cancer: Development of the Advanced Cancer Patients' Distress Scale. *The American Journal of Hospice & Palliative Care* 30: 339–46.

Genia, Vickly. 2001. Evaluation of the Spiritual Well-Being Scale in a Sample of College Students. *The International Journal for the Psychology of Religion* 11: 25–33.

Gherghina, Viorel, I. Cindea, R. Popescu, and A. Balcan. 2014. Spiritual distress assessment tool a valid instrument for elderly patients in the perioperative period: 18AP3-7. *European Journal of Anaesthesiology* 31: 267. [CrossRef]

Ghodsbin, Fariba, Marzieh Safaei, Iahanbin Jahanbin, Mohammed A. Ostovan, and Sareh Keshvarzi. 2015. The effect of positive thinking training on the level of spiritual well-being among the patients with coronary artery diseases referred to Imam Reza specialty and subspecialty clinic in Shiraz, Iran: A randomized controlled clinical trial. *ARYA Atherosclerosis* 11: 341–48. [PubMed]

Hatch, Robert L., Mary A. Burg, Debra S. Naberhaus, and Linda K. Hellmich. 1998. The Spiritual Involvement and Beliefs Scale. Development and testing of a new instrument. *The Journal of Family Practice* 46: 476–86. [PubMed]

Hermann, Carla. 2006. Development and testing of the spiritual needs inventory for patients near the end of life. *Oncology Nursing Forum* 33: 737–44. [CrossRef] [PubMed]

Hill, Peter C., and Kenneth I. Pargament. 2003. Advances in the conceptualization and measurement of religion and spirituality. Implications for physical and mental health research. *The American Psychologist* 58: 64–74. [CrossRef] [PubMed]

Hood, Ralph W., and Bernard Spilka. 2003. *The Psychology of Religion: An Empirical Approach*, 3rd ed. New York: Guilford Press.

Hyman, Corine, and Paul J. Handal. 2006. Definitions and Evaluation of Religion and Spirituality Items by Religious Professionals: A Pilot Study. *Journal of Religion and Health* 45: 264–82. [CrossRef]

Ironson, Gail, George F. Solomon, Elizabeth G. Balbin, Conall O'Cleirigh, Annie George, Mahendra Kumar, David Larson, and Teresa E. Woods. 2002. The Ironson-woods Spirituality/Religiousness Index is associated with long survival, health behaviors, less distress, and low cortisol in people with HIV/AIDS. *Annals of Behavioral Medicine: A Publication of the Society of Behavioral Medicine* 24: 34–48. [CrossRef]

Johnstone, Brick, Dong P. Yoon, Kelly L. Franklin, Laura Schopp, and Joseph Hinkebein. 2009. Re-conceptualizing the factor structure of the brief multidimensional measure of religiousness/spirituality. *Journal of Religion and Health* 48: 146–63. [CrossRef]

Kimura, Miako, Acacia L. de Oliveira, Lina S. Mishima, and Lynn G. Underwood. 2012. Cultural adaptation and validation of the Underwood's Daily Spiritual Experience Scale—Brazilian version. *Revista da Escola de Enfermagem da U S P* 46: 99–106. [CrossRef] [PubMed]

Koenig, Harold G. 2009. Research on religion, spirituality, and mental health: A review. *Canadian Journal of Psychiatry Revue Canadienne de Psychiatrie* 54: 283–91. [CrossRef] [PubMed]

Koenig, Harold G. 2012. Religion, Spirituality, and Health: The Research and Clinical Implications. *ISRN Psychiatry* 2012: 33. [CrossRef] [PubMed]

Koenig, Harold G., Nathan A. Boucher, and Michelle J. Pearce. 2017. Rationale for Spiritually Oriented Cognitive Processing Therapy for Moral Injury in Active Duty Military and Veterans with Posttraumatic Stress Disorder. *The Journal of Nervous and Mental Disease* 205: 147–53. [PubMed]

Kouloulias, Vassilis, John Kokakis, Nikolaos Kelekis, and John Kouvaris. 2017. A New Questionnaire (QRFPC25) Regarding the Religiosity and Spirituality in People with Life-Threatening Disease: Reliability and Validity in a Population of Cancer Patients Undergoing Radiotherapy. *Journal of Religion and Health* 56: 1137–54. [CrossRef]

Kreitzer, Mary J., Cynthia R. Gross, On A. Waleekhachonloet, Maryanne Reilly-Spong, and Marcia Byrd. 2009. The brief serenity scale: A psychometric analysis of a measure of spirituality and well-being. *Journal of Holistic Nursing* 27: 7–16. [CrossRef]

Ku, Ya L., Shih M. Kuo, and Ching Y. Yao. 2010. Establishing the validity of a spiritual distress scale for cancer patients hospitalized in southern Taiwan. *International Journal of Palliative Nursing* 16: 134–38. [CrossRef] [PubMed]

Lucchetti, Giancarlo, Alessandra Lamas Granero Lucchetti, and Homero Vallada. 2013. Measuring spirituality and religiosity in clinical research: A systematic review of instruments available in the Portuguese language. *Sao Paulo Medical Journal = Revista paulista de medicina* 131: 112–22. [CrossRef] [PubMed]

MacLeod, Rod, Donna M. Wilson, Jackie Crandall, and Phil Austin. 2017. Death Anxiety among New Zealanders: The Predictive Roles of Religion, Spirituality, and Family Connection. *Omega*. [CrossRef] [PubMed]

Mateen, Farrah J., Jiwon Oh, Ana I. Tergas, Neil Bhayani, and Biren Bharat Kamdar. 2013. Titles versus titles and abstracts for initial screening of articles for systematic reviews. *Clinical Epidemiology* 5: 89–95. [CrossRef] [PubMed]

McBride, J.L., G. Arthur, R. Brooks, and L. Pilkington. 1998a. The relationship between a patient's spirituality and health experiences. *Family Medicine* 30: 122–6.

McBride, J.L., L. Pilkington, and G. Arthur. 1998b. Development of brief pictorial instruments for assessing spirituality in primary care. *The Journal of Ambulatory care Management* 21: 53–61. [CrossRef]

McSherry, Wilfred, Peter Draper, and Don Kendrick. 2002. The construct validity of a rating scale designed to assess spirituality and spiritual care. *International Journal of Nursing Studies* 39: 723–34. [CrossRef]

Mistretta, Erin G., Danetta Sloan, Karlynn BrintzenhofeSzoc, Kathleen M. Weber, and Ann Berger. 2017. Testing domains of the healing experiences in all life stressors questionnaire in a cohort of HIV-infected and HIV-uninfected Chicago women. *Psychology Research and Behavior Management* 10: 201–8. [CrossRef] [PubMed]

Moeini, Babak, Hadi Zamanian, Zahra Taheri-Kharameh, Tehereh Ramezani, Mohamadhasan Saati-Asr, Mohamadhasan Hajrahimian, and Mohammadali Amini-TehraniMscb. 2018. Translation and Psychometric Testing of the Persian Version of the Spiritual Needs Questionnaire Among Elders with Chronic Diseases. *Journal of Pain and Symptom Management* 55: 94–100. [CrossRef] [PubMed]

Monod, Stefanie M., Etienne Rochat, Christophe J. Bula, Guy Jobin, Estelle Martin, and Brenda Spencer. 2010. The spiritual distress assessment tool: An instrument to assess spiritual distress in hospitalised elderly persons. *BMC Geriatrics* 10: 88. [CrossRef] [PubMed]

Monod, Stefanie, Mark Brennan, Etienne Rochat, Estelle Martin, Stephane Rochat, and Chrisotphe J. Büla. 2011. Instruments Measuring Spirituality in Clinical Research: A Systematic Review. *Journal of General Internal Medicine* 26: 1345–57. [CrossRef] [PubMed]

Monod, Stefanie, Estelle Martin, Brenda Spencer, Etienne Rochat, and Christophe Bula. 2012. Validation of the Spiritual Distress Assessment Tool in older hospitalized patients. *BMC Geriatrics* 12: 13. [CrossRef] [PubMed]

Monod, Stepfanie, Estelle Martin, Brenda Spencer, Etienne Rochat, and Christophe Büla. 2012. Validation of the spiritual distress assessment tool in older hospitalized patients. *BMC Geriatrics* 12: 13. [CrossRef] [PubMed]

Munoz, Alexis R., John M. Salsman, Kevin D. Stein, and David Cella. 2015. Reference Values of the Functional Assessment of Chronic Illness Therapy—Spiritual Well-Being (FACIT-Sp-12): A Report from the American Cancer Society's Studies of Cancer Survivors. *Cancer* 121: 1838–44. [CrossRef] [PubMed]

Mystakidou, Kyriaki, Eleni Tsilika, Efi Parpa, M. Smyrnioti, and Lambros Vlahos. 2006. Assessing spirituality and religiousness in advanced cancer patients. *The American Journal of Hospice & Palliative Care* 23: 457–63.

Mystakidou, Kyriaki, Eleni Tsilika, Efi Parpa, Maria Pathiaki, Elisabeth Patiraki, Antonis Galanos, and Lambros Vlahos. 2007. Exploring the relationships between depression, hopelessness, cognitive status, pain, and spirituality in patients with advanced cancer. *Archives of Psychiatric Nursing* 21: 150–61. [CrossRef] [PubMed]

Mystakidou, Kyriaki, Eleni Tsilika, Efi Parpa, Ioanna Hatzipli, Marilena Smyrnioti, Antonis Galanos, and Lambros Vlahos. 2008. Demographic and clinical predictors of spirituality in advanced cancer patients: a randomized control study. *Journal of Clinical Nursing* 17: 1779–85. [CrossRef] [PubMed]

Mystakidou, Kyriaki, Eleni Tsilika, Efi Prapa, Marilena Smyrnioti, Anna Pagoropoulou, and Lambros Vlahos. 2008. Predictors of spirituality at the end of life. *Canadian Family Physician Medecin de Famille Canadien* 54: 1720-21.e5. [PubMed]

Oji, V.U., L.C. Hung, R. Abbasgholizadeh, Hamilton F. Terrell, E.J. Essien, and E. Nwulia. 2017. Spiritual care may impact mental health and medication adherence in HIV+ populations. *HIV/AIDS (Auckland, NZ)* 9: 101–109. [CrossRef] [PubMed]

Peterman, Amy H., George Fitchett, Marianne J. Brady, Lesbia Hernandez, and David Cella. 2002. Measuring spiritual well-being in people with cancer: The functional assessment of chronic illness therapy—Spiritual well-being scale (FACIT-Sp). *Annals of Behavioral Medicine* 24: 49–58. [CrossRef] [PubMed]

Puchalski, Christina M. 2001. The role of spirituality in health care. *Proceedings (Baylor University Medical Center)* 14: 352–57. [CrossRef]

Puchalski, Christina, Betty Ferrell, Rose Virani, Shirley Otis-Green, Pamela Baird, Janet Bull, Harvey Chochinov, George Handzo, Holly Nelson-Becker, Maryjo Prince-Paul, and et al. 2009. Improving the Quality of Spiritual Care as a Dimension of Palliative Care: The Report of the Consensus Conference. *Journal of Palliative Medicine* 12: 885–904. [CrossRef] [PubMed]

Rasinski, Kenneth A., Y.G. Kalad, J.D. Yoon, and F.A. Curlin. 2011. An assessment of US physicians' training in religion, spirituality, and medicine. *Medical Teacher* 33: 944–45. [CrossRef] [PubMed]

Rusa, Suzana Gabriela Rusa, Gabriele Ibanhes Peripato, Sofia Cristina Iost Pavarini, Keika Inouye, Marisa Silvana Zazzetta, and Fabiana de Souza Orlandi. 2014. Quality of life/spirituality, religion and personal beliefs of adult and elderly chronic kidney patients under hemodialysis. *Revista Latino-Americana de Enfermagem* 22: 911–17. [CrossRef] [PubMed]

Sharma, Rashmi K., Alan B. Astrow, Kenneth Texeira, and Daniel P. Sulmasy. 2012. The Spiritual Needs Assessment for Patients (SNAP): development and validation of a comprehensive instrument to assess unmet spiritual needs. *Journal of Pain and Symptom Management* 44: 44–51. [CrossRef] [PubMed]

Simao, Talita P., Erika de Cássia Lopes Chaves, Emília Campos de Carvalho, Denismar Alves Nogueira, Camila Csizmar Carvalho, Ya-Li Ku, and Denise Hollanda Iunes. 2016. Cultural adaptation and analysis of the psychometric properties of the Brazilian version of the Spiritual Distress Scale. *Journal of Clinical Nursing* 25: 231–39. [CrossRef] [PubMed]

Steinhauser, Karen E., Stewart C. Alexander, Ira R. Byock, Linda K. George, Maren K. Olsen, and James A. Tulsky. 2008. Do preparation and life completion discussions improve functioning and quality of life in seriously ill patients? Pilot randomized control trial. *Journal of Palliative Medicine* 11: 1234–40. [CrossRef] [PubMed]

Van Leeuwen, Rene, Lucas J. Tiesinga, Berrie Middel, Doeke Post, and Henk Jochemsen. 2009. The validity and reliability of an instrument to assess nursing competencies in spiritual care. *Journal of Clinical Nursing* 18: 2857–69. [CrossRef] [PubMed]

VandeCreek, Larry, Susan Ayres, and Meredith Bassham. 1995. Using INSPIRIT to conduct spiritual assessments. *Journal of Pastoral Care* 49: 83–89. [CrossRef] [PubMed]

Vivat, Bella, Teresa E. Young, J. Winstanley, J.I. Arraras, K. Black, F. Boyle, A. Bredart, A. Costantini, J. Guo, M.E. Irarrazaval, and et al. 2017. The international phase 4 validation study of the EORTC QLQ-SWB32: A stand-alone measure of spiritual well-being for people receiving palliative care for cancer. *European Journal of Cancer Care (England)* 26. [CrossRef] [PubMed]

WHOQOL SRPB Group. 2006. A cross-cultural study of spirituality, religion, and personal beliefs as components of quality of life. *Social Science & Medicine* 62: 1486–97.

Wu, Li-Fen, and Lih-Ying Lin. 2011. Exploration of clinical nurses' perceptions of spirituality and spiritual care. *The Journal of Nursing Research: JNR* 19: 250–6. [CrossRef] [PubMed]

Wu, Li-Fen, Shu-Hui Yang, and Malcolm Koo. 2017. Psychometric properties of the Chinese version of Spiritual Index of Well-Being in elderly Taiwanese. *BMC Geriatrics* 17: 3. [CrossRef] [PubMed]

Xue, S., S. Arya, A. Embuldeniya, H. Narammalage, Tricia da Silva, Shehan Williams, and A. Ravindran. 2016. Perceived functional impairment and spirituality/religiosity as predictors of depression in a Sri Lankan spinal cord injury patient population. *Spinal Cord* 54: 1158–63. [CrossRef] [PubMed]

Zimmer, Zachary, Carol Jagger, Chi-Tsun Chiu, Mary Beth Ofstedal, Florencia Rojo, and Yasuhiko Saito. 2016. Spirituality, religiosity, aging and health in global perspective: A review. *SSM—Population Health* 2: 373–81. [CrossRef] [PubMed]

© 2018 by the authors. Licensee MDPI, Basel, Switzerland. This article is an open access article distributed under the terms and conditions of the Creative Commons Attribution (CC BY) license (http://creativecommons.org/licenses/by/4.0/).

Article

Factor Structure of the Spiritual Needs Questionnaire (SpNQ) in Persons with Chronic Diseases, Elderly and Healthy Individuals

Arndt Büssing [1,2,*], Daniela Rodrigues Recchia [1,3], Harold Koenig [4,5], Klaus Baumann [6] and Eckhard Frick [7]

[1] Professorship Quality of Life, Spirituality and Coping, Faculty of Health, Witten/Herdecke University, 58313 Herdecke, Germany; Daniela.RodriguesRecchia@uni-wh.de
[2] IUNCTUS—Competence Center for Christian Spirituality, Philosophical-Theological Academy, 48149 Münster, Germany
[3] Chair of Research Methodology and Statistics in Psychology Department of Psychology, Faculty of Health, University of Witten-Herdecke, 58455 Witten, Germany
[4] Department of Psychiatry and Behavioral Sciences, Duke University Medical Center, Durham, NC 27710, USA; Harold.Koenig@duke.edu
[5] Department of Medicine, King Abdulaziz University, Jeddah 21589, Saudi Arabia
[6] Caritas Science and Christian Social Work, Faculty of Theology, Albert-Ludwigs University, 79098 Freiburg, Germany; klaus.baumann@theol.uni-freiburg.de
[7] Munich School of Philosophy & Research Centre Spiritual Care, Technical University Munich, 80333 München, Germany; Eckhard.Frick@hfph.mwn.de
* Correspondence: arndt.buessing@uni-wh.de; Tel.: +49-233-062-3246

Received: 18 December 2017; Accepted: 3 January 2018; Published: 5 January 2018

Abstract: The Spiritual Needs Questionnaire (SpNQ) is an established measure of psychosocial, existential and spiritual needs. Its 4-factor structure has been primarily validated in persons with chronic diseases, but until now has not been done in elderly and stressed healthy populations. Therefore, we tested the factor structure of the SpNQ in: (1) persons with chronic diseases (n = 627); (2) persons with chronic disease plus elderly (n = 940); (3) healthy persons (i.e., adults and elderly) (n = 1468); and (4) chronically ill, elderly, and healthy persons together (n = 2095). The suggested structure was then validated using structured equation modelling (SEM). The 4-factor structure of the 20-item SpNQ (SpNQ-20) was confirmed, differentiating *Religious Needs*, *Existential Needs*, *Inner Peace Needs*, and *Giving/Generativity Needs*. The psychometric properties of the measure indicated (CFI = 0.96, TLI = 0.95, RMSEA = 0.04 and SRMR = 0.03), with good reliability indices (Cronbach's alpha varying from 0.71 to 0.81). This latest version of the SpNQ provides researchers with a reliable and valid instrument that can now be used in comparative studies. Cultural and religious differences can be addressed using their different language versions, assuming the SpNQ's structure is maintained.

Keywords: spiritual needs; questionnaire; factorial structure; validation; structural equation modeling; patients; chronic disease; healthy persons; elderly

1. Introduction

Confronted with chronic and life-threatening diseases, patients often wish to talk with someone about their existential and spiritual needs, but have difficulties finding a person who they trust enough to talk about such 'private' aspects of their lives. Health professionals may have limited time to address patients' specific existential and spiritual needs, and often see this task as going beyond their professional training. Consequently, they may call a board-certified chaplain. However, one study of

German cancer patients found that these patients wanted their physicians to know about their spiritual orientation (Frick et al. 2006). In a study of German out-patients with diseases associated with chronic pain, researchers found that "23% talked with a chaplain/priest about their spiritual needs, 20% had no partner to talk about these needs, while for 37% it was important to talk with their medical doctor about these needs" (Büssing et al. 2009). A majority (72%) of patients with advanced cancer from the USA felt minimally or not at all supported in their spiritual needs (Balboni et al. 2007), and one may argue that this is not the primary task of the health care system. However, about half of these patients (47%) also did not feel supported by their religious community. This means that a large proportion of persons with chronic and life-threatening diseases have unmet spiritual needs that no one seems to care about. Despite the clear recommendations of a US Consensus Conference (Puchalski et al. 2009) that a patient's spirituality should be adequately assessed (i.e., spiritual history) and integrated into the treatment plan by addressing patients' spiritual needs, this is often not done. These recommendations were intended to improve the quality of palliative care. In contrast to this focus, one may ask why the topic of spirituality as a resource should be considered relevant only during the late stages of disease and not early on when patients are first confronted with the diagnosis.

Addressing unmet spiritual needs requires specific knowledge about what the individual persons require and expect. Therefore, these unmet needs have to be operationalized and measured. Health professionals, chaplains and patients´ relatives will then have a chance to respond to those needs.

In a narrative review, Seddigh et al. (2016) described eight measures currently being used to assess patients' spiritual needs. They highlighted the Spiritual Needs Questionnaire (SpNQ), describing it as "the most important assigned questionnaire for the evaluation of spiritual needs of particular patients". This instrument was developed in 2009 to measure a person's unmet psychosocial, existential and spiritual needs in a standardized way (Büssing et al. 2009, 2010). It was distinguished from other measures by not focusing on "patients close to death as opposed to those with chronic illness" (Seddigh et al. 2016). The underlying theoretical basis for the SpNQ refers to four core dimensions of spiritual needs, i.e., Connection, Peace, Meaning/Purpose, and Transcendence (Büssing and Koenig 2010). These were divided into categories of social, emotional, existential, and religious needs. These dimensions of spiritual needs can be further categorized according to Alderfer´s model of Relational, Existential and Growth needs (Büssing 2010), i.e., Relational in terms of a connection with others or the Sacred, Existential in terms of needs to find states of inner peace, hope and forgiveness, and Growth in terms of meaning in life, self-realization, etc.

The primary structure of the SpNQ (Cronbach's alpha ranging from 0.82 to 0.90) involved four main factors, i.e., *Religious Needs, Needs for Inner Peace, Existential Needs (Reflection/Meaning)* and *Giving Needs* (Büssing et al. 2010, 2012). The 4-factorial structure was verified with a sample of patients with chronic diseases (i.e., cancer and pain diseases). The German language version of the instrument was examined not only in persons with chronic diseases (Büssing et al. 2013a; Offenbaecher et al. 2013; Höcker et al. 2014; Haußmann et al. 2017), but also in elderly persons living in retirement and nursing homes (Erichsen and Büssing 2013; Man-Ging et al. 2015), in soldiers with and without posttraumatic stress disorder symptoms (Büssing et al. 2015), and in stressed mothers with sick new born or premature infants (Büssing et al. 2017). Further, the instrument has been translated into many different languages and used to identify spiritual needs in different countries (e.g., China, Poland, Croatia, Iran, Australia, Indonesia, Brazil, and others) (Büssing et al. 2013b, 2015; Glavas et al. 2017; Nuraeni et al. 2015; Nejat et al. 2016; Munirruzzaman et al. 2017; Hatamipour et al. 2018; Valente et al. 2018).

2. Factorial Structure of the SpNQ in Persons with Chronic Diseases, Elderly and Healthy Persons

The instrument's factorial structure has thus far not been tested in healthy populations which may not share the same life experiences and spiritual challenges that persons with chronic illness or elderly persons living in retirement homes must confront. For example, item N10 addresses finding meaning in illness and/or suffering, and may thus not be applicable to healthy persons who have no experience with suffering and illness. In addition, reflecting back on one's life (item N4) is of less relevance to healthy younger persons, but of particular importance to elderly persons and those with life-threatening diseases.

The purpose of our study is to psychometrically test and refine the SpNQ so it could be used to compare spiritual needs of different populations, including those who are healthy and those with chronic illness. Therefore, we tested the factorial structure of the SpNQ in existing datasets that involved both ill and healthy persons (Table 1).

Table 1. Included data sets and distribution by age and gender.

		Patients with Chronic Diseases	Healthy Persons	Elderly in Retirement Homes	All Persons
Number of persons		627	1158	313	2095
Gender	Women	65.5%	18.0%	76.0%	40.4%
	Men	34.5%	82.0%	24.0%	59.6%
	All	100.0%	100.0%	100.0%	100.0%
Age groups	<31 years	6.5%	39.1%	0.0%	24.5%
	31–40 years	9.0%	36.2%	0.0%	23.4%
	41–50 years	23.1%	19.1%	0.0%	17.1%
	51–60 years	27.6%	5.6%	0.6%	10.5%
	60–70 years	19.0%	0.0%	3.9%	5.5%
	>70 years	14.9%	0.0%	95.5%	18.9%
	All	100.0%	100.0%	100.0%	100.0%

3. Materials and Methods

3.1. Participants

To test the instrument's factorial structure, we relied on existing datasets that involved both ill and healthy persons from Germany (Table 1), i.e., 448 patients with chronic pain diseases, 116 persons with cancer, and 63 persons psychiatric/neurological diseases (Büssing et al. 2013b; Offenbaecher et al. 2013), 1033 adults (Büssing and Recchia 2016), 125 mothers with sick newborns (Büssing et al. 2017), and 313 elderly persons (Erichsen and Büssing 2013; Man-Ging et al. 2015; Mayr et al. unpublished). All groups differed significantly with respect to gender and age ($p < 0.0001$; χ^2).

All persons except the very old persons responded to anonymous questionnaires by themselves; elderly persons were offered assistance in self-reporting (i.e., an external person read the questionnaires and filled in their responses).

3.2. Methods

The factorial structure (exploratory factor analysis: principle component analysis with Varimax rotation) and internal consistency (Cronbach's alpha) was examined in the following manner: (1) in persons with chronic diseases; (2) in persons with chronic disease and elderly; (3) in healthy persons (i.e., adults and elderly); and (4) in diseased and healthy persons together (see Table 1). To determine the factor structure of the measure, we conducted factor analysis using structural equation modelling (SEM) using the entire sample.

3.3. Spiritual Needs Questionnaire

The SpNQ can be used either as a diagnostic tool with 27 items or as a research instrument which does not use all items. The initial version of the SpNQ (version 1.2) used 19 items to which two new items were added to strengthen the 3-item *Giving* factor (Büssing et al. 2012): N27 (assured that your life was meaningful and of value) and N26 (pass own life experiences to others). Some of the initial items were not used in the following 2.1 version, i.e., items N1 (more attention by others), N3 (someone from your community cares), N24 (becoming completely well), and N25 (connected with the family), which were regarded as 'informative' marker items.

However, due to a weak item-to-scale correlation and weak factor loadings for two additional items, these two items were eliminated from version 2.1 of the SpNQ, i.e., items N5 (dissolve open aspects of your life) and N14 (give away something from yourself). These were still regarded as conceptually relevant, however, and were included again in the current item pool that was to be tested in the present analysis. Thus, we tested the items of the previous version 2.1 and some of the relevant items of the initial version 1.2 together.

The intensity of unmet needs was scored using a 4-point scale ranging from disagreement to agreement (0—*not at all*; 1—*somewhat*; 2—*strong*; 3—*very strong*).

3.4. Factor Structure in the Different Samples

In all four samples, the items N4 (reflect back on your life) and N13 (turn to someone in a loving attitude) loaded too weakly on the respective factors and were thus removed from the item pool. As shown in Table 2, among persons with chronic diseases the 4 factors were replicated. In that sample, item N2 (talk with someone about fears and worries) loaded weakly on both the *Existential Needs* factor and the *Inner Peace Needs* factor. Adding elderly persons to the sample of those with chronic diseases resulted in a split of the *Existential Needs* items (Table 2), with a three-item factor consisting of forgiveness and dissolving open aspects in life, and a two to three item factor consisting of relieving talks about life after death, meaning of life, and finding meaning in life. The item N2 had a weak loading on all three factors. Testing the SpNQ exclusively in a sample of non-diseased persons (i.e., healthy adults and elderly) again resulted in a split of the *Existential Needs* factor items. Combining all data sets of persons with chronic diseases, elderly, and healthy persons, the four-factor structure of the SpNQ was confirmed. Here, item N2 (talk with someone about fears and worries) loaded best on the *Inner Peace Needs* factor, as was initially found.

Thus, the SpNQ in its new version (SpNQ-20) consists of 20 items, i.e., 6 items addressing *Religious Needs*, 6 items addressing *Existential Needs*, 4 items addressing *Inner Peace Needs*, and 4 items addressing *Giving/Generativity Needs*. The internal reliability of these factors was good (Cronbach's alphas ranging from 0.71 to 0.87) (Table 2).

Table 2. Synopsis of factor loadings in diseased, elderly and healthy persons.

	Persons with Chronic Diseases (n = 627)				Persons with Chronic Diseases + Elderly (n = 940)					Healthy Persons (n = 1468)					All Persons (n = 2095)			
	1	2	3	4	1	2	3	4	5	1	2	3	4	5	1	2	3	4
Cronbach's alpha	0.88	0.77	0.75	0.74	0.87	0.66	0.71	0.68	0.70	0.87	0.66	0.69	0.64	0.60	0.87	0.73	0.74	0.71
N20 pray for yourself	0.797				0.824					0.837					0.828			
N23 turn to a higher presence (i.e., God, Allah, Angels)	0.745				0.773					0.780					0.784			
N21 participate at a religious ceremony (i.e., service)	0.812				0.816					0.772					0.764			
N18 pray with someone	0.782				0.744					0.765					0.755			
N19 someone prays for you	0.775				0.747					0.746					0.746			
N22 read religious/spiritual books	0.603	0.335			0.605					0.618					0.642			
N17 be forgiven	0.313	0.534				0.707							0.769				0.682	
N16 forgive someone from a distinct period of your life		0.503				0.639							0.731				0.641	0.349
N5 dissolve open aspects of your life		0.515	0.381			0.666							0.670				0.563	
N11 talk about the question of meaning in life		0.758						0.752						0.801		0.364	0.541	
N12 talk about the possibility of life after death	0.351	0.644						0.706						0.745	0.316		0.534	
N10 find meaning in illness and/or suffering		0.608						0.592				0.335		0.441	0.381	0.457	0.371	
N7 dwell at a place of quietness and peace			0.801			0.369			0.713			0.766				0.762		
N6 plunge into beauty of nature			0.755				0.363		0.702		0.470	0.469				0.590		
N8 find inner peace		0.381	0.721			0.478			0.653			0.743				0.721		0.408
N2 talk with someone about fears and worries		0.390	0.373			0.483		0.301	0.313			0.610				0.576	0.337	
N26 pass own life experiences to others				0.789			0.668				0.565							0.626
N27 assured that your life was meaningful and of value				0.730			0.613				0.459							0.534
N15 give solace to someone				0.599			0.646				0.719							0.698
N14 give away something from yourself		0.365		0.520			0.631				0.729							0.661

Main component analysis (Variamax rotation with Kaiser normalization); only factor loadings are depicted < 0.03; items loading on a specific factor > 0.5 are highlighted (bold).

3.5. Structured Equation Modelling

After defining the most reasonable factor structure for the pooled data, a structural equation modeling (SEM) was used to confirm the structure. This advanced statistical tool includes many statistical techniques, such as regression modeling, factor and correlation analysis combined in one model. Model fit was determined using Root Mean Square Error of Approximation (RMSEA), Standardized Root Mean Square Residual (SRMR), Comparative Fit Index (CFI) and Tucker-Lewis Index (TLI). The thresholds for a good fit are CFI and TLI > 0.95, SRMR < 0.06 and RMSEA < 0.05.

These indices for the SpNQ-20 were CFI = 0.96, TLI = 0.95, RMSEA = 0.04 and SRMR = 0.03, with good to very good reliability scores (Chronbach's alphas ranging from 0.71 to 0.81). Two variables loaded on two different factors; such cross-loadings are quite common in such models allowing variables to move freely from one factor to another (Asparouhov and Muthén 2009). Figure 1 shows that the variable N5 (dissolve open aspects of your life) loaded on both *Religious Needs* and *Existential Needs*; however, the loading on the *Religious Needs* factor was relativley weak, while on the *Existential Needs* factor, the loading was strong. Variable N6 (plunge into beauty of nature) loaded positively on both the *Inner Peace Needs* and *Giving/Generativity Needs* factors.

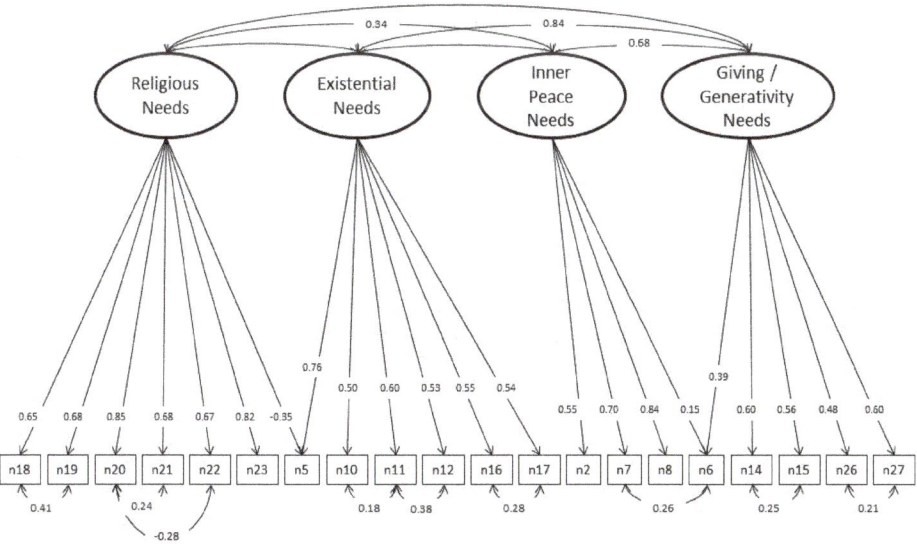

Figure 1. SEM model for pooled data. Values on arrows between items (in boxes) and factors (in circles) represent loadings, while items between boxes and circles, respectively, represent correlations.

3.6. Differences between the Mean Scores of Previous and Current Version of the SpNQ

The mean scores obtained on the previous SpNQ 2.1 version and on the new version (SpNQ-20) were comparable (Table 3), i.e., the *Religious Needs* mean scores were identical, the *Existential Needs* score was lower in the new version, the *Inner Peace Needs* was marginally higher, and the *Giving/Generativity Needs* was marginally lower in the new version. Thus, the largest differences in mean score were found in the *Existential Needs* subscale.

Table 3. SpNQ scores of previous and new version.

	Religious Needs		Existential Needs		Inner Peace Needs		Giving/Generativity Needs	
	Version 2.1	New SpNQ-20	Version 2.1	New SpNQ-20	Version 2.1	New SpNQ-20	Version 2.1	New SpNQ-20
Mean	0.51	0.51	0.55	0.48	1.21	1.23	1.09	1.00
SD	0.74	0.74	0.62	0.61	0.79	0.90	0.87	0.82

3.7. Profiles of Unmet Needs

As shown in Table 4, the mean scores differed significantly between non-ill ("healthy") persons and persons with chronic diseases, particularly on the *Existential Needs* and *Inner Peace Needs* subscales. There were also significant differences on gender and age with regard to the expression of spiritual needs, particularly on the *Religious Needs* subscale.

Table 4. SpNQ scores analyzed with respect to gender, age and sample.

		Religious Needs	Existential Needs	Inner Peace Needs	Giving/Generativity Needs
Healthy/Diseased					
Non-diseased (healthy) persons ($n = 1468$)	Mean	0.46	0.36	1.05	0.90
	SD	0.71	0.49	0.82	0.76
Chronically diseased persons ($n = 627$)	Mean	0.61	0.77	1.64	1.28
	SD	0.80	0.75	0.93	0.89
All persons ($n = 2085$)	Mean	0.51	0.48	1.23	1.01
	SD	0.74	0.61	0.90	0.82
	F value	17.3	213.6	208.5	99.3
	p value	<0.0001	<0.0001	<0.0001	<0.0001
Gender					
Women ($n = 826$)	Mean	0.78	0.64	1.49	1.18
	SD	0.84	0.67	0.87	0.85
Men ($n = 1219$)	Mean	0.32	0.37	1.04	0.88
	SD	0.60	0.53	0.86	0.77
All persons ($n = 2045$)	Mean	0.51	0.48	1.22	1.00
	SD	0.74	0.60	0.89	0.81
	F value	209.2	103.3	137.0	66.8
	p value	<0.0001	<0.0001	<0.0001	<0.0001
Age groups					
<31 years ($n = 482$)	Mean	0.78	0.64	1.49	1.18
	SD	0.23	0.31	0.92	0.71
31–40 years ($n = 462$)	Mean	0.48	0.45	0.78	0.68
	SD	0.30	0.38	1.18	0.83
41–50 years ($n = 338$)	Mean	0.56	0.53	0.87	0.73
	SD	0.44	0.49	1.28	1.03
51–60 years ($n = 207$)	Mean	0.69	0.65	0.98	0.84
	SD	0.56	0.72	1.62	1.25
61–70 years ($n = 109$)	Mean	0.74	0.76	0.95	0.85
	SD	0.80	0.75	1.62	1.49
>70 years ($n = 373$)	Mean	0.86	0.77	0.85	0.88
	SD	1.06	0.54	1.25	1.27
All ages ($n = 1971$)	Mean	0.89	0.57	0.82	0.81
	SD	0.51	0.47	1.22	1.00
	F value	80.2	22.8	25.3	39.9
	p value	<0.0001	<0.0001	<0.0001	<0.0001

Because all three variables (gender, age and disease vs healthy) had a significant influence on scores, we performed univariate variance analyses to test inter-subject effects with the SpNQ factors as dependent variables, producing the following findings:

- For *Religious Needs*, there were age ($F = 23.8$; $p < 0.0001$) and gender ($F = 13.4$; $p < 0.0001$) differences, but not disease/healthy differences ($F = 2.2$; $p = 0.139$). No significant interaction effects were present.
- For *Existential Needs*, there were significant gender ($F = 13.6$; $p < 0.0001$) and disease/healthy ($F = 7.8$; $p = 0.005$) differences, but differences in age were only at the trend level ($F = 3.0$; $p = 0.010$). There was a difference at the trend level for the combined effect of all three variables ($F = 2.9$; $p = 0.013$).
- For *Inner Peace Needs*, there were significant gender ($F = 13.8$; $p < 0.0001$) and disease/healthy ($F = 9.8$; $p = 0.002$) differences, but not for age ($F = 1.9$; $p = 0.096$). Again, there was a difference at the trend level for the combined effects of all three variables ($F = 2.7$; $p = 0.018$).
- For *Giving/Generativity Needs*, only a significant difference was found for age ($F = 7.9$; $p < 0.0001$), not for gender ($F = 3.5$; $p = 0.062$) or disease/healthy ($F = 1.7$; $p = 0.197$). There were no significant interaction effects for these three variables ($F = 2.1$; $p = 0.064$).

4. Discussion

The purpose of this study was to examine the psychometric properties of an instrument which is not only suited for persons with chronic diseases or alternatively only for those who are healthy, but also for use in both, persons with chronic diseases and in those who are healthy.

Compared to the previous version of the SpNQ (version 2.1), the *Religious Needs* factor did not change and was stable with its 6 items in all samples. The *Existential Needs* factor initially had five items and consists of six items now; item N4 (reflect back on your life) was deleted and items N5 and N17 were added. The *Inner Peace Needs* factor initially consisted of six items and is composed of four items now; item N5 was switched to the *Existential Needs* factor and N13 (turn to someone in a loving attitude) was removed. The *Giving/Generativity Needs* factor initially consisted of three items and now consists of four items; item N14 (give away something from yourself) was added. With this 6 + 6 + 4 + 4 item structure, which was confirmed by structural equitation modeling, the SpNQ-20 is better balanced compared to the previous version.

Two items are worth discussing. In persons with chronic diseases, item N2 (talk with someone about fears and worries) loaded weakly on two factors, *Existential Needs* and *Inner Peace Needs*. This means that talking with others about fears and worries can be a matter of life reflection and subsequent intention to let go of fears and worries, resulting in a state of inner peace. In healthy persons, this item clearly belonged to the *Inner Peace Needs* domain. Thus, because of its relevance and connection to states of peacefulness particularly in healthy persons, this item is best included as part of the *Inner Peace Needs* domain for the entire sample. In a similar vein, item N10 (finding meaning in illness and/or suffering) clearly belongs to the *Existential Needs* domain in persons with chronic disease, but also loaded weakly on the *Inner Peace Needs* domain in healthy persons. Thus, this item belongs best in the *Existential Needs* domain. The ambivalence of both items, however, should be considered in future studies.

A further interesting aspect is that the *Existential Needs* factor splits into two constructs when examined in elderly and healthy persons instead of persons with chronic diseases, i.e., into a domain of reflection and forgiveness and a domain of relieving talks with others. However, the internal consistency of both of these domains was too weak to be used as independent scales, and thus these six items were considered as one factor.

5. Associations with Spirituality and Quality of Life

In persons with chronic diseases, *Religious Needs* were strongly and *Existential Needs* moderately correlated with both religious Trust (SpREUK) and Search for spiritual support (SpREUK), while *Inner Peace Needs* and *Giving/Generativity Needs* were weakly to moderately related to Search or Trust (Büssing et al. 2013a; Offenbaecher et al. 2013). Thus, the scales *Religious Needs* and *Existential Needs* have clear spiritual/religious connections.

With respect to spiritual well-being (FACIT-Sp), it was found that the Faith subscale was strongly and positively related to *Religious Needs*, while the Peace subscale correlated moderately in a negative direction with *Inner Peace Needs* and *Existential Needs*, and the Meaning subscale correlated moderately in a negative direction with *Existential Needs* (Büssing et al. 2013a). The Meaning subscale was also weakly positively correlated with *Giving/Generativity Needs*. This suggests that the scales *Inner Peace Needs* and *Existential Needs* indicate a lack of something that is missing, while in contrast *Religious Needs* may indicate a positive resource which is principally available and one thus can call for.

Addressing quality of life associated variables in patients with chronic pain, it was found that *Inner Peace Needs* and *Existential Needs* were moderately associated with anxiety (and depression) (HADS) and with reduced mental health (SF-36), while *Religious Needs* and *Giving/Generativity Needs* were not significantly related to any mental health outcomes (Offenbaecher et al. 2013). In line with this finding, *Existential Needs* and *Inner Peace Needs* of German soldiers were moderately correlated with perceptions of stress (PSS) and with posttraumatic stress disorder symptoms (PCL-M), while *Religious Needs* and *Giving/Generativity Needs* were marginally to weakly related to these mental health indicators (Büssing and Recchia 2016). Furthermore, among elderly persons living in retirement homes, *Existential Needs* were moderately related to tiredness (ASTS) and *Inner Peace Needs* with grief and tiredness, while *Religious Needs* and *Giving/Generativity Needs* were weakly associated with emotional tiredness (Erichsen and Büssing 2013). This suggests that *Religious Needs* and *Giving/Generativity Needs* are not necessarily indicators of a reduced quality of life. Multivariate linear regression analyses revealed that tumor patients' anxiety (HADS) was the strongest predictor of *Existential Needs*, *Inner Peace Needs* and *Giving Needs*, while coherence (LAP-R) predicted *Religious Needs* and *Inner Peace Needs* (Höcker et al. 2014). However, patients' symptom scores (VAS) and pain disability (PDI) were not significantly related to any of the SpNQ scales (Büssing et al. 2013a).

With regard to interpretations of illness (IIQ) of persons with chronic pain diseases, *Religious Needs* were moderately associated with interpretations of illness as something of value, as a call for help, and as a relieving break from the demands of life; *Existential Needs* were moderately correlated with illness as something of value and as a relieving break from the demands of life (Büssing et al. 2013a). In contrast, *Inner Peace Needs* were weakly related to illness as both an interruption and something of value, and *Giving/Generativity Needs* were weakly correlated with illness as a call for help (Büssing et al. 2013a).

6. Conclusions

The SpNQ-20 provides researchers with a reliable and valid measure for use in comparative studies. Cultural and religious differences can be addressed using different language versions, assuming the SpNQ's structure is maintained (so far, the instrument is available in the following languages: German, English, Italian, French, Portuguese, Polish, Danish, Chinese, Indonesian, Farsi, Croatian, Lithuanian).

The Farsi version of the SpNQ (termed 'Spiritual Needs Assessment Scale of Patients with Cancer'), for example, has a 5-factorial structure (Hatamipour et al. 2018), i.e., the four main factors were retained and an additional culturally specific new fifth factor emerged and was called "Support and Nationalism", however, with a rather low internal consistency (Cronbach's alpha = 0.67).

The Portuguese version of the SpNQ differentiates *Religious Needs*, *Existentialistic Needs*, *Inner Peace*, *Actively Giving* and *Family Support Needs* (Valente et al. 2018). The items of the *Family Support Needs* scale are optional items which can be found in the SpNQ, but may not represent a specific 'spiritual' topic. Nevertheless, this domain is of high relevance and can thus be used as an additional scale.

The Chinese version of the instrument differentiates *Religious Needs* (with two subscales, Praying and Sources), *Reflection/Release Needs*, *Inner Peace Needs*, and *Giving/Generativity Needs* (Büssing et al. 2013b). Here, the scores of the *Reflection/Release Needs* (which uses only 3 items of the *Existential Needs* scale) might be less comparable than in other samples. The same is true for the Polish version of the SpNQ which also differentiates the four established domains (Büssing et al. 2015), but with only two items in its *Inner Peace Needs* domain.

Acknowledgments: There was no external funding for this analysis. We are grateful to all collaborators.

Author Contributions: A.B. designed the questionnaire, has analyzed the data and written the manuscript; D.R.R. performed SEM analyses; H.K., K.B. and E.F. contributed to write the manuscript and finally approved the manuscript.

Conflicts of Interest: The authors declare no conflict of interest.

References

Asparouhov, Tihomir, and Bengt Muthén. 2009. Exploratory structural equation modeling. *Structural Equation Modeling* 16: 397–438. [CrossRef]

Balboni, Tracy A., Lauren C. Vanderwerker, Susan D. Block, M. Elizabeth Paulk, Christopher S. Lathan, John R. Peteet, and Holly G. Prigerson. 2007. Religiousness and spiritual support among advanced cancer patients and associations with end-of-life treatment preferences and quality of life. *Journal of Clinical Oncology* 25: 555–60. [CrossRef] [PubMed]

Büssing, Arndt. 2010. Measures of Spirituality in Health Care. In *Oxford Textbook of Spirituality in Healthcare*. Edited by Mark R. Cobb, Christina M. Puchalski and Bruce Rumbold. Oxford: Oxford University Press, pp. 323–31. ISBN 978-0-19-957139-0.

Büssing, Arndt, and Harold G. Koenig. 2010. Spiritual Needs of Patients with Chronic Diseases. *Religions* 1: 18–27. [CrossRef]

Büssing, Arndt, and Daniela Rodrigues Recchia. 2016. Spiritual and Non-spiritual Needs Among German Soldiers and their Relation to Stress Perception, PTDS Symptoms, and Life Satisfaction—Results from a Structural Equation Modeling Approach. *Journal of Religion and Health* 55: 747–64.

Büssing, Arndt, Hans-Joachim Balzat, and Peter Heusser. 2009. Spirituelle Bedürfnisse von Patienten mit chronischen Schmerz- und Tumorerkrankungen. *Perioperative Medizin* 1: 248. [CrossRef]

Büssing, Arndt, Hans-Joachim Balzat, and Peter Heusser. 2010. Spiritual needs of patients with chronic pain diseases and cancer—Validation of the spiritual needs questionnaire. *European Journal of Medical Research* 15: 266–73.

Büssing, Arndt, Annina Janko, Andreas Kopf, Eberhard Albert Lux, and Eckhard Frick. 2012. Zusammenhänge zwischen psychosozialen und spirituellen Bedürfnissen und Bewertung von Krankheit bei Patienten mit chronischen Erkrankungen. *Spiritual Care* 1: 57–73.

Büssing, Arndt, Annina Janko, Klaus Baumann, Niels Christian Hvidt, and Andreas Kopf. 2013a. Spiritual Needs among Patients with Chronic Pain Diseases and Cancer Living in a Secular Society. *Pain Medicine* 14: 1362–73.

Büssing, Arndt, Zhai Xiao-Feng, Wen-bo Peng, and Chang-quan Ling. 2013b. Psychosocial and spiritual needs of patients with chronic diseases: Validation of the Chinese version of the Spiritual Needs Questionnaire. *Journal of Integrative Medicine* 11: 106–15. [CrossRef] [PubMed]

Büssing, Arndt, Iwoan Pilchowska, and Janusz Surzykiewicz. 2015. Spiritual Needs of Polish patients with chronic diseases. *Journal of Religion and Health* 54: 1524–42. [CrossRef] [PubMed]

Büssing, Arndt, Undine Wassermann, Niels Christian Hvidt, Alfred Längler, and Michael Thiel. 2017. Spiritual needs of mothers with sick new born or premature infants. *Woman and Birth*. [CrossRef] [PubMed]

Erichsen, Nora Beata, and Arndt Büssing. 2013. Spiritual Needs of Elderly living in Retirement/Nursing Homes. *Evidence-Based Complementary and Alternative Medicine*, 913247. [CrossRef]

Frick, Eckhard, Carola Riedner, Martin J. Fegg, S. Hauf, and Gian Domenico Borasio. 2006. A clinical interview assessing cancer patients' spiritual needs and preferences. *European Journal of Cancer Care* 15: 238–43. [CrossRef] [PubMed]

Glavas, Andrijana, Karin Jors, Arndt Büssing, and Klaus Baumann. 2017. Spiritual needs of PTSD patients in Croatia and Bosnia-Herzegovina: A quantitative pilot study. *Psychiatria Danubina* 29: 282–90. [CrossRef] [PubMed]

Hatamipour, Khadijeh, Maryam Rassouli, Farideh Yaghmaie, Kazem Zendedel, and Hamid Alavi Majd. 2018. Development and Psychometrics of a 'Spiritual Needs Assessment Scale of Patients with Cancer': A mixed exploratory study. *International Journal of Cancer Management*. in press.

Haußmann, Annette, Norbert Schäffeler, Martin Hautzinger, Birgit Weyel, Thomas Eigentler, Stephan Zipfel, and Martin Teufel. 2017. Religiöse/spirituelle Bedürfnisse und psychosoziale Belastung von Patienten mit malignem Melanom. *Psychotherapie, Psychosomatik, Medizinische Psychologie* 67: 413–19. [CrossRef] [PubMed]

Höcker, Anja, Andreas Krüll, Uwe Koch, and Anja Mehnert A. 2014. Exploring spiritual needs and their associated factors in an urban sample of early and advanced cancer patients. *European Journal of Cancer Care* 23: 786–94. [CrossRef] [PubMed]

Man-Ging, Carlos Ignacio, Jülyet Öven Uslucan, Martin Fegg, Eckhard Frick, and Arndt Büssing. 2015. Reporting Spiritual Needs of Older Adults Living in Bavarian Residential and Nursing Homes. *Journal of Mental Health, Religion and Spirituality* 18: 809–21. [CrossRef]

Munirruzzaman, Muhammad, Yuni Sapto Edi R, and Ahus Prasetyo. 2017. Gambaran Tingkat Kebutuhan Spiritual Pada Pasien Gagal Ginjal Kronik Yang Menjalani Hemodialisis Di Ruang Hemodialisa Rsud Cilacap. In *Proceeding Management Communication in Health Team Collaboration of Giving High Alert for Patient Safety*. Cilacap: STIKES Al-Irsyad Al-Islamiyyah Cilacap, pp. 1–8. ISBN 978-602-60725-1-1.

Nejat, Nazi, Lisa Whitehead, and Marie Crowe. 2016. Exploratory Psychometric Properties of the Farsi and English Versions of the Spiritual Needs Questionnaire (SpNQ). *Religions* 7: 84. [CrossRef]

Nuraeni, Aan, Ikeu Nurhidayah, Nuroktavia Hidayati, Citra Windani Mambang Sari, and Ristina Mirwanti. 2015. Kebutuhan Spiritual pada Pasien Kanker. *Jurnal Keperawatan Padjadjaran* 3: 57–66. Available online: http://jkp.fkep.unpad.ac.id/index.php/jkp/article/view/101 (accessed on 10 December 2017). [CrossRef]

Offenbaecher, Martin, Nico Kohls, Loren L. Toussaint, Claudia Sigl, Andreas Winkelmann, Robin Hieblinger, Albrecht Walther, and Arndt Büssing. 2013. Spiritual needs in patients suffering from fibromyalgia. *Evidence-Based Complementary and Alternative Medicine*, 178547. [CrossRef] [PubMed]

Puchalski, Christina, Betty Ferrell, Rose Virani, Shirley Otis-Green, Pamela Baird, Janet Bull, Harvey Chochinov, George Handzo, Holly Nelson-Becker, Maryjo Prince-Paul, and et al. 2009. Improving the quality of spiritual care as a dimension of palliative care: The report of the Consensus Conference. *Journal of Palliative Medicine* 12: 885–904. [CrossRef] [PubMed]

Seddigh, Ruohollah, Amir-Abbas Keshavarz-Akhlaghi, and Somayeh Azarnik. 2016. Questionnaires Measuring Patients' Spiritual Needs: A Narrative Literature Review. *Iranian Journal of Psychiatry and Behavioral Sciences* 10: e4011. [CrossRef] [PubMed]

Valente, Tania Christina de Oliveira, Ana Paula R. Cavalcanti, Arndt Büssing, and Clóvis Pereira da Costa Júnior. 2018. Transcultural adaptation and psychometric properties of Portuguese version of the Spiritual Needs Questionnaire among HIB positive patients in Brasil. Paper presented at 6th European Conference on Religion, Spirituality and Health and 5th International Conference of the British Association for the Study of Spirituality, Coventry, UK, May 17–19. forthcoming.

© 2018 by the authors. Licensee MDPI, Basel, Switzerland. This article is an open access article distributed under the terms and conditions of the Creative Commons Attribution (CC BY) license (http://creativecommons.org/licenses/by/4.0/).

Article

Translation, Cultural Adaptation of Spiritual Needs Questionnaire in Pakistan

Aisha Kashif [1,*] and Zaira Kanwal [2]

1. Faculty of Humanitites, COMSATS University, Park Road, Chak Shehzad, Islamabad 45550, Pakistan
2. Department of Humanities, COMSATS University, Park Road, Chak Shehzad, Islamabad 45550, Pakistan; zaira_kanwal@yahoo.com
* Correspondence: aisha.kashif@comsats.edu.pk

Received: 1 March 2018; Accepted: 3 May 2018; Published: 18 May 2018

Abstract: The current study was conducted with the aim of translating, adapting, and exploring the factor structure of Spiritual Needs Questionnaire (SpNQ) in chronically ill patients. To meet this objective, the English-version SpNQ was translated into Urdu for Pakistan following standard methods of translation and adaptation. The Urdu version was then used to collect data from a sample of 150 chronically ill patients. The results showed that spiritual needs were significantly associated with each other. Compared to the previous English-version that proposed a four-factor solution, the exploratory factor analysis revealed a three-factor structure for the Urdu version with good internal consistency coefficients, indicating the new version to be a reliable measure.

Keywords: spiritual needs; translation; exploratory factor analysis; internal consistency

1. Introduction

Spirituality is a multifaceted term that is represented diversely in practice and perception. Spirituality originated from the Latin word *Spiritus*, which means to breathe, and while *spirit* refers to purity of soul. The concept of spirituality emerged from Christianity, denoting a life oriented toward the Holy Spirit (Mok et al. 2010). Some authors suggest spirituality to be a form of religious transformation, a process of redeeming originality of an individual directed toward an image of God in terms of divinity and self-actualization (Saucier and Skrzypińska 2006). For achieving this transformation in every belief system, there are different codes of submission. For example, there is the Torah in Judaism, Christ in Christianity, the Buddha in Buddhism, and the Prophet Muhammad (peace be upon him) in Islam (McMahan 2008).

According to (Ellison 2006), spirituality is a motivational force or power that leads an individual towards path of curiosity, surge, purpose, direction and meaning in life. It is the totality of human existence and does not exist independent of mind and body (psyche, soma). Spirituality can also be defined as way individuals experience their relatedness with their family, self, others and the transcendent (Puchalski et al. 2009). Spirituality is a common human attribute found in all individuals whether they are religious or not (Woll et al. 2008). Koenig et al. (2012) maintained that spirituality is sanctity within as well as at the extrinsic level. In the Islamic context, *sufism* is considered a form of spirituality in which a spiritual leader or peer transmits spiritual knowledge to his students. Tasawwuf or Sufiism is a mystical aspect of Islam (Azeemi 2005).

Spirituality has been indicated as a significant factor in wellbeing and quality of life amongst the patient population, especially those diagnosed with cancer (Balboni et al. 2007). The quality of life for patients constitutes psychosocial, physical, and spiritual wellbeing that helps individuals to grow in totality (Oh and Kang 2005). Spiritual wellbeing is an overall state that fosters positive growth and survival that is responsible for an increased sense of connectivity with a divine power

(Shahbaz and Shahbaz 2015). Literature suggests a positive correlation between spiritual wellbeing and psychological wellbeing (Moreira-Almeida et al. 2006).

The existence of individuals as humans depends on the relation between biological, psychological, spiritual, and social dimensions. The biopsychosocial–spiritual model supplements holistic grounds for treating and healing individuals and also provides a conceptual basis for addressing overall health and care (Sulmasy 2002). Spiritual needs exist in both the clinical and non-clinical population. Spirituality serves as a significant factor in making a contribution toward physical health, most prominently in cancer patients. It also escalates their self-worth, emotional support, coping with illness, and hope (Thune-Boyle et al. 2006). A relatively recent study (Büssing et al. 2010) assessed the spiritual, psychosocial, and existential needs of patients with chronic pain disease.

The study investigated spirituality/religiosity as significant source of healing and coping amongst European patients with chronic illnesses (Büssing et al. 2010). In the following study, the psychosocial needs, spiritual, and existential needs of patients were assessed among those chronically ill patients who did not consider themselves to be religious (Büssing et al. 2009, 2007a, 2007b). The results of this study showed that need for inner peace and actively giving were significantly high, whereas religious needs were of least importance among European cancer patients. It was additionally found that there is an association between spirituality and religiosity and coping mechanism against disease (Büssing et al. 2007a). In cancer patients particularly, spirituality serves to provide emotional support, hope, and meaning in life and therefore helped them to better cope with their illness. Another study revealed that cancer patients have a relatively high level of unmet spiritual needs in comparison to biological and psychosocial needs (Rainbird et al. 2009). These needs are associated with improved life quality and hope in life. The cancer patients in which these needs are less able to cope with their illness and have a reduced quality of life (Zamanzadeh et al. 2014).

The major objective of the present research is to translate and adapt the spiritual needs questionnaire (SpNQ). The instrument was developed by Büssing et al. (2010) considering patient population as spirituality and religion were perceived as an imperative technique of coping. Previous attempts concentrated on spiritual needs of ill, close to death while SpNQ was administered to chronically ill patients. SpNQ has been studied in different countries, including Malaysia, Nigeria, Poland (Büssing et al. 2015), France, China (Büssing et al. 2013), Germany (Büssing et al. 2018), England, and Iran (Moeini et al. 2018). The instrument has been normalized in Iran with negligible revisions. In gauging spiritual needs, it is important for the respondents' inner self to be revealed (Seddigh et al. 2016). The spiritual needs are stated to be interrelated; thus, cautious administration of instrument is suggested.

Some concepts included in the spiritual needs questionnaires are culturally dependent. For example, in western cultures, music was added as a putative need in patient care. but in later research, it was deleted. In Islamic contexts, listening to or reading the Quran (holy book) holds spiritual significance. Likewise, contingent upon the culture where the questionnaire is being used, the importance of needs will vary. For example, in the Chinese version, the need for active giving was found to be most important compared to the need for inner peace that emerged in German norms. Previous literature highlights a need for translation of the spiritual needs questionnaires as they are culturally dependent, according to different cultures with adjustment of certain items conveying culture-specific meaning. Considering the above commentary, the current research endeavored to translate, adapt, and validate the SpNQ in a Pakistani sample of chronically ill patients.

2. Method

2.1. Measure

Spiritual Needs Questionnaire. The original version of spiritual needs questionnaire (SpNQ) was developed by Büssing et al. (2010) to assess spiritual needs of patients with chronic illness. SpNQ is a 29-item tool with four subscales i.e., religious needs, existential needs, need for inner peace, and need for actively giving or generativity. SpNQ is rated on a four-point Likert scale ranging from 0 = not at all, 1 = somewhat, 2 = very, and 3 = extremely. The Cronbach alpha for religious needs = 0.92, existential needs = 0.82, need for inner peace = 0.82, need for active giving and generativity = 0.74. The spiritual needs questionnaire is free from religious bias and is suitable to use both in secular states as well as religious states. The current study translated the original version into Urdu according to the following steps after obtaining permissions from the original author.

Phase 1: Tool Translation and Adaptation of English Version of the Spiritual Needs Questionnaire

The translation and adaptation process were completed in two phases. In the first phase, translation and adaptation of SpNQ was accomplished, and in second phase, the exploration of factor structure and validity of tool was established. All steps in tool translation were considered.

Step 1: Forward translation. Four translators from the Army Public School and College were approached who were bilingual and had postgraduate academic qualifications. The translators were requested to translate the original English tool into Urdu so that the inherent meaning of the items was unchanged and explicit i.e., ensure a parallel value of item content in both versions without any adaptation. After the translation, the translated versions were subjected to the committee approach step.

Step 2: Evaluation of translated items by a committee of experts. The objective of step 2 was to determine the unqualified items. In order to accomplish this, all translated statements from four translations were written down under the corresponding item. These items were then evaluated by members of a committee. The committee members included two Ph.D. professors—one from Quaid-e-Azam University and the other from COMSATS Institute of Information Technology Islamabad. Both were bilingual. All items were carefully assessed, and items having the most appropriate correspondence with original items in semantic terms were selected. Subsequently, items conveying approximately exact meaning of original English-version were chosen for back translation.

Step 3: Back Translation of the selected items into English. In order to corroborate equivalence of translated items, items of the Urdu version were translated back into English. For back translation, the translated version was given to five bilinguals who were not involved in the prior translation. The back translators were Ph.D. professors from Riphah University and Government College. Five translations were later given to committee for evaluation.

Step 4: Evaluation of back-translated items in to English. The back-translated items were written down under their corresponding original items for comparison. The committee constituted same members who were involved in back translation. No incomprehensibility was reported in back translated items. The comparison between back translated and original items to affirmed accuracy of translated version.

Step 5: Cultural equivalence. The Urdu version of the SpNQ was administered to patients with various chronic illnesses for at least three months. The main focus of this step was evaluating the comprehension of items and format. It was observed that, instead of self-administration, it was best to use it in a personal interview format.

The only change relative to the original was the format of administration of the questionnaire. The original English version was designed as self-applicable, whereas for the Brazilian-Portuguese (de Araujo Toloi et al. 2016) version, reading the questionnaire out loud to the patient during a personal interview due to the rate of illiteracy among patients was conducted. Thus, the phrase "when you read these statements" was changed to "when you listen to these statements," followed by the instruction to answer yes or no. The statements could be understood and answered by at least 95% of the patients, thus proving to be easy to understand, and no objections of cultural inappropriateness was reported.

Phase 2: Exploration of Factor Structure for SpNQ Urdu Version

The objectives of phase 2 included exploration of factor structure and psychometric examination for the newly translated Urdu version. To meet the phase 2 objectives, the newly translated Urdu version was administered to a local sample of chronically ill patients.

2.2. Sample and Procedure

The sample consisted of 150 in- and out-patients with chronic illnesses, having pathological conditions prevailing for three or more months along with persistent or recurring illness as diagnostic criteria. The patients included had illnesses histories of up to 12 years and above and under medical supervision with periodic visit to their physicians. The age ranged between 17 to 75. The demographic properties included gender, marital status, chronic illness, and duration of chronic illness. The objective of including these variables was to observe gender differences concerning spiritual needs keeping in view previous findings. There were 46 males and 104 females. Marital status association with respect to spiritual needs in chronically ill patients has not previously explored, which present study intended to explore. There were no educational criteria for the sample population. The chronic illnesses included were classified in order of their chronicity, intensity, and frequency. The duration of the chronic illness has been found to be associated with increased spiritual concerns. To examine its impact, this variable duration was chosen. The sample was selected from hospitals in Islamabad and Rawalpindi using a purposive or selective sampling technique. The present sample and participants were interviewed with the translated Urdu version to gain insight along with accuracy of their responses. The same procedure was used for those patients who were confined to bed. Prior to the administration of the questionnaire, the patients were given instructions in simple language, and their consent was obtained. The codes of ethics for research were strictly followed, and typically, each participant took 15–20 min for a complete administration.

3. Results

The main aim of the present study was to translate, adapt, and explore the factor structure of the translated Urdu version of the Spiritual Needs Questionnaire. To meet the above objective, exploratory factor analysis (EFA) was conducted after considering the assumptions of EFA e.g., interval level and normality. The sample size was checked for adequacy of sample size, indicated by a Kaiser-Meyer-Olkin score greater than 0.5 (KMO = 0.78, $p < 0.001$). The communality pattern matrix in Table 1 explains the variance explained by each item. Principle component analysis was used to extract the maximum number of positive eigen-values in determining the dimensions without losing any information. It was observed that the maximum amount of variance was explained in the first two factors. According to indications that showed spiritual needs to be correlated, an oblique rotation with varimax strategy was employed. The results display that some items were cross-loaded when compared with the original English version. The cross-loading items were handled by retaining items in the factors where highest loadings were observed and loadings greater than 0.4 (Costello and Osborne 2005). It was observed that approximately 30% of the variance was explained by the two factors, a third factor explain 5%, and the rest explaining 3% of the variance. The scree plot also indicated a bent after the third factor, which was suggestive of a prominent role of the initial three-factor structure.

The EFA was rerun was after being restricted to a three-factor solution based on the information received from eigen-values (greater than 1), and scree plot, rejecting factors with fewer than three-items. After the re-execution of EFA, the first factor explained about 28% of the variance, with the second explaining 16%, and the third factor explaining 12% of the variance with 52% of cumulative explained variance.

Table 1. Communalities pattern matrix.

	Extraction
To talk with others about your fears and worries?	0.38
That someone of your religious community (i.e., Alim, peer, imam.guru, padri) cares for you?	0.05
To reflect your previous life?	0.52
To dissolve open aspects of your life?	0.28
To plunge into beauty of nature?	0.30
To dwell at a place of quietness and peace?	0.19
To find inner peace?	0.43
To find meaning in illness and/or suffering?	0.32
To talk with someone about the question of meaning in life?	0.33
To talk with someone about the possibility of life after death?	0.52
To turn to someone in a loving attitude?	0.28
To give away something from yourself?	0.36
To solace someone?	0.27
To forgive someone from a distinct period of your life?	0.53

The rotated component matrix with fixed 3-factors solution (see Table 2) represented a balanced structure with eigen-values ranging between 0.41 to 0.72. Further, the new factor structure showed that items in the inner peace need subscale in the original English version loaded onto the family social support needs after factor rotation. The final 15-item SpNQ questionnaire is available in an Urdu version that constitutes the spirituality needs within religious, family social support and existential needs. The number of items in each factor were 10, 6, and 7, respectively.

Table 2. Rotated component matrix for the three-factor solution with oblique ($N = 150$).

Items	Factors			M	SD
	1	2	3		
That someone prays for you?	0.73			22.21	5.64
To pray with someone?	0.72			22.14	5.62
To turn to a higher presence (i.e., God, Allah, Angels)	0.72			22.14	5.62
To pray for yourself?	0.67			19.61	5.44
To be forgiven?	0.62			18.92	5.35
To forgive someone from a distinct period of your life?	0.60			17.65	5.31
To find inner peace?	0.58			16.94	4.97
To read religious/spiritual books?	0.51			14.95	4.68
To participate at a religious ceremony	0.43			13.98	3.47
To dwell at a place of quietness and peace?	0.41			12.97	3.41
That someone of your religious community (i.e., Alim, peer, imam.guru, padri) cares for you?					
For being complete and safe?		0.66		17.92	4.35
To feel connected with family?		0.65		17.65	4.31
To receive more support from your family?		0.64		17.61	3.97
To pass own life experiences to others?		0.63		15.95	3.68
To be re-involved by your family in their life concerns?		0.62		15.78	3.47
To be assured that your life was meaningful and of value?		0.59		13.97	3.41
To talk with someone about the possibility of life after death?			0.70	18.72	5.35
To reflect your previous life?			0.68	17.55	5.31
To give away something from yourself?			0.59	15.94	4.97
To talk with others about your fears and worries?			0.59	15.94	4.97
To talk with someone about the question of meaning in life?			0.54	14.98	3.67
To find meaning in illness and/or suffering?			0.49	13.97	3.41
To plunge into beauty of nature?			0.45	11.92	2.35
To dissolve open aspects of your life?					
To solace someone?					
To turn to someone in a loving attitude?					

The new factor structure for the Urdu version was evaluated for internal consistency though Cronbach alpha. The results showed psychometrically sound values presented in the Table 3. The correlation analysis revealed all subscales to be positively significantly correlated with each other, suggesting similar direction of elevation of decline for either.

Table 3. Correlation coefficients for the Urdu version subscales (N = 150).

	Factors	1	2	3	Items	M	SD	α
1	Religious Needs	-	0.46 **	0.26 **	10	24.13	5.78	0.82
2	Family Social Support Needs		-	0.19 *	7	11.35	5.04	0.70
3	Existential Needs			-	6	12.66	4.41	0.75

* $p < 0.05$, ** $p < 0.01$.

4. Discussion

The Spiritual Needs Questionnaire was designed to measure spirituality in patients, especially those suffering from chronic illnesses where the duration of illness is long-term and the illness is enduring in nature. In such conditions, the psychological and emotional wellbeing of patients is especially at stake. Spiritual coping is one of the ways the patients combat the challenges of chronic illnesses. Spirituality is a varied concept that is indicated previously to be embedded within religious, cultural, and ethnic practices. This is especially in Pakistan, where the spiritual practices follow religious teachings as well as an influence of Indo-Pak historical influences. Nevertheless, the spiritual needs emerge in the lifespan of every individual and may surface early when faced with life-threatening challenges.

Presently, the current study contributed in broadening the scope of existing Spiritual Needs Questionnaire by translating, adapting, and establishing psychometrics for the tool. Büssing et al. (2010) suggested that when using Spiritual Needs Questionnaire, it must consider that these needs may follow different patterns or dimensions e.g., in the Iranian version, a four-factor structure emerged. Similarly, in the Portuguese version, a five-factor structure differentiated inner peace, religious, existential, actively giving/generativity needs, and family social support needs. The Chinese and Polish versions hold similar factor structures (Büssing et al. 2018). Therefore, the need for further exploration of factor structure in different contexts is highlighted. The current findings presented a diverse picture of the construct compared to the original version. Previously conducted research has identified four dimensions of needs in patients with any chronic or terminal illness. These needs include religious needs, existential needs, inner peace needs, and giving or generativity needs. The factor structure of spiritual needs in Pakistan is different as compared to given structures prevailing in western states. In Pakistan, these four needs cluster in three factors, into which all other needs are accommodated. These needs include religious needs, family social support needs, and existential needs. The inner peace need items were found to merge with family social support needs. The family social support needs were not primarily intended to be spiritual in nature. After exploratory and confirmatory factor analysis, it was found that the spiritual need items merged with family social support needs.

The collectivistic context of present study provides a logical explanation for this merger. Commonly, family plays a pertinent role in an experience of illness and also provides spiritual or religious support, particularly coming from the elderly members of the family. A common practice reflecting such behaviors is asking elderly members of family to conduct praying rituals for the ill. The family also serves as spiritual mentors especially in the lives of chronically ill patients. Family members create an active collaboration with patient to improve their socialization practices during course of illness (Rosland and Piette 2010). Family members also provide spiritual care to patients, thereby helping them in acceptance of disease and to develop the potential for painful treatment procedures. Therefore, family social support needs are surfaced as spiritual items within the context of Pakistan.

Religious needs include being involved in religious services to form a transcendent connection with God. In the context of Pakistan, religious needs occupy a prominent locus in people's lives because of strong religious and spiritual beliefs. An inclination toward religion and spirituality after diagnosis is used as mechanism to adapt disease conditions (Lim 2013) in that family social support works as a moderator, palliating them to fulfill their religious needs. Although this can further be attributed to the larger portion of the sample being married, the unmarried participants also relied on family members for meeting their spiritual needs.

The existential needs include discussing life after death, solutiosn for apparent problems, reflecting on one's previous life, and discussing the meaning in life. The majority of chronically ill patients reported that soliciting contiguity to Allah is a very powerful way to cope with disease. Many patients responded that they are not afraid of disease because the illness comes from God and he will alleviate it. This was consistent with the findings of (Nixon et al. 2013). They also believed that this illness might be their trial in this world for which there will be a reward in the afterlife.

This translated version of the spiritual need questionnaire measures the spiritual need of only chronically ill patients. The scope should be further broadened to assess the spiritual needs of those people who are not chronically ill.

Author Contributions: Conceptualization, A.K. and Z.K.; Methodology, A.K.; Software, SPSS (version 22); Validation, A.K. and Z.K.; Formal Analysis, A.K.; Investigation, A.K. and Z.K.; Resources, A.K. and Z.K.; Data Curation, Z.K.; Writing-Original Draft Preparation, Z.K.; Writing-Review & Editing, A.K.; Visualization, A.K. and Z.K.; Supervision, A.K.; Project Administration, A.K.

Funding: This research received no external funding.

Conflicts of Interest: The authors declare no conflict of interest.

References

Azeemi, Khwaja Shamsuddin. 2005. *Muraqaba: The Art and Science of Sufi Meditation*. Houston: Plato Publishing Inc.

Balboni, Tracy A., Lauren C. Vanderwerker, Susan D. Block, M. Elizabeth Paulk, Christopher S. Lathan, John R. Peteet, and Holly G. Prigerson. 2007. Religiousness and spiritual support among advanced cancer patients and associations with end-of-life treatment preferences and quality of life. *Journal of Clinical Oncology* 25: 555–60. [CrossRef] [PubMed]

Büssing, Arndt, Thomas Ostermann, and Peter F. Matthiessen. 2007a. Adaptive coping and spirituality as a resource in cancer patients. *Breast Care* 2: 195–202. [CrossRef]

Büssing, Arndt, Thomas Ostermann, and Harold G. Koenig. 2007b. Relevance of religion and spirituality in German patients with chronic diseases. *The International Journal of Psychiatry in Medicine* 37: 39–57. [CrossRef] [PubMed]

Büssing, Arndt, Andreas Michalsen, Hans-Joachim Balzat, Ralf-Achim Grünther, Thomas Ostermann, Edmund A. M. Neugebauer, and Peter F. Matthiessen. 2009. Are spirituality and religiosity resources for patients with chronic pain conditions? *Pain Medicine* 10: 327–39. [CrossRef] [PubMed]

Büssing, Arndt, Hans-Joachim Balzat, and Peter Heusser. 2010. Spiritual needs of patients with chronic pain diseases and cancer-validation of the spiritual needs questionnaire. *European Journal of Medical Research* 15: 266. [CrossRef] [PubMed]

Büssing, Arndt, Xiao-Feng Zhai, Wen-Bo Peng, and Chang-Quan Ling. 2013. Psychosocial and spiritual needs of patients with chronic diseases: Validation of the Chinese version of the Spiritual Needs Questionnaire. *Journal of Integrative Medicine* 11: 106–15. [CrossRef] [PubMed]

Büssing, Arndt, Iwona Pilchowska, and Janusz Surzykiewicz. 2015. Spiritual needs of Polish patients with chronic diseases. *Journal of Religion and Health* 54: 1524–42. [CrossRef] [PubMed]

Büssing, Arndt, Daniela Rodrigues Recchia, Harold Koenig, Klaus Baumann, and Eckhard Frick. 2018. Factor Structure of the Spiritual Needs Questionnaire (SpNQ) in Persons with Chronic Diseases, Elderly and Healthy Individuals. *Religions* 9: 13. [CrossRef]

Costello, Anna B., and Jason W. Osborne. 2005. Best practices in exploratory factor analysis: Four recommendations for getting the most from your analysis. *Practical Assessment, Research & Evaluation* 10: 1–9.

de Araujo Toloi, Diego, Deise Uema, Felipe Matsushita, Paulo Antonio da Silva Andrade, Tiago Pugliese Branco, Fabiana Tomie Becker de Carvalho Chino, and Daniel P. Sulmasy. 2016. Validation of questionnaire on the Spiritual Needs Assessment for Patients (SNAP) questionnaire in Brazilian Portuguese. *Ecancermedicalscience*, 10. [CrossRef] [PubMed]

Ellison, Lori L. 2006. The Spiritual Well-Being Scale. *NewsNotes*. 44. Available online: http://mds.marshall.edu/co_faculty/9/ (accessed on 16 July 2006).

Koenig, Harold George, Dana King, and Verna B. Carson. 2012. *Handbook of Religion and Health*. New York: Oup Usa.

Lim, Kokkwang. 2013. Clinical hypnosis in the management of panic disorder with cognitive-behavioural and spiritual strategies. *Australian Journal of Clinical & Experimental Hypnosis* 41: 213–24.

McMahan, David L. 2008. *The Making of Buddhist Modernism*. Oxford: Oxford University Press.

Mok, Esther, Frances Wong, and Daniel Wong. 2010. The meaning of spirituality and spiritual care among the Hong Kong Chinese terminally ill. *Journal of Advanced Nursing* 66: 360–70. [CrossRef] [PubMed]

Moreira-Almeida, Alexander, Francisco Lotufo Neto, and Harold G. Koenig. 2006. Religiousness and mental health: A review. *Revista Brasileira de Psiquiatria* 28: 242–50. [CrossRef] [PubMed]

Moeini, Babak, Hadi Zamanian, Zahra Taheri-Kharameh, Tahereh Ramezani, Mohamadhasan Saati-Asr, Mohamadhasan Hajrahimian, and Mohammadali Amini-Tehrani. 2018. Translation and Psychometric Testing of the Persian Version of the Spiritual Needs Questionnaire among elders with chronic diseases. *Journal of Pain and Symptom Management* 55: 94–100. [CrossRef] [PubMed]

Nixon, Aline Victoria, Aru Narayanasamy, and Vivian Penny. 2013. An investigation into the spiritual needs of neuro-oncology patients from a nurse perspective. *BMC Nursing* 12: 2. [CrossRef] [PubMed]

Oh, Pok Ja, and Kyung Ah Kang. 2005. Spirituality: Concept analysis based on hybrid model. *Journal of Korean Academy of Nursing* 35: 709–20. [CrossRef] [PubMed]

Puchalski, Christina, Betty Ferrell, Rose Virani, Shirley Otis-Green, Pamela Baird, Janet Bull, Harvey Chochinov, George Handzo, Holly Nelson-Becker, Maryjo Prince-Paul, and et al. 2009. Improving the quality of spiritual care as a dimension of palliative care: The report of the Consensus Conference. *Journal of Palliative Medicine* 12: 885–904. [CrossRef] [PubMed]

Rainbird, Kathy, J. Perkins, Robert Sanson-Fisher, I. Rolfe, and Paul Anseline. 2009. The needs of patients with advanced, incurable cancer. *British Journal of Cancer* 101: 759. [CrossRef] [PubMed]

Rosland, Ann-Marie, and John D. Piette. 2010. Emerging models for mobilizing family support for chronic disease management: a structured review. *Chronic Illness* 6: 7–21. [CrossRef] [PubMed]

Saucier, Gerard, and Katarzyna Skrzypińska. 2006. Spiritual but not religious? Evidence for two independent dispositions. *Journal of Personality* 74: 1257–92. [CrossRef] [PubMed]

Seddigh, Ruohollah, Amir-Abbas Keshavarz-Akhlaghi, and Somayeh Azarnik. 2016. Questionnaires Measuring Patients' Spiritual Needs: A Narrative Literature Review. *Iranian Journal of Psychiatry and Behavioral Sciences* 10: e4011. [CrossRef] [PubMed]

Shahbaz, Kanwai, and Kiran Shahbaz. 2015. Relationship between Spiritual Well-being and Quality of Life among Chronically Ill Individuals. *The International Journal of Indian Psychology* 2: 128–42.

Sulmasy, Daniel P. 2002. A biopsychosocial-spiritual model for the care of patients at the end of life. *The Gerontologist* 42 S3: 24–33. [CrossRef]

Thune-Boyle, Ingela C., Jan A. Stygall, Mohammed R. Keshtgar, and Stanton P. Newman. 2006. Do religious/spiritual coping strategies affect illness adjustment in patients with cancer? A systematic review of the literature. *Social Science & Medicine* 63: 151–64.

Woll, Monica L., Daniel B. Hinshaw, and Timothy M. Pawlik. 2008. Spirituality and religion in the care of surgical oncology patients with life-threatening or advanced illnesses. *Annals of Surgical Oncology* 15: 3048–57. [CrossRef] [PubMed]

Zamanzadeh, Vahid, Maryam Rassouli, Abbas Abbaszadeh, Alireza Nikanfar, Hamid Alavi-Majd, and Akram Ghahramanian. 2014. Factors influencing communication between the patients with cancer and their nurses in oncology wards. *Indian Journal of Palliative Care* 20: 12. [PubMed]

© 2018 by the authors. Licensee MDPI, Basel, Switzerland. This article is an open access article distributed under the terms and conditions of the Creative Commons Attribution (CC BY) license (http://creativecommons.org/licenses/by/4.0/).

Article

Transcultural Adaptation and Psychometric Properties of Portuguese Version of the Spiritual Needs Questionnaire (SpNQ) Among HIV Positive Patients in Brazil

Tânia Cristina de Oliveira Valente [1,*], Ana Paula Rodrigues Cavalcanti [2], Arndt Büssing [3], Clóvis Pereira da Costa Junior [4] and Rogerio Neves Motta [5]

[1] Interdisciplinary Medical Anthropologic Studies and Research Laboratory, Rio de Janeiro State Federal University, 20211-040 Rio de Janeiro, Brazil
[2] Department of Sciences of Religions, Universidade Federal da Paraíba, 58051-900 João Pessoa, Paraíba, Brazil; anapaulacavalcanti.ufpb@gmail.com
[3] Professorship Quality of Life, Spirituality and Coping, Faculty of Health, Witten/Herdecke University, 58313 Herdecke, Germany; arndt.buessing@uni-wh.de
[4] Complexo Hospitalar de Mangabeira Governador Tarcísio Burity, 58056-384 João Pessoa, Paraíba, Brazil; costajunior.cp@gmail.com
[5] Rio de Janeiro Federal State University Medical School HIV/AIDS Outpatient Clinic, 20270-001 Rio de Janeiro, Brazil; nevesmotta@cremerj.org.br
* Correspondence: valenteunirio@gmail.com; Tel.: +55-21-25317677

Received: 28 February 2018; Accepted: 11 April 2018; Published: 18 April 2018

Abstract: The Spiritual Needs Questionnaire (SpNQ), originally written in the German language, was translated and validated into 11 languages, but not Latin languages, such as Brazilian Portuguese. This study aimed to determine the psychometric properties of the SpNQ after translation and transcultural adaptation to the Portuguese language, identifying unmet spiritual needs in a sample of patients living with HIV in Brazil. This pioneering study conformed a four-factor structure of 20 items, differentiating Religious Needs (α = 0.887), Giving/Generativity Needs (α = 0.848), Inner Peace (α = 0.813) and a new item: Family Support Needs (α = 0.778). The Brazilian version of the SpNQ (SpNQ-BR) had good internal validity criteria and can be used for research of the spiritual needs for Brazilian patients. The cross-cultural adaptation and comparison with previous studies showed that the SpNQ is sensitive to the cultural characteristics of different countries.

Keywords: psychometric properties; transcultural adaptation; spiritual needs; people living with HIV

1. Introduction

The World Health Organization defines a four-fold approach as a health concept to assess individual and community well-being that includes biological, psychological, social, and spiritual aspects (World Health Organization 1998). Among them, spirituality/religiosity has been deeply studied in the last decade and its positive effects on health are well established (Koenig 2015). Spirituality is defined as "dynamic and intrinsic aspect of humanity through which persons seek ultimate meaning, purpose, and transcendence, and experience relationship to self, family, others, community, society, nature, and the significant or sacred, expressed through beliefs, values, traditions, and practices" (Puchalski et al. 2014). A further, rather broad definition assumes "spirituality as all attempts to find meaning, purpose, and hope in relation to the sacred or significant (which may have a secular, religious, philosophical, humanist, or personal dimension)", and the related "spiritual practices have commitment to values, beliefs, practices, or philosophies which may have an impact on patients' cognition, emotion, and behavior" (Büssing et al. 2014). Although spirituality is often used as an opposite dimension to religiosity, "spirituality can be found through religious engagement", but also independent from specific religion "through an individual experience of the Divine, and/or through a connection to other people, the environment and the Sacred" (Büssing 2015).

Acquired immunodeficiency syndrome (AIDS) is one of the chronic diseases that most mobilizes human beings from a bio-psycho-socio-spiritual view. People with this disease often face isolation, anxiety, stress, depression, stigma and discrimination, characterizing a situation where subjective, supportive, and resilience need to be addressed in physical and mental healthcare (Tuck et al. 2001). Although AIDS has figured in the scientific literature since 1981, study on the importance given to spirituality by AIDS patients has been directed toward the role of spirituality/religiosity (S/R) on coping with their illness (Coleman et al. 2006; Kemppainen et al. 2006) or the disease in its final phase. Few studies have focused on the spiritual needs (Van Wyngaard 2013) of people living with HIV (PLHIV—seropositive patients who still do not show signs of disease progression), and none have been done in Brazil.

To help health services reflect the spiritual angle, several questionnaires have been proposed to check the relevance of S/R for chronic disease patients. The Spiritual Needs Questionnaire (SpNQ) is one of the most widely used. Originally written in the German language, by Büssing et al. (2009, 2010), this instrument can be used as a diagnostic instrument with 29 items and as a 20-item research instrument, which was validated in persons with chronic diseases, and also in (healthy) elderly and stressed people (Büssing et al. 2018). It avoids the exclusive use of religious terminology and is, thus, applicable also to persons living in secular societies and atheist/agnostic populations, relying on the bio-psycho-socio-spiritual or a "holistic" perspective of health. It has been translated into English, Italian, Polish, Danish, Chinese, Indonesian, Farsi, Croatian, and Lithuanian (Büssing et al. 2018), but not Latin languages, such as Brazilian Portuguese.

In this study, we aimed to identify spiritual needs in a sample of PLHIV in Brazil, translating SpNQ to the Portuguese Language and adapting it for cross-cultural purposes. It may highlight high-priority spiritual needs in a transdisciplinary perspective, contributing to a whole-person healthcare for these patients in Brazil.

2. Materials and Methods

2.1. Participants

The cross-sectional, longitudinal validation study included application of the SpNQ-BR and a demographic information questionnaire (including age, educational status, gender and religious organizational or non-organizational practices) for 200 seropositive patients, randomly selected among patients who followed up at the AIDS Outpatient Clinic of the Medical School Hospital, located in Rio de Janeiro, Brazil. This hospital is accredited as a National Aids Reference Center by the Brazilian Ministry of Health and it is the largest clinic with this specialty in Rio de Janeiro State. The inclusion criteria was to be older than or equal to 18 years of age, of all genders, HIV positive followed at Rio de Janeiro Federal State University Medical School HIV/AIDS Outpatient Clinic, to have the capacity to read, understand, fill out the instrument at the time of application. Patients with some level of clinical disorientation, unable to read, to understand, and to fill out the instrument, or those who refuse to sign the informed consent form were excluded. All participants were informed about confidentiality assurance and the purpose of the study and freely signed the informed consent form, consented to participate.

The study was carried out according to ethical principles in research and was approved by the Rio de Janeiro Federal State University (UNIRIO) Ethics Committee on Research in Human Beings (2.316.525/2017).

2.2. Questionnaire and Translation Process

To measure patients' spiritual needs, we used the Spiritual Needs Questionnaire (SpNQ) (Büssing et al. 2010, 2012). In its primary version, it differentiates between four main factors:

1. Religious Needs (Cronbach's alpha = 0.92), e.g., praying for and with others, praying alone, participating in a religious ceremony, reading spiritual/religious books, turning to a higher presence (e.g., God, angels);
2. Existential Needs (Reflection/Meaning) (alpha = 0.82), e.g., reflecting on one's life, talking with someone about the meaning of life/suffering, resolving open aspects in life, talking about the possibility of life after death, etc.;
3. Need for Inner Peace (alpha = 0.82), e.g., wish to dwell in places of quietness and peace, plunge into the beauty of nature, finding inner peace, talking with others about fears and worries, turning to someone in a loving attitude;
4. Need for Active Giving/Generativity (alpha = 0.74), e.g., active and autonomous intention to provide solace to someone, passing along one's own life experiences to others, and to be assured that life was meaningful and of value.

All items were scored with respect to self-ascribed importance on a 4-point scale from disagreement to agreement (0—not at all; 1—somewhat; 2—very; 3—extremely). For all analyses, we used the mean scores of the respective scales described above; the higher the scores, the stronger the respective needs were.

Translation and validation of the questionnaire was performed using the World Health Organization recommendations for the translation and adaptation of instruments (WHO 2014). After reading other papers about SpNQ transcultural adaptation, we asked the author for authorization, and the transcultural translation procedure followed the steps described below:

Step 1:

Translation of the 27-item English version into Portuguese by two bilingual professionals, aware of the objectives of the study, resulting in two Portuguese versions of SpNQ.

Step 2:

The versions were compared by another bilingual researcher, resulting in a reconciled version in Portuguese.

Step 3:

The reconciled version was translated back into English by two other bilingual professionals, and the versions were compared by another bilingual researcher, resulting in an SpNQ reconciled version in English.

Step 4:

The English and Portuguese versions were sent to the author of the instrument for review and approval.

Step 5:

The final version was approved by the author and was revised for Portuguese grammar, punctuation and formatting, obtaining a translated version of SpNQ for the pre-test.

Step 6:

The translated instrument was presented to 26 outpatients in 4 Brazilian health services, and individual interviews were conducted with each of them to identify problems in understanding the instrument's questions, obtaining the 27-item SpNQ Portuguese final version (27 SpNQ-BR).

2.3. Statistical Analyses

Descriptive statistics, internal consistency (Cronbach's coefficient α) and factor analyses (principal component analysis using Varimax rotation with Kaiser's normalization), as well as first order correlations, were computed using SPSS 21.0 and 23.0.

3. Results

3.1. Participants

Data were collected in July, 2017. In the studied population, most were male (57%), with age ranging from 30–49 years old (57%) and 61% had a high school level education. Spiritists and religious organizational practices were the majority in the religious aspect (27%), as shown on Table 1.

Table 1. Demographic characteristics and religion of HIV positive Brazilian participants ($N = 200$).

Participants Characteristics	N	%
GENDER		
Male	114	57
Female	82	41
Other	4	2
AGE		
Less than 29 year	60	30
30–49 year	114	57
50–70 year	26	13
EDUCATIONAL STATUS		
Primary School Complete	6	3
High School Incomplete	67	33.5
High School Graduate	54	27
University Incomplete	49	24.5
Missing Values	24	12
RELIGION		
Christian	46	23
Kardecist Spiritist	54	27
Other (Jewish, Ecumenic, Seicho-no-iê, Hare-Krishna, Adventist of the Seventh-day, White Table Rituals, Wicca, Buddhist, Messianic, Jehovah's Witness)	17	8.5
Prefer not to say/missing values	83	41.5
PRACTICE OF RELIGION		
Organizational	116	58
No-organizational	43	21.5
Missing values	41	20.5

3.2. Validation of the Questionnaire

With KMO indexes = 0.89 and Bartlett's sphericity test, $X^2(351) = 2775.405$, $p < 0.001$ the item pool was suited for factor analysis. Together, they showed the association between items, which corroborated the factorial validity of the instrument and allowed us to continue analyses. The second step was the factorial analysis, fixing the number of factors to 4, as noted by Büssing et al. (2009). To do so, we used the method for main components, with orthogonal rotation types. It is important to point out that, in fact, this solution presented the best statistical parameters, compared with other alternatives (example: Trifactorial, bifactorial, or unifactorial). The quadrifactorial structure obtained values (eigenvalues) of 9.58; 2.22; 1.74 and 1.48 (shown in Figure 1), explaining 55.6% of the total variance.

Thus, the Portuguese version of the SpNQ (SpNQ-BR) included 20 items and differentiated four factors. The first factor was composed of seven items, accounting for 18.5% of the explained variance and with an eigenvalue of 9.58. From its semantic content, it was named "Religious Needs", and obtained loads between 0.52 and 0.83 factorials. The second factor was comprised of six items, explaining 14.9% of the variance, with an eigenvalue of 2.22 and factorial loads ranging from 0.51 to 0.69, and was called "Giving/Generativity Needs". The third factor was labeled "Inner Peace", and was composed of three items, explaining 11.6% of variance, with an eigenvalue of 1.74 and factorial loads ranging from 0.79 to 0.83. Finally, the fourth factor, named "Family Support Needs", contained three items which were intended as additional 'psychosocial' items of the SpNQ, and explained 10.5% of the variance, showed a 1.48 eigenvalue and factorial loads between 0.64 and 0.72. The factorial structure obtained can be seen in Table 2.

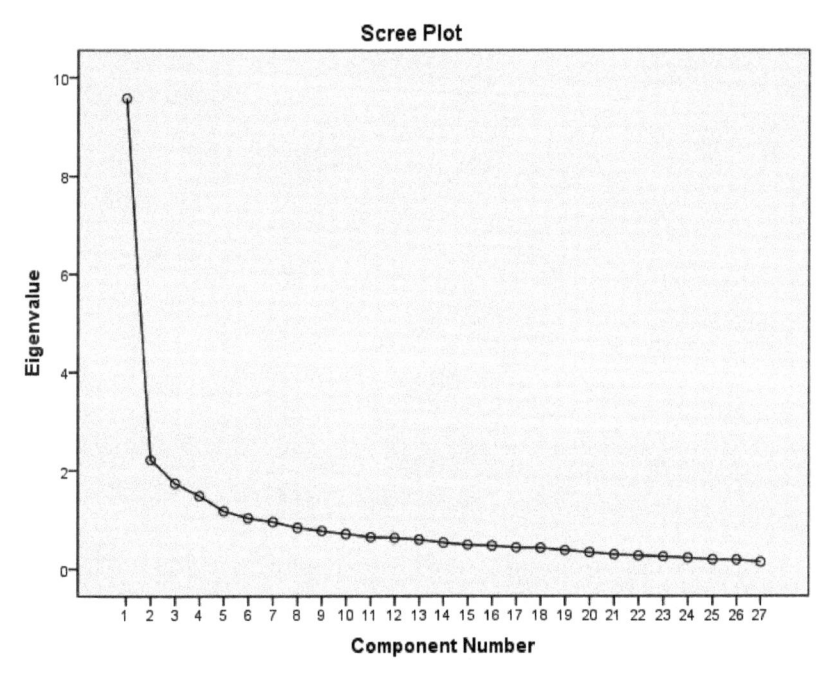

Figure 1. Graphical distribution of eigen values of Spiritual Needs Questionnaire —Portuguese Version (SpNQ-BR).

Table 2. Factorial structure, means, standard deviations, correlation items and factorial loads of the 20 Spiritual Needs Questionnaire Portuguese Version (SpNQ-BR) in a four-factors structure.

	Factors and Items	Mean	SD	Correlation Item-Total	Alfa if Item Deleted	I	II	III	IV
	1—Religious Needs (eigenvalue 9.58; α = 0.887)								
N21	Participate at a religious ceremony (e.g., service)	0.95	0.98	0.569	0.925	0.836			
N23	Turn to a higher presence (e.g., God, Allah)	1.36	1.00	0.656	0.923	0.836			
N19	Someone prays for you	1.08	0.94	0.666	0.923	0.786			
N20	Pray for yourself	0.94	0.91	0.685	0.923	0.778			
N18	Pray with someone	0.62	0.81	0.656	0.924	0.639	0.335		0.330
N03	Someone of your religious community (e.g., pastor) cares for you	0.39	0.67	0.430	0.927	0.564			0.379
N22	Read religious/ spiritual books	0.63	0.89	0.545	0.925	0.523	0.519		

Table 2. Cont.

	Factors and Items	Mean	SD	Correlation Item-Total	Alfa if Item Deleted	Factorial Loads I	II	III	IV
	2—Giving/Generativity Needs (eigenvalue 2.22; α = 0.848)								
N10	Find meaning in illness and/or suffering	0.60	0.85	0.540	0.925		0.692		
N11	Talk about the question of meaning in life	1.07	0.90	0.657	0.923	0.377	0.617		
N13	Turn to someone in a loving attitude	1.18	0.77	0.632	0.924	0.333	0.601		
N12	Talk about the possibility of life after death	0.75	0.97	0.559	0.925	0.438	0.595		
N17	Be forgiven	1.08	0.98	0.554	0.925		0.551		
N14	Give away something from yourself	0.98	0.82				0.510		0.323
	3—Inner Peace (eigenvalue 1.74; α = 0.813)								
N07	Dwell at a place of quietness and peace	1.78	0.77	0.501	0.926			0.837	
N08	Find inner peace	1.86	0.80	0.546	0.925			0.835	
N06	Plunge into beauty of nature	1.63	0.80	0.489	0.926			0.792	
N04	Reflect your previous life	0.99	0.86	0.440	0.927		0.387	0.469	
	4—Family Support Needs (eigenvalue 1.48; α = 0.778)								
N30	Receive more support from your family	1.09	0.73	0.543	0.925			0.302	0.722
N25	Feel connected with your family	1.14	0.74	0.537	0.925				0.665
N28	Be inserted again on your family concerns	0.38	0.68	0.418	0.927		0.325		0.649

A solution of five factors (supposing Family Support Needs to be an additional dimension), Varimax rotation, and main axis extraction (Valente et al. 2018) was also considered. However, it was not observed to be statistically well grounded: Giving/Generativity Needs consisted, on this solution, of only two items, as can be seen in Table 3. Also on this statistical version many items (N27, N24, N02, N14, N15, N04, and N05) would have to be excluded making five factors version use inappropriate.

Table 3. Factorial structure, means and standard deviations of the SpNQ—Portuguese Version in a structure of five factors.

	Factors and Items	Mean	SD	Correlation Item-Total	Alfa if Item Deleted	Factorial Loads I	II	III	IV
	1—Religious Needs (eigenvalue 9.58; α = 0.892)								
N23	Turn to a higher presence (i.e., God, Allah)	1.36	1.00	0.680	0.908	0.809			
N21	Participate at a religious ceremony (e.g., service)	0.95	0.98	0.594	0.910	0.780			
N19	Someone prays for you	1.08	0.94	0.686	0.908	0.767			
N20	Pray for yourself	0.94	0.91	0.699	0.908	0.749			
N18	Pray with someone	0.62	0.81	0.668	0.909	0.594			
N03	Someone of your religious community cares for you	0.39	0.67	0.453	0.913	0.513			

Table 3. Cont.

	Factors and Items	Mean	SD	Correlation Item-Total	Alfa if Item Deleted	I	II	III	IV
						\multicolumn{4}{c}{Factorial Loads}
\multicolumn{10}{c}{2—Existential Needs (eigenvalue 2.22; α = 0.834)}
N12	Talk about the posibility of life after death	0.75	0.97	0.556		0.693			
N11	Talk with someone about the question of meaning in life	1.07	0.90	0.640		0.568			
N22	Read religious/ spiritual books	0.63	0.89	0.551		0.567			
N10	Find meaning in illness and/or suffering	0.60	0.85	0.522		0.547			
N13	Turn to someone in a loving attitude	1.18	0.77	0.610		0.527			
N26	Pass own life experiences to others	1.00	0.81	0.673		0.415			
\multicolumn{10}{c}{3—Inner Peace (eigenvalue 1.74; alpha = 0.876)}
N08	Find inner peace	1.86	0.80	0.515			0.819		
N07	Dwell at a place of quietness and peace	1.78	0.77	0.484			0.813		
N06	Plunge into the beauty of nature	1.63	0.80	0.485			0.727		
\multicolumn{10}{c}{4—Family Support Needs (eigenvalue 1.48; alpha = 0.778)}
N30	Receive more support from your family	1.00	0.75	0.526				0.815	
N25	Feel connected with your family	1.14	0.74	0.525				0.682	
N28	Be inserted again on your family concerns	0.38	0.68	0.401				0.538	
\multicolumn{10}{c}{5—Giving/Generativity Needs (eigenvalue 1.17; α = 0.821)}
N16	Forgive someone from a distinct period of your life	0.95	0.92	0.482	0.913				0.759
N17	Be forgiven	1.08	0.98	0.545	0.912				0.736

4. Discussion

Spirituality is one of the aspects that differentiates human beings from other creatures, and a way to highlight differences among societies and individuals. In Brazil, we do not have data regarding PLHIV spiritual needs, as such, this is a pioneering study.

The SpNQ was originally written in German by Büssing et al. (2010, 2012), and included 29 items that are not all used for the construct (19 items were used for the research instrument). In the Polish language (Büssing et al. 2015) 20 items were tested and two items were deleted during the factorial analyses (item N4W and N6W). The Chinese version (Büssing et al. 2013) was tested with 20 items, resulting in 17 items due to a weak factor loading of N2, N11, and N14. The Polynesian version (Nuraeni et al. 2015) tested 19 items and for the Iranian and New Zealand English Languages translation there is no information about the tested items (Nejat et al. 2016); however, all these translations processes included the four-factor structure: Religious Needs, Existential Needs, Inner Peace Needs, and Giving/Generativity Needs. In the Croatian Language translation process (Glavas et al. 2017) version 20 + 3 items was used to calculate the five factor scales, and, as an additional "non-spiritual" category, Social Support Needs (which is like our Family Support Needs scale). For the Persian version, the 19-item version was tested, and the five factors were tested and approved.

Nevertheless, there was stability of the four main factors with some variances, because some 'existential' items could be also be called 'inner peace' items, and vice versa. However, one has to take into account cultural and religious differences, because spirituality is a highly diverse set of beliefs, attitudes, and practices, and probably also needs. Moreover, the validation process of an interculturally-used instrument requires larger and more heterogeneous samples. This is also true for our sample of HIV positive patients, with 42% of them not stating their religious/spiritual orientation.

The diversity of translated versions caused a great deal of doubt in choosing the model to be tested in Brazil. Due to this, in the pilot test, we applied the SpNQ—27-item version to 26 in-patients with other diseases, using a five factor scale: Religious Needs, Existential Needs, Inner Peace Needs, Giving/Generativity Needs, and adding a category called Family Support Needs, which included questions regarding: Feeling connected with family, transmitting one's own life experiences to others, being assured that your life was meaningful and of value, being rather involved by your family in their life concerns, and receiving more support from your family. These questions were present in former SpNQ versions. In that pilot test, Family Support Needs was the most important domain to the interviewed Brazilian patients (Büssing et al. 2016).

Family Support Needs was also found to be relevant in the Brazilian PLHIV sample, confirming the former pilot test results; this was different from other countries, where SpNQ was previously translated (Büssing et al. 2018; Glavas et al. 2017; Hatamipour et al. 2018; Offenbaecher et al. 2013), where these items were used only as 'informative' items because of their lack of a 'spiritual' connotation. Data about the spiritual needs of PLHIV in other countries were not found, making it impossible to compare data.

This fact, and the way in which spiritual needs are linked to religious needs in the researched Brazilian population, is probably linked to the cultural characteristics of the Brazilian people, who are markedly religious, so that it is reflected in their everyday lives, in the capacity of expression of multiple forms of religious faith. These cultural and religious beliefs account for a fundamental part of the ethos of Brazilian culture and are often confused with spirituality (De Andrade 2009).

These results reinforce the need to have a spiritual needs measure that, not only can be translated into several languages, but also fits the cultural characteristics of each country, allowing comparison of the obtained results. SpNQ has promising characteristics to be a measure that strengthens efforts that are being done to broaden the integration of spiritual care as an essential aspect of person-centered healthcare in many countries, as proposed by the Global Network for Spirituality and Health (Puchalski et al. 2016).

The main limitation of this study is the rather small and young sample, as well as its exclusive focus on persons living with HIV. Therefore, further studies that enroll other persons from Brazil with chronic diseases are needed. With a more heterogeneous sample, the factorial structure may change slightly. The current validation process of the 20-item version (Büssing et al. 2018), enrolling healthy elderly and persons with chronic diseases showed that some items have a distinct relevance to persons with different life and health.

5. Conclusions

The translation of SpNQ showed that this measure had good internal validity and that its 20-item version can be used for research on the spiritual needs of Brazilian patients.

Cross-cultural adaptation and comparison with previous studies showed that the SpNQ can be adjusted to the cultural characteristics of different countries, especially regarding to the role and importance that societies give to religion and spirituality, remembering that the results of modifications to be proposed will certainly be influenced by the disease, the size of the sample to be researched and the study design.

We encourage subsequent studies regarding the theme in the largest Brazilian populations and in other Latin countries to confirm the results of this research.

Acknowledgments: No sources of funding are reported. We sincerely are grateful to Bussing who helped in the translation process and presented our work at the international meetings. We are very grateful to the undergraduate students, especially Anderson Tarocco Junior, that collaborated in the SpNQ translation and pilot test and Thiago Falheiros, undergraduate social sciences student that did the data collection

Author Contributions: Tania C. O. Valente and Ana Paula R. Cavalcanti conceived and designed the study. Rogerio N. Motta conducted data collection. Tania C. O. Valente, Ana Paula Cavalcanti, Clovis P. Costa Junior and Arndt Bussing analyzed the data. Tania C. O. Valente, Ana Paula R. Cavalcanti and Arndt Bussing wrote and revised the paper.

Conflicts of Interest: The authors declare no conflicts of interest.

References

Büssing, Arndt. 2015. Spirituality/Religiosity as a Resource for Coping in Soldiers: A Summary Report. *Medical Acupuncture* 27: 360–66. [CrossRef]

Büssing, Arndt, Hans-Joachim Balzat, and Peter Heusser. 2009. Spirituelle Bedürfnisse von Patienten mit chronischen Schmerz- und Tumorerkrankungen. *Perioperative Medizin* 1: 248. [CrossRef]

Büssing, Arndt, Hans-Joachim Balzat, and Peter Heusser. 2010. Spiritual needs of patients with chronic pain diseases and cancer—Validation of the spiritual needs questionnaire. *European Journal of Medical Research* 15: 266–73. Available online: https://www.ncbi.nlm.nih.gov/pubmed/20696636 (accessed on 19 February 2018).

Büssing, Arndt, J. Janko, Andreas Kopf, Eberhard Lux, and Eckhard Frick. 2012. Zusammenhänge zwischen psychosozialen und spirituellen Bedürfnissen und Bewertung von Krankheit bei Patienten mit chronischen Erkrankungen. *Spiritual Care* 1: 57–73.

Büssing, Arndt, Xiao-Feng Zhai, Wen-Bo Peng, and Chang-Quan Ling. 2013. Validation of the Chinese Version of the Spiritual Needs Questionnaire. *Journal of Integrative Medicine* 11: 106–15. [CrossRef] [PubMed]

Büssing, Arndt, Klaus Baumann, Niels Christian Hvidt, Harold G. Koenig, Christina M. Puchalski, and John Swinton. 2014. Spirituality and Health. *Evidence-Based Complementary and Alternative Medicine* 2014: 682817. [CrossRef] [PubMed]

Büssing, Arndt, Iwona Pilchowska, and Janusz Surzykiewicz. 2015. Spiritual Needs of Polish Patients with Chronic Diseases. *Journal of Religion and Health* 54: 1524–42. [CrossRef]

Büssing, Arndt, Tânia Cristina de Oliveira Valente, Ana Paula Rodrigues Cavalcanti, Anderson Luís Carvalho Tarocco Jr., and Daniela Rodrigues Recchia. 2016. Brazilian Transcultural of Patient's Spiritual Needs Questionnaire. Paper presented at 5th European Conference on Religion, Spirituality and Health and 4th International Conference of the British Association for the Study of Spirituality, Gdansk, Poland, May 12–14.

Büssing, Arndt, Daniela Rodrigues Recchia, Harold Koenig, Klaus Baumann, and Eckhard Frick. 2018. Factor Structure of the Spiritual Needs Questionnaire (SpNQ) in Persons with Chronic Diseases, Elderly and Healthy Individuals. *Religions* 9: 13. [CrossRef]

Coleman, Christopher Lance, Jeanne K. Kemppainen, William L. Holzemer, Lucille Sanzero Eller, Inge Corless, Nancy Reynolds, Kathleen M. Nokes, Pam Dole, Kenn Kirksey, Liz Seficik, and et al. 2006. Gender Differences in Use of Prayer as a Self-Care Strategy for Managing Symptoms in African Americans Living with HIV/AIDS. *Journal of the Association of Nurses in AIDS Care* 17: 16–23. Available online: https://www.ncbi.nlm.nih.gov/pubmed/16849085 (accessed on 19 February 2018). [CrossRef] [PubMed]

De Andrade, Maristela Oliveira. 2009. Brazilian Religiosity: Religious Pluralism, Diversity of Beliefs and the Syncretic Process. *CAOS-Revista Eletrônica de Ciências Sociais* 14: 106–18. Available online: http://www.cchla.ufpb.br/caos/n14/6A%20religiosidade%20brasileira.pdf (accessed on 19 February 2018).

Glavas, Andrijana, Karin Jors, Arndt Büssing, and Klaus Baumann. 2017. Spiritual Needs of PTSD Patients in Croatia and Bosnia-Herzegovina: A Quantitative Pilot Study. *Psychiatria Danubina* 29: 282–90. [CrossRef] [PubMed]

Hatamipour, Khadijeh, Maryam Rassouli, Farideh Yaghmaie, Kazem Zendedel, and Hamid Alavi Majd. 2018. Development and Psychometrics of a 'Spiritual Assessment Scale of Patients with Cancer': A Mixed Exploratory Study. *International Journal of Cancer Management* 11: e10083. Available online: http://dx.doi.org/10.5812/ijcm.10083 (accessed on 25 January 2018). [CrossRef]

Kemppainen, Jeanne, Lucille Sanzero Eller, Eli Haugen Bunch, Mary J. Hamilton, Pamela J. Dole, William L. Holzemer, Kenn Kirksey, Patrice K. Nicholas, Inge Corless, Christopher Lance Coleman, and et al. 2006. Strategies for Self-Management of HIV-Related Anxiety. *AIDS Care* 18: 597–607. [CrossRef] [PubMed]

Koenig, Harold G. 2015. Religion, Spirituality, and Health: A Review and Update. *Advances* 29: 11–18. Available online: https://www.ncbi.nlm.nih.gov/pubmed/26026153 (accessed on 19 February 2018).

Nejat, Nazi, Lisa Whitehead, and Marie Crowe. 2016. Exploratory Psychometric Properties of the Farsi and English Versions of the Spiritual Needs Questionnaire (SpNQ). *Religions* 7: 84. [CrossRef]

Nuraeni, Aan, Ikeu Nurhidayah, Nuroktavia Hidayati, Citra Windani Mambang Sari, and Ristina Mirwanti. 2015. Kebutuhan Spiritual pada Pasien Kanker. *Jurnal Keperawatan Padjadjaran* 3: 57–66. Available online: http://jkp.fkep.unpad.ac.id/index.php/jkp/article/view/101 (accessed on 2 February 2018). [CrossRef]

Offenbaecher, M., N. Kohls, L. L. Toussant, C. Sigl, A. Winkelmann, R. Hieblinger, A. Whalter, and A. Büssing. 2013. Spiritual Needs in Patients Suffering from Fibromyalgia. *Evidence-Based Complementary and Alternative Medicine* 2013: 178547. Available online: http://dx.doi.org/10.1155/2013/178547 (accessed on 25 January 2018). [CrossRef] [PubMed]

Puchalski, Christina M., Robert Vitillo, Sharon K. Hull, and Nancy Reller. 2014. Improving the Spiritual Dimension of Whole Person Care: Reaching National and International Consensus. *Journal of Palliative Medicine* 17: 642–65. Available online: https://www.ncbi.nlm.nih.gov/pubmed/24842136 (accessed on 19 February 2018). [CrossRef] [PubMed]

Puchalski, Christina M., Robert J. Vitillo, and Najmeh Jafari. 2016. Global Network for Spirituality and Health (GNSAH): Seeking More Compassionate Health Systems. *Journal for the Study of Spirituality* 1: 106–12. [CrossRef]

Tuck, Inez, Nancy L. McCain, and Ronald K. Elswick Jr. 2001. Spirituality and psychosocial factors in persons living with HIV. *Journal of Advanced Nursing* 33: 776–83. [CrossRef] [PubMed]

Valente, Tânia Cristina de Oliveira, Cavalcanti Ana Paula Rodrigues, Büssing Arndt, and Clóvis Pereira Costa Júnior. 2018. Transcultural adaptation and psychometric properties of Portuguese version of the Spiritual Needs Questionnaire among people living with HIV in Brazil. Paper presented at 6th European Conference on Religion, Spirituality and Health and 5th International Conference of the British Association for the Study of Spirituality, Coventry, UK, May 17–19. forthcoming.

Van Wyngaard, Arnau. 2013. Addressing the Spiritual Needs of People Infected with and Affected by HIV and AIDS in Swaziland. *Journal of Social Work in End-of-Life & Palliative Care* 9: 226–40.

World Health Organization. 1998. *WHOQOL and Spirituality, Religiousness and Personal Beliefs (SRPB)—Report on WHO Consultation*. WHO/MSA/MHP/98.2, 2-23; Geneva: WHO.

World Health Organization (WHO). 2014. Process of Translation and Adaptation of Instruments. Available online: http://www.who.int/substance_abuse/research_tools/translation/en/ (accessed on 19 February 2018).

© 2018 by the authors. Licensee MDPI, Basel, Switzerland. This article is an open access article distributed under the terms and conditions of the Creative Commons Attribution (CC BY) license (http://creativecommons.org/licenses/by/4.0/).

Article

Spiritual Jihad among U.S. Muslims: Preliminary Measurement and Associations with Well-Being and Growth

Seyma N. Saritoprak, Julie J. Exline * and Nick Stauner

Department of Psychological Sciences, Case Western Reserve University, Cleveland, OH 44106-7123, USA; seyma.saritoprak@case.edu (S.N.S.); nickstauner@gmail.com (N.S.)
* Correspondence: julie.exline@case.edu

Received: 2 March 2018; Accepted: 10 May 2018; Published: 13 May 2018

Abstract: Religious and spiritual (r/s) struggles entail tension and conflict regarding religious and spiritual aspects of life. R/s struggles relate to distress, but may also relate to growth. Growth from struggles is prominent in Islamic spirituality and is sometimes referred to as spiritual jihad. This work's main hypothesis was that in the context of moral struggles, incorporating a spiritual jihad mindset would relate to well-being, spiritual growth, and virtue. The project included two samples of U.S. Muslims: an online sample from Amazon's Mechanical Turk (MTurk) worker database website (*N* = 280) and a community sample (*N* = 74). Preliminary evidence of reliability and validity emerged for a new measure of a spiritual jihad mindset. Results revealed that Islamic religiousness and daily spiritual experiences with God predicted greater endorsement of a spiritual jihad mindset among participants from both samples. A spiritual jihad mindset predicted greater levels of positive religious coping (both samples), spiritual and post-traumatic growth (both samples), and virtuous behaviors (MTurk sample), and less depression and anxiety (MTurk sample). Results suggest that some Muslims incorporate a spiritual jihad mindset in the face of moral struggles. Muslims who endorse greater religiousness and spirituality may specifically benefit from implementing a spiritual jihad mindset in coping with religious and spiritual struggles.

Keywords: spiritual jihad; Islam; Muslims; struggles; growth

---

1. Introduction

Numerous studies have investigated the beneficial effects of religion and spirituality on health and well-being (Seybold and Hill 2001; Miller and Thoresen 2003). While religious and spiritual involvement can yield various benefits, they can also be a source of struggle. Religious and spiritual (r/s) struggles transpire when a person's beliefs, practices, or experiences regarding r/s matters cause conflict or distress (for reviews, see Exline 2013; Exline and Rose 2013; Pargament 2007; Stauner et al. 2016).

There are several forms of general r/s struggles (Exline et al. 2014). Divine struggles occur when one experiences negative thoughts or feelings about God. Demonic struggles involve concerns about being attacked by a devil or various forms of evil spirits. Interpersonal struggles refer to conflicts surrounding religious people, groups, or institutions. Moral struggles involve concerns about obedience to moral principles and guilt surrounding violations of those principles. Doubt-related struggles involve concerns about religious doubts and questions. Finally, ultimate meaning struggles involve concerns regarding a perceived absence of meaning or purpose in life (Exline et al. 2014).

Many individuals experience r/s struggles. For example, in a study of undergraduates from U.S. colleges and universities (Astin et al. 2005), a majority of first-year students reported occasionally feeling distant from God (65%) and questioning their religious beliefs (57%). Furthermore, recent studies have documented r/s struggles among diverse cultural and religious groups. For example, self-reports on the Religious and Spiritual Struggles (RSS) scale among Israeli-Jewish university students indicated as many as 30% of students experience r/s struggles (Abu-Raiya et al. 2016). Religious and spiritual struggles have also been reported among broad samples of U.S. adults (Stauner et al. 2015/2016). Using a large, nationally representative sample of adults, Ellison and Lee (2010) examined troubled relationships with God, negative social encounters within religious contexts, and chronic religious doubt and found that most people reported low levels of these struggles; nevertheless, the struggles were positively associated with psychological distress. Similarly, Abu-Raiya et al. (2015) found that, although participants that reported low levels of r/s struggle on average, all forms of struggle were positively related to depressive and anxious symptomology.

R/s struggles often imply tension and conflict regarding one's core beliefs and behaviors. Thus, it is not surprising that many studies have found r/s struggles to be linked with psychological distress (e.g., Ellison and Lee 2010; Exline et al. 2000). A meta-analysis on religious coping and psychological adjustment revealed a direct link between r/s struggles and indicators of distress such as anxiety, anger, and depression (Ano and Vasconcelles 2005). Such links with psychological distress have been found even after controlling demographic variables such as race and socioeconomic status (Ellison and Lee 2010). R/s struggles have also been associated with greater thoughts of suicide (Exline et al. 2000), lower levels of life satisfaction (Abu-Raiya et al. 2016; Abu-Raiya et al. 2015), and less happiness, even after controlling overall religiousness, personality factors, and social isolation (Abu-Raiya et al. 2015). Although there is not enough evidence to infer a causal relationship between r/s struggles and emotional distress, research suggests a strong connection between the two domains.

In contrast to the significant body of research on the distressing aspects of r/s struggles, relatively little attention has been given to the potential of r/s struggles to promote personal growth. The existing research on the relationship between r/s struggles and growth is mixed (for a review, see Pargament et al. 2006). Although some researchers have found a connection (Pargament et al. 2000), others have not (e.g., Phillips and Stein 2007), and some studies have even found negative links between struggle and growth (e.g., Park et al. 2009). The lack of concurrent findings in the literature suggest that it may be the actual coping response to the r/s struggle, rather than the struggle itself, that predicts spiritual growth or decline (Exline and Rose 2013; Exline et al. 2017). Similarly, growth from struggle has been linked with positive religious coping (Exline et al. 2017), perception of a secure relationship with God (for a review, see Granqvist and Granqvist and Kirkpatrick 2013), integrating religion into everyday life (Desai 2006), having religious support (Desai 2006), and perceived support or intervention from God (Pargament et al. 2006; Wilt et al. 2017).

Although studies have demonstrated that r/s struggles can be linked with growth-related outcomes, more research needs to be conducted to examine the growth processes that could accompany r/s struggles. Looking at the process of growth from a religious perspective, individuals may intentionally embrace the experience of struggle for a greater purpose, such as for the sake of becoming closer to God or eliminating their perceived shortcomings; such struggles may be intentional in nature for the purpose of spiritual growth. People of faith who may desire to become more devoted believers may embrace struggle as a medium through which they can develop a stronger relationship with the Divine. Struggling for growth purposes is prominent in the religion of Islam, and is sometimes referred to as spiritual jihad. Hence, a natural place to initiate an empirical investigation of such processes is within the context of the religion of Islam.

1.1. Spiritual Jihad: An Islamic Perspective

Much of the research conducted on r/s struggles has made use of predominantly Christian samples. The aim of the current project was to focus primarily on struggles and growth among Muslims, framed in terms of spiritual jihad. A brief review of relevant Islamic theology and psychological research will be addressed. The Arabic noun "jihad" is derived from the Arabic verb "jahada", which is translated as "struggle" or "hardships" (Al-Khalil 1986). Some traditions within Islam, such as the Sufi tradition, categorize jihad into two types: the greater and the lesser jihad. The greater jihad (al-jihad al-akbar), contrary to popular thought, refers to an internal spiritual struggle in the path of God against the various trials of life (Nizami 1997). On the other hand, the lesser jihad (al-jihad al-asghar) refers to an external endeavor for the sake of Islam (Al-Zabidi 1987). Examples of the lesser jihad include fighting for God's cause on the battlefield, stepping out of a conversation due to religious objections, or speaking out for God's sake. Notably, the lesser jihad (often simply referred to as "jihad") has become increasingly aligned with popular views of Muslims in recent years (Amin 2015; Afsaruddin 2013). The term jihad has particularly become increasingly associated with acts of terrorism, thereby promoting the notion that terrorism is a fundamental aspect of Islam (Turner 2007). Such interpretations of the term jihad not only ignore the majority of forms of the lesser jihad that are completely nonviolent, but also fail to acknowledge the meaning of greater jihad for many Muslims. Islamic spirituality, as reflected largely in the Sufi heritage, considers the greater spiritual jihad a fundamental component of spiritual growth and development. Spiritual jihad is a process that requires a conscious effort in "struggling against the soul (al-nafs) for the sake of God" (Picken 2011). In Islam, the nafs are thought to be responsible for a wide variety of dangerous, unsocialized impulses; this psychological influence is roughly analogous to the Freud (1923/1962) concept of the id. For further information regarding the role of the nafs in the process of spiritual jihad, please request a copy of Saritoprak et al. (2018).

The ongoing journey of spiritual jihad may be a common experience among practicing Muslims. Numerous Qur'anic verses promote an intentional, continuous engagement in spiritual jihad, such as these: "And those who strive for us, we will surely guide them to our ways. And indeed, Allah is with the doers of good" (29:69), and, "The ones who have believed, emigrated, and striven in the cause of Allah with their wealth and their lives are greater in rank in the sight of Allah. And it is those who are the attainers [of success]" (9:20). Similarly, as narrated by Al-Bayhaqi (1996), after a successful defeat and arrival from the Battle of Badr, Prophet Muhammad stated, "We have returned from the lesser jihad to the greater jihad." When his companions inquired about the greater jihad's meaning, the Prophet replied, "It is the struggle that one must make against one's carnal self (*nafs*)." As the Day of Judgment is one of the six articles of the Islamic faith, practicing Muslims often engage in a conscious examination of their nafs with the aim of striving to better themselves as believers in return for not only an eternal afterlife, but also for the sole sake of God. Thus, introspection regarding one's behaviors, words, and thoughts throughout life on earth promotes a sense of preparedness for the final Judgment and a path toward spiritual refinement.

Nevertheless, despite the theological emphasis on spiritual jihad within Islam, no study to date has examined the construct of spiritual jihad within the field of psychology. A review of the current literature on r/s struggles and growth indicates a gap in both the conceptualization and measurement of spiritual jihad. As a preliminary attempt to address this gap, the aim of the current article is to investigate the process by which individuals engage in spiritual jihad and the outcomes associated with such engagement.

1.2. Spiritual Jihad: Attributing Wrongdoings to the Nafs

Attribution theory (Weiner 1985) emphasizes the need to assign responsibility for events. In the face of certain events, people often look for information regarding the cause of why an event occurred, and this is especially true for unexpected and negative events. In such cases, people may often think, "Why did this event occur?" or, "Why did I do what I did?" in attempting to explain why a particular incident took place. By seeking knowledge to explain certain outcomes, including successes and failures, the individual can learn to adapt their behavior accordingly in order to prevent or promote a certain incident in the future.

This line of research is relevant to the concept of spiritual jihad. Within a spiritual jihad framework, Muslims who are faced with certain desires or temptations may attribute such inclinations to their nafs. For example, one may think, "I have a sexual desire because my nafs wants it." Along similar lines, in the face of perceived wrongdoings or moral failures, a Muslim may think, "I engaged in the behavior because of the desires of my nafs", thereby attributing either thoughts or actions to such proclivities of their nafs. By attributing certain thoughts and behaviors to their nafs, Muslims incorporating a spiritual jihad approach into their life may be more likely to become aware of such inclinations in the future and engage in greater efforts in struggling against such desires. Speculatively speaking, cognitively separating the source of motivation for undesirable behaviors from one's own consciousness may help Muslims resolve cognitive dissonance and reject their unwanted impulses.

1.3. Spiritual Jihad and Positive Religious Coping

The mechanism of meaning-making may play a role in positive emotional experiences (Folkman 1997). Because religious and spiritual beliefs and practices may play a significant role in making meaning (e.g., Park 2012), they can also be major component of the coping process (Pargament 1997). Religious coping has been proposed to play five main functions: providing a sense of comfort in times of struggle, bringing a feeling of connectedness with others, bringing meaning to a distressing life experience, providing a framework for controlling events that are beyond one's direct personal control and resources, and providing help in making life transformations (Pargament et al. 2000). Additionally, religious coping may take both positive and negative forms.

Positive religious coping may involve being spiritually connected with the world and others, having a secure relationship with God, and/or finding a greater meaning in life (Pargament et al. 1998). On the other hand, negative religious coping methods may reflect religious/spiritual struggles such as being spiritually discontent, appraising a stressor as a punishment from God, viewing the stressor as an act of demonic forces, and/or being dissatisfied with other religious people or institutions (Pargament et al. 1998). Research has shown that negative and positive forms of religious coping can exhibit differing outcomes related to mental and physical health (e.g., Hebert et al. 2009; Trevino et al. 2010). For example, negative religious coping has been associated with greater symptoms of depression and lower quality of life, whereas positive religious coping has been linked with lower levels of psychological distress and greater well-being (Pargament et al. 1998).

Similarly, spiritual jihad may be framed as a form of positive religious coping. It may be a way in which some Muslims approach life experiences and a process that fosters making meaning of negative life events and coping in a proactive manner. In the face of adversities and struggle, Muslims may appraise the situation through a spiritual jihad-based interpretive lens. For example, they may regard a distressing life event as a test that will bring them closer to their faith, a test of their nafs that they must overcome, a way in which they can earn greater sawab (good deeds) in the afterlife, or an opportunity to ask for Divine forgiveness. Incorporating such a mindset may allow the individual to make meaning of their experience in a positive manner, and may promote perceptions of spiritual growth. Within the writings of some Islamic scholars, spiritual jihad has been considered an essential component of spiritual growth (Al-Ghazali 1982; Al-Bursawi 1990). It requires a constant and conscious struggle against one's nafs with the aim of developing a closer relationship with God and becoming a more devout Muslim.

1.4. Spiritual Jihad: Implications for Virtues, Vices, and Well-Being

Spiritual jihad is not only intended to promote positive religious coping, but it is also intended to promote virtues. From an Islamic perspective, there are several overarching themes rooted in the Qur'an and Sunnah of the Prophet that promote actively bettering oneself in the path of God through virtuous behavior. For the purpose of this study, we will focus on patience, gratitude, and forgiveness with an emphasis on their potential links with spiritual and psychological well-being.

The cultivation of sabr (often translated from Arabic as "patience"), is an essential component in the active engagement of spiritual jihad. Differing from the traditional understanding of the English word patience, in the Islamic tradition, sabr can essentially be described as the active restraining of oneself from wrongdoings, limiting objections and complaints in the face of calamities, and putting all trust in God (Khan 2000). In order to ensure that we use the term as close as possible to the original Arabic term, herein, a nuanced presentation of the word patience is the most accurate way to present the information. One of the earliest examples of patience in Islamic history can be traced back to the time when the Prophet was being persecuted by the pagan Meccans of the time. During such times of hardship, the Qur'anic verse, "And whoever is patient and forgives ... indeed, that is of the matters [requiring] determination" (42:42–43) encouraged Muslims to maintain a steadfast approach and patiently endure wrongdoings in a forgiving and non-combative manner (Afsaruddin 2007). From a psychological perspective, approaching situations in a patient manner enhances resilience in times of hardship, thereby promoting better coping ability (Connor and Zhang 2006). The act of being patient involves a proactive approach in coping with negative emotions such as anger and frustration. Therefore, it may encourage a less hostile approach to life experiences, a positive perspective, and increased resilience in the face of adversity.

Gratitude, referred to as shukr in Arabic, is an essential aspect of Islamic spirituality. Gratefulness towards God and other people is reflected through one's appreciation and acknowledgement of the surrounding blessings. Gratitude is a manner through which one remembers God and brings a religious perspective of life to conscious awareness, which may be regarded as a vital component of spiritual jihad. Numerous themes of gratitude can be found in the Qur'an and hadith (sayings of the Prophet Muhammad). For example, an emphasis on gratitude is evident in such sayings of the Prophet: "One who does not thank for the little does not thank for the abundant, and one who does not thank people does not thank God" (Al-Muslim 2006; hadith 2734). Psychological literature has considered gratitude to be a part of one's larger framework of life that fosters noticing and appreciating the positive in the world (Wood et al. 2010). Gratitude has also been linked with less anger and hostility and with more warmth, altruism, and trust (Wood et al. 2008), in addition to greater happiness and positive affect (e.g., Emmons and McCullough 2003; Watkins et al. 2003).

The act of forgiving can be regarded as an inevitable aspect of one's spiritual jihad and holds a distinguished place in Islamic theology. As humans are vulnerable to sins, mistakes, and transgressions, forgiveness promotes an opportunity for spiritual reformation. The act of forgiving fosters both one's relationship with God and with other humans. The Qur'an highlights both God's forgiveness and the act of forgiving others, as evident in the verse: "And let not those of virtue among you and wealth swear not to give [aid] to their relatives and the needy and the emigrants for the cause of Allah, and let them pardon and overlook. Would you not like that Allah should forgive you? And Allah is forgiving and merciful" (24:22). Within psychology, forgiveness has been studied as a positive and prosocial response to transgressions (for reviews, see Fehr et al. 2010; Riek and Mania 2012; Worthington 2005). Historically, researchers have found that individuals who tend to forgive others are more altruistic, caring, generous, and empathic (Ashton et al. 1998). More recent studies show that people who forgive are more likely to be in relationships described as "close", "committed", and "satisfactory" (Tsang et al. 2006). For a more detailed overview of virtues rooted in the Qur'an and Sunnah, please request a copy of Saritoprak et al. (2018).

Forgiveness can also take the form of self-forgiveness. Research has shown a positive association between self-forgiveness and perceived forgiveness from God (Martin 2008; McConnell and Dixon 2012). Feeling unforgiven by God may contribute to one's general view of the self (e.g., feeling unworthy) and/or of God (e.g., punitive and angry). Such experiences may form r/s struggles (Exline et al. 2017) and adversely impact an individual's spiritual and mental wellness. This possibility suggests another way in which forgiveness may facilitate growth: if taking a spiritual jihad mindset toward one's r/s struggles can help a person feel forgiven by God, that perception may then lead to self-forgiveness and allow healing to occur.

In addition to promoting virtuous behaviors, the greater jihad also fosters an active strife against the everyday malevolent temptations of the nafs as a means towards improving the self in the way of God. The individual must struggle to control sinful desires for the purpose of gaining God's favor and eternal Paradise, as evident in the verse, "But as for he who feared the position of his Lord and prevented the soul from [unlawful] inclination, then indeed, paradise will be [his] refuge" (79:40–41). Such a strife can take form against the many evils the Qur'an and Sunnah put forward. For example, the Qur'an presents numerous verses on the consequences of exhibiting arrogance and pride, such as, "And do not turn your cheek [in contempt] toward people and do not walk through the earth exultantly. Indeed, Allah does not like everyone self-deluded and boastful" (31:18). Similarly, other vices are also cautioned against among the Qur'anic verses and the life of the Prophet. For example, the Qur'an states "So fear Allah as much as you are able and listen and obey and spend [in the way of Allah]; it is better for yourselves. And whoever is protected from the stinginess of his soul—it is those who will be the successful" (64:16) highlights the strife to deter oneself from sinful traits such as greed and stinginess. Similarly, the saying of the Prophet "Do not spy upon one another and do not feel envy with the other, and nurse no malice, and nurse no aversion and hostility against one another. And be fellow-brothers and servants of Allah" (Al-Bukhari 1990) discourages Muslims from vices such as envy and hatred.

1.5. The Present Study

We are not aware of any empirical studies that have examined spiritual jihad, a growth-oriented mindset that Muslims may bring to r/s struggles. Our aim was to attempt to assess the mindset associated with spiritual jihad and to begin to examine its associations with perceptions of personal growth (including spiritual and posttraumatic growth), well-being, and virtues among U.S. Muslims. Although a mindset of spiritual jihad could be brought to almost any type of r/s struggle, we began with an emphasis on moral struggles, because these are struggles in which an internal conflict against one's unwanted inclinations would be especially salient.

1.6. Hypotheses

We expected positive associations between endorsement of a spiritual jihad mindset and two indicators of religious engagement: general religiousness and daily spiritual experiences with God while controlling social desirability. In response to a specific moral struggle, we hypothesized that greater endorsement of a spiritual jihad mindset would relate to higher levels of positive religious coping, spiritual growth, posttraumatic growth, and lower levels of spiritual decline. In terms of general well-being, we expected that endorsement of the spiritual jihad mindset would be associated with greater life satisfaction and fewer symptoms of anxiety and depression. Finally, we predicted that endorsement of the spiritual jihad mindset would be associated with reports of more virtuous behaviors in terms of greater endorsement of traits related to patience, forgiveness, and gratitude. All hypotheses were preregistered with the Open Science Framework (Saritoprak and Exline 2017a, embargoed until 2021).

2. Method

2.1. Participants and Procedure

We included participants from two samples. The first was an adult Muslim sample ($N = 280$) obtained from Amazon's Mechanical Turk (MTurk) website. The second sample was comprised of an adult Muslim community sample ($N = 74$). To obtain the community sample, we contacted Muslim leaders throughout Northeast Ohio via email and asked them to forward an invitation to members of their congregations. All participants completed a battery of questionnaires assessing predictor and outcome variables related to spiritual jihad. Participants read the consent form prior to initiating the questionnaires and received a small monetary incentive for their participation (MTurk participants received $3; community participants received $10 to mitigate recruitment difficulty).

Table 1 summarizes demographic information for both samples. Both samples were comprised mostly of Middle Eastern participants, with the median age for both samples being in the range of early thirties to mid thirties. The participants in the MTurk sample comprised a larger percent of

U.S.-born participants compared to the community sample, in addition to more participants identifying as single. In terms of English language proficiency, both samples were composed predominantly of native English speakers, followed by advanced English speakers.

Table 1. Descriptive statistics for demographics.

	Community N = 74	MTurk N = 280
	Median (SD) (Range)	
Age	31 (14.2) (19–77)	28 (9.2) (18–65)
	N (%)	N (%)
Gender		
Male	50 (68%)	131 (46%)
Female	24 (32%)	130 (47%)
Transgender Female	0 (0%)	9 (3.2%)
Transgender Male	0 (0%)	9 (3.2%)
Genderqueer	0 (0%)	1 (0.4%)
Race/Ethnicity		
Middle Eastern	30 (38%)	131 (50%)
White/Caucasian/European American	19 (24%)	54 (21%)
Indian	13 (16%)	27 (10%)
African American/Black	6 (8%)	28 (11%)
Asian/Pacific Islander	11 (14%)	15 (6%)
Latino/Hispanic/Native American	0 (0%)	6 (2%)
USA Born		
Yes	34 (46%)	233 (83%)
No	40 (54%)	47 (17%)
Relationship Status		
Single	29 (39%)	148 (55%)
Married	44 (59%)	77 (28%)
Living w/Romantic Partner	1 (1%)	26 (10%)
Engaged	0 (0%)	15 (6%)
Seperated/Divorced	1 (1%)	2 (1%)
Widowed	0 (0%)	3 (1%)
Years in the USA		
20+ years	46 (62%)	210 (75%)
16–20 years	7 (9%)	19 (7%)
11–15 years	2 (3%)	25 (9%)
6–10 years	8 (11%)	18 (6%)
0–5 years	11 (15%)	8 (3%)
English Proficiency		
Beginner	0 (0%)	7 (2%)
Intermediate	3 (4%)	18 (6%)
Advanced	31 (42%)	58 (21%)
Native	40 (54%)	197 (70%)

2.2. Measures

Table 2 (which appears at the start of the Results section) lists descriptive statistics (means, standard deviations, ranges) for all study variables. For a brief description of all of the measures, please see Appendix B.

Demographic questionnaire. Participants completed a demographic questionnaire. The items provided further information on participants' genders, ages, religious/spiritual traditions, ethnicities, places of birth, relationship statuses, years of residence in the United States, and degrees of proficiency in the English language.

We initially developed a 16-item measure to examine the extent to which participants endorse a spiritual jihad interpretive framework in reference to a specific struggle. Note that spiritual jihad is our technical term for the Islamic concept; items did not use the term "jihad" to avoid unwanted connotations. Items were sent to academic scholars in the field of Islamic spirituality in order to develop content validity. The three scholars provided feedback regarding the content of items. Feedback from the scholarly experts primarily involved suggestions towards developing a working definition of the term spiritual jihad, translating Arabic terminology, and the rewording of items to better align with an Islamic framework. Participants were instructed to rate each item on a seven-point scale (1 = strongly disagree, 7 = strongly agree) pertaining to how they viewed a specific moral struggle they recently encountered. Sample items included "It is a test that will make me closer to God" and "It is a desire of my nafs that I must work against." Reverse-scored items such as "The struggle has no meaning for me" and "Allah plays no role in my struggle" were also included in the measure to address issues of response biases (e.g., acquiescence). As detailed in the results section, an exploratory factor analysis was conducted to evaluate the structure of the measure. One item was dropped as a result of the analysis, as described in the results section. The current study provided initial tests of this new measure's reliability and validity. See Appendix A for the complete measure.

Religious coping was measured with select, abbreviated (three-item) subscales from the Religious Coping Questionnaire (RCOPE; Pargament et al. 2000). The RCOPE consists of subscales assessing coping responses to stressful experiences within a religious context including Benevolent Religious Appraisal (e.g., "Thought the event might bring me closer to God"), Active Religious Surrender (e.g., "Did my best and turned the situation over to God"), Seeking Spiritual Support (e.g., "Looked to God for strength, support, and guidance"), Religious Focus (e.g., "Prayed to get my mind off problems"), Religious Purification (e.g., "Asked forgiveness for my sins"), Spiritual Connection (e.g., "Looked for a stronger connection with God") and Religious Forgiving (e.g., "Sought help from God in letting go of my anger"). Subscale average scores and an overall average score were examined.

Islamic religiousness was measured with the five Islamic Dimensions subscales of the Psychological Measure of Islamic Religiousness (PMIR; Abu Raiya et al. 2008): Beliefs Dimension (e.g., "I believe in the Day of Judgment"), Practices Dimension (e.g., "How often do you fast?"), Ethical Conduct-Do Dimension (e.g., "Islam is the major reason why I honor my parents"), Ethical Conduct-Do Not Dimension (e.g., "Islam is the major reason why I do not drink alcohol"), and Islamic Universality Dimension (e.g., "I identify with the suffering of every Muslim in the world"). An average score was obtained from each subscale, in addition to an overall average score, in order to measure levels of Islamic religiousness.

Daily spiritual experiences were measured with the Daily Spiritual Experiences Scale (DSES; Underwood and Teresi 2002). The DSES examines spiritual experiences such as a perceived connection with the transcendent (e.g., "I feel God's presence"). Our focus was on the first 15 items, which were presented in the form of a six-point scale (1 = never, or almost never, 6 = many times a day). The word "Allah" was substituted for "God" for the purpose of the current study. An overall average score was obtained, with larger scores indicating greater perceived closeness with Allah.

The short form of the Post-Traumatic Growth Inventory (PTGI-S; Calhoun and Tedeschi 1999) assessed the extent to which participants perceived themselves as having grown from their reported crisis with 13 items (e.g., "A willingness to express my emotions"). Ratings were averaged.

Spiritual growth and decline were measured via abbreviated versions of the Spiritual Growth (e.g., "Spirituality has become more important to me") and Spiritual Decline (e.g., In some ways I have shut down spiritually") subscales of the Spiritual Transformation Scale (STS; Cole et al. 2008). A shortened version of the STS (eight items), using the highest-loading items from each subscale, was administered for the current study, with permission from the scale author. Similar shortened forms have been used in other published studies of religious/spiritual struggles (Exline et al. 2017; Wilt et al. 2016). Participants were asked to rate their degree of agreement regarding spiritual growth and decline on a seven-point scale (1 = not at all, 7 = very true). An overall average score was calculated for both subscales.

The five-item Satisfaction with Life Scale (SWLS; Diener et al. 1985) was used in order to measure satisfaction with life (e.g., "So far I have gotten the important things I want in life"). Participants responded to items on a seven-point scale (1 = strongly disagree, 7 = strongly agree). An overall score was obtained from all five items, including reverse-scored items, with higher scores indicating greater self-reported life satisfaction.

Generalized anxiety was measured with the Generalized Anxiety Disorder seven-item scale (GAD-7; Spitzer et al. 2006). The GAD-7 assesses generalized anxiety symptoms by asking participants to report their frequency of anxiety-related concerns (e.g., "Worrying too much about different things") on a four-point scale ranging from 0 (not at all) to 3 (nearly every day). Scores were summed.

Depressed mood was assessed with the Center for Epidemiological Studies of Depression Short Form (CES-D-10; Radloff 1977), which includes 10 items (e.g., "I was bothered by things that usually don't bother me"). Participants responded to statements measuring depressive symptoms in the past week on a four-point scale ranging from 0 (rarely or none of the time) to 3 (all of the time). Ratings were summed.

Dispositional gratitude was measured with the Gratitude Questionnaire-Six Item Form (GQ-6; McCullough et al. 2002). Participants responded to six items addressing gratefulness (e.g., "I have so much in life to be thankful for"). Items were answered on a seven-point scale (1 = strongly disagree, 7 = strongly agree). Item ratings were summed.

A general tendency to forgive was measured with the Heartland Forgiveness Scale (HFS; Thompson and Snyder 2003), a self-report questionnaire with 18 items (e.g., "Learning from bad things that I've done helps me get over them"). Participants responded on a scale ranging from 1 (almost always false of me) to 7 (almost always true of me). An overall scale score was calculated from ratings of the 18 items, including reverse-scored items.

Patience was measured with the 3-Factor Patience Scale (3-FPS, Schnitker 2012). The scale is comprised of 11 items (e.g., "I am able to wait-out tough times"). A composite patience score was calculated by summing ratings of all items, including reverse-scored items.

Social desirability: the five-item short form of the Marlowe–Crowne Social Desirability Scale (MCSDS; Reynolds 1982) was included. Items (e.g., "No matter whom I am talking to, I am always a good listener") were rated true or false. The MCSDS has exhibited good internal consistency and test-retest reliability in prior research (Reynolds 1982). Ratings were summed, including reverse-scored items, with higher scores indicating greater endorsement of socially desirable responses.

3. Results

All analyses were conducted in R (R Core Team 2017) using the psych (Revelle 2017), robustbase (Maechler et al. 2018), lmtest (Zeileis and Hothorn 2002), and car (Fox and Weisberg 2011) packages.

3.1. Descriptive Statistics

Frequency and descriptive statistics for the demographics and main variables were examined for the MTurk and community samples. Participants were asked to skip any questions they may feel uncomfortable answering. The ability to skip items resulted in increased missing data and lower sample sizes for various variables, particularly within the community sample. In the interest of validity, we eliminated participant responses reporting no current moral struggles and/or responding in incomprehensible ways to qualitative items (MTurk, n = 39; Community, n = 12). Preliminary analyses were performed to examine any violations of the assumptions of approximate normality. Negligible violations of normality (defined provisionally as skew and excess kurtosis $\leq$ 1) were observed within the MTurk sample. However, substantial violations of normality were observed (in spiritual decline, Islamic religiousness, gratitude, and daily spiritual experiences) within the community sample. In this sample, the distribution of spiritual decline had a skewness of 1.11 and kurtosis of 0.32 (i.e., excess kurtosis, which is ordinary kurtosis −3; we only refer to this excess kurtosis throughout this report). Islamic religiousness had a skewness of −1.63 and kurtosis of 3.48. Gratitude had a skewness of −1.43 and kurtosis of 1.78. Daily spiritual experiences had a skewness of −1.01 and kurtosis of 1.19. Square root transformations (except daily spiritual experiences, which was squared) reduced skew and kurtosis to less than one in magnitude for all four variables.

Table 2 provides descriptive statistics for the main variables. Mann–Whitney U tests evaluated the evidence for any tendency of either population to score higher or lower than the other on each variable. A Benjamini and Yekutieli (2001) correction maintained $\alpha = 0.05$ across this set of dependent pairwise comparisons. Specifically, in comparison to those in the MTurk sample, participants in the community sample endorsed higher levels of incorporating a spiritual jihad mindset when approaching struggles. Similarly, they reported greater religiousness and higher levels of daily spiritual experiences and life satisfaction. Those in the community sample were also significantly more likely to endorse dispositions toward forgiveness and gratitude. Finally, the community sample participants indicated lower levels of spiritual decline.

Table 2. Descriptive statistics and differences between MTurk and community samples for main study variables.

	MTurk (n = 267–276) M (SD) (Range)	Community (n = 48–68) M (SD) (Range)	Mann–Whitney Test U, FDR-adjusted p
Anxiety	14.00 (5.3) (7–28)	13.40 (5.1) (7–28)	7893, 1.000
Depression	21.30 (5.7) (10–36)	19.89 (4.2) (12–30)	8085, 0.416
Daily Spiritual Experiences	4.08 (1.2) (1–6)	4.69 (1.0) (1–6)	5053, 0.002 *
Forgiveness	81.63 (16.0) (47–126)	89.08 (13.1) (65–118)	4161, <0.001 *
Gratitude	29.70 (6.9) (11–42)	38.04 (4.4) (23–42)	2231, <0.001 *
Islamic Religiousness	3.31 (0.8) (1–5)	3.85 (0.6) (1–5)	4012, <0.001 *
Patience	39.34 (7.6) (17–55)	40.83 (6.5) (30–55)	5693, 0.717
Post-Traumatic Growth	2.72 (0.6) (1–4)	2.91 (0.7) (1–4)	7047, 0.387
Life Satisfaction	21.50 (7.0) (5–35)	24.82 (5.1) (13–34)	5289, 0.003 *
Positive Religious Coping	2.67 (0.7) (1–4)	2.91 (0.7) (1–4)	6457, 0.048 *
Spiritual Jihad Mindset (all items averaged)	4.75 (1.1) (1–7)	5.86 (1.1) (3–7)	4310, <0.001 *
Spiritual Growth	4.35 (1.5) (1–7)	4.83 (1.5) (1–7)	6641, 0.056
Spiritual Decline	3.53 (1.6) (1–7)	1.98 (1.1) (1–6)	12,739, <0.001 *
Social Desirability	7.88 (1.5) (5–10)	8.22 (1.1) (5–10)	5808, 0.675

Note. * $p < 0.05$. All p values are adjusted using the Benjamini and Yekutieli (2001) correction for inflation of the false discovery rate (FDR).

3.2. Exploratory Factor Analysis

All 16 items from the spiritual jihad mindset questionnaire (MTurk sample) were entered into an exploratory factor analysis using ordinary least squares estimation from a polychoric correlation matrix. (A factor analysis was not conducted with the community sample data due to the small sample size.) The Kaiser–Meyer–Olkin overall measure of sampling adequacy value was 0.92, indicating excellent factorability. Barlett's sphericity test of the polychoric correlation matrix rejected the null hypothesis ($\chi^2_{(120)} = 2340$, $p < 0.001$), further supporting the factor analysis. The first and second eigenvalues (6.5 and 1.4, respectively) substantially exceeded the others (eigenvalues 3–16 < 0.5), which did not differ meaningfully from each other or from resampled eigenvalues in parallel analysis (all differences < 0.3; see Figure 1). This test indicated that a two-factor model accounts for the majority of variance (51%) with optimal efficiency and parsimony.

Examination of direct oblimin-rotated factor loadings revealed one item (i.e., "I believe this struggle is ultimately weakening my faith") that had a weak factor loading ($\lambda = 0.38$). This item was dropped from the overall measure, which improved its average interitem correlation ($\Delta \bar{r} = 0.03$). A second factor analysis of the remaining 15 items revealed that two factors explained 54% of the variance. This model fit the data acceptably (Tucker–Lewis index = 0.908, RMSEA = 0.085, root mean square of residuals corrected for degrees of freedom = 0.05). The first factor ($\sum \lambda^2 = 5.40$) explained 36% of the variance, and the second factor ($\sum \lambda^2 = 2.72$) explained 18% of the variance. Table 3 shows all items' factor loadings, which exhibit fairly simple structure (all primary $\lambda > 0.5$, all secondary $|\lambda| < 0.2$). Overall, these results were compatible with the theoretical framework proposed in development of the measure, although a second factor was not anticipated. Conceptually, we interpreted the two factors as endorsing a spiritual jihad mindset (SJM) and rejecting a SJM, respectively. These factors correlated negatively and strongly (r = −0.50, p < 0.001).

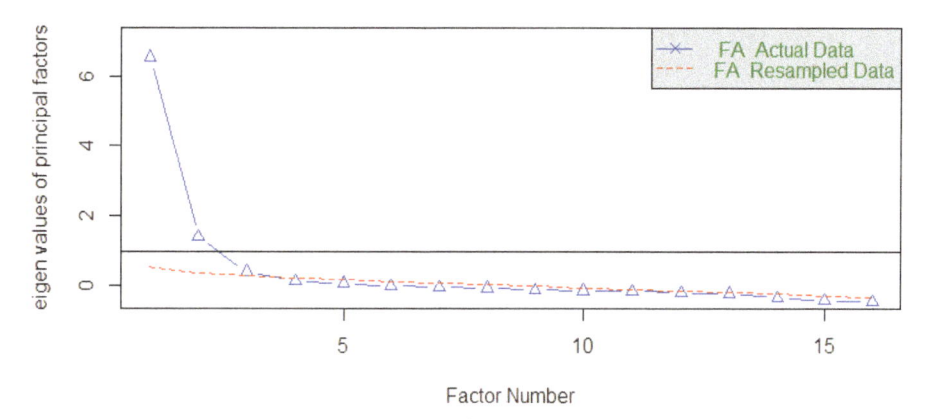

Figure 1. Scree plot and parallel analysis.

Table 3. Summary of the exploratory factor analysis of the spiritual jihad measure using ordinary least squares estimation from a polychoric correlation matrix and direct oblimin rotation.

		Factor Loadings	
		Endorse SJM	Reject SJM
Items [1]	Omega total reliability	0.91	0.82
I have been thinking of my struggle as a test that will make me closer to Allah.		**0.81**	0.00
The struggle is an opportunity for me to seeks Allah's forgiveness.		**0.63**	0.07
I see the struggle as an opportunity to pray and ask Allah for guidance.		**0.77**	−0.04
The struggle is an opportunity for me to seeks Allah's forgiveness.		**0.76**	−0.04
I have been thinking of my struggle as a trial through which I will become a better Muslim.		**0.76**	−0.08
I view the struggle as means of earning more thawab (good deeds) for the afterlife.		**0.79**	0.16
I know that there is khair (good) in the struggle because there is khair (good) in everything Allah does.		**0.62**	−0.20
The struggle is an opportunity for me to seeks Allah's forgiveness.		**0.69**	−0.12
I tend to think that the struggle is for my best interest because Allah is al-Alim (All-Knowing).		**0.80**	0.08
I believe the struggle is a way in which I can understand my imperfect nature.		**0.53**	−0.09
I do not view the struggle as means to become closer to Allah.		−0.19	**0.58**
The struggle has no meaning for me.		0.07	**0.73**
Allah plays no role in my struggle.		−0.02	**0.76**
There is no place for Islam in my struggle.		0.03	**0.81**
I do not see the struggle as part of my spiritual growth.		−0.17	**0.59**

[1] Boldfaced text indicates items assigned to each factor.

3.3. Internal Consistency

Results from the factor analysis were used to generate subscales. Estimates of omega total were calculated for the factor analytically derived subscales. The Endorsing a Spiritual Jihad Mindset subscale revealed excellent internal consistency (ω_{total} = 0.91). The Rejecting a Spiritual Jihad Mindset subscale revealed good internal consistency (ω_{total} = 0.82). With both subscales combined after reversing the coding of responses to items on the Rejecting a Spiritual Jihad Mindset subscale, the total measure revealed excellent internal consistency (ω_{total} = 0.92). This total score is presented as a composite that represents the overall consistency of responses with a spiritual jihad mindset—both endorsing and not rejecting it—rather than as a unidimensional latent factor, since the factor analysis indicated greater complexity than that. Item-total correlations (calculated from the polychoric correlation matrix with corrections for item overlap and scale reliability) were between 0.48 and 0.78. If the complexity was due to acquiescence bias or true ambivalence or indifference, then the distinctions between these possibilities were largely set aside in the composite score, which would have represented each of these configurations as middling scores. To best enable multiple interpretive perspectives, many of the analyses below will be examined in reference to both the two subscales and the total composite score. Each score was calculated by coding response options as consecutive integers (1–7) and averaging responses across items. Items on the Rejecting a Spiritual Jihad Mindset subscale were reverse-coded for the purposes of calculating composite scores.

3.4. Spiritual Jihad, Daily Spiritual Experiences, and Islamic Religiousness

Associations of the spiritual jihad mindset with Islamic religiousness and daily spiritual experiences were estimated as Pearson product–moment correlations (Table 4). As predicted, results within the MTurk sample revealed that incorporating a spiritual jihad mindset correlated significantly and positively with Islamic religiousness and daily spiritual experiences. Similar results were found among participants in the community sample.

Table 4. Pearson product–moment correlations between the Spiritual Jihad Measure and main variables.

	Endorsing SJ MTurk (n = 267)	Endorsing SJ Community (n = 52)	Rejecting SJ MTurk (n = 267)	Rejecting SJ Community (n = 52)	Composite MTurk (n = 267)	Composite Community (n = 52)
Daily Spiritual Experiences	0.62 **	0.66 **	−0.35 **	−0.42 *	0.61 **	0.64 **
Islamic Religiousness	0.62 **	0.69 **	−0.36 **	−0.50 **	0.62 **	0.68 **
Anxiety	−0.06	0.08	0.19 *	−0.15	−0.12	0.11
Depression	−0.05	0.19	0.19 *	−0.15	−0.11	0.18
Spiritual Growth	0.60 **	0.66 **	−0.27 **	−0.45 **	0.57 **	0.63 **
Spiritual Decline	−0.17 *	0.05	0.37 **	−0.08	−0.28 **	0.06
Post-Traumatic Growth	0.52 **	0.47 **	−0.22 **	−0.35	0.49 **	0.46 **
Life Satisfaction	0.09	0.12	−0.07	−0.04	0.10	0.11

* $p < 0.05$ (2-tailed); ** $p < 0.01$ (2-tailed). Adjusted to maintain $\alpha = 0.05$ across dependent tests (Benjamini and Yekutieli 2001).

The spiritual jihad mindset composite was regressed onto Islamic religiousness ($\beta = 0.35$, $t_{(262)} = 4.41$, and $p < 0.001$) and daily spiritual experiences ($\beta = 0.37$, $t_{(262)} = 4.18$, and $p < 0.001$) simultaneously (adjusted $R^2 = 0.44$) by using the iteratively reweighted least squares estimation (by default a bisquare redescending score function with other defaults suggested in Koller and Stahel 2017), revealing independent predictive effects. This model's residuals approximated a normal distribution (|skew| and |kurtosis| = 0.11) and passed a test of independence (H_0: no first-order autocorrelation; Durbin–Watson d = 2.2, $p = 0.210$). A Breusch–Pagan test retained the null hypothesis of homoskedasticity ($\chi^2_{(2)} = 0.70$ and $p = 0.703$). The variance inflation factor (VIF = 2.3) indicated minimal multicollinearity. Effects appeared roughly linear, though exploratory analysis of a third-order polynomial model suggested positive quadratic ($\beta = 0.19$, $t_{(262)} = 4.24$, and $p < 0.001$) and cubic ($\beta = 0.10$, $t_{(262)} = 3.42$, and $p < 0.001$) effects of Islamic religiousness could partly explain and reduce its linear effect ($\beta = 0.20$, $t_{(262)} = 1.80$, and $p = 0.073$) while improving the model fit significantly (robust Wald $\chi^2_{(2)} = 19.3$, $p < 0.001$; $\Delta R^2_{adj.} = 0.04$). Despite this model's robustness to high-leverage and outlying observations, the curvilinear effects seemed to reflect the influence of a few very low scores in both Islamic religiousness and the spiritual jihad mindset, which strengthened their positive relationship at low levels of both factors. The sparseness of data at these low levels and the exploratory nature of this model precluded confident interpretation of curvilinear effects, and the model's close resemblance to a linear relationship above low levels favored the originally predicted model of simple main effects.

Slightly stronger results were found within the community sample, where both Islamic religiousness ($\beta = 0.55$, $t_{(47)} = 6.34$, and $p < 0.001$) and daily spiritual experiences ($\beta = 0.30$, $t_{(47)} = 3.29$, and $p = 0.002$) predicted unique variance in the spiritual jihad mindset composite ($R^2_{adj.} = 0.67$). This model's residuals were somewhat leptokurtic (kurtosis = 1.49), but independent (d = 2.1 and $p = 0.734$)

and homoskedastic ($\chi^2_{(2)}$ = 4.07 and p = 0.131). This model had minimal multicollinearity (VIF = 1.7), and exploratory alternatives yielded insignificant evidence of any curvilinear effects.

Partial correlation analysis was used to explore the relationship between Islamic religiousness and endorsing a spiritual jihad mindset, while controlling scores on the Marlowe–Crowne Social Desirability Scale within the MTurk and community samples. There was a strong, positive, partial correlation between Islamic religiousness and endorsing a spiritual jihad mindset when controlling social desirability (MTurk sample: $r_{(264)}$ = 0.61, p < 0.001; community sample: $r_{(43)}$ = 0.69, p < 0.001). Similar results were found between Islamic religiousness and participants' composite spiritual jihad mindset score (MTurk sample: $r_{(264)}$ = 0.60, p < 0.001; community sample: $r_{(43)}$ = 0.70, p < 0.001).

3.5. Spiritual Jihad and Religious Coping

Correlations between a spiritual jihad mindset and various forms of positive religious coping (as measured by subscales of the RCOPE) were investigated (see Table 5). As expected, there were moderate to strong, positive correlations between incorporating a spiritual jihad mindset and positive religious coping subscales, with high levels of a spiritual jihad mindset associated with higher levels of all forms of positive religious coping within both the MTurk and community samples, indicating strong support for the hypotheses. Similar results were found in regard to participants' composite spiritual jihad mindset scores. Consistently, rejecting a spiritual jihad mindset was significantly negatively correlated with all forms of positive religious coping within both samples (except religious purification coping in the community sample: $r_{(61)}$ = −0.23, p = 0.07).

Table 5. Pearson product–moment correlations between the Spiritual Jihad Measure and Forms of Positive Religious Coping.

	Endorsing SJ		Rejecting SJ		Composite	
	MTurk (n = 270)	Community (n = 60)	MTurk (n = 270)	Community (n = 60)	MTurk (n = 270)	Community (n = 60)
Spiritual Connection Coping	0.64 **	0.72 **	−0.36 **	−0.50 **	0.63 **	0.69 **
Benevolent Religious Appraisal Coping	0.55 **	0.72 **	−0.30 **	−0.44 **	0.54 **	0.68 **
Active Religious Surrender Coping	0.55 **	0.62 **	−0.29 **	−0.36 *	0.53 **	0.57 **
Spiritual Support Coping	0.63 **	0.67 **	−0.42 **	−0.50 **	0.65 **	0.67 **
Religious Forgiving Coping	0.55 **	0.63 **	−0.28 **	−0.39 *	0.53 **	0.59 **
Religious Focus Coping	0.53 **	0.58 **	−0.30 **	−0.34 *	0.53 **	0.54 **
Religious Purification Coping	0.56 **	0.55 **	−0.32 **	−0.23	0.55 **	0.48 **

* p < 0.05 (2-tailed); ** p < 0.01 (2-tailed). Adjusted to maintain α = 0.05 across dependent tests (Benjamini and Yekutieli 2001).

3.6. Spiritual Jihad, Growth, and Decline

As expected, significant, fairly strong, positive correlations with post-traumatic growth were found for the spiritual jihad mindset endorsement subscale and composite score in both the MTurk and community samples (Table 4). Also as expected, in the MTurk sample, a significant, moderate, negative correlation was found between the spiritual jihad mindset composite and spiritual decline, whereas rejecting a spiritual jihad mindset was positively associated with spiritual decline. Though negative in valence as hypothesized, these same correlations in the community sample between one's spiritual jihad mindset scores and spiritual decline did not differ from zero significantly.

Within the MTurk sample, endorsing a spiritual jihad mindset was found to predict spiritual growth strongly and positively (β = 0.48, $t_{(265)}$ = 6.05, and p < 0.001) after controlling Islamic religiousness (β = 0.26, $t_{(265)}$ = 2.83, and p = 0.005; $R^2_{adj.}$ = 0.45, $\Delta R^2_{adj.}$ = 0.13). Likewise, within the community sample, endorsing a spiritual jihad mindset predicted greater spiritual growth strongly, significantly (β = 0.60, $t_{(49)}$ = 4.81, and p < 0.001), and independently of Islamic religiousness, which had essentially no independent effect (β = 0.04, $t_{(49)}$ = 0.26, and p = 0.793; $R^2_{adj.}$ = 0.38, $\Delta R^2_{adj.}$ = 0.17), though its bivariate correlation was strong ($\beta = 0.47$ as the only predictor in robust regression, $t_{(50)} = 3.57$, and $p < 0.001$). However, these models' residuals exhibited heteroskedasticity (MTurk $\chi^2_{(2)} = 10.99$, $p = 0.004$; community $\chi^2_{(2)} = 1.86$, $p = 0.400$, but a pattern was visible in a scatterplot of residuals vs. fitted values; also, community residuals' kurtosis = -1.1), and spiritual growth in the community sample was predicted slightly better by an exploratory model with a negative quadratic effect of Islamic religiousness ($\beta = -0.08$, $t_{(48)} = -2.02$, and $p = 0.049$; linear $\beta = -0.09$, $t_{(48)} = -0.58$, and $p = 0.568$; $R^2_{adj.} = 0.39$; $\Delta R^2_{adj.} = 0.01$, Wald $\chi^2_{(1)} = 4.1$, and $p = 0.043$). These violations of regression assumptions (linear effects and homoskedastic, normally distributed residuals) may have biased the model's primary results.

Similar results were found when examining the prediction of post-traumatic growth. Endorsing a spiritual jihad mindset was found to explain additional unique variance in post-traumatic growth after controlling Islamic religiousness within the members of the MTurk sample ($\beta = 0.47$, $t_{(264)} = 5.64$, $p < 0.001$, $R^2 = 0.31$) and the community sample ($\beta = 0.67$, $t_{(48)} = 3.48$, $p = 0.001$, $R^2_{adj.} = 0.27$). These models met all regression assumptions (|skew| and |kurtosis| of residuals < 1, Breusch–Pagan and Durbin–Watson $p > 0.05$, VIF < 5) except linearity of effects; an exploratory alternative improved the MTurk model with a quadratic effect of spiritual jihad endorsement ($\beta = 0.13$, $t_{(263)} = 4.11$; linear $\beta = 0.51$, $t_{(263)} = 6.32$; both $p < 0.001$; $\Delta R^2_{adj.} = 0.03$, Wald $\chi^2_{(1)} = 16.9$, $p < 0.001$).

3.7. Spiritual Jihad, Psychological Well-Being, and Life Satisfaction

When controlling Islamic religiousness, endorsement of a spiritual jihad mindset showed negative, significant, partial correlations with both anxiety and depression in the MTurk sample, but not in the community sample (Table 6). No significant correlations were found between life satisfaction and incorporating a spiritual jihad mindset within either sample.

Table 6. Partial Pearson product–moment correlations between spiritual jihad scores, depressive symptoms, and anxiety, controlling Islamic religiousness.

	Endorsing SJ		Rejecting SJ		Composite	
	MTurk ($n = 267$)	Community ($n = 52$)	MTurk ($n = 267$)	Community ($n = 52$)	MTurk ($n = 267$)	Community ($n = 52$)
Depressive Symptoms	−0.11	0.07	0.23 **	−0.05	−0.19 *	0.06
Anxiety	−0.11	−0.01	0.22 **	−0.10	−0.19 *	0.03

* $p < 0.05$ (2-tailed); ** $p < 0.01$ (2-tailed). Adjusted to maintain $\alpha = 0.05$ across dependent tests (Benjamini and Yekutieli 2001).

3.8. Spiritual Jihad and Virtues

The correlations between a spiritual jihad mindset and virtuous behaviors such as patience, forgiveness, and gratitude were investigated. Results in the MTurk sample revealed significant, positive correlations between all virtues, patience, forgiveness, and gratitude (Table 7) and incorporating a spiritual jihad mindset, thereby providing support for hypotheses. Similarly, rejecting a spiritual jihad mindset correlated significantly and negatively with all virtues, patience, forgiveness, and gratitude in the MTurk sample. No significant correlations were found within the community sample.

Table 7. Pearson product–moment correlations between the Spiritual Jihad Measure and virtues.

	Endorsing SJ		Rejecting SJ		Composite	
	MTurk ($n = 267$)	Community ($n = 48$)	MTurk ($n = 267$)	Community ($n = 48$)	MTurk ($n = 267$)	Community ($n = 48$)
Patience	0.31 **	−0.08	−0.29 **	0.14	0.36 **	−0.11
Forgiveness	0.22 **	0.10	−0.27 **	0.02	0.28 **	0.08
Gratitude	0.36 **	−0.11	−0.40 **	−0.02	0.44 **	−0.07

* $p < 0.05$ (2-tailed); ** $p < 0.01$ (2-tailed). Adjusted to maintain $\alpha = 0.05$ across dependent tests (Benjamini and Yekutieli 2001).

4. Discussion

The goal of the present study was to investigate the process of approaching moral struggles with a spiritual jihad mindset among Muslims living in the United States, and the outcomes associated with incorporating such a mindset. One aim was to create a new measure to assess the construct of spiritual jihad. Participants were obtained from two samples: an online platform (MTurk) and a community sample. The following sections will examine key findings of the current study, in addition to research and practical implications, and limitations and directions for future research.

4.1. Key Findings

The results of the current study provided preliminary support for the Spiritual Jihad Measure. An exploratory factor analysis revealed a two-factor solution (Endorsing SJ Mindset, Rejecting SJ Mindset). Both subscales showed good to excellent internal consistency. Examining the measure, the two subscales and the total composite scale provided complementary results regarding associations. Though we reported results using both the individual subscales and the composite scale for completeness, we suggest using the composite scale to measure respondents' overall consistency with the spiritual jihad mindset in general applications of this measure. Internal consistency was still very good when the subscales were combined, and the inclusion of both Endorsing SJ and Rejecting SJ items may help to mitigate any influence of acquiescence bias on total scores. However, this scoring system conflates general non-endorsement (i.e., low scores on both subscales) with ambivalence (high scores on both), which might represent legitimate perspectives on the spiritual jihad mindset rather than acquiescence bias. The moderate correlation between the subscales implies that such perspectives may not be rare. Therefore, methodologists and any researchers with interests in ambivalence toward the spiritual jihad mindset or the potential for acquiescence bias in its measurement should consider the endorsement and rejection factors separately or within a bifactor model.

The findings of the present study revealed that Islamic religiousness and daily spiritual experiences both significantly predict incorporating a spiritual jihad mindset when Muslims face moral struggles, even when controlling social desirability. These close associations between greater religious devotion and a spiritual jihad mindset are consistent with the construct of spiritual jihad, which implies a conscious effort in striving to become a more devout Muslim by working against the temptations and desires of the nafs. Furthermore, the results indicated that Muslims in both samples who endorsed higher levels of a spiritual jihad mindset were more likely to make use of positive religious coping. For example, they were more likely to see stressors as beneficial for them or to view stressors as part of God's plan. The findings provided strong support for the hypotheses in the current study.

A further key finding was that Muslims in both samples who endorsed a spiritual jihad mindset when faced with moral struggles also reported greater levels of perceived spiritual and post-traumatic growth. Importantly, the results remained significant even after controlling Islamic religiousness, implying that a spiritual jihad mindset may be contributing additional unique variance in Muslims' perceived spiritual and post-traumatic growth experiences. Although research on the relationship between r/s struggles and growth is mixed, the current findings add preliminary evidence to proposed suggestions in the literature that the actual response to the r/s struggle, rather than the struggle itself, may be what predicts spiritual growth or decline (Exline and Rose 2013; Exline et al. 2016; Wilt et al. 2017). Similar results emerged in regard to the association between a spiritual jihad mindset and perceived spiritual decline. As expected, Muslims in the MTurk sample who were more likely to endorse a spiritual jihad mindset were also less likely to endorse perceived spiritual decline. However, this relationship was not clear for participants in the community sample.

In terms of mental health outcomes, results revealed negative associations between participants' spiritual jihad mindset scores and their levels of anxious and depressive symptoms, as expected, within the MTurk sample. However, these results should be interpreted with caution and will need further investigation, as the associations were weak, and no significant correlations were found within the community sample. Given that moral struggles themselves are usually associated with distress (see, e.g., Exline et al. 2014), these results suggest that endorsement of a spiritual jihad mindset may not play a large role in attenuating this overall level of distress. It is important to note that the measures of anxiety and depression used here are not specific to the struggle situation, and instead represent a broader picture of recent mental health symptoms. As such, it makes sense that their associations with the struggle-specific endorsement of the spiritual jihad mindset would be modest in magnitude. In addition, it is of course possible that a person might see a struggle as personally beneficial (i.e., leading to growth) without necessarily experiencing immediate, widespread mood benefits from this mindset. This same logic may also help to explain the (unexpected) lack of conclusive evidence for an association with life satisfaction.

Finally, Muslims who were more likely to endorse a spiritual jihad mindset were found to also endorse greater levels of virtue traits such as gratitude, patience, and forgiveness, as we predicted—but only in the MTurk sample. The lack of associations within the community sample may be a result of devout Muslims portraying themselves with greater humility when inquired about virtues. On the other hand, these Muslims may be more likely to be honest regarding their negative inclinations or be more aware of their lower self-tendencies, potentially due to having very high moral standards. Granted, these are only speculations; these issues can be addressed systematically in future studies with supplementary measures such as implicit or behavioral assessments of virtues or morality.

4.2. Implications for Research and Practice

The proposed psychological construct of spiritual jihad and the associated findings of the present study have noteworthy implications for both research and practice. First and foremost, spiritual jihad is a construct that had never before been studied in the field of psychology. As a result of the current study, researchers can begin to learn more, not only about Islamic spirituality, but also the emerging field of Islamic psychology in a quantifiable manner. The proposed new measure also showed good internal consistency. In addition, by correlating with variables such as Islamic religiousness, daily spiritual experiences, spiritual growth, post-traumatic growth, forgiveness, patience, and gratitude, the measure shows preliminary evidence of validity for future use. Second, although we chose not to use the term jihad within the measure itself, the study may begin to highlight the importance of a more positive and beneficial understanding of the term jihad, a term that can often be misunderstood by non-Muslims and/or Muslims practicing in extremist manners.

Third, the results indicate the importance of considering Muslims' religious beliefs and practices within therapeutic settings. The practice of spiritual jihad can be brought to attention within the therapeutic setting when working with Muslim clients who may identify themselves as practicing. This may specifically be important for practicing Muslims experiencing struggles related to their religion and spirituality. Fourth, the findings of the study add further evidence that r/s struggles do not necessarily result in only negative psychological outcomes. In circumstances such as those of Muslims who apply a spiritual jihad mindset to their moral struggles, perceived growth may follow. Finally, the results from the current study suggest the possibility of some parallels between Muslims and those of other faith traditions, as many faith traditions are likely to emphasize the idea of seeing moral struggles as a personal challenge that can lead to growth. Further similar constructs may be researched with Christians and other groups residing in the United States (see, e.g., Saritoprak and Exline 2017b). Though Islam may be unique and distinct in certain beliefs and practices, it also shares great overlap with other traditions, specifically Abrahamic traditions, which may open doors for greater cross-cultural research of theory and practice.

4.3. Limitations and Future Directions

It is important to note several limitations of the current study. First, we aimed to develop a self-report measure of a spiritual jihad mindset, in addition to evaluating the newly developed measure's reliability and validity. Self-report measures have limitations such as susceptibilities to participants responding in biased ways, participants lacking adequate introspective ability to respond accurately, and participants interpreting items in unintended manners. Second, to the best of our knowledge, the construct of spiritual jihad has never been empirically assessed prior to the current study. Hence, the reported findings are preliminary and should be interpreted with caution. Third, the presented data were cross-sectional. Hence, results do not indicate any causal inferences regarding the construct of spiritual jihad. In future research, it will be important to conduct research regarding Muslims and spiritual jihad with longitudinal analyses, and it may be feasible to develop and test experimental interventions.

Fourth, the community sample was local and smaller than intended, which limited the conclusiveness and generalizability of results within the group. In addition, some community sample distributions were less approximately normal, which may have biased hypothesis tests in that sample. Subsequent studies should focus on gathering larger samples from the community, in addition to gathering clinical samples to investigate the role of spiritual jihad among Muslims seeking mental health treatment. Fifth, it is important that future research focuses on more refined and nuanced research predictors and outcomes associated with a spiritual jihad mindset. For example, what factors may mediate or moderate the relationship between Islamic religiousness and having a spiritual jihad mindset?

Additionally, future studies that utilize different research methods such as qualitative analyses and implicit or behavioral measurement can provide further tests of the hypotheses considered here. It is also recommended that researchers translate the Spiritual Jihad Measure into other languages in order to promote greater applicability for non-English speaking Muslims within or outside of the United States. Similarly, it will be important for researchers to modify the measure in regards to its specific terminology that is grounded within an Islamic framework, with the aim of better accommodating other theistic and nontheistic religious orientations. Finally, it will be important for future studies with larger sample sizes to conduct confirmatory factor analyses of the measure.

Author Contributions: S.N.S. designed the study, did the primary data analyses, and served as first author for the introduction, method, results, and discussion sections. J.J.E. gave input on the study design, collected data, and reviewed the manuscript. N.S. also did a majority of data analyses, wrote parts of the method and results sections and gave input on the manuscript draft.

Acknowledgments: We wish to express our gratitude to the John Templeton Foundation for funding this research (Grants #36094 and 59916). We would also like to acknowledge Elliott Bazzano, Whitney Bodman, and Zeki Saritoprak for their contributions.

Conflicts of Interest: The authors declare no conflicts of interest.

Appendix A. Spiritual Jihad Measure

Think of a type of moral struggle you have experienced or are currently experiencing in life, how did/do you view the struggle you experienced/are experiencing?

Strongly Disagree   Disagree   Somewhat Disagree   Neither   Somewhat Agree   Agree   Strongly Agree

The following items are examples of moral struggles:

- I want to do more positive things, however, I'm having trouble doing them (e.g., praying the recommended prayer, tahajjud, and becoming more conscious of Allah)
- I'm struggling with the temptation to do something wrong (e.g., engaging in sexual desires, skipping my prayers, and eating unhealthy)
- I'm feeling guilty because I have done something wrong.
- I'm having trouble telling what is morally wrong and right.

    1. I have been thinking of my struggle as a test that will make me closer to Allah.
    2. I have been thinking of my struggle as a desire of my nafs (soul/self) that I must work against.
    3. I see the struggle as an opportunity to pray and ask Allah for guidance.

4. I believe that through this struggle, my iman (faith) will become stronger.
5. I have been thinking of my struggle as a trial through which I will become a better Muslim.
6. I view the struggle as means of earning more thawāb (good deeds) for the afterlife.
7. I know that there is khair (good) in the struggle because there is khair (good) in everything Allah does.
8. The struggle is an opportunity for me to seek Allah's forgiveness.
9. I tend to think that the struggle is for my best interest because Allah is al-Alim (all-knowing).
10. I believe that the struggle is a way in which I can understand my imperfect human nature.
11. I do not see the struggle as part of my spiritual growth (reverse).
12. The struggle has no meaning for me (reverse).
13. There is no place for Islam in my struggle (reverse).
14. I do not view the struggle as means to become closer to Allah (reverse).
15. Allah plays no role in my struggle (reverse).

Appendix B. Measure Descriptions

Measure	Description	Example Item
Spiritual Jihad Measure	A 16-item measure to examine the extent to which participants endorse a spiritual jihad interpretive framework in reference to a specific moral struggle. Participants were instructed to rate each item on a seven-point scale (1 = strongly disagree, 7 = strongly agree)	"I have been thinking of my struggle as a test that will make me closer to Allah"
Religious Coping Questionnaire (RCOPE; Pargament et al. 2000)	Abbreviated subscales of the RCOPE were used to measure coping responses to stressful experiences	"Thought the event might bring me closer to God"
Psychological Measure of Islamic Religiousness (PMIR; Abu Raiya et al. 2008)	A measure of Islamic religiousness assessing five dimensions	"I believe in the Day of Judgment"
Daily Spiritual Experiences Scale (DSES; Underwood and Teresi 2002)	A 16-item measure assessing spiritual experiences such as a perceived connection with the transcendent	"I feel God's presence"
Post-Traumatic Growth Inventory: Short form (PTGI-S; Calhoun and Tedeschi 1999)	A 13-item measure examining the extent to which individuals perceive themselves as having grown from a reported crisis	"A willingness to express my emotions"
Spiritual Transformation Scale (STS; Cole et al. 2008).	A shortened version of the STS assessing perceived spiritual growth and spiritual decline	"In some ways I have shut down spiritually"
Satisfaction with Life Scale (SWLS; Diener et al. 1985)	A five-item measure of satisfaction with life	"So far I have gotten the important things I want in life"
Generalized Anxiety Disorder, seven-item scale (GAD-7; Spitzer et al. 2006)	A seven-item measure examining frequency of anxiety-related concerns	"Worrying too much about different things"
Center for Epidemiological Studies of Depression Short Form (CES-D-10; Radloff 1977)	A 10-item scale measuring depressive symptoms.	"I was bothered by things that usually don't bother me"
Gratitude Questionnaire-Six Item Form (GQ-6; McCullough et al. 2002)	A six-item scale addressing gratefulness	"I have so much in life to be thankful for"
Heartland Forgiveness Scale (HFS; Thompson and Snyder 2003)	An 18-item self-report questionnaire examining individuals' general tendency to forgive	"Learning from bad things that I've done helps me get over them"
3-Factor Patience Scale (3-FPS, Schnitker 2012)	An 11-item measure of patience	"I am able to wait-out tough times"
Marlowe–Crowne Social Desirability Scale, 5-item version (MCSDS; Reynolds 1982)	A five-item scale of social desirability	"No matter whom I am talking to, I am always a good listener"

References

Abu-Raiya, Hisham, Kenneth I. Pargament, Andra Weissberger, and Julie Exline. 2016. An empirical examination of religious/spiritual struggle among Israeli Jews. *The International Journal for the Psychology of Religion* 26: 61–79. [CrossRef]

Abu-Raiya, Hisham, Kenneth I. Pargament, Neal Krause, and Gail Ironson. 2015. Robust links between religious/spiritual struggles, psychological distress, and well-being in a national sample of American adults. *American Journal of Orthopsychiatry* 85: 565–75. [CrossRef] [PubMed]

Abu Raiya, Hisham, Kenneth I. Pargament, Annette Mahoney, and Catherine Stein. 2008. A psychological measure of Islamic religiousness: Development and evidence for reliability and validity. *The International Journal for the Psychology of Religion* 18: 291–315. [CrossRef]

Afsaruddin, Asma. 2013. *Striving in the Path of God: Jihad and Martyrdom in Islamic Thought*. Oxford: Oxford University Press.

Afsaruddin, Asma. 2007. Striving in the Path of God: Fethullah Gülen's Views on Jihad. Paper presented as part of the Muslim World in Transition: Contributions of the Gülen Movement conference, London, UK; pp. 494–502.

Al-Bayhaqi. 1996. *Kitab al-Zuhd al-Kabir (The Book of Great Asceticism)*. Edited by Amir Ahmad Haydar. Beirut: Muassasat al-Kutub al-Thaqafiyya, vol. 1, p. 165.

Al-Bukhari. 1990. *Al-Sahih*. Edited by Mustafa Dayb al-Bugha. Damascus: Dar Ibn Kathir, book 32, hadith 6214.

Al-Bursawi. 1990. *Ruh al-Bayan*. Beirut: Dar al-Fikr, vol 3, p. 424.

Al-Ghazali. 1982. *Ihya Ulum-al-Din*. Translated by al-Haj Maulana Fazul-ul-Karim. New Delhi: Kitab Bhavan, vol. 1.

Al-Khalil. 1986. *Kitab al-'Ayn*. Edited by Mahdi al-Makhzumi and Ibrahim al-Samarai. Beirut: Maktabat al-Hilal, vol. 3, p. 386.

Al-Muslim. 2006. *Sahih Muslim*. Edited by Muhammad Fuad Abd al-Baqi. Istanbul: al-Maktabat al-Islamiyya, Riyadh: Dar Tayba.

Al-Zabidi. 1987. *Taj al-Arus*. Beirut: Darul Hidaye, vol. 27, p. 236.

Amin, ElSayed M. A. 2015. *Reclaiming Jihad: A Qur'anic Critique of Terrorism*. Markfield: Kube Publishing Ltd., pp. 1–103.

Ano, Gene G., and Erin B. Vasconcelles. 2005. Religious coping and psychological adjustment to stress: A meta-analysis. *Journal of Clinical Psychology* 61: 461–80. [CrossRef] [PubMed]

Ashton, Michael C., Sampo V. Paunonen, Edward Helmes, and Douglas N. Jackson. 1998. Kin altruism, reciprocal altruism, and the Big Five personality factors. *Evolution and Human Behavior* 19: 243–55. [CrossRef]

Astin, Alexander W., Helen S. Astin, Jennifer A. Lindholm, Alyssa N. Bryant, K. Szelényi, and S. Calderone. 2005. *The Spiritual Life of College Students: A National Study of College Students' Search for Meaning and Purpose*. Los Angeles: UCLA Higher Education Research Institute.

Benjamini, Yoav, and Daniel Yekutieli. 2001. The control of the false discovery rate in multiple testing under dependency. *The Annals of Statistics* 29: 1165–88.

Calhoun, Lawrence G., and Richard G. Tedeschi, eds. 1999. *Facilitating Posttraumatic Growth: A Clinician's Guide*. New York: Routledge.

Cole, Brenda S., Clare M. Hopkins, John Tisak, Jennifer L. Steel, and Brian I. Carr. 2008. Assessing spiritual growth and spiritual decline following a diagnosis of cancer: Reliability and validity of the spiritual transformation scale. *Psycho-Oncology* 17: 112–21. [CrossRef] [PubMed]

Connor, Kathryn M., and Wei Zhang. 2006. Resilience: Determinants, measurement, and treatment responsiveness. *CNS Spectrums* 11: 5–12. [CrossRef] [PubMed]

Desai, Kavita M. 2006. Predictors of Growth and Decline Following Spiritual Struggles. Doctoral dissertation, Bowling Green State University, Bowling Green, OH, USA.

Diener, Edward D., Robert A. Emmons, Randy J. Larsen, and Sharon Griffin. 1985. The satisfaction with life scale. *Journal of Personality Assessment* 49: 71–75. [CrossRef] [PubMed]

Ellison, Christopher G., and Jinwoo Lee. 2010. Spiritual struggles and psychological distress: Is there a dark side of religion? *Social Indicators Research* 98: 501–517. [CrossRef]

Emmons, Robert A., and Michael E. McCullough. 2003. Counting blessings versus burdens: an experimental investigation of gratitude and subjective well-being in daily life. *Journal of Personality and Social Psychology* 84: 377. [CrossRef] [PubMed]

Exline, Julie J., Joshua A. Wilt, Nick Stauner, Valencia A. Harriott, and Seyma N. Saritoprak. 2017. Self-Forgiveness and Religious/Spiritual Struggles. In *Handbook of the Psychology of Self-Forgiveness*. Berlin: Springer, pp. 131–45.

Exline, Julie J., Todd W. Hall, Kenneth I. Pargament, and Valencia A. Harriott. 2016. Predictors of growth from spiritual struggle among Christian undergraduates: Religious coping and perceptions of helpful action by God are both important. *The Journal of Positive Psychology* 12: 501–8. [CrossRef]

Exline, Julie J., Kenneth I. Pargament, Joshua B. Grubbs, and Ann Marie Yali. 2014. The Religious and Spiritual Struggles Scale: Development and initial validation. *Psychology of Religion and Spirituality* 6: 208–22. [CrossRef]

Exline, Julie J. 2013. Religious and spiritual struggles. In *APA Handbook of Psychology*. Edited by Kenneth I. Pargament, Julie J. Exline and James W. Jones. Washington: American Psychological Association, pp. 497–75.

Exline, Julie J., and Eric D. Rose. 2013. Religious and spiritual struggles. In *Handbook of the Psychology of Religion and Spirituality*. Edited by Raymond F. Paloutzian and Crystal L. Park. New York: The Guilford Press, pp. 380–98.

Exline, Julie J., Ann Marie Yali, and William C. Sanderson. 2000. Guilt, discord, and alienation: The role of religious strain in depression and suicidality. *Journal of Clinical Psychology* 56: 1481–96. [CrossRef]

Fehr, Ryan, Michele J. Gelfand, and Monisha Nag. 2010. The road to forgiveness: A meta-analytic synthesis of its situational and dispositional correlates. *Psychological Bulletin* 136: 894. [CrossRef] [PubMed]

Folkman, Susan. 1997. Positive psychological states and coping with severe stress. *Social Science & Medicine* 45: 1207–21.

Fox, John, and Sanford Weisberg. 2011. *An {R} Companion to Applied Regression*, 2nd ed. Thousand Oaks: Sage, Available online: http://socserv.socsci.mcmaster.ca/jfox/Books/Companion (accessed on 11 May 2018).

Freud, Sigmund. 1923/1962. *The ego and the id*. New York: Norton.

Granqvist, Pehr, and Lee A. Kirkpatrick. 2013. Religion, spirituality, and assessment. In *APA Handbook of Psychology, Religion, and Spirituality (Vol 1): Context, Theory, and Research*. Edited by Kenneth I. Pargament, Julie J. Exline and James W. Jones. Washington: American Psychological Association, pp. 139–55.

Hebert, Randy, Bozena Zdaniuk, Richard Schulz, and Michael Scheier. 2009. Positive and negative religious coping and well-being in women with breast cancer. *Journal of Palliative Medicine* 12: 537–45. [CrossRef] [PubMed]

Khan, Vahiduddin. 2000. Patience (Sabr). In *Principles of Islam*. Noida: Goodword, pp. 100–2.

Koller, Manuel, and Werner A. Stahel. 2017. Nonsingular subsampling for regression S~estimators with categorical predictors. *Computational Statistics* 32: 631–46. [CrossRef]

Maechler, Martin, Peter Rousseeuw, Christophe Croux, Valentin Todorov, Andreas Ruckstuhl, Matias Salibian-Barrera, Tobias Verbeke, Manuel Koller, Eduardo L. T. Conceicao, and Maria Anna di Palma. 2018. Robustbase: Basic Robust Statistics R Package Version 0.93-0. Available online: http://CRAN.R-project.org/package=robustbase (accessed on 11 May 2018).

Martin, Alyce M. 2008. Exploring Forgiveness: The Relationship between Feeling Forgiven by God and Self-forgiveness for a Interpersonal Offense. Doctoral dissertation, Case Western Reserve University, Cleveland, OH, USA.

McConnell, John M., and David N. Dixon. 2012. Perceived forgiveness from God and self-forgiveness. *Journal of Psychology and Christianity* 31: 31–40.

McCullough, Michael E., Robert A. Emmons, and Jo-Ann Tsang. 2002. The grateful disposition: A conceptual and empirical topography. *Journal of Personality and Social Psychology* 82: 112. [CrossRef] [PubMed]

Miller, William R., and Carl E. Thoresen. 2003. Spirituality, religion, and health: An emerging research field. *American Psychologist* 58: 24–35. [CrossRef] [PubMed]

Nizami, Ahmad K. 1997. The Naqshbandiyyah order. In *Islamic Spirituality: Manifestations*. Edited by Seyyed H. Nasr. New York: Crossroad Publishing, pp. 162–93.

Pargament, Kenneth I. 2007. *Spiritually Integrated Psychotherapy: Understanding and Addressing the Sacred*. New York: Guilford.

Pargament, Kenneth I., Kavita M. Desai, Kelly M. McConnell, Lawrence G. Calhoun, and Richard G. Tedeschi. 2006. Spirituality: A pathway to posttraumatic growth or decline. In *Handbook of Posttraumatic Growth: Research and Practice*. New York and London: Lawrence Erlbaum Associates, pp. 121–37.

Pargament, Kenneth I., Harold G. Koenig, and Lisa M. Perez. 2000. The many methods of religious coping: Development and initial validation of the RCOPE. *Journal of Clinical Psychology* 56: 519–43. [CrossRef]

Pargament, Kenneth I., Bruce W. Smith, Harold G. Koenig, and Lisa Perez. 1998. Patterns of positive and negative religious coping with major life stressors. *Journal for the Scientific Study of Religion* 1: 710–24. [CrossRef]

Pargament, Kenneth I. 1997. *The Psychology of Religion and Coping: Theory, Research, Practice*. New York: Guilford Press.

Park, Crystal L. 2012. Religious and spiritual aspects of meaning in the context of work life. *Psychology of Religion and Workplace Spirituality* 1: 25–42.

Park, Crystal L., Mohamad A. Brooks, and Jessica Sussman. 2009. Dimensions of religion and spirituality in psychological adjustment in older adults living with congestive heart failure. *Faith and Well-Being in Later Life* 2009: 41–58.

Phillips, Russell E., and Catherine H. Stein. 2007. God's will, God's punishment, or God's limitations? Religious coping strategies reported by young adults living with serious mental illness. *Journal of Clinical Psychology* 63: 529–40. [CrossRef] [PubMed]

Picken, Gavin. 2011. *Spiritual Purification in Islam: The Life and Works of al-Muhasibi*. Abingdon: Routledge.

R Core Team. 2017. *R: A Language and Environment for Statistical Computing*. Vienna: R Foundation for Statistical Computing, Available online: https://www.R-project.org/Version=3.4.1 (accessed on 11 May 2018).

Radloff, Lenore S. 1977. The CES-D scale: A self-report depression scale for research in the general population. *Applied Psychological Measurement* 1: 385–401. [CrossRef]

Revelle, W. 2017. *Psych: Procedures for Personality and Psychological Research*. Evanston: Northwestern University, Available online: https://CRAN.R-project.org/package=psychVersion=1.7.5 (accessed on 11 May 2018).

Reynolds, William M. 1982. Development of reliable and valid short forms of the Marlowe-Crowne Social Desirability Scale. *Journal of Clinical Psychology* 38: 119–25. [CrossRef]

Riek, Blake M., and Eric W. Mania. 2012. The antecedents and consequences of interpersonal forgiveness: A meta-analytic review. *Personal Relationships* 19: 304–25. [CrossRef]

Saritoprak, Seyma N., Julie J. Exline, and Hisham Abu-Raiya. 2018. Spiritual jihad: Implications for struggle and growth. Manuscript in preparation.

Saritoprak, Seyma N., and Julie J. Exline. 2017a. Muslims and Spiritual Jihad Study. Open Science Framework. Available online: https://osf.io/yxf8s (accessed on 9 February 2018).

Saritoprak, Seyma N., and Julie J. Exline. 2017b. Does God Use Struggles to Transform Us? Both Christians and Muslims Can Approach Struggles with a Transformational Mindset. Presented as Part of a Symposium at the American Psychological Association, Division 36, Annual Mid-Year Conference on Religion and Spirituality, Chattanooga, TN.

Schnitker, Sarah A. 2012. An examination of patience and well-being. *The Journal of Positive Psychology* 7: 263–80. [CrossRef]

Seybold, Kevin S., and Peter C. Hill. 2001. The role of religion and spirituality in mental and physical health. *Current Directions in Psychological Science* 10: 21–24. [CrossRef]

Spitzer, Robert L., Kurt Kroenke, Janet B. Williams, and Bernd Lowe. 2006. A brief measure for assessing generalized anxiety disorder: the GAD-7. *Archives of Internal Medicine* 166: 1092–97. [CrossRef] [PubMed]

Stauner, Nick, Julie J. Exline, and Kenneth I. Pargament. 2016. Religious and spiritual struggles as concerns for health and well-being. *Horizonte* 14: 48–75. [CrossRef]

Stauner, Nick, Julie J. Exline, and Kenneth I. Pargament. 2015/2016. The demographics of religious and spiritual struggles in the USA. In Thomas J. Coleman, III (chair), Belief and Nonbelief are Complex: Longitudinal, Demographical, and Cognitive Perspectives. Paper presented at the Convention of the Society for the Scientific Study of Religion, Newport Beach, CA, USA, October 23–25, and at the 31st International Congress of Psychology, Yokohama, Japan, July 24–29.

Thompson, Laura Y., and Charles R. Snyder. 2003. Measuring forgiveness. In *Positive Psychological Assessment: A Handbook of Models and Measures*. Edited by Shane J. Lopez and Charles R. Snyder. Washington: American Psychological Association, pp. 301–12.

Trevino, Kelly M., Kenneth I. Pargament, Sian Cotton, Anthony C. Leonard, June Hahn, Carol Ann Caprini-Faigin, and Joel Tsevat. 2010. Religious coping and physiological, psychological, social, and spiritual outcomes in patients with HIV/AIDS: Cross-sectional and longitudinal findings. *AIDS and Behavior* 14: 379–89. [CrossRef] [PubMed]

Tsang, Jo-Ann, Michael McCullough, and Frank D. Fincham. 2006. Forgiveness and the psychological dimension of reconciliation: A longitudinal analysis. *Journal of Social and Clinical Psychology* 25: 404–28.

Turner, Colin. 2007. Reconsidering Jihad: The Perspective of Bediüzzaman Said Nursi. *Nova Religio: The Journal of Alternative and Emergent Religions* 11: 94–111. [CrossRef]

Underwood, Lynn G., and Jeanne A. Teresi. 2002. The daily spiritual experience scale: Development, theoretical description, reliability, exploratory factor analysis, and preliminary construct validity using health-related data. *Annals of Behavioral Medicine* 24: 22–33. [CrossRef] [PubMed]

Watkins, Philip C., Kathrane Woodward, Tamara Stone, and Russell L. Kolts. 2003. Gratitude and happiness: Development of a measure of gratitude, and relationships with subjective well-being. *Social Behavior and Personality: An International Journal* 31: 431–51. [CrossRef]

Weiner, Bernard. 1985. An attributional theory of achievement motivation and emotion. *Psychological review* 92: 548. [CrossRef] [PubMed]

Wilt, Joshua A., Valencia A. Harriott, Julie J. Exline, and Kenneth I. Pargament. 2017. Partnering with God: Religious coping and perceptions of divine intervention predict spiritual transformation in response to religious/spiritual struggle. Manuscript submitted for publication.

Wilt, Joshua A., Joshua B. Grubbs, Julie J. Exline, and Kenneth I. Pargament. 2016. Personality, religious and spiritual struggles, and well-being. *Psychology of Religion and Spirituality* 8: 341. [CrossRef]

Wood, Alex M., Jeffrey J. Froh, and Adam WA Geraghty. 2010. Gratitude and well-being: A review and theoretical integration. *Clinical Psychology Review* 30: 890–905. [CrossRef] [PubMed]

Wood, Alex M., Stephen Joseph, and John Maltby. 2008. Gratitude uniquely predicts satisfaction with life: Incremental validity above the domains and facets of the five factor model. *Personality and Individual Differences* 45: 49–54. [CrossRef]

Worthington, Everett L., Jr. 2005. More questions about forgiveness: Research agenda for 2005–2015. In *Handbook of Forgiveness*. Edited by Everett L. Worthington. New York: Routledge, pp. 557–73.

Zeileis, Achim, and Torsten Hothorn. 2002. Diagnostic checking in regression relationships. *R News* 2/3: 7–10. Available online: https://CRAN.R-project.org/doc/Rnews/Rnews_2002-3.pdf (accessed on 11 May 2018).

© 2018 by the authors. Licensee MDPI, Basel, Switzerland. This article is an open access article distributed under the terms and conditions of the Creative Commons Attribution (CC BY) license (http://creativecommons.org/licenses/by/4.0/).

Article

Translation and Validation of Spiritual Well-Being Questionnaire SHALOM in Lithuanian Language, Culture and Health Care Practice

Olga Riklikiene [1,*], Snieguole Kaseliene [2] and John Fisher [3]

[1] Department of Nursing and Care, Faculty of Nursing, Lithuanian University of Health Sciences, Kaunas 44307, Lithuania
[2] Department of Health Management, Faculty of Public Health, Lithuanian University of Health Sciences, Kaunas 44307, Lithuania; snieguole.kaseliene@lsmuni.lt
[3] Department of Rural Health, Faculty of Medicine, Dentistry & Health Sciences, University of Melbourne, Parkville VIC 3010, Australia; jwfisher@unimelb.edu.au
* Correspondence: olga.riklikiene@lsmuni.lt; Tel.: +370-37-787382

Received: 3 April 2018; Accepted: 9 May 2018; Published: 11 May 2018

Abstract: Awareness of patients' and healthy people's spiritual well-being allows for care professionals to support individual spiritual concerns in a timely and appropriate manner, performing a whole-person approach to care. To date, there have been no validated measures of spiritual well-being for use with healthy or illness-affected Lithuanian people. This paper reports the translation and validation procedures of the Spiritual Well-Being Questionnaire, SHALOM, for its use with Lithuanian people regarding the self-assessment of spiritual health. A convenience sample of 171 hospitalized non-terminally ill oncology patients was interviewed face-to-face during a field-test of a Lithuanian version of SHALOM. Overall scale reliability of the SHALOM-Ideals section was 0.909, with overall scale reliability of the SHALOM-Lived Experience section being 0.888. Culturally relevant translation resulted in very good stability over time with a seven-day break between repeat application (Ideals section: Spearman-Brown coefficient was 0.927; Lived Experience section: Spearman-Brown coefficient was 0.942). The construct validity of the scale was determined using exploratory factor analysis. The research perspective on spirituality and spiritual well-being in Lithuania indicates the desirability for larger scale quantitative and qualitative studies with different populations applying cross-sectional and cross-cultural comparisons.

Keywords: spirituality; spiritual well-being; translation; validation; SHALOM; Lithuania

---

1. Introduction

Spirituality, as a dimension of health and health care, has not fitted well in the usual rational or objective medical paradigm that focuses on the physical demands of illness and treatment (Rumbold 2003). Spiritual health disorders often remain unrecognized due to the lack of healthcare professionals' knowledge and preparation to meet those requirements, or no attention at all being paid to the spiritual health domain (Valiuliene 2013).

Despite a high emphasis on spirituality in patients' health and nursing care, deliberation about what spirituality is, by a personal and professional understanding of health care specialists, and how it has to be recognized, assessed, and provided for those seeking it, continues. It may be an expression, framework, source of, or searching for, transcendent meaning to life (Ferrell et al. 2003; Puchalski et al. 2009). It may be immediate experience or reactions to life (Lazenby 2010), or it may be the way people "experience their connectedness to the moment, to self, to others, to nature, and to the significant or sacred" (Puchalski et al. 2009, p. 887). Stern and James (2006) compiled a framework, from the point of view of relationships, to exemplify spirituality. This includes the continuum of relationships, ranging from that with self, to others, and the whole world, including God, gods, or nature. This broad view, as the authors' suggested, underscores the ambiguity of spirituality, which then forces nurses to consider the full realm and intensity of beliefs and practices, rather than oversimplifying or dismissing them.

Lithuanians have a deep and complex history around spiritual expression (Riklikiene et al. 2016, 2018), which may impact their experience of health and well-being, as well as comprehension of links between spirituality and religiosity. In a country in which Christianity is largely practiced, spiritual matters are closely associated with religion and the practice of faith among healthy or ill people, their relatives and health care professionals. Many people express their spirituality in religious practice, possibly because religion also provides a searching for transcendent meaning, but in a particular way, generally on the basis of belief in a deity. Thus, although not everyone has a religion, everyone who searches for ultimate or transcendent meaning can be said to have a spirituality (Sulmasy 2002). Simply put, and for the purposes of this study, spirituality is reflected through the meaning or purpose that one individually ascribes to life.

Spiritual health is a fundamental dimension of people's overall health and well-being, permeating and integrating all the other dimensions of health (i.e., the physical, mental, emotional, social, and vocational). Spiritual health/well-being is understood as a dynamic state of being that is reflected in relationships in four areas, namely with self, others, environment, and/or Transcendent Other (Fisher 2012).

Nursing tradition goes beyond the medical to integrate physical, mental, social and spiritual dimensions of patients' lives in care. This holistic paradigm guides nurses towards a careful assessment of a spiritual dimension of human beings, recognizing the fact that expression of any form of spirituality has strong cultural underpinnings. A traditional approach toward spiritual matters affects familiarity of terminology used by a population, adoption, and comprehension of novel concepts, recognition of patients' spiritual issues as targets for health care providers, finally, the readiness and comfort of individuals to discuss their spiritual health concerns with others unreservedly. Nurses' understanding of spiritual health domains contributes to the quality of spiritual care and overall care delivery.

To date, there have been no measures and validated tools of spiritual well-being for use with healthy or illness-affected Lithuanian people. This paper reports the translation and validation of the Spiritual Well-Being Questionnaire called SHALOM for its use with Lithuanian respondents regarding self-assessment of spiritual health and needs for spiritual support. The title of the instrument SHALOM was chosen to represent the very essence of Spiritual Well-Being (SWB). The Hebrew word *Shalom* means "completeness, wholeness, health, peace, welfare, safety, soundness, tranquillity, prosperity, fullness, rest, harmony, the absence of agitation or discord." (Strong 1979). The acronym SHALOM reveals its two components—Spiritual Health Measure (SHM) and Life-Orientation Measure (LOM). The LOM elicits the 'ideals' that people have for Spiritual Health in four sets of relationships with self, others, environment, and/or God. The SHM asks people to reflect on 'lived experience/how they feel each item reflects their personal experience most of the time' (Fisher 2010).

The purpose of our study was to psychometrically test a translated and validated Lithuanian version of the Spiritual Well-Being Questionnaire SHALOM in non-terminally ill hospitalized oncology patients. This article also provides the primary results on the state of spiritual well-being and its relationship with sociodemographic factors in hospitalized non-terminally ill oncology patients.

2. Material and Methods

2.1. Study Design and Methods

A descriptive, multisite, cross-sectional survey design was employed for this study. A face-to-face individual interview method was employed to investigate the spiritual well-being of non-terminally ill oncology adult patients hospitalized in nursing care and oncology units of a tertiary level hospital in one of the largest city of Lithuania.

2.2. Field Testing

The study sample consisted of patients that were diagnosed with an oncology disease and undergoing treatment at an oncology unit. Before data collection, the principal reseacher provided sufficient consultations with the interviewers regarding instructions for completing the instrument, the specific language, and the meaning of terms. The researcher and her assistant (last year student of a university nursing program) visited the hospital and introduced the study to nurse managers at the units. The managers directed the researchers to patients that met the inclusion criteria: oncology illness diagnosed, non-terminal phase of the disease, patient is conscious, able to understand the informed consent, and to answer the questions. During face-to-face interviews, trained interviewers (oncology nurse and final year bachelor of nursing student) administered the questionnaire on a one-to-one basis, at the most convenient time for patients, in a calm and private place, for an average duration of 5–10 min, depending on the health status and the age of the respondent.

2.3. Participants

Responses were obtained from 171 patients in nursing and supportive treatment units at public hospitals. Response rate was 100% because of the face-to face interview method that was applied for the survey. The results are therefore not necessarily representative of the institutions surveyed.

There were more female patients (55.6%) than male. The age of patients varied from 25 years to 96 years, mean age was 65.82 ± 12.15 years. Most of the patients (N = 140) were affiliated with the Roman Catholic religion (95.9%), two (1.4%) patients were Russian Orthodox, and three (2.1%) were Old Believers (Table 1). The duration of chronic disease varied from one month to 59 years (mean 3.98 ± 3.33).

Table 1. Sociodemographic characteristics of respondents.

Characteristics	Groups	N	%
Gender	Female	95	55.6
	Male	76	44.4
	All	171	100
Age groups in years	<51	19	11.2
	51–60	37	21.9
	61–70	50	29.6
	71–80	47	27.8
	>80	16	9.5
	All	169	100
Place of residence	Urban	90	52.6
	Rural	81	47.4
	All	171	100
Education	Primary	59	34.9
	Secondary	49	29
	Vocational	45	26.6
	Higher	12	7.1
	Other	4	2.4
	All	169	100
Marital status	Married	103	60.8
	Divorced	34	20.1
	Widowed	17	10.1
	Live with a partner	9	5.3
	Not married	6	3.6
	All	169	100

Table 1. Cont.

Characteristics	Groups	N	%
Religiosity	Religious	117	68.4
	Non-religious	22	12.9
	Can not answer	32	18.7
	All	171	100

2.4. Study Instrument

After written permission for SHALOM translation and validation into Lithuanian was granted by the author, Fisher's Spiritual Health And Life-Orientation Measure (SHALOM) was used for the study (Fisher 2010). The 20-item questionnaire sought two responses to indicate: (1) patients' ideals for SWB where participants rate the importance of each item for their optimum spiritual health as well as (2) the lived experience where participants rate how they feel each item reflects their personal experience most of the time. Comparing these two responses provides a measure of spiritual harmony or dissonance in each of the four domains of SWB. The set of sociodemographic characteristics was collected using an investigator-developed form.

2.5. Procedures

The SHALOM questionnaire was forward-translated into the Lithuanian language and back-translated into English following the methodological considerations for double translation and reconciliation (Maneesriwongul and Dixon 2004). A nurse educator and nursing student were invited, as two native, local culture and language translators, to make the initial translation of the instrument from the original, English, language to the target language—Lithuanian. An in-depth knowledge of culture, English language proficiency and confidence in health care practice was essential for maintaining cultural equivalence of the translated items and concepts. Later, both of the translated Lithuanian versions were compared and a consensus reached during group conversation with a third translator—a nursing professor with fluent knowledge of English, rich clinical experience, as well as competence of subject matter and knowledge of instrument development/translation/adaptation principles. Afterwards, the back translation of the newly translated version of SHALOM was conducted by English language specialists, for identification of errors in meaning of terms, concepts and constructs, before validity and reliability testing of the new version of SHALOM (Jones et al. 2001). During the translation and adaptation processes linguistic, psychological, and cultural differences in the Lithuanian population and peculiarities in health care practices were considered through the choice of experts with relevant expertise, e.g., spiritual services, knowledge of anthropology, and proficiency in Lithuanian language. The equivalency checking between the original and translated versions of the instrument was accomplished by the author (J. Fisher), following the three level congruence structure that was defined in advance by the researchers. Any discrepancies were corrected seeking greatest agreement. During the translation procedure the Lithuanian language style, syntax, and grammar were corrected several times. Field validation of the SHALOM-Lithuanian version was conducted with hospitalized oncology patients in November 2017–February 2018.

2.6. Ethical Considerations

The Lithuanian Regional Committee on Bioethics issued permission to conduct the study (5 December 2017, No. BE-2-84). Participants received written and oral information about the aim of the survey and gave their informed consent by participating in the face-to-face interview. Data confidentiality was guaranteed by no identifying information being recorded on answers.

2.7. Statistical Analysis

Data were recorded and analyzed using the Statistical Package for Social Sciences (IBM SPSS Statistics) version 22.0. Descriptive statistics and parametric tests for two and more than two independent samples (*t*-test and One-Way ANOVA with post hoc Tukey multiple comparisons) were used. We used Paired samples *t*-test to compare spiritual dimensions' mean scores between the Ideals and Lived Experience sections. A *p*-value of 0.05 or less was used to define statistical significance. To assess the psychometric properties of the scale, Cronbach's alpha, split half test, average inter-item, and item-total correlations were calculated for internal consistency. Cronbach's alpha coefficient was calculated for both individual domains and the whole scale in two sections; internal consistency that exceeds α 0.6 was considered to be acceptable (Bland and Altman 1997). Test-retest was conducted with 28 student nurses, with an interval of one week, and construct stability-in-time was tested using Spearman-Brown coefficient; the value of 0.80 and above identified adequate construct stability, or 0.90 and above—good construct stability of the instrument (Kaplan and Saccuzzo 2001). Items scoring below 0.15 have poor inter-item correlations, suggesting that they are really not that well related to each other. Items that correlate above 0.50 tend to be very similar to each other.

An exploratory factor analysis was used to confirm the construct validity of the translated version of SHALOM. Principal Component Analysis with Varimax rotation was applied. The Kaiser-Meyer-Olkin and Bartlett's Test of Sphericity were used to assess the appropriateness of the sample for the factor analysis. Eigen values of above one and the scree plot were used to determine the number of factors.

3. Results

3.1. Face and Content Validity of the SHALOM Lithuanian Version

A specific language constitutes a symbolical expression of tradition and culture of a particular geographical territory. Lithuanian language is related to Latvian and dead Prussian, and it is the Eastern Baltic language with the highest number of users. Lithuanian, as a separate branch of Eastern Baltic languages, started to be developed from the VIIth century. The oldest known Lithuanian script—"Tractatus sacerdotalis"—originated at the begining of 1600s. The strong roots of the Lithuanian language have led to it retaining ancient grammar forms and morphology and, from a linguistic perspective, it is as worthy to study as Latin or ancient Greek. Lithuanian grammar is very similar to all ancient Indo-European language forms and even older language forms. The Lithuanian language has the greatest resemblance to its archaic forms than any other Indo-European language in use.

SHALOM was developed in the belief that an instrument should have appropriate language and conceptual clarity for studies of Spiritual Health within general populations and individuals. Homogeneity of cultures usually results in separate linguistic systems, whose identity rests on a typical, essential for a given language, grammatical and intonation system and lexical resources. The advantage of SHALOM relates to its construction of items. The instrument lists the items in a very short form using a single or a few words—not a sentence. That is much easier for ill patients to get the sense of what is being asked rather than listening to long sentences.

During the translation process, primary attention was assigned by the researchers to instrument applicability and comprehensiveness. Expressions such as *awe at a breathtaking view, peace with God, prayer life, meaning in life, kindness towards other people* and *a sense of 'magic' in the environment* were difficult to find culturally and linguistically appropriate equivalents, that would be familiar to the general public. Consultations between the Lithuanian researchers and the author of SHALOM (J. Fisher) provided a wider exploration of meaning, which led to an accurate interpretation and avoidance of semantic errors, during the translation process. Achievement of equivalency and congruence was achieved when the authors of SHALOM made a comparison of both English versions: original and back translated, providing comments on discrepancies and their corrections.

The conversational manner of the data collection enabled interviewers to obtain criticisms of the Lithuanian version of SHALOM itself. The field notes and the oral feedback from interviewers revealed the fact that younger patients of better health status and no feeling of pain were easier to interview. Those respondents who experienced difficulty concentrating well enough on the items, because of their weak condition, noticed the repetition of rather similar aspects and had difficulty distinguishing between them. It was also noted by interviewers that for older, and usually rural, respondents, the items *sense of 'magic' in the environment, connection with nature, harmony with the environment* appeared strange as they had never given thought to this. American English terms and combinations *a sense of identity, self-consciousness, oneness with nature, inner peace, meaning in life* were rather novel for older Lithuanians. A patient of an oncology unit asked the interviewer to explore the meaning of those concepts. The reflection from the interviewers was that respondents nearly always associated spirituality with religiosity.

To test the face validity of the Lithuanian version of the SHALOM, the clarity of the instrument, firstly, was discussed in a group with the student nurses (N = 28), who participated in a test-retest study. To ensure that item content had similar meaning for the intended population, the pilot testing of the instrument was conducted with non-terminally ill oncology hospitalized patients during the first two weeks of the survey. Additional minimal corrections were incorporated in response to the interviewers' comments and suggestions.

3.2. Field Testing of the Lithuanian Version of SHALOM

To prove that the Lithuanian version of SHALOM measures the spiritual well-being concept in reproducible fashion, a set of tests were employed to assess the psychometric properties of the the newly translated instrument.

Internal consistency. The four domains of two SHALOM sections (SHALOM-Ideals and SHALOM-Lived Experience) had Cronbach's alpha (α) values ranging from 0.578 to 0.949. The Personal domain in both sections had the lowest values of alpha in relation to other domains (Table 2).

Table 2. Reliability statistics for the two sections of Spiritual Well-Being Questionnaire (SHALOM).

Domain-Items	Ideals Item-Total Correlation	Ideals α If Item Deleted	α	Lived Experience Item-Total Correlation	Lived Experience α If Item Deleted	α
Personal	-	-		-	-	
5. Sense of identity	0.481	0.695		0.167	0.630	
9. Self-awareness	0.631	0.617	0.725	0.331	0.526	0.578
14. Joy in life	0.539	0.666		0.423	0.473	
16. Inner peace	0.632	0.629		0.440	0.464	
18. Meaning in life	0.238	0.765		0.364	0.510	
Communal	-	-		-	-	
1. Love for other people	0.688	0.871		0.532	0.783	
3. Forgiveness toward others	0.705	0.866		0.571	0.769	
8. Trust between individuals	0.684	0.871	0.886	0.582	0.766	0.802
17. Respect for others	0.743	0.858		0.599	0.761	
19. Kindness toward other people	0.817	0.839		0.652	0.743	
Environmental	-	-		-	-	
4. Connection with nature	0.709	0.782		0.677	0.707	
7. Awe at a breath-taking view	0.632	0.804		0.472	0.773	
10. Oneness with nature	0.753	0.766	0.834	0.709	0.692	0.784
12. Harmony with the environment	0.582	0.818		0.518	0.757	
20. Sense of 'magic' in the environment	0.550	0.829		0.459	0.782	
Transcendental	-	-		-	-	
2. Personal relationship with transcendent	0.838	0.940		0.859	0.924	
6. Worship of the transcendent	0.806	0.945		0.782	0.937	
11. Oneness with transcendent	0.911	0.927	0.949	0.871	0.921	0.941
13. Peace with transcendent	0.860	0.936		0.838	0.927	
15. Prayer life	0.879	0.933		0.850	0.925	
Total	-	-	0.909	-	-	0.888

Item-total correlations were inspected for the five items in each of the four domains comprising SHALOM. For the Personal domain, the corrected item-total correlation ranged from 0.238 to 0.632 in the SHALOM-Ideals section and from 0.167 to 0.440 in the SHALOM-Lived Experience section; the item-total correlation of this domain was the lowest in comparison with the other three domains. For the Transcendental domain, the corrected item-total correlation was the strongest and ranged from 0.806 to 0.911 in the section for Ideals and from 0.782 to 0.871 in the section of Lived Experience (Table 2).

Stability in time. Test-retest correlation with seven days interval showed good construct stability of the SHALOM Lithuanian version. The correlation (Spearman-Brown coefficient) between the responses of the two surveys was 0.927 on Ideals and 0.942 on Lived Experiences.

Average inter-item correlation was calculated. In the Personal domain of Ideals, the correlation coefficient ranged from 0.009 to 0.609; the Communal domain correlation coefficients ranged from 0.525 to 0.731; in the Environmental domain—0.35–0.738 and in the Transcendental domain correlation coefficients varied from 0.721 to 0.871. The inter-item correlation in Lived Experiences section was: in the Personal domain from 0.096 to 0.538, in the Communal domain from 0.369 to 0.538, in the Environmental domain from 0.278 to 0.711 and in the Transcendental domain inter-item correlation ranged from 0.679 to 0.821.

Construct validity. The goal of factor analyses was to confirm the equivalence of the structure of the SHALOM Lithuanian version. The Kaiser-Meyer-Olkin (KMO) values indicated that data and sample size were adequate for factor analysis. Moreover, the approximate Chi-square values of Bartlett's test of sphericity confirmed that the factor model is appropriate. These two tests showed the suitability of the respondent data for exploratory factor analysis, which was performed on the 20 Ideal and Lived Experience items using the principal component factor analysis with Varimax rotation.

Following the Varimax rotation, the Ideals items loaded significantly on four factors. These four factors had an eigenvalue greater than 1 with an explained variance of 72%. All of the items had a loading range higher than 0.5, above the minimum acceptable value of 0.4. The first factor was related to the communal (1, 3, 8, 17, 19)/personal (9, 14, 16) SWB with one additional item (12) from environmental SWB. The second factor related to the transcendental dimension of SWB and the third factor was for environmental SWB; the fourth factor was associated with personal SWB (Table 3, Figure 1).

As shown in Table 3 and Figure 2, the five factors that reported a eigenvalue greater than 1, accounting for 69 % of variance, were extracted in the section of Lived Experience. Factor 1 and factor 2 items in Lived experience section were consistent with the factor 2 and factor 3 items in the Ideals section and corresponded with the environmental and transcendental domains of the original version of SHALOM. In accordance to factorisation, in Lived experience, factors 4 and 5 together make up/comprise the Personal domain. The results on other domains fit the normal pattern quite well.

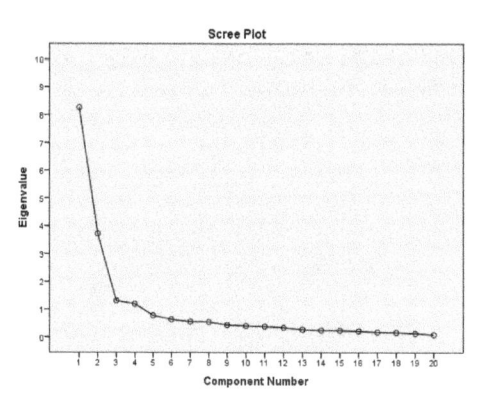

Figure 1. Scree plot of SHALOM–Ideals.

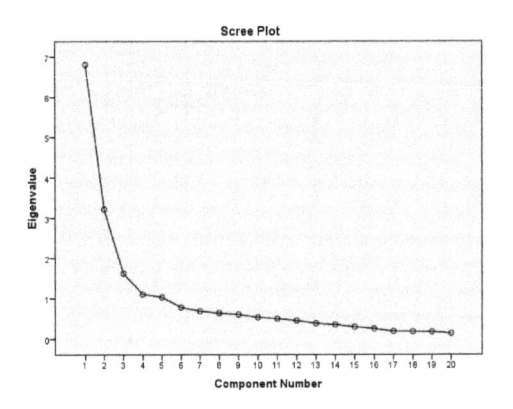

Figure 2. Scree plot of SHALOM–Lived Experience.

Table 3. Exploratory factor loadings for the two sections of SHALOM.

		Ideals						Lived Experiences				
			Factor Loading						Factor Loading			
Item No.	h^2	1	2	3	4	Item No.	h^2	1	2	3	4	5
Factor 1						Factor 2						
12	0.775	**0.836**				3	0.681		**0.809**			
19	0.756	**0.836**				8	0.548		**0.641**			
17	0.738	**0.833**				1	0.549		**0.621**			
3	0.685	**0.796**				19	0.629		**0.615**			
8	0.658	**0.779**				17	0.579		**0.593**		0.404	
1	0.653	**0.722**				12	0.584		0.472	0.411	0.423	
14	0.625	**0.716**										
16	0.574	**0.674**										
9	0.666	**0.584**		0.313	0.465							
Factor 2						Factor 1						
11	0.899		**0.938**			2	0.843	**0.891**				
15	0.849		**0.91**			11	0.842	**0.888**				
13	0.834		**0.894**			15	0.822	**0.888**				
2	0.801		**0.88**			13	0.827	**0.859**				
6	0.81		**0.87**			6	0.804	**0.857**				
Factor 3						Factor 3						
10	0.775	0.308		**0.812**		10	0.795			**0.855**		
4	0.712	0.375		**0.743**		4	0.707			**0.761**		
20	0.62			**0.741**		7	0.573			**0.589**		0.355
7	0.639	**0.505**		**0.55**		20	0.463		0.345	**0.562**		
Factor 4						Factor 4						
5	0.755	0.419		0.372	**0.657**	14	0.753				**0.836**	
18	0.648	0.362		0.34	**−0.632**	16	0.695				**0.755**	
						18	0.625				**0.668**	
						Factor 5						
						5	0.785					**0.856**
						9	0.689					**0.746**
	KMO			0.891			KMO				0.871	
Bartlett's test of sphericity: c^2						Bartlett's test of sphericity:					69	
df				2453.063		χ^2					1763.843	
				190		df					190	
p				<0.001		p					<0.001	
% variance explained				72.4		% variance explained					69	

KMO: Kaiser-Meyer-Olkin Measure of Sampling Adequacy; h^2: communalities. Principal component analysis (Varimax rotation with Kaiser normalization). Factor loadings <0.3 are not depicted; factor loadings greater than 0.5 are in bold type, that is above the minimum acceptable value of 0.4.

3.3. Spiritual Well-Being of Non-Terminally Ill Hospitalized Oncology Patients

The results revealed that summative scores of the domain and the mean scores of each item on Ideals were significantly higher than the same domain and the same item on Lived Experience section. Communal domain of spiritual well-being in both of the sections had higher mean scores than the three other domains (Table 4).

Table 4. Summary statistics for each item/domain of the Ideals and Lived Experience sections of SHALOM.

Domain-Item No.	Ideals N	%	Mean ± SD	Median (Minimum–Maximum)	Lived Experience N	%	Mean ± SD	Median (Minimum–Maximum)	p (Paired Samples t-Test)
Personal	167	97.7	21.10 ± 3.28	22 (5–25)	167	97.7	18.60 ± 3.26	19 (5–25)	<0.001
5	169	98.8	3.83 ± 1.23	4 (1–5)	169	98.8	3.62 ± 1.23	4 (1–5)	<0.001
9	169	98.8	4.17 ± 0.96	4 (1–5)	169	98.8	4.01 ± 1.01	4 (1–5)	0.001
14	171	100.0	4.58 ± 0.76	5 (1–5)	171	100.0	3.67 ± 1.06	4 (1–5)	<0.001
16	171	100.0	4.54 ± 0.82	5 (1–5)	171	100.0	3.62 ± 1.04	4 (1–5)	<0.001
18	171	100.0	3.95 ± 0.91	4 (1–5)	171	100.0	3.71 ± 0.96	4 (1–5)	<0.001
Communal	170	99.4	22.68 ± 3.20	24 (5–25)	169	98.8	21.02 ± 3.36	22 (5–25)	<0.001
1	171	100.0	4.41 ± 0.85	5 (1–5)	171	100.0	4.20 ± 0.98	5 (1–5)	<0.001
3	171	100.0	4.53 ± 0.75	5 (1–5)	171	100.0	4.12 ± 0.92	4 (1–5)	<0.001
8	171	100.0	4.67 ± 0.69	5 (1–5)	171	100.0	4.37 ± 0.84	5 (1–5)	<0.001
17	171	100.0	4.65 ± 0.72	5 (1–5)	171	100.0	4.26 ± 0.84	4 (1–5)	<0.001
19	170	99.4	4.40 ± 0.85	5 (1–5)	169	98.8	4.05 ± 0.94	4 (1–5)	<0.001
Environmental	169	98.8	20.02 ± 4.14	21 (5–25)	168	98.2	18.61 ± 3.98	19 (5–25)	<0.001
4	171	100.0	4.23 ± 0.97	5 (1–5)	171	100.0	4.01 ± 1.01	4 (1–5)	<0.001
7	170	99.4	3.79 ± 1.22	4 (1–5)	170	99.4	3.26 ± 1.12	3 (1–5)	<0.001
10	170	99.4	4.05 ± 1.06	4 (1–5)	171	100.0	3.82 ± 1.10	4 (1–5)	<0.001
12	171	100.0	4.47 ± 0.82	5 (1–5)	171	100.0	4.14 ± 0.98	4 (1–5)	<0.001
20	171	100.0	3.47 ± 1.20	4 (1–5)	169	98.8	3.34 ± 1.21	3 (1–5)	<0.001
Transcendental	170	99.4	16.59 ± 6.46	17 (5–25)	168	98.2	15.71 ± 6.39	18 (5–25)	<0.001
2	171	100.0	3.48 ± 1.40	4 (1–5)	171	100.0	3.36 ± 1.41	4 (1–5)	0.011
6	171	100.0	3.04 ± 1.36	3 (1–5)	171	100.0	2.85 ± 1.39	3 (1–5)	<0.001
11	171	100.0	3.26 ± 1.46	3 (1–5)	169	98.8	3.08 ± 1.43	3 (1–5)	<0.001
13	170	99.4	3.57 ± 1.47	4 (1–5)	170	99.4	3.40 ± 1.44	4 (1–5)	<0.001
15	171	100.0	3.19 ± 1.43	3 (1–5)	171	100.0	3.04 ± 1.44	3 (1–5)	0.001
Total	164	95.9	80.36 ± 12.99	81 (20–100)	161	94.2	73.86 ± 12.78	76 (20–100)	<0.001

According to Fisher (2006), spiritual dissonance is indicated by a difference in mean value of greater than 1.0 between the 'ideal' and 'lived experience' in any domain of SWB. The result on all four domains of the SHALOM scale indicated limited spiritual dissonance in the Personal domain ($n = 20$, 11.7%), Communal domain ($n = 12$, 7.0%), Environmental domain ($n = 6$, 3.5%), as well as the Transcendental domain ($n = 6$, 3.5%).

The scores on each scale of a SWB measure were compared in relation to the sociodemographic characteristics of respondents. The results on Ideals and Lived Experience sections revealed significant differences on two domains of SWB in accordance with patients' gender: females rated the environmental and transcendental domains more highly than males; on Lived Experience sections the gender difference was additionally determined on the Communal domain. Place of residence was significant for the respondents in assessing the transcendental domain in both sections: the rural respondents rated the items of Ideals and Lived Experience more highly than urban residents. Those respondents who were not able to identify their religiosity rated the items of the transcendental domain of both SHALOM sections lower in comparison with religious but higher in comparison with non-religious respondents. In addition, the communal domain of Lived Experience was rated higher by religious respondents than the non-religious. Scoring of the transcendental domains of both sections, and the communal domain of Ideals, were significantly related to patients' age (Tables 5 and 6).

Table 5. Comparison of SHALOM–Ideals between sociodemographic characteristics (N = 171).

Variables	Personal (Mean ± SD)	Communal (Mean ± SD)	Environmental (Mean ± SD)	Transcendental (Mean ± SD)
Gender				
Male	20.8 ± 3.2	22.1 ± 3.3	19.2 ± 3.9	13.8 ± 6.5
Female	21.1 ± 3.4	23.0 ± 3.2	20.6 ± 4.2	18.7 ± 5.7
p (t-test)	0.606 (0.516)	0.071 (1.817)	**0.031 (2.170)**	**<0.001 (5.235)**
Place of Residence				
Urban	21.1 ± 3.5	22.6 ± 3.6	20.0 ± 4.2	15.5 ± 6.7
Rural	20.8 ± 3.2	22.7 ± 2.8	20.0 ± 4.0	16.7 ± 6.1
p (t-test)	0.549 (0.600)	0.820 (−0.228)	0.960 (−0.050)	**0.028 (−2.220)**
Age by years				
<51	21.4 ± 2.9	22.6 ± 2.7 [ab]	20.6 ± 3.4	15.6 ± 5.8 [abc]
51–60	20.8 ± 3.2	22.4 ± 2.9 [ab]	20.2 ± 3.9	14.8 ± 6.2 [ab]
61–70	20.7 ± 3.2	22.7 ± 3.0 [ab]	19.4 ± 4.1	15.4 ± 6.6 [b]
71–80	21.9 ± 2.4	23.7 ± 2.0 [a]	21.1 ± 3.8	19.7 ± 5.6 [c]
>80	19.8 ± 5.6	21.1 ± 5.5 [b]	18.1 ± 5.3	16.6 ± 7.5 [abc]
p	0.2	**0.048**	0.072	**0.003**
Education				
Primary	21.0 ± 3.8	22.9 ± 3.9	20.2 ± 4.3	17.4 ± 6.7
Secondary	21.3 ± 3.0	22.4 ± 3.4	19.3 ± 4.5	14.6 ± 7.2
Vocational	20.7 ± 3.2	22.7 ± 2.2	19.8 ± 3.9	16.8 ± 5.6
Higher	22.1 ± 2.0	22.5 ± 3.0	22.0 ± 3.3	19.1 ± 4.8
p	0.611	0.866	0.245	0.067
Religiosity				
Religious	20.9 ± 3.2	22.8 ± 2.9	20.3 ± 4.0	19.8 ± 4.2 [a]
Non-religious	21.9 ± 3.2	22.5 ± 2.6	19.9 ± 3.5	5.9 ± 1.9 [a]
Can't to answer	20.7 ± 3.9	22.0 ± 4.6	18.8 ± 5.0	11.9 ± 4.6 [c]
p	0.386	0.386	0.162	**<0.001**

[abc] ANOVA equal letters do not differ on Tukey post hoc comparison ($p < 0.05$).

Table 6. Comparison of SHALOM–Lived Experience by sociodemographic characteristics (N = 171).

Variables	Personal (Mean ± SD)	Communal (Mean ± SD)	Environmental (Mean ± SD)	Transcendental (Mean ± SD)
Gender				
Male	18.0 ± 3.4	20.1 ± 3.6	17.8 ± 4.1	12.6 ± 6.2
Female	19.0 ± 3.1	21.6 ± 3.1	19.1 ± 3.9	18.1 ± 5.4
p (t-test)	0.055 (1.930)	**0.005 (2.847)**	**0.026 (2.240)**	**<0.001 (6.110)**
Place of Residence				
Urban	18.7 ± 3.4	20.6 ± 3.7	18.4 ± 4.1	14.7 ± 6.6
Rural	18.4 ± 3.1	21.3 ± 3.0	16.7 ± 3.9	16.7 ± 5.9
p (t-test)	0.603 (0.521)	0.194 (−1.303)	0.624 (−0.491)	**0.038 (−2.096)**
Age by years				
<51	19.2 ± 2.7	20.5 ± 3.0	19.0 ± 3.7	14.8 ± 5.8 [abc]
51–60	19.0 ± 2.9	21.1 ± 2.9	19.3 ± 3.9	14.1 ± 6.0 [ab]
61–70	18.4 ± 3.3	20.7 ± 3.5	18.1 ± 3.9	14.5 ± 6.7 [b]
71–80	18.9 ± 2.6	22.1 ± 2.7	19.1 ± 3.8	18.5 ± 5.6 [c]
>80	16.6 ± 5.2	19.8 ± 4.2	16.6 ± 4.6	16.6 ± 6.8 [abc]
p	0.095	0.079	0.16	**0.006**

Table 6. Cont.

Variables	Personal (Mean ± SD)	Communal (Mean ± SD)	Environmental (Mean ± SD)	Transcendental (Mean ± SD)
Education				
Primary	18.2 ± 3.8	21.4 ± 3.6	18.5 ± 4.0	16.5 ± 6.2 [a]
Secondary	18.3 ± 2.8	20.1 ± 3.7	17.7 ± 4.3	13.3 ± 6.9 [b]
Vocational	19.3 ± 3.0	21.4 ± 2.6	19.0 ± 3.8	16.4 ± 5.6 [ab]
Higher	16.7 ± 2.2	21.1 ± 3.0	20.1 ± 3.4	18.5 ± 5.3 [ab]
p	0.212	0.153	0.225	**0.013**
Religiosity				
Religious	18.8 ± 2.9	21.5 ± 3.0 [a]	19.0 ± 3.7	18.9 ± 4.2 [a]
Non-religious	18.4 ± 4.0	19.2 ± 2.8 [b]	17.6 ± 3.7	5.6 ± 1.4 [b]
Can't to answer	17.8 ± 3.8	20.0 ± 4.5 [ab]	17.5 ± 5.1	11.0 ± 4.7 [c]
p	0.3	**0.002**	0.099	**<0.001**

[abc] ANOVA equal letters do not differ on Tukey post hoc comparison ($p < 0.05$).

The marital status showed no difference on ratings of both sections of SHALOM. No significant difference was shown in Ideals items in relation to the education level of respondents, but the Lived Experience of the transcendental domain was scored significantly higher by those with primary education than those with secondary (Tables 5 and 6).

4. Discussion

It is evident that the development of proper measures and methods to assess subjective attributes, including spiritual well-being, as such, is a complex task and time consuming activity that requires considerable human, technical, and financial resources. Keeping in mind that no instrument can give an absolute measure of spiritual well-being (Fisher 2016) and by realistically estimating all of the effort required, and challenges to develop an adequate new measure, we decided to make a critical review of the evidence and to find the most appropriate instrument for our study's aims and research perspectives in the area of spiritual well-being of ill and healthy people. We chose the Spiritual Health And Life-Orientation Measure (SHALOM) relying on the review results of de Jager Meezenbroek et al. (2012), with recognition that the multidimensional Spiritual Well-being Questionnaire (SWBQ) from Gomez and Fisher (2003) is promising for measuring spirituality as an experience or attitude that transcends any particular religion. The Spiritual Well-Being Questionnaire (SWBQ) is the 'lived experience' component of SHALOM (Gomez and Fisher 2003). This questionnaire has the advantage that it can be used among people who adhere to a faith or no faith at all. This is a strong argument, as our intention for this study was, and for further studies will be, to assess spirituality as a universal phenomenon, not excluding people on the basis of their religious background.

The Lithuanian version of SHALOM demonstrated high comprehensiveness and adequate psychometric properties of the instrument. Assessment of the 'linguistic and cultural distance' between the source and target language and cultural groups (van de Vijver and Leung 1997) might include the considerations of differences in language, religion, lifestyle, and values. Such distance is obvious between Western countries and Lithuania in speaking about the developments of health care models, professional competences and scope of practice of medical staff, a history of freedom of thoughts, faith, and human rights. To maximize the cultural suitability of the instrument to the Lithuanian population, the wording of particular items, which were novel or not very familiar to Lithuanians (especially to older populations), should be further tested and modified to feel much more natural and be acceptable, with functional, rather than literal, equivalence. The additional consideration of appropriate Lithuanian terms for 'identity', 'self-confidence', and 'inner peace' is feasible and is recommended.

It is assumed that the response to any one question is subject to error: the person may misinterpret the item, respond in a biased manner, or to make a mistake in transcribing the reply to the answer sheet (Streiner and Norman 2009). In our study the effect of these errors was minimized by the selection of a conversational approach with respondents being questioned via face-to-face interviews by an experienced researcher or final year nursing student, as a part of her final thesis on the topic. Thus, the interviewer was able to determine if the respondent had any difficulty in understanding any items because of older age, limited intelligence, lower health literacy, problems in concentration because of illness and weak health status, or whether due to unfamiliar terms of spirituality language. Interviewers reflected that they often were asked to rephrase particular questions for better understanding.

In addition to the primary aim of this study, which was to translate and to validate the Spiritual Well-Being Questionnaire SHALOM in Lithuanian language and culture, a field test also provided results on spiritual well-being of non-terminally ill hospitalized oncology patients. These results are preliminary and confirmation of them by a larger scale study will follow. This paper reports on the main tendencies. The Communal domain of spiritual well-being, representing the individual's relationship with others, revealed the highest mean score and Transcendental domain the lowest. Significant differences were found between respondents' Lived experiences and their Ideals. Gender plays a significant role for the sense of spiritual well-being of non-terminally ill oncology patients, with females perceiving their relationship with others, with the environment and with a Transcendent Other, to be better than males, as indicated by more highly-scored responses.

Importantly, the place of residence was significant for the respondents in assessing the Transcendental domain, where individuals from rural areas reported a better relationship with a higher power when compared with the urban population. In addition, patients without a clear identification of their religiosity assess the transcendental domain of spiritual well-being lower in comparison with the religious, but higher in comparison with non-religious, respondents. In addition, the communal domain of Lived Experience was rated higher by religious respondents than non-religious.

The Lithuanian version of SHALOM was translated and validated for its further use in larger scale research studies on terminally ill hospitalized oncology patients and for cross-cultural comparisons, which may be valid only if the same questionnaire is understood in the same way across language and cultural groups. In perspective, the instruments will be applied to other samples as well: student nurses, nurse educators, family caregivers to investigate their spiritual well-being and link it with other influential factors, such as sociodemographic characteristics, religion affiliation, satisfaction with life, happiness, and spiritual needs. Furthermore, qualitative evidence collection from healthy and ill persons, care-providers, and experts would help to clarify the construct of spiritual health/well-being and to know exactly what sense it makes in Lithuanian culture. Deeper understanding of concepts' interpretation would enable us to minimize the influence of any cultural and linguistic differences that are irrelevant to the Lithuanian uses of the SHALOM.

The process that was used to validate this Lithuanian version of SHALOM has some limitations. Firstly, the instrument requires evidence for its concurrent validity, by comparing the findings with data from other sources and applying congruent or divergent measurement tools. Secondly, the Lithuanian version of SHALOM was only used with one homogenous sample. More variety would be advisable. Thirdly, the face-to-face interview method that was employed during the validation process has to be taken into consideration in making overall conclusions about the reliability of newly adapted instrument. Repeated testing of psychometric properties is recommended for data collected by other means, such as independent responding.

5. Conclusions

In Lithuanian society, attention to the spiritual dimension of healthy and ill individuals, and society overall, is increasing with a high need of standardized and high quality measurement tools for different spiritual dimensions. The Lithuanian version of the Spiritual Health And Life-

Orientation Measure (SHALOM) is a valid and reliable instrument for assessing spiritual well-being of non-terminally ill oncology patients in hospital settings. Further testing of this newly validated instrument will include different research approaches with multiple populations of ill, as well as healthy people, and a more comprehensive investigation of the spiritual well-being phenomenon.

Author Contributions: O.R. performed the study conception and design, participated in the translation process, coordinated data collection and drafted the manuscript; S.K. analyzed the data and provided statistical expertise; J.F. contributed to the interpretation of data, critical revision and editing of the manuscript. All authors approved the final version of the manuscript.

Acknowledgments: The authors appreciate final year BSN student nurse Ernesta Sliuburyte who participated in data collection conducting face-to-face interviews with patients. We also express our gratitude to student nurses who participated in the test-retest study. The study was supported by The Research Council of Lithuania Grant for Young scientists' project No. S-MIP-17-19.

Conflicts of Interest: The authors declare no conflicts of interest.

References

Bland, J. Martin, and Douglas G. Altman. 1997. Statistics notes: Cronbach's alpha. *British Medical Journal* 314: 572. [CrossRef] [PubMed]

de Jager Meezenbroek, Eltica, Bert Garssen, Machteld van den Berg, Dirk van Dierendonck, Adriaan Visser, and Wilmar Schaufeli. 2012. Measuring Spirituality as a Universal Human Experience: A Review of Spirituality Questionnaires. *Journal of Religion & Health* 51: 336–54. [CrossRef]

Ferrell, Betty, Stephany Smith, Gloria Juarez, and Cindy Melancon. 2003. Meaning of illness and spirituality in ovarian cancer survivors. *Oncology Nursing Forum* 30: 249–57. [CrossRef] [PubMed]

Fisher, John. 2006. Using secondary students' views about influences on their spiritual well-being to inform pastoral care. *International Journal of Children's Spirituality* 11: 347–56. [CrossRef]

Fisher, John. 2010. Development and application of a spiritual well-being questionnaire called SHALOM. *Religions* 1: 105–21. [CrossRef]

Fisher, John. 2012. Staff's and family members' spiritual well-being in relation to help for residents with dementia. *Journal of Nursing Education and Practice* 2: 77–85. [CrossRef]

Fisher, John. 2016. Selecting the best version of SHALOM to assess spiritual well-being. *Religions* 7: 45. [CrossRef]

Gomez, Rapson, and John Fisher. 2003. Domains of spiritual well-being and development and validation of the Spiritual Well-Being Questionnaire. *Personality and Individual Differences* 35: 1975–91. [CrossRef]

Jones, Paticia, Jerry Lee, Linda Phillips, Xinwei Zhang, and Karen Jacelbo. 2001. An adaptation of Brislin's translational model for cross-cultural research. *Nursing Research* 50: 300–4. [CrossRef] [PubMed]

Kaplan, Robert M., and Dennis P. Saccuzzo. 2001. *Psychological Testing: Principle, Applications and Issues*, 5th ed. Belmont: Wadswoth.

Lazenby, Mark. 2010. On "spirituality," "religion," and "religions": A concept analysis. *Palliative and Supportive Care* 8: 469–76. [CrossRef] [PubMed]

Maneesriwongul, Wantana, and Jane K. Dixon. 2004. Instrument translation process: A methods review. *Journal of Advanced Nursing* 48: 175–86. [CrossRef] [PubMed]

Puchalski, Christina, Betty Ferrell, Rose Virani, Shirley Otis-Green, Pamela Baird, Janet Bull, Harvey Chochinov, George Handzo, Holly Nelson-Becker, Maryjo Prince-Paul, and et al. 2009. Improving the quality of spiritual care as a dimension of palliatve care: The report of the Consensus Conference. *Journal of Palliative Medicine* 12: 885–904. [CrossRef] [PubMed]

Riklikiene, Olga, Inga Vozgirdiene, Laima Karosas, and Mark Lazenby. 2016. Spiritual care as perceived by Lithuanian student nurses and nurse educators: A national survey. *Nurse Education Today* 36: 207–13. [CrossRef] [PubMed]

Riklikiene, Olga, Laima Karosas, and Snieguole Kaseliene. 2018. General and professional values of student nurses and nurse educators. *Journal of Advanced Nursing* 74: 666–76. [CrossRef] [PubMed]

Rumbold, B. 2003. Attending to spiritual care. *Health Issues* 77: 14–17.

Stern, Julian, and Sarah James. 2006. Every person matters: Enabling spirituality education for nurses. *Journal of Clinical Nursing* 15: 897–904. [CrossRef] [PubMed]

Streiner, David, and Geoffrey Norman. 2009. *Health Measurement Scales: A Practical Guide to Their Development and Use*. Oxford: Oxford University Press. [CrossRef]

Strong, James. 1979. *Strong's Exhaustive Concordance of the Bible*. Nashville: Thomas Nelson Publishers.

Sulmasy, Daniel. 2002. A Biopsychosocial-Spiritual Model for the Care of Patients at the End of Life. *The Gerontologist* 42: 24–33. [CrossRef] [PubMed]

Valiuliene, Zaneta. 2013. Health Problems of Palliative Care Patients with Oncological and Heart Diseases and Their Associations with Spirituality. Ph.D. Disseration, Lithuanian University of Health Sciences, Medical Academy, Kaunas, Lithuania.

van de Vijver, Fons, and Kwok Leung. 1997. *Methods and Data Analysis for Cross-Cultural Research*. Newbury Park: Sage.

© 2018 by the authors. Licensee MDPI, Basel, Switzerland. This article is an open access article distributed under the terms and conditions of the Creative Commons Attribution (CC BY) license (http://creativecommons.org/licenses/by/4.0/).

Article

Brazilian Validation of the Attachment to God Inventory (IAD-Br)

Hartmut August [1], Mary Rute G. Esperandio [2,*] and Fabiana Thiele Escudero [3]

1. Department of Theology, Fidelis College, Curitiba-PR 80050-540, Brazil; hart@ausland.com.br
2. Postgraduate Program in Theology/Postgraduate Program in Bioethics, Pontifical Catholic University of Parana, Curitiba, Curitiba-PR 80215-901, Brazil
3. Business School, Pontifical Catholic University of Parana, Curitiba-PR 80215-901, Brazil; fabiana.escudero@pucpr.br
* Correspondence: mary.esperandio@pucpr.br or mresperandio@gmail.com; Tel.: +55-419-9229-8339

Received: 12 March 2018; Accepted: 27 March 2018; Published: 30 March 2018

Abstract: Bowlby's Attachment Theory proposes that the person seeks protection and security with his or her caregiver, establishing a significant bond, which Bowlby characterizes as "attachment relationship". The relationship with God can also be understood as an attachment relationship. Until now, there are no instruments in Brazil to measure one's attachment to God. The purpose of this article is to present the adaptation and validation process of the Attachment to God Inventory for the Brazilian context, resulting in a Brazilian version of the Attachment to God Inventory (IAD-Br). The validation methodology for the IAD-Br consisted of Portuguese translation, reverse translation to English, pre-test, data collection, and validation through confirmatory factorial analysis (CFA). A total of 470 people participated in the study: 179 men and 291 women. Confirmatory factorial analysis presented unsatisfactory statistical parameters. Of the 28 items of the instrument, 11 items did not present adequate Item-Total Correlation. After excluding these 11 items, the instrument presented adequate adjustment indices. The IAD-Br, composed of 17 items, is able to be used to measure attachment to God in Brazil and constitutes a relevant instrument to identify the attachment to God style, being useful for application in the psychotherapeutic clinic and in contexts of spiritual care.

Keywords: Attachment to God Inventory; IAD-Br; styles of attachment; attachment theory; Validation; Brazil

1. Introduction

In researching the links between young children and their caregivers, the British psychiatrist Bowlby (2002, 2004a, 2004b) structured what has come to be called the Attachment Theory, thus providing a solid conceptual basis on the formation, maintenance, and modification of affective bonds. Unlike the classic Freudian psychoanalysis perspective, which emphasizes the exploration of the fantasy world of adults and children, Bowlby directs his attention to real experiences and the real world of people. He deals with the impact of parents' emotional problems on children (Bowlby 1988, pp. 43–44). He himself states that he distances himself from classical psychoanalysis and, in his most recent works, presents an approach based on the principles of cognitive psychology (Bowlby 2004a, p. 37). For Bowlby, "attachment behavior is interpreted as any form of behavior that results in a person attaining or retaining proximity to some other differentiated and preferred individual" (Bowlby 2004a, p. 38) and it "contributes to the survival of the individual" (Bowlby 2004a, p. 40), insofar as the caregiver (the person or persons responsible for the care of the child) protects and cares for the attached person. Over time, "attachment behavior leads to the development of bonds or attachments" (Bowlby 2004a, p. 38). Attachment behaviors "are active throughout the life cycle" (Bowlby 2004a,

p. 39). Thus, the patterns of attachment between the person and his or her caregiver are established through search mechanisms for protection and security for the exploration of the environment (Bowlby 2004a, p. 41).

When the child feels threatened or otherwise anguished, he or she engages in attachment behaviors such as crying and clinging to the caregiver. When possible, the child turns to the caregiver in order to reinforce closeness and, consequently, a sense of security (Kirkpatrick and Shaver 1990, p. 317). On the other hand, when the child feels safe, he or she voluntarily steps away from the caregiver to explore the environment, periodically checking to see if the base of her security remains attentive and available. Thus, through these search mechanisms of protection and security for the exploration of the environment, the patterns of attachment between the child and his or her caregiver are established.

With each experience with their caregivers, children seek to understand, even if unconsciously, how their mother and father will react to their need for protection and comfort. This response of caregivers to the needs of the child will lead to a secure or more insecure attachment (Esperandio and August 2014, p. 248). The Attachment models developed throughout personal history (through relationships) "are integrated into our personality structure in the form of general internal working models that will determine the characteristics of the self in the different life situations" (Abreu 2005, p. 15).

Differently from what occurs in childhood attachment, in healthy adult attachment there is reciprocity, and two people can perform the attachment function on each other. Although attachment styles learned in childhood tend to be reproduced in adulthood, new experiences provide opportunities for changes in the attachment style, as exemplified in a love relationship. While at least one partner has a secure attachment style, the person with insecure attachment style can be positively affected by the secure attachment style of his/her loving partner. Thus, throughout the existential process there are possibilities for change in the attachment styles. These bonding and dependence feelings shape the way one relates to other people. The attachment style influences the formation of identity, self-assessment and the assessment of others, expectations about the partner and marital relationship, the way sexuality is viewed and practiced, and the way a person relates to others in a professional environment and how he or she handles conflicts (Mario and Shaver 2010).

Recently, there have been studies proposing to approach the field of research of science of religion with cognitive psychology using the perspective of the Theory of Attachment. The reference researcher in this area is Kirkpatrick (2005), a psychologist of religion who proposes to characterize the relationship of believers with God as a relation of attachment. Research on the nature and functions of attachment to God provided new ways of understanding psycho-spiritual health through analogies with interpersonal attachment relationships (Granqvist and Kirkpatrick 2013). Kirkpatrick (2005) shows that for the person who professes a religious belief in a personal God, God will play the role of an attachment figure. Thus, in the relationship with God, the attachment styles constructed in the relationship with the caregivers can be reproduced or be a "substitute" (compensatory) of an insecure attachment relationship (Granqvist and Kirkpatrick 2004). In Brazil, a pioneering study in the perspective of Psychology of Religion is the article published under the title Attachment Theory and Religious Behavior (Teoria do Apego e Comportamento Religioso (Esperandio and August 2014)).

In an article published in 2004, Richard Beck & Angie McDonald proposed an instrument for measuring attachment to God and described the methodology used for its preparation. Following the recommendations of Brennan et al. (1998), the purpose of the authors was to develop an instrument for measuring the dimensions of Avoidance of Intimacy and Anxiety about Abandonment in the person's relationship with God. For this reason, the Experiences in Close Relationships (ECR) scale of Brennan et al. became the model for the construction of the instrument Attachment to God Inventory—AGI.

Up to the present moment, there is no instrument adapted to the Brazilian context that allows us to measure the style of a person's attachment to God. For this reason, a study was conducted with the objective of validating the AGI (Beck and McDonald 2004) for the Brazilian context.

Before presenting the validation process of the AGI for the Brazilian context, a brief description of the processes of validation and application of this instrument in other cultural contexts will be made.

2. Attachment to God Inventory—A Brief Theoretical Background

For the structuring and validation of the AGI, Beck and McDonald (2004) organized their work in three studies. Study 1 contemplated the construction of the questionnaire. In Study 2, a first validation of the questionnaire was made with the participation of 507 US students, of which 80.2% were of Evangelical Protestant churches (Churches of Christ, Baptists, and Methodists); 6.5% did not belong to a denomination, and 3.4% were Catholics. In Study 3, a new validation was performed on a sample with a higher level of religious diversity. This stage had the participation of 118 US students, of which 75.4% were from of Protestant evangelical churches (Churches of Christ, Baptists, and Methodists); 6.8% did not belong to a denomination, and 6.8% were Catholics. The final selection of the items was based on the simultaneous obtaining of the best balance between three psychometric properties: factorial structure (load of dominant factors ≥ 0.40, load of cross factors ≤ 0.25), internal consistency (Cronbach's alpha > 0.80), and minimum shared variation between the subscales (r2 < 0.10). Thus, 28 items (14 items of avoidance and 14 items of anxiety) were selected to compose the Attachment to God Inventory.

The original AGI was constructed and validated in the USA. Subsequently, several researchers conducted studies aimed at its validation in other cultural contexts. The results obtained in these studies will be presented in the next section in order to contextualize, among those processes of validation, the validation process of this instrument in Brazil.

2.1. Validation of the Attachment to God Inventory (AGI) In the USA and Canada

The US concentrates 84% of the localized publications that used the AGI as an instrument of measuring the attachment to God. All 21 studies of the US that applied the AGI did so with individuals from Christian teaching institutions or Christian churches (Beck (2006a, 2006b); Bruce et al. 2011; Cooper et al. 2009; Dumont et al. 2012; Freeze and Ditommaso 2014, 2015; Hall et al. 2009; Homan 2012, 2014; Homan and Lemmon 2014, 2015; Homan and Boyatzis 2010; Houser and Welch 2013; Knabb and Pelletier 2014; Limke and Mayfield 2011; Olson et al. 2016; Prout et al. 2012; Rasar et al. 2013; Reiner et al. 2010; Thomas et al. 2011).

Among these publications, the four that published the psychometric data of the research presented satisfactory reliability indexes: Prout et al. (2012) surveyed 46 individuals, 60% of whom were Catholics, 28% of whom were Protestant evangelicals, 6% of whom had other affiliations, and 6% of whom had no religious affiliation. Homan and Lemmon (2014) collected data on 186 women, of whom 43% declared themselves Protestant and 48% from other Christian religions; 7% were Catholics, and 2% had no religious affiliation. In the study by Knabb and Pelletier (2014), the 187 university students reported the following religious affiliations: 45% Christians, 18% Protestant or Pentecostal Evangelicals, 17% Catholics, and 9% non-affiliated; 11% did not inform. The studies of Homan (2012) and Houser and Welch (2013) did not report data on religious affiliation.

The research conducted in Canada by Freeze and Ditommaso (2014) had the participation of 185 members of Baptist churches and 19 students of a Baptist institution and also presented adequate reliability indexes.

2.2. Validation of the AGI in Taiwan

Yeo (2011) conducted a psychometric study to validate the AGI scale for the Taiwanese reality. Four hundred people, recruited from Protestant (Baptists, Presbyterians, Charismatic, and Lutheran) and Catholic churches from Taipei, participated in the survey. The results of his research only presented the necessary consistency for validation after the exclusion of fifteen items of the instrument. The hypothesis raised by the author is that cultural differences may have influenced the responses. Yeo argues that the AGI was developed for American individualist culture, while in Taiwan, a collectivist culture prevails. According to Yeo, in a collectivist culture, being jealous of the way God answers the prayers of others, for example, is seen as inadequate. Thus, these and other issues that make up the original instrument and that aim to measure the level of anxiety and avoidance in the person's attachment to God may have very different weights for the respondent, depending on the cultural context in which he or she was raised.

2.3. Validation of the AGI in Italy

Rossi and Tagini (2011) conducted an AGI validation study for Italy. The work counted with 751 participants, of whom 73% declared themselves Catholics, 13% declared that they did not believe in God, 9% declared themselves Christians (of which the majority declared themselves Seventh-day Adventists), and the remaining 5% identified themselves with other religions. The AGI scale only met the psychometric requirements after the exclusion of five items from the scale. The authors argue that

> The original instrument was mainly developed on a sample of believers, protestant groups with a high percentage of women, while our sample is more heterogeneous and more balanced for sex. (Rossi and Tagini 2011)

Therefore, the hypothesis proposed by the authors for this divergence is that it was influenced by the profile of the respondents.

2.4. Validation of the AGI in Korea

Kim et al. (2017) validated the AGI scale with Christian Koreans who immigrated to the United States. The study participants were recruited from Christian communities, 220 were Catholics, and 43 were Methodists (Protestant evangelicals). In their studies, the scale only presented reliable indexes after the exclusion of 17 of the 28 items. The hypothesis raised by the authors is that the original scale did not present necessary consistency in view of the fact that Korean immigrants maintain different spiritual and religious traditions from the American tradition (p. 21), which may have interfered with the responses to the instrument. Christianity in Korea is strongly influenced by Confucianism and Shamanism, demonstrating characteristics of a religious syncretism. In this cultural context, the expression of emotions is not seen with good eyes, which may have contributed to the discarding of items dealing with emotional relationship with God (Kim et al. 2017, p. 23).

The validation of this instrument in other contexts demonstrated the need to exclude some items from the original instrument so that the model reached the necessary minimum parameters. Some hypotheses for these exclusions are presented in item 4.2.

3. Method

3.1. Translation and Adaptation

The adaptation and adaptation of the Attachment to God Inventory (AGI) to the Brazilian context, hereinafter called the *Inventário de Apego a Deus*—Brazilian Version (IAD-Br), was carried out according to the methodological and descriptive method, following the procedures of translation, cross-cultural adaptation, and validation, which are applicable to measuring instruments used in social sciences (Reichenheim and Moraes 2007).

All participants gave their informed consent for inclusion before participated in the study. The study was conducted in accordance with the declaration of Helsinki, and the protocol was approved on 20 October 2015 by PUCPR Research Ethics Committee, Protocol No. 49743315.4.0000.0020, Approval No. 2.365.692.

The process of translation, adaptation, and validation of the Attachment to God Inventory for its use in the Brazilian context went through a number of phases:

Phase 1—Translation to Portuguese. At this phase, the original instrument was sent to a sworn translator, who produced the Portuguese version of the instrument. Version 2 of the IAD-Br instrument was forwarded separately to four experts, who were asked to give their individual opinion on the version. Each specialist analyzed whether the Portuguese version had the original meaning. Based on the opinions of the specialists, the necessary adjustments were made, generating a new version of the instrument in Portuguese.

Phase 2—Reverse Translation to English. In this phase, the Portuguese version was translated into English, aiming to evaluate if the terms adopted in Portuguese maintained fidelity with the original terms of the instrument. This translation was done by a professional whose native language is English and who was qualified in this area. From the confrontation between the original English text and the translated text from Portuguese to English, some adjustments were made to the instrument, thus generating a new Portuguese version.

Phase 3—Pilot study. The new version of the IAD-Br instrument was fed into the Qualtrics® system, an online data collection and analysis tool, in order to evaluate the degree of comprehension and the ease of responding to the instrument. The participants were asked to inform bio-socio-demographic data and to answer some questions pertinent to the study. The sample consisted of 49 (forty-nine) online participants and 22 (twenty-two) presential participants. It was found that the scale issues were clearly described, and therefore no adjustments were necessary in the instrument.

Phase 4—Data Collection. At this phase, the final version of the instrument, together with the bio-socio-demographic data and the added questions, was fed back into the Qualtrics® system. The virtual questionnaire link was posted on random email lists and social networks. Participants were selected for convenience, aiming to compose a heterogeneous group in socioeconomic, religious, educational, ethnic, and racial terms. As the research could generate some emotional discomfort, participation was directed toward people older than 18 (eighteen) years old.

Phase 5—Confirmatory Factor Analysis. Confirmatory factorial tests were performed to extract the main components. The results of this analysis, as well as the refinements made in the IAD-Br instrument, are described in the following topic.

3.2. Sample

541 individuals participated in the study. Considering that the AGI was validated only or predominantly with Christian individuals (as seen in item 2 above), individuals who do not believe in God, as well as those who belong to other beliefs or who do not belong to any religious group, were excluded. The content of religious beliefs tends to vary between religious groups (Ghorbani-Bonab et al. 2013; Miner et al. 2014), indicating that in the case of religious groups that do not emphasize belief in a personal and relational God, the application of this instrument proves to be of little use, since the purpose of the Inventory is to measure the quality of attachment to God. Thus, subjects who declared themselves Kardecist Spiritists ($N = 10$) and/or those affiliated with Afro-Brazilian religious groups (Candomblé and Umbanda, $N = 5$) were excluded from the sample. Although this number was not very representative, the decision to exclude them was based on the consideration that such samples would be potential confounders. Given the religious characteristics of the Kardecist Spiritists, who believe in spiritual evolution through successive reincarnations, and of Afro-Brazilian religious groups, which are not categorized as Christians in Brazilian sociology, the inclusion of such data could cause some distortion in the results. For the same reason, 34 samples from the "non-religion" group were excluded. Participants under the age of eighteen were also excluded. After these exclusions, there were 470 participants ($N = 470$), more than the minimum of 300 individuals, as recommended by Guilford (1954) and MacCallum et al. (1999), to evaluate the reliability of an instrument.

The participants are divided into the following age groups: 54 individuals between 18 and 25 years old (11%), 112 between 26 and 36 (24%), 108 between 36 and 45 (23%), 111 between 46 and 55 (24%), 64 between 56 and 65 (14%), and 21 older than 65 (4%). Of the total, 179 are men (38%) and 291 are women (62%). In terms of schooling, 56 have a high school education (12%), 103 have an incomplete university degree (22%), 126 have a university degree (27%), and 185 have a postgraduate degree

(39%). As for marital status, 59% are married, 26% are single, 11% are separated or divorced, and 4% are widowed. In terms of monthly family income, 13% reported having income lower than R$ 1760, 65% reported having income between R$ 1760 and R$ 8800 and 22% reported an income above R$ 8800. As for the place of residence, 80% are from the South Region, 9% from the Southeast Region, 7% from the Central-West Region, 3% from the Northeast Region, and 1% from the Northern Region of Brazil, so that individuals from all geographic regions of the country participated in the study.

As for religiousness, 57% consider themselves religious and spiritual, 28% consider themselves religious, and 15% consider themselves spiritual, but not religious. Regarding religious services, 11% participate in religious services at most every two weeks, 43% participate once a week, and 46% participate several times a week. As for the religious community, 51% are Protestant evangelicals, 37% are Catholics, 8% are Pentecostal evangelicals, 2% are neo-Pentecostal evangelicals, and 2% are independent Christians.

4. Results and Discussion

4.1. Confirmatory Factor Analysis and Refinements of the IAD-Br

The answers to the questionnaire were analyzed through the use of two statistical software, the IBM SPSS Software 17.0, and the IBM SPSS Amos 22.0. Considering that the AGI instrument is structured in two factors (Anxiety about Abandonment by God and Avoidance of Intimacy with God), a confirmatory factorial analysis of the collected data was performed, consisting of a "multivariate technique used to test (confirm) a prespecified relationship" (Hair et al. 2009, p. 540). For this analysis, the factorial analysis software SPSS AMOS version 22 was adopted.

According to recommendations applicable to analyzes of data on human behavior, the adherence to the model was evaluated using values recommended by Hair et al. (2009). The loading of the data generated Model 1. Since the statistical indices of Model 1 do not fit within the required satisfactory parameters, the items of the instrument were refined. This refinement was performed by excluding the items with the Item-Total Correlation lower than 0.40, until the model reached all the necessary minimum adjustment parameters (Hair et al. 2009, p. 122). The recommended loading indexes were achieved after the exclusion of eleven items.

Table 1 presents the Total-Item Correlation indices obtained in Model 1 (with 28 items) and in Model 2 (with 17 items).

Table 1. Total-Item Correlation in Models 1 and 2.

	Model 1	Model 2
1. I worry a lot about my relationship with God (Eu me preocupo muito com meu relacionamento com Deus)	−0.09	–
2. I just don't feel a deep need to be close to God (Eu não sinto uma necessidade tão grande de estar próximo(a) a Deus)	0.20	–
3. If I can't see God working in my life, I get upset or angry (Se eu não vejo Deus agindo em minha vida, eu fico chateado(a) ou com raiva)	0.53	0.51
4. I am totally dependent upon God for everything in my life (R) (Sou totalmente dependente de Deus para tudo na minha vida)	0.70	0.74
5. I am jealous at how God seems to care more for others than for me (Tenho ciúmes da forma como Deus parece cuidar mais dos outros do que de mim)	0.78	0.74
6. It is uncommon for me to cry when sharing with God (Não é habitual eu chorar quando estou em comunhão com Deus)	0.31	–
7. Sometimes I feel that God loves others more than me (Às vezes sinto que Deus ama os outros mais do que a mim)	0.70	0.69
8. My experiences with God are very intimate and emotional (R) (Minhas experiências com Deus são muito íntimas e emocionais)	0.43	–

Table 1. *Cont.*

	Model 1	Model 2
9. I am jealous at how close some people are to God (*Tenho ciúmes da proximidade que algumas pessoas têm com Deus*)	0.67	0.64
10. I prefer not to depend too much on God (*Prefiro não depender muito de Deus*)	0.64	0.62
11. I often worry about whether God is pleased with me (*Com frequência me preocupo se Deus está satisfeito comigo*)	0.11	–
12. I am uncomfortable being emotional in my communication with God (*Sinto-me desconfortável se minha comunicação com Deus é emocional*)	0.15	–
13. Even if I fail, I never question that God is pleased with me (R) (*Mesmo quando eu falho, nunca me pergunto se Deus está contente comigo*)	−0.01	–
14. My prayers to God are often matter-of-fact and not very personal (*Minhas orações a Deus frequentemente são práticas e não muito pessoais*)	0.28	–
15. Almost daily, I feel that my relationship with God goes back and forth from "hot" to "cold" (*Quase diariamente sinto que minha relação com Deus é oscilante, vai de "intensa" a "fria"*)	0.48	0.48
16. I am uncomfortable with emotional displays of affection to God (*Sinto-me desconfortável com demonstrações emocionais de afeto a Deus*)	0.33	–
17. I fear God does not accept me when I do wrong (*Temo que Deus não me aceite quando faço algo errado*)	0.45	0.45
18. Without God I could not function at all (R) (*Sem Deus eu não consigo fazer nada*)	0.61	0.63
19. I often feel angry with God for not responding to me when I want (*Muitas vezes fico bravo(a) com Deus quando Ele não me responde quando quero*)	0.64	0.62
20. I believe people should not depend on God for things they should do for themselves (*Eu acredito que as pessoas não deveriam depender de Deus para fazer as coisas que elas deveriam fazer sozinhas*)	0.49	0.48
21. I crave reassurance from God that God loves me (*Eu preciso intensamente que Deus reafirme o seu amor por mim*)	0.42	0.42
22. Daily I discuss all of my problems and concerns with God (R) (*Diariamente eu discuto todos os meus problemas e preocupações com Deus*)	0.45	0.42
23. I am jealous when others feel God's presence when I cannot (*Eu fico com ciúmes quando outros sentem a presença de Deus e eu não*)	0.68	0.70
24. I am uncomfortable allowing God to control every aspect of my life (*Eu fico desconfortável em deixar que Deus controle cada aspecto da minha vida*)	0.52	0.51
25. I worry a lot about damaging my relationship with God (*Preocupo-me bastante com a possibilidade de eu prejudicar meu relacionamento com Deus*)	0.11	–
26. My prayers to God are very emotional (R) (*Minhas orações a Deus são muito emocionais*)	0.21	–
27. I get upset when I feel God helps others, but forgets about me (*Eu fico chateado(a) quando sinto que Deus ajuda outros, mas se esquece de mim*)	0.81	0.83
28. I let God make most of the decisions in my life (R) (*Eu deixo que Deus tome a maior parte das decisões na minha vida*)	0.67	0.69

Source: Data study analysis.

Table 2 presents the reliability and convergent validity before and after the exclusion of eleven items.

As can be verified, all indices showed significant improvements after the exclusion of the 11 items. Table 3 presents the adjustment rates for Model 2.

The adjustment of the model was calculated through several indices, all within parameters considered good or excellent. On the other hand, the reliability was calculated through the Composite Reliability, which should be above 0.70. Finally, the convergent validity was calculated through the Average Variance Extracted (AVE), which should be considered valid if above 0.5 (Hu and Bentler 1999).

Table 2. Reliability and Convergent Validity in Models 1 and 2.

	Model 1	Model 2
Anxiety about Abandonment by God		
Cronbach's Alpha	0.80	0.85
Composite Reliability	0.80	0.91
Average Variance Extracted	0.29	0.50
Avoidance of Intimacy with God		
Cronbach's Alpha	0.76	0.77
Composite Reliability	0.77	0.87
Average Variance Extracted	0.22	0.50

Source: Data study analysis.

Table 3. Adjustment Rates for Model 2.

	P	X2	DF	X2/DF	RMSEA	GFI	AGFI	CFI	NFI	SRMR
Model 2	<0.001	244.860	114	2.148	0.049	0.942	0.922	0.949	0.909	0.067

Source: Data study analysis.

Confirmatory factorial analysis of Model 1 presented unsatisfactory statistical parameters. This required the refinement of the instrument, excluding the eleven items that presented Item-Total Correlation below the recommended one (0.40).

After the exclusion of these items, a new confirmatory factorial analysis (Model 2) was generated, which presented adequate adjustment indexes, indicating that the IAD-Br instrument measures the phenomenon adequately, being therefore able to be used to measure attachment of people to God for the Brazilian population (see Appendixs A and B).

A person's attachment to God style can be represented through the indices of anxiety and avoidance obtained in the IAD-Br. The closer to 1 (one) the rates of Anxiety about Abandonment by God and Avoidance of Intimacy with God, the more secure the person's style of attachment to God. On the other hand, the closer to 7 (seven) the rates of Anxiety about Abandonment by God and Avoidance of Intimacy with God, the greater the anxiety and avoidance in the attachment to God, respectively.

Figure 1 shows the dispersion of the Anxiety about Abandonment by God and Avoidance of Intimacy with God rates of the study participants. Each point on the chart reproduces the responses of one individual.

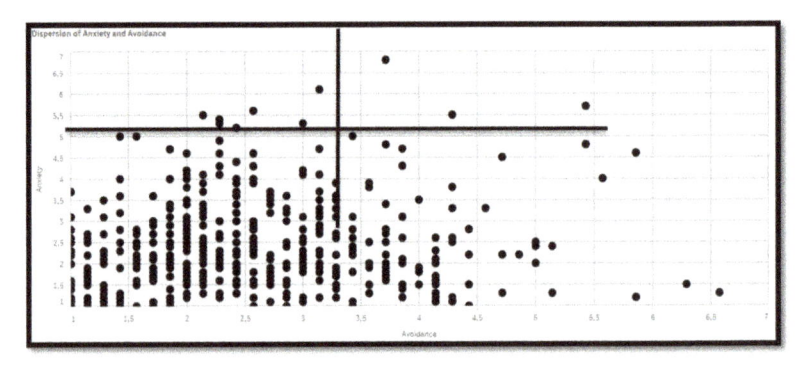

Figure 1. Dispersion of Anxiety and Avoidance Rates. Source: data study analysis.

The individuals are distributed in the most different positions in the graph, in which the horizontal axis 'x' represents the Anxiety about Abandonment by God, and the vertical axis 'y' represents the

Avoidance of Intimacy with God. The closer to 1 (both on the x-axis and the y-axis), the more secure the person's relationship with God. On the other hand, the more to the right the person is on the chart, the more anxious his or her relationship with God. Finally, the higher the point in the chart, the more avoidant the person's relationship with God.

It is noticed that 85% of the individuals are within the quadrant of security in relationship with God (anxiety and avoidance less than 4), 7% are in the quadrant of anxiety, 7% are in the avoidance quadrant, and 1% in the anxiety-avoidance quadrant. However, even among those in a given quadrant, there is infinite variation in anxiety and avoidance rates.

Attachment mechanisms are universal. However, insofar as religion includes the activation and operationalization of the attachment system, the parameters of the attachment system act differently in different people (Kirkpatrick 2005, p. 126). These differences in attachment styles are evidenced in the correlations between the Attachment to God anxiety and avoidance rates, and the following sample variables: (a) age group, (b) gender, (c) schooling, (d) marital status, (e) religious frequency, and (f) membership in the religious community.

4.1.1. Attachment to God Style and Age Group

Figures 2 and 3 present the average rates of Anxiety about Abandonment by God and Avoidance of Intimacy with God, sorted by age group.

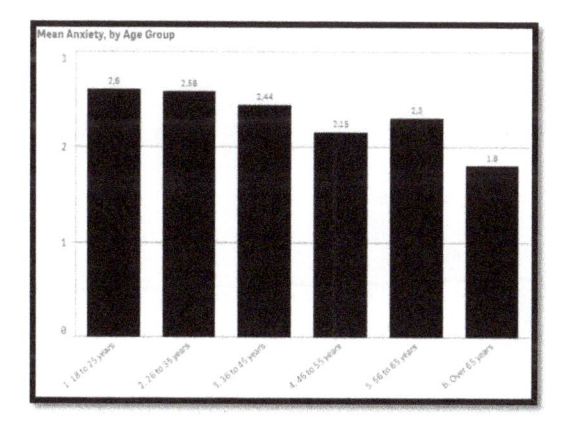

Figure 2. Anxiety, by age. Source: data study analysis.

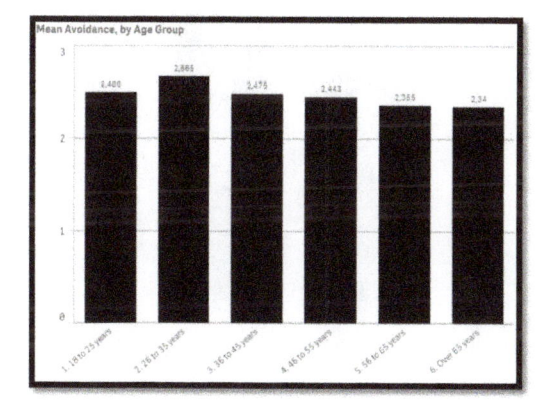

Figure 3. Avoidance, by age. Source: data study analysis.

There is a slight decrease in the Anxiety about Abandonment by God as the age ranges go up. However, when applying the Pearson correlation method, this decrease is evidenced (r = −0.179; $p < 0.001$). Regarding the Avoidance of Intimacy with God, there is a marginal trend to lower scores with increasing age (r = −0.079; $p = 0.088$). Van Assche et al. (2013), in a study on the impact of the attachment on behavioral and psychological symptoms in dementia, identified that "anxiety in close relations appears to diminish as people age". These authors also noted in their research that "attachment avoidance remains relatively stable" among the elderly. One possible explanation for greater security in the attachment to God among older people is raised by Cicirelli: "The nature and identities of attachment figures changed from those of earlier adult life to adult children, deceased loved ones, and God" (Cicirelli 2010).

4.1.2. Attachment to God Style and Gender

Figures 4 and 5 present the mean rates of Anxiety about Abandonment by God and Avoidance of Intimacy with God, grouped by gender.

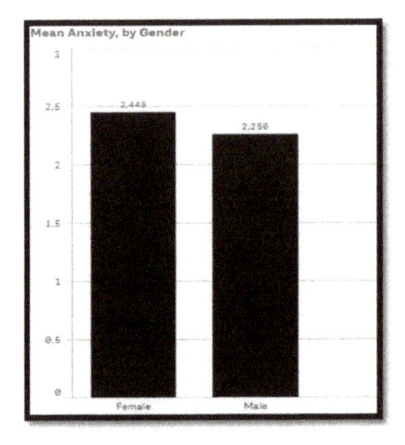

Figure 4. Anxiety, by Gender. Source: data study analysis.

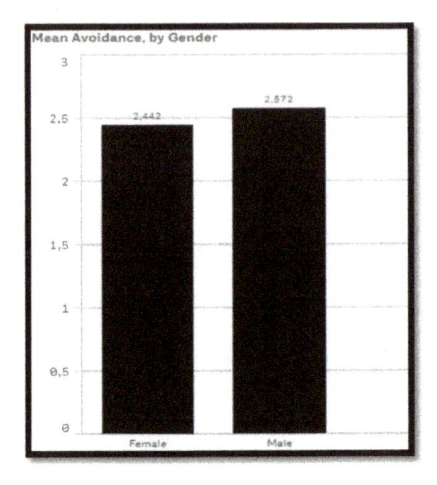

Figure 5. Avoidance, by Gender. Source: data study analysis.

The mean of the Anxiety about Abandonment by God is higher in the female sample (M = 2.44; SD = 1.10) than in the male sample (M = 2.25; SD = 0.90). To indicate which items of the IAD-Br instrument best express this tendency to greater anxiety in women's attachment to God, the Student's t-test was applied for independent samples. Thus, it has been identified that the statements that best illustrate this greater anxiety of women in attachment to God are the items 21 "I crave reassurance from God that God loves me" (t(405.059) = −2.343, p = 0.02), 23 "I am jealous when others feel God's presence when I cannot" (t(416.024) = −2.185, p = 0.029), and 27 "I get upset when I feel God helps others, but forgets about me" (t(426.341) = −2.251, p = 0.025).

Figure 5 shows that the mean of Avoidance of Intimacy with God is higher in the male sample (M = 2.57; SD = 1.04) than in the female sample (M = 2.44; SD = 1.00). However, differences in avoidance of attachment to God between men and women are statistically insignificant, as found in applying the Student's t-test on independent samples (t(468) = 1.336, p = 0.18). The statement that best illustrates the tendency toward greater avoidance of men in their relationship with God is item 24 "I am uncomfortable allowing God to control every aspect of my life" (t(335.696) = 2.087, p = 0.03).

4.1.3. Attachment to God Style and Schooling

Regarding Anxiety about Abandonment by God, a correlation with schooling of the individuals was not identified. Figure 6 shows the mean rates of Avoidance of Intimacy with God, classified by schooling.

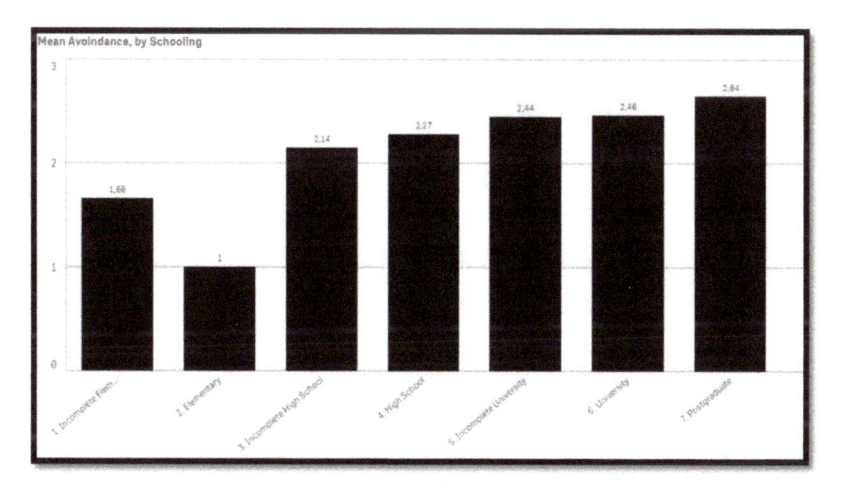

Figure 6. Avoidance, by Schooling. Source: data study analysis.

The rates of avoidance of intimacy with God increase as the degree of instruction rises, which was validated by the Pearson's correlation test (r = 0.150; p < 0.001).

4.1.4. Attachment to God Style and Marital Status

Figures 7 and 8 present the mean rates of Anxiety about Abandonment by God and Avoidance of Intimacy with God, comparing single and married people.

[Figure 7 chart: Mean Anxiety, by Marital Status — Married 2.249, Single 2.728]

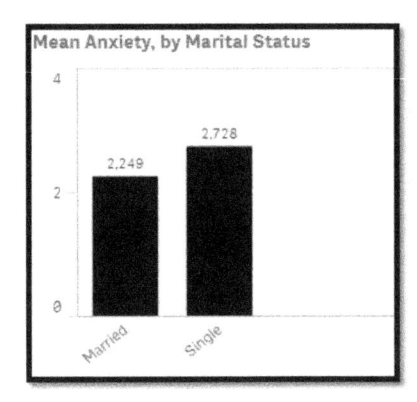

Figure 7. Anxiety, by Marital Status. Source: data study analysis.

[Figure 8 chart: Mean Avoidance, by Marital Status — Married 2.48, Single 2.704]

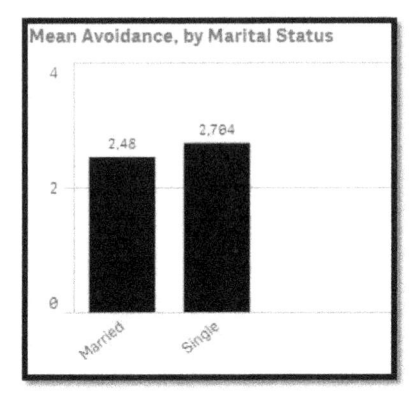

Figure 8. Avoidance, by Marital Status. Source: data study analysis.

Both anxiety and avoidance of attachment to God vary according to marital status. Compared with married people (M = 2.24; SD = 0.90), single people (M = 2.72; SD = 1.24) had higher mean values for both Anxiety about Abandonment by God (t(181.205) = 3.841; p = 0.000) and Avoidance of Intimacy with God, in which single people presented a higher mean (M = 2.70; SD = 1.09) than those married (M = 2.48; SD = 0.96), and the t-test was also significant for this difference of means (t(208) = 1.948; p = 0.041).

In comparison to married people, single people provided more anxious answers on all ten questions that measure Anxiety about Abandonment by God, as demonstrated by the Student's t-test rates: Item 3 (t(217.700) = 2.405; p = 0.074), Item 5 (t(180.765) = 2.386; p = 0.000), Item 7 (t(173.075) = 1.991; p = 0.000), Item 9 (t(196.192) = 2.261; p = 0.001), Item 15 (t(209.808) = 3.691; p = 0.001), Item 17 (t(217.881) = 2.559; p = 0.033), Item 19 (t(187.973) = 03.597, p = 0.000, Item 21 (t(223.049) = 2.026; p = 0.150), Item 23 (t(187.151) = 2.825, p = 0.000), and Item 27 (t(186.845) = 2.310; p = 0.001).

Of the seven questions that measure the avoidant dimension attachment to God, the statements that best represent this behavior are items 10 "I prefer not to depend too much on God" (t(176.066) = 2.375; p = 0.000) and 24 "I am uncomfortable allowing God to control every aspect of my life" (t(190.871) = 2.155; p = 0.000).

4.1.5. Attachment to God Style and Religious Frequency

A marginal correlation between the religious frequency reported by the participants and Anxiety about Abandonment by God was identified. Figure 9 shows the averages of Avoidance of Intimacy with God, ranked according to the religious frequency reported.

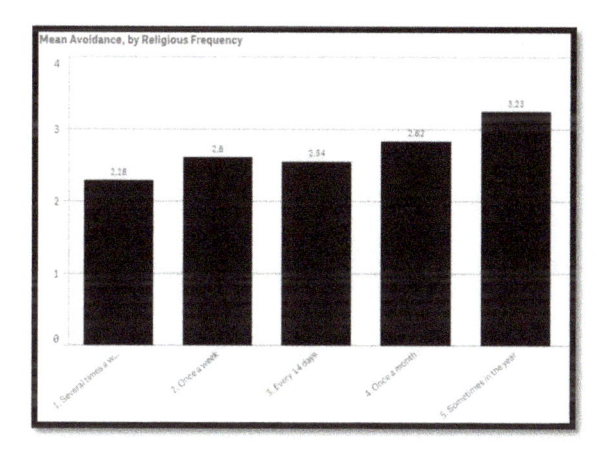

Figure 9. Avoidance, by Religious Frequency. Source: data study analysis.

Avoidance of Intimacy with God is lower among those who most attend religious activities, whether they are church services, masses, sessions, Bible studies, meetings, prayer groups, etc. In studying the attachment to God behavior in people who pray, Maeland (2013) concludes that "the experience of predictability and responsiveness is what allows a corrective relational experience, which in turn changes the pattern of connection". Another study with individuals from a Protestant community noted that "a secure attachment to God was related to an increase in religious behaviors and spirituality. It seems that increases in these religious and spiritual variables are related to less emotional distress" (Freeze and Ditommaso 2014, pp. 699–700).

These studies suggest that the participation in religious activities helps a person to regulate their security in God, reducing the rates of avoidance of intimacy with God. Another possibility is that people with secure attachment to God are more motivated to participate in religious activities in their community. In any case, these factors deserve specific studies, in order to better understand this phenomenon.

4.1.6. Attachment to God Style and Belonging to the Religious Community

When analyzing the data of the present research, only marginal differences of means were observed between the religious community frequented by the participants of the research and their Anxiety about Abandonment by God.

However, there were significant differences in Avoidance of Intimacy with God, depending on the religious community to which the person belongs. Applying the Student's t-test for independent samples on the Avoidance of Intimacy with God rates of statistically representative communities ($N > 30$) and comparing groups two to two, the following differences were found: Catholics (M = 2.94; SD = 1.13) are more avoidant in their relationship to God than Pentecostal evangelicals (M = 1.92; SD = 0.67) (t(93.349) = 7.414; p = 0.000). Catholics (M = 2.94; SD = 1.13) are also more avoidant in their relationship with God than Protestant evangelicals (M = 2.26; SD = 0.87) (t(310.997) = 6.631; p = 0.000). Finally, Protestant evangelicals (M = 2.26; SD = 0.87) are more avoidant in their relationship with God than Pentecostal evangelicals (M = 1.92; SD = 0.67) (t(61.053) = −2.792; p = 0.007).

Participant data analysis showed that anxiety about abandonment by God is greater among younger people, among women, and among single people. On the other hand, avoidance of intimacy with God is greater among people with higher schooling and among single people. It was also observed that the attachment to God style differs among people from different religious communities.

These indicators suggest that a person's attachment to God suffers multiple influences, since their relationship with God does not occur isolated of the context of the person. In the same way, attachment to God has repercussions in other spheres of the person's life. Further studies could deepen research in this field.

It is also necessary to raise some possible explanations for the exclusion of the 11 items of the IAD-Br scale.

4.2. Culture Influences the Expression of Faith

As for the cultural question and the way in which it affects a process of adaptation/validation of an instrument that was constructed in another cultural context, at least two aspects can be raised: each culture has its way of expressing faith, and an individualist culture will express its faith in a different way than a relational culture.

Regarding the first aspect, it is observed that only one item of the 14 items that measure Anxiety about Abandonment by God in the original scale remained in all four validations. It is item 17 (I fear God does not accept me when I do wrong). Of the 14 items that measure Avoidance of Intimacy with God in the original scale, only three items remained in all four validations. These are item 4 (I am totally dependent upon God for everything in my life), item 18 (Without God I couldn't function at all) and item 22 (Daily I discuss all of my problems and concerns with God). This analysis suggests that in the original scale there is a variation of the factors and that it is sensitive to the cultural context in which it is applied.

As for the aspect of difference in the expression of faith in an individualist culture if compared to a relational culture, the philosopher Ales Bello emphasizes that the religious moment is central to each cultural expression (Ales Bello 1998, p. 147). Since the human being presents himself basically as a religious being, the way in which he expresses his religiosity is closely related to the culture to which he belongs. Culture "is the artificial, 'secondary environment', which man superimposes on the natural. It encompasses language, habits, ideas, beliefs, customs, social organization, inherited artifacts, technical processes, and values" (Niebuhr 1967, p. 53). And as an environment produced by society, culture is constituted in the environment in which faith is expressed (Niebuhr 1967, p. 16). Therefore, the comparison between different cultures allows us to understand the differences between the expressions of faith of these cultures (Ales Bello 1998, p. 148).

Roberto DaMatta, a renowned Brazilian sociologist, defends the thesis that

> The Brazilian ritual system is a complex mode of establishing and even proposing a permanent and strong relation between the house and the street, between 'this world' and the 'other world'. In other words, the festivity, ceremonial, ritual and solemn moment are modalities of relating separate and complementary sets of the same social system. (DaMatta 1997, p. 56)

The house, the street, and the other world are sociological categories that are "fundamental for the understanding of the Brazilian society", proposed DaMatta (1997, p. 14). As 'house', DaMatta understands the private, personal, familiar, intimate world of the Brazilian. The 'street' refers to the public, juridical/legal, impersonal, anonymous, and torn environment. However, the 'other world' comprises the environment of the 'supernatural', of religion, beliefs, rituals, and the dead. According to this proposition, the understanding of Brazilian society takes place through the observation of the mediations that appear in the interface between the three worlds (the house, the street, and the other world). Thus, for DaMatta, Brazilian society is characterized by being essentially relational, where the meaning of the person is in the way he or she relates to the interface between these worlds.

This relational characteristic that differentiates Brazilian culture also impacts the way individuals view and practice their faith (DaMatta 1997, p. 58).

Whereas the "American society would be homogeneous, individualistic and exclusive; in Brazil it would be heterogeneous, unequal, relational and inclusive. In one situation, what counts is the individual and the citizen; in another, it is the relationship" (DaMatta 1997, pp. 70–71). Thus, "in the United States there is exclusion and separation; in Brazil, there is junction and hierarchy. In one situation the creed says: equal, but separate; in another, it decrees: different, but together" (DaMatta 1997, p. 97).

Therefore, items that were adequately correlated with the factor they should measure (Anxiety about Abandonment by God and Avoidance of Intimacy with God) in the Anglo-Saxon context in which the AGI was constructed; they behaved differently in collectivist (Taiwan), secularized (Italy), syncretic (Korea), and relational (Brazil) contexts.

Even considering the cultural differences noted, the IAD-Br is able to be used to measure attachment to God in the Brazilian context, since attachment to God is a universal element of the manifestation of faith. Cultural differences in the measurement of attachment to God are restricted to items that measure anxiety and avoidance in attachment to God, without compromising the basic conceptual structure of the original instrument. Understanding God as a figure of attachment who acts as a safe haven and secure base for those who trust Him remains a common value in all cultures.

4.3. Limitations and Future Studies

Since the IAD-Br instrument aims to measure the person's relationship with God, the results of applying the instrument will only make sense to people who believe in God and who in some way maintain a relationship with Him.

The use of a self-assessment tool brings with it the risk of the participant's self-misunderstanding. In addition, responses may also be influenced by socially desirable patterns (Olson et al. 2016, p. 87). Therefore, the interpretation of the data should take these elements into account.

The results suggest a correlation between the style of Attachment to God and the different ways of experiencing faith in each community of faith, which could be the object of future studies. In addition, the exclusion of some specific religious groups, such as Kardecist Spiritists and Afro-Brazilian religions, leave open the question about the applicability of the Inventory in these groups and whether such applicability would actually demonstrate significantly different results from those presented here. Thus, it is suggested to apply this instrument in these groups, as well as in other religious groups, such as Muslims and Jews. Although there have been changes in the Brazilian religious map, as evidenced in the last religious census, Brazil remains a predominantly Christian country (IBGE 2010). The changes show a decline in the number of Catholics (from 73.8% in 2000 to 64.6% in 2010) and an increase of 22.2% in the number of Evangelicals (Protestants, Pentecostals and Neo-Pentecostals) between 2000 and 2010. Muslims and Jews are still a minority, with 35,000 Muslims and 107,329 Jews (IBGE 2010).

Given that none of the participants identified themselves as affiliated to Jewish or Islamic religions, it is suggested that future studies should include these groups in order to verify the instrument's reliability with them. It is worth highlighting that in the study of Miner et al. (2017), the authors note that in the Islamic context it is recommended to use a specific instrument to measure attachment to God because of the differences between Christians and Muslims in the understanding of God (Miner et al. 2017, p.184).

5. Conclusions

This article demonstrated the validation process of the Inventário de Apego a Deus (IAD-Br) for the Brazilian context. The purpose of IAD-Br is to measure the person's attachment to God, considering the existence of two factors: Anxiety about Abandonment by God and Avoidance of Intimacy with God. After the reduction from 28 to 17 items, the model presented adequate psychometric qualities.

The results indicated that the IAD-Br is a useful tool for use in the Brazilian cultural context, as it will allow researchers to make comparisons between data obtained in different contexts and samples. It will also make it possible to add important content in the curricula of training courses for theologians, spiritual caregivers, counselors, pastors, and spiritual leaders.

In addition, it is important to emphasize that the use of this instrument and consequently the studies on its application in the most diverse contexts may impact theological reflection (mainly the practical theology), especially in the questions about the provision of spiritual care in the most diverse contexts and situations of the cycles of life.

The analysis of the data collected during the validation process shows that the indices of anxiety about abandonment by God and avoidance of intimacy with God vary according to age, schooling, gender, marital status, and religious community. As already argued, the person's affective relationship with God undergoes multiple influences.

Although the validation of the IAD-Br expands the wide field of research on religious behavior in Brazil, further studies are required with the application of the Inventory. It is suggested that it be applied in specific populations, such as groups with different religious traditions and in health-disease contexts. It is believed that the use of IAD-Br will allow an application of the concepts of the attachment theory and the verification of the Inventory as a reliable instrument for the measurement of attachment to God in clinical and research use. Such studies would be promising, especially if applied with other instruments such as the Spiritual/Religious Coping Scale, the Religious and Spiritual Struggle Scale, and the Centrality of Religiousness Scale.

Acknowledgments: This study was partially subsidized by CAPES—Coordination for the Improvement of Higher Education Personnel. We are thankful to Beck and McDonald (2004), the original authors of the Attachment to God Inventory.

Author Contributions: All the authors contributed equally to the manuscript.

Conflicts of Interest: The authors declare no conflict of interest.

Appendix A. Inventário de Apego a Deus—Versão Brasileira (IAD-Br)—In Portuguese

Adaptado de Beck and McDonald (2004).

As seguintes afirmações se referem a como você se sente em seu relacionamento com Deus. Estamos interessados em como você de modo geral experimenta sua relação com Deus, não apenas no que está acontecendo atualmente, nessa relação. Assinale em cada afirmação o quanto você concorda ou discorda dela.

		Discordo Fortemente	Discordo	Discordo Moderadamente	Não Concordo; Nem Discordo	Concordo Moderadamente	Concordo	Concordo Fortemente
1	Sou totalmente dependente de Deus para tudo na minha vida.	7	6	5	4	3	2	1
2	Prefiro não depender muito de Deus	1	2	3	4	5	6	7
3	Sem Deus eu não consigo fazer nada.	7	6	5	4	3	2	1
4	Eu acredito que as pessoas não deveriam depender de Deus para fazer as coisas que elas deveriam fazer sozinhas.	1	2	3	4	5	6	7
5	Diariamente eu discuto todos os meus problemas e preocupações com Deus.	7	6	5	4	3	2	1
6	Eu fico desconfortável em deixar que Deus controle cada aspecto da minha vida.	1	2	3	4	5	6	7
7	Eu deixo que Deus tome a maior parte das decisões na minha vida.	7	6	5	4	3	2	1
						Soma 1		
8	Se eu não vejo Deus agindo em minha vida, eu fico chateado(a) ou com raiva.	1	2	3	4	5	6	7
9	Tenho ciúmes da forma como Deus parece cuidar mais dos outros do que de mim.	1	2	3	4	5	6	7
10	Às vezes sinto que Deus ama os outros mais do que a mim.	1	2	3	4	5	6	7
11	Tenho ciúmes da proximidade que algumas pessoas têm com Deus.	1	2	3	4	5	6	7
12	Quase diariamente sinto que minha relação com Deus é oscilante, vai de "intensa" a "fria".	1	2	3	4	5	6	7
13	Temo que Deus não me aceite quando faço algo errado.	1	2	3	4	5	6	7
14	Muitas vezes fico bravo(a) com Deus quando Ele não me responde quando quero.	1	2	3	4	5	6	7
15	Eu preciso intensamente que Deus reafirme o seu amor por mim.	1	2	3	4	5	6	7
16	Eu fico com ciúmes quando outros sentem a presença de Deus e eu não.	1	2	3	4	5	6	7
17	Eu fico chateado(a) quando sinto que Deus ajuda outros, mas se esquece de mim.	1	2	3	4	5	6	7
						Soma 2		

Dimensão da Evitação a Deus Dimensão da Ansiedade a Deus
Soma 1: _____ : 7 = _____ . Soma 2: _____ : 10 = _____

Appendix B. The Attachment to God Inventory

The following statements concern how you feel about your relationship with God. We are interested in how you generally experience your relationship with God, not just in what is happening in that relationship currently. Respond to each statement by indicating how much you agree or disagree with it. Write the number in the space provided, using the following rating scale:

1	2	3	4	5	6	7
Disagree Strongly			Neutral/Mixed			Agree Strongly

_____ 1. I worry a lot about my relationship with God.
_____ 2. I just do not feel a deep need to be close to God.
_____ 3. If I cannot see God working in my life, I get upset or angry.
_____ 4. I am totally dependent upon God for everything in my life. (R)
_____ 5. I am jealous at how God seems to care more for others than for me.
_____ 6. It is uncommon for me to cry when sharing with God.
_____ 7. Sometimes I feel that God loves others more than me.
_____ 8. My experiences with God are very intimate and emotional. (R)
_____ 9. I am jealous at how close some people are to God.
_____10. I prefer not to depend too much on God.
_____11. I often worry about whether God is pleased with me.
_____12. I am uncomfortable being emotional in my communication with God.
_____13. Even if I fail, I never question that God is pleased with me. (R)
_____14. My prayers to God are often matter-of-fact and not very personal.*
_____15. Almost daily I feel that my relationship with God goes back and forth from "hot" to "cold."
_____16. I am uncomfortable with emotional displays of affection to God.*
_____17. I fear God does not accept me when I do wrong.
_____18. Without God I could not function at all. (R)
_____19. I often feel angry with God for not responding to me when I want.
_____20. I believe people should not depend on God for things they should do for themselves.
_____21. I crave reassurance from God that God loves me.
_____22. Daily I discuss all of my problems and concerns with God. (R)
_____23. I am jealous when others feel God's presence when I cannot.
_____24. I am uncomfortable allowing God to control every aspect of my life.
_____25. I worry a lot about damaging my relationship with God.
_____26. My prayers to God are very emotional. (R)
_____27. I get upset when I feel God helps others, but forgets about me.
_____28. I let God make most of the decisions in my life. (R)

Scoring:

Avoidance = sum of even numbered items
Anxiety = sum of odd numbered items
Items 4, 8, 13, 18, 22, 26, and 28 are reverse scored
* Researchers may want to consider dropping these items (14 and 16)

References

Abreu, Cristiano Nabuco de. 2005. *Teoria do Apego—Fundamentos, Pesquisas e Implicações Clínicas*. São Paulo: Casa do Psicólogo. (In Portuguese)
Ales Bello, Angela. 1998. *Culturas e Religiões: Uma Leitura Fenomenológica*. Bauru: EDUSC. (In Portuguese)
Beck, Richard. 2006a. Communion and Complaint: Attachment, object-relations, and triangular love perspectives on relationship with God. *Journal of Psychology and Theology* 34: 43–53. [CrossRef]

Beck, Richard. 2006b. God as a secure base: Attachment to God and theological exploration. *Journal of Psychology and Theology* 34: 125–33. [CrossRef]

Beck, Richard, and Angie McDonald. 2004. Attachment to God: The Attachment to God Inventory, Tests of Working Model Correspondence, and an Exploration of Faith Group Differences. *Journal of Psychology and Theology* 32: 92–103. [CrossRef]

Bowlby, John. 1988. *A Secure Base: Parent-Child Attachment and Healthy Human Development*. New York: Basic Books.

Bowlby, John. 2002. *Apego e Perda: Apego, V. 1 Da Trilogia*, 3rd ed. São Paulo: Martins Fontes. (In Portuguese)

Bowlby, John. 2004a. *Apego e Perda: Perda: Tristeza e Depressão. V. 3 Da Trilogia*. São Paulo: Martins Fontes. (In Portuguese)

Bowlby, John. 2004b. *Apego e Perda: Separação: Angústia e Raiva. V. 2 Da Trilogia*. São Paulo: Martins Fontes. (In Portuguese)

Brennan, Kelly A., Catherine L. Clark, and Phillip R. Shaver. 1998. Self-report measures of adult romantic attachment. An integrative overview. In *Attachment Theory and Close Relationships*. Edited by Jeffry A. Simpson and William Steven Rholes. New York: Guilford Press.

Bruce, A. Jerry, Laura B. Cooper, S. Thomas Kordinak, and Marsha J. Harman. 2011. God and Sin after 50: Gender and Religious Affiliation. *Journal of Religion, Spirituality & Aging* 23: 224–35.

Cicirelli, Victor G. 2010. Attachment relationships in old age. *Journal of Social & Personal Relationships* 27: 191–99.

Cooper, Laura B., A. Jerry Bruce, Marsha J. Harman, and Marcus T. Boccaccini. 2009. Differentiated styles of attachment to God and varying religious coping efforts. *Journal of Psychology and Theology* 37: 134–42. [CrossRef]

DaMatta, Roberto. 1997. *A Casa & a Rua: Espaço, Cidadania, Mulher e Morte No Brasil*, 5th ed. Rio de Janeiro: Rocco. (In Portuguese)

Dumont, Karin, David Jenkins, Victor Hinson, and Gary Sibcy. 2012. God's shield: The relationship between god attachment, relationship satisfaction, and adult child of an alcoholic (ACOA) status in a sample of evangelical graduate counseling students. *Journal of Psychology and Christianity* 31: 51–66.

Esperandio, Mary Rute G., and Hartmut August. 2014. Teoria do Apego e Comportamento Religioso. *Interações—Cultura e Comunidade, Belo Horizonte, Brasil* 16: 243–65. (In Portuguese)

Freeze, Tracy A., and Enrico Ditommaso. 2014. An examination of attachment, religiousness, spirituality and well-being in a Baptist faith sample. *Mental Health, Religion & Culture* 17: 690–702.

Freeze, Tracy A., and Enrico Ditommaso. 2015. Attachment to God and church family: Predictors of spiritual and psychological well-being. *Journal of Psychology and Christianity* 34: 60–73.

Ghorbani-Bonab, Bagher, Maureen Miner, and Marie-Therese Proctor. 2013. Attachment to God in Islamic spirituality. *Journal of Muslim Mental Health* 7: 77–104.

Granqvist, Pehr, and Lee A. Kirkpatrick. 2004. Religious Conversion and Perceived Childhood Attachment: A Meta-Analysis. *The International Journal for the Psychology of Religion* 4: 223–250. [CrossRef]

Granqvist, Pehr, and Lee A. Kirkpatrick. 2013. Religion, spirituality, and attachment. In *APA Handbook for the Psychology of Religion and Spirituality (Vol 1): Context, Theory, and Research*. Edited by Kenneth I. Pargament. Washington: American Psychological Association, pp. 129–55.

Guilford, Joy Paul. 1954. *Psychometric Methods*, 2nd ed. New York: McGraw-Hill.

Hair, Joseph F., Jr., Rolph E. Anderson, Ronald L. Tatham, and William. C. Black. 2009. *Análise Multivariada de Dados*, 6th ed. Porto Alegre: Bookman. (In Portuguese)

Hall, Todd W., Annie Fujikawa, Sarah R. Halcrow, Peter C. Hill, and Harold Delaney. 2009. Attachment to god and implicit spirituality: Clarifying correspondence and compensation models. *Journal of Psychology and Theology* 37: 227–45. [CrossRef]

Homan, Kristin J. 2012. Attachment to God mitigates negative effect of media exposure on women's body image. *Psychology of Religion and Spirituality* 4: 324–31. [CrossRef]

Homan, Kristin J. 2014. A mediation model linking attachment to God, self-compassion, and mental health. *Mental Health, Religion & Culture* 17: 977–89.

Homan, Kristin J., and Chris J. Boyatzis. 2010. The protective role of attachment to God against eating disorder risk factors: Concurrent and prospective evidence. *Eating Disorder* 18: 239–58. [CrossRef] [PubMed]

Homan, Kristin J., and Valerie A. Lemmon. 2014. Attachment to God and eating disorder tendencies: The mediating role of social comparison. *Psychology of Religion and Spirituality* 6: 349–57. [CrossRef]

Homan, Kristin J., and Valerie A. Lemmon. 2015. Perceived relationship with God moderates the relationship between social comparison and body appreciation. *Mental Health, Religion & Culture* 18: 425–39.

Houser, Melissa E., and Ronald D. Welch. 2013. Hope, religious behaviors, and attachment to god: A trinitarian perspective. *Journal of Psychology and Theology* 41: 281–317. [CrossRef]

Hu, Li-tze, and Peter M. Bentler. 1999. Cutoff Criteria for Fit Indices in Covariance Structure Analysis: Conventional Criteria Versus New Alternatives. *Structural Equation Modeling: A Multidisciplinary Journal* 6: 1–55. [CrossRef]

IBGE. 2010. Censo Demográfico. Rio de Janeiro: IBGE, 2000. Available online: https://www.ibge.gov.br/index.php (accessed on 18 March 2018).

Kim, Pio, Sangwon Kim, Fran Blumberg, and Jihee Cho. 2017. Validation of the Korean Attachment to God Inventory. *Psychology of Religion and Spirituality* 9. [CrossRef]

Kirkpatrick, Lee. 2005. *Attachment, Evolution, and the Psychology of Religion*. New York: Guilford.

Kirkpatrick, Lee A., and Phillip R. Shaver. 1990. Attachment Theory and Religion. Childhood Attachments, Religious Beliefs and Conversion. *Journal for the Scientific Study of Religion* 29: 315–34. [CrossRef]

Knabb, Joshua J., and Joseph Pelletier. 2014. The relationship between problematic Internet use, God attachment, and psychological functioning among adults at a Christian university. *Mental Health, Religion & Culture* 17: 239–51.

Limke, Alicia, and Patrick B. Mayfield. 2011. Attachment to God: Differentiating the contributions of fathers and mothers using the experiences in parental relationships scale. *Journal of Psychology and Theology* 39: 122–30. [CrossRef]

MacCallum, Robert C., Keith Widaman, Shaobo Zhang, and Sehee Hong. 1999. Sample size in factor analysis. *Psychological Methods* 4: 84–99. [CrossRef]

Maeland, Elisabeth. 2013. Attachment and Prayer a Critical Analysis of Relationships among Attachment Experiences and Perceived Relation to God in Prayer. Master's thesis, Det Teologiske Menighetsfakultet, Oslo, Norway.

Mario, Mikulincer, and Philip R. Shaver. 2010. *Attachment in Adulthood—Structure, Dynamics, and Change*. New York: Guilford.

Miner, Maureen, Bagher Ghorbany-Bonab, Martin Dowson, and Marie-Therese Proctor. 2014. Spiritual attachment in Islam and Christianity. *Mental Health, Religion and Culture* 17: 79–93. [CrossRef]

Miner, Maureen, Bagher Ghobary-Bonab, and Martin Dowson. 2017. Development of a Measure of Attachment to God for Muslims. *Review of Religious Research* 59: 183–206. [CrossRef]

Niebuhr, H. Richard. 1967. *Cristo e Cultura. Série Encontros e Diálogos*. Rio de Janeiro: Paz e Terra, vol. 3. (In Portuguese)

Olson, Trevor, Theresa Clement Tisdale, Edward B. Davis, Elizabeth A. Park, Jiyun Nam, Glendon L. Moriarty, Don E. Davis, Michael J. Thomas, Andrew D. Cuthbert, and Lance W. Hays. 2016. God image narrative therapy: A mixed-methods investigation of a controlled group-based spiritual intervention. *Spirituality in Clinical Practice* 3: 77–91. [CrossRef]

Prout, Tracy A., John Cecero, and Dianna Dragatsi. 2012. Parental object representations, attachment to God, and recovery among individuals with psychosis. *Mental Health, Religion & Culture* 15: 449–66.

Rasar, Jacqueline D., Fernando L. Garzon, Frederick Volk, Carlmella A. O'Hare, and Glendon L. Moriarty. 2013. The efficacy of a manualized group treatment protocol for changing god image, attachment to god, religious coping, and love of god, others, and self. *Journal of Psychology and Theology* 41: 267–81. [CrossRef]

Reichenheim, Michael, and Claudia Moraes. 2007. Operacionalização de adaptação transcultural de instrumentos de aferição usados em epidemiologia. *Revista de Saúde Pública* 41: 665–73. (In Portuguese)[CrossRef]

Reiner, Sarah R., Tamara L. Anderson, M. Elizabeth Lewis Hall, and Todd W. Hall. 2010. Adult attachment, God attachment and gender in relation to perceived stress. *Journal of Psychology and Theology* 38: 175–211. [CrossRef]

Rossi, Germano, and Angela Tagini. 2011. The Attachment to God Inventory (AGI, Beck & MacDonald, 2004): An Italian Adaptation. Available online: http://www.germanorossi.it/pubb/C71_2011_RosTag.pdf (accessed on 27 December 2016).

Thomas, Michael J., Glendon L. Moriarty, Edward B. Davis, and Elizabeth L. Anderson. 2011. The effects of a manualized group-psychotherapy intervention on client God images and attachment to God: A pilot study. *Journal of Psychology and Theology* 39: 44–59. [CrossRef]

Van Assche, Lies, Patrick Luyten, Lucas Van de Ven, and Mathieu Vandenbulcke. 2013. The impact of attachment on behavioral and psychological symptoms in dementia. *Tijdschr Gerontol Geriatr* 44: 157–65.

Yeo, Ju-Ping Chiao. 2011. The Psychometric Study of the Attachment to God Inventory and the Brief Religious Coping Scale in a Taiwanese Christian Sample. Ph.D. dissertation, Liberty University, Lynchburg, VA, USA. Available online: http://digitalcommons.liberty.edu/doctoral/458 (accessed on 27 October 2016).

© 2018 by the authors. Licensee MDPI, Basel, Switzerland. This article is an open access article distributed under the terms and conditions of the Creative Commons Attribution (CC BY) license (http://creativecommons.org/licenses/by/4.0/).

religions

Article

Filipino College Students' Attitudes towards Religion: An Analysis of the Underlying Factors

Rito Baring [1,*], Philip Joseph Sarmiento [2], Nestor Sibug [3], Paolo Lumanlan [4], Benita Bonus [5], Cristina Samia [2] and Stephen Reysen [6]

1. Theology & Religious Education Department, De La Salle University, Manila 0927, Philippines
2. Christian Living Education Department, Holy Angel University, Angeles City 2009, Philippines; pjsarmiento@hau.edu.ph (P.J.S.); csamia@hau.edu.ph (C.S.)
3. Psychology Department, Holy Angel University, Angeles City 2009, Philippines; nsibug@hau.edu.ph
4. College of Social Sciences & Philosophy, Don Honorio Ventura Technological State University, Bacolor 2001, Philippines; plumanlan@dhvtsu.edu.ph
5. School of Education, Holy Angel University, Angeles City 2009, Philippines; bbonus@hau.ed.ph
6. Department of Psychology, Counseling and Special Education, Texas A&M-Commerce, TX 75429, USA; Stephen.Reysen@tamuc.edu
* Correspondence: rito.baring@dlsu.edu.ph; Tel.: +63-524-4611 (local 534)

Received: 18 January 2018; Accepted: 13 March 2018; Published: 17 March 2018

Abstract: In the last 50 years, measures of religious constructs have been the subject of much scientific attention. Cross-cultural considerations necessitate that empirical claims on assessments about religion are validated by local data. While religion is typically viewed in terms of spirituality and religiosity, recent empirical studies indicate a shift in the interpretation of these dimensions in a more diffused and relaxed appreciation. Building up from these developments, in the present research, we develop and test the structure and reliability of a scale to assess students' attitudes towards religion. Using a sample (n = 2733) of college students from two provincial universities in the Philippines, we employed data reduction techniques to understand the underlying factor structure. The results showed a three-factor measure of attitudes towards religion.

Keywords: attitudes towards religion; Filipino students; religiosity; spirituality; self-report measure of religion

---

1. Introduction

Poll surveys in the Philippines often assess attitudes towards religion in terms of religiosity and spirituality. These studies favor the impression that religion is essentially about faith and practice. Sociological inquiries generally frame these studies using "religious beliefs and practices" (Mangahas and Guerrero 1992), reflecting the inward and outward dimensions of belief. The inquiries gravitate around religious affiliation, e.g., Christianity, personal obligation such as religious practice and spiritual norms. The thin dividing line between the religious and spiritual dimensions suggested in local literature (Abad 2001) offers some new insights about how local contemporary studies in religion could be theorized. Recent empirical studies in religion see the fluid interaction between the institutional, obligatory, and spiritual dimensions. In a recent national youth survey (CBCP-ECY and CEAP 2014) in the country, religiosity and religious domains is assessed to include "private practice" and "religious experience." These measures, however, are specifically directed towards forming baseline data for population profile regarding religion rather than investigate the underlying dimensions that characterize respondents' notions of religion. Considering the missing inquiry that provides an in-depth analysis of latent dimensions representing youth attitudes towards religion in the Philippines and in an ASEAN (Association of Southeast Asian Nations) setting, the researchers decided to embark on this study. Attempts to locate assessment scales in the local and regional context intended to measure student attitudes toward religion did not yield favorable results. However, related scales developed from the West to assess attitudes towards Christianity (Francis et al. 1995) among undergraduate students are prevalent but are missing some peculiar characteristics of student perspectives found in recent local studies (Baring et al. 2016a; Batara 2015). Another assessment scale developed to assess attitudes towards religion is the Astley–Francis Scale of attitude towards theistic faith (Astley et al. 2012). This assessment is validated for internal consistency and reliability in varied Western settings. However, no validation was conducted for the Southeast Asian context. Obviously, these measures carry out delimiting objectives or context that are very specific to their design and development (Büssing 2017). A previous study (MacDonald et al. 2015) involving university students in eight countries evaluated the validity and reliability of the Expressions of Spirituality Inventory (ESI-R) and the Spirituality Adjective List (SAL). From the empirical findings, we considered that certain cultural factors (Hambleton 2005), e.g., ethnicity, may affect the outcomes of empirical designs and results. After reviewing the Astley–Francis Scale and the other related scales, we noted that certain atypical characteristics of student perspectives in our setting need to be articulated in our desire to develop an assessment tool for college students' attitudes towards religion. We were looking at the diffused interaction between the religious and spiritual, the moral/ethical perspectives and personal views (Baring et al. 2016b) which emerged in a previous study in the local setting. In saying this, we did consider how contrasting studies have operationalized assessments that dealt with spirituality as being distinct from religiosity but inter-related (MacDonald et al. 2015). We fully understand that introducing a diffused conceptualization of spirituality and religiosity incorporated in a single construct looks unlikely in traditional empirical studies involving attitudes towards religion. The diffused state is not preferred in some Western settings where religiosity is distinguished from spirituality (Zwingmann et al. 2011) due to the secular context. However, the recent use of both Spirituality/Religiosity as a single construct in a growing number of studies (Baring et al. 2016b; Good and Willoughby 2014) from different environments supports our intent. The study of Religiosity/Spirituality as one construct in many other investigations render this pairing highly plausible.

2. The Need for a New Measure: Peculiar Traits

This recent development henceforth takes note of the increasing attention given to the collapse of the distinction itself. Recent studies on Filipino youth articulations of religious belief already show a diffused appreciation of religion, morals and spiritual life (Baring and Cacho 2015). A growing recognition in the literature (Baring et al. 2016a, 2016b) studying Filipino youth profile records the loosening of the boundaries and distinctions proposed in the previous sacred–profane model. This observation is also noted in other Western literature (Koenig 2009) which sees the distinction of spirituality from religiosity as problematic for assessment purposes. In effect, this profound shift has given way to a new awareness which this inquiry is interested to explore and verify. Adolescence is a strategic period to understand the youths' spiritual and religious engagements (King and Boyatzis 2004). Understanding the essential role of spirituality vis-à-vis religiosity in Filipino youth development (Ocampo et al. 2013) can be a significant step towards deepening the appreciation of local scholarship towards spirituality and religiosity among adolescents. To clarify therefore the peculiar turn of the youth's appreciation of the spiritual and religious and how these are interspersed presents itself as a logical scope towards a study of youth attitudes towards religion. Locally, thus far, no research has attempted to provide an empirical explanation of the youth's underlying attitudes towards religion. Youth studies in relation to religion are the usual demographic profiles mostly assessed with respect to other psycho-social variables reported in social weather stations and in commissioned reports. The present study will serve to bridge the un-articulated spaces between numerous baseline data serving to describe youth profile and students' fundamental attitudes towards religion.

Previous scales designed to assess attitudes towards religion claim correspondence with specific religious traditions (Francis 1993). However, the recent shifts in meaning of the youth's appreciation of religion and the sacred necessitates that an approach to an attitude towards religion will have to consider religious and non-religious domains. Studying attitudes towards religion therefore necessitate expanding the meanings for religiosity and spirituality. In the present study the concept "religion" is understood in an inclusive sense, i.e., not exclusive to Christianity.

Religiosity is traditionally considered with respect to specific religious traditions while spirituality is understood in either way: as a function of religious lifestyle irrespective of one's religious affiliation or as a purely interior mindset. In recent sociological studies, religiosity is measured in terms of religious affiliation, behavior and commitment (Voas 2007). MacDonald et al. (2015) sees how spirituality can be treated distinctly from religiosity, as a multidimensional concept, as a psychological issue, and as a "universal domain of functioning" beyond its traditional associations with age and gender. The theme of transcendence vis a vis the subjective dispositions (David Elkins et al. 1988) is also associated with this notion. Spirituality is also examined as a humanistic concept (Koenig 2010). This differentiated description of religiosity and spirituality also provide interconnections. Literature review suggests that both notions offer humanistic and spiritual features. These features are gleaned when initial interviews conducted prior to the construction of the scale suggested non-traditional dimensions of spirituality that include human traits and motivations. We considered that these variables are essential to their attitude towards religion. Previous studies already see (Baring et al. 2016b; Hernandez 2011) the essential constitution of the human and social elements in the spiritual and religious domains. The present study sees the renewed interest towards youth spirituality in negotiated forms as an essential dimension of religion that sees a thriving experience-based spirituality (McQuillan 2006). Local data see spirituality and religiosity in previous literature as complementing aspects of the Filipino religious experience (Dy-Liacco et al. 2009; Mansukhani and Resurreccion 2009). The diffused character of the notions of religiosity and spirituality among the young (Baring et al. 2016b; Giordan and Swatos 2012; Tan 2009) partly explains the loosening of the youth distinctions of the religious and the spiritual. Citing Alexander and McLaughlin (2003), Tan's characterization of "tethered" and "untethered" spirituality (2009) describes the changed religious attitudes of the youth in an Asian setting.

3. Present Study

The purpose of the present study is to develop a self-report measure to assess Filipino Students' Attitudes towards Religion (FSAR) and test its validity and reliability. This is in response to an urgent need to provide empirical measures of religion in the region particularly in the Philippines. This collaborative effort is the first attempt to articulate an empirical basis for students' attitudes towards religion in the country. Secondly, we want to present the peculiar traits of the Filipino youth perspective towards religion which accommodates both Christian, personal and religiously diverse points of view.

4. Participants and Procedure

Participants (N = 2733, 58.1% female; M_{age} = 19.03, SD = 2.03) included college students in two Philippine universities. Participants indicated their age, sex, and college, and then completed an initial pool of 80 items regarding attitudes toward religion. They come from a private and government managed university in the province. These institutions cater to students who come from varied cultural, religious, and regional backgrounds. Participant profile included gender, university affiliation, academic course, and age. Since we considered religion in the inclusive sense, we decided that FSAR be administered to students with religious affiliation after its development.

To develop the self-report measure (FSAR), free essays and Focus Group Discussions (FGDs) were initiated in both participating institutions using the Concept Analysis Response model (Prasad and Mohan 2009) to help us understand how students view religion. Due to the highly varied composition of students per class the researchers decided to pick 8–10 students for selection from each year level. An equal number of students were also selected for the free essay writing. The basic intent of study was explained to the participants upon selection. The aim of these essays and FGDs was meant to identify the orientation of their perceptions and attitudes towards religion. It was supposed to assist us in further framing students' attitudes towards religion and complement literature review. The FGD generated a large base of student perspectives that led to the construction of the items. We took note of their responses during the conversations and constructed an initial pool of 80 items thought to tap attitudes toward religion (see Table 1).

Table 1. Initial Item Composition from FGD and Free Essays (Level 1).

RELIGIOSITY	SPIRITUALITY
RELIGIOUS Dimension	RELIGIOUS Dimension
a. Religious affiliation [Sees religiosity in terms of the person's institutional engagements] (5)	**a. Religious affiliation** [sees spirituality in terms of institutional identification] (8)
1. A religious person follows his/her religion. 2. I believe in the doctrines of the Church. 3. I love God but hate religion. 4. The religious people are easily persuaded to believe in something. 5. I think religion keeps us blinded from the truths. (* eliminated items) I am presently affiliated to a religion. (1) Religious people are intolerant of those who hold different opinions (2) I honor Church doctrine through my speech and actions. (2) I know who to follow without religion. (3) I always depend on my faith. (1) My religion makes me religious. (1)	1. Spirituality is about believing in God. 2. For me spirituality is concerned with religious matters. 3. Spirituality is beyond any religion. 4. The spiritual person is one who loves religion. 5. Spirituality indicates how one's beliefs are practiced in daily life. 6. I leave everything to God. 7. I am happy to see different religions in my midst. 8. The religious person knows many things about Scriptures. (* eliminated items) Spirituality is about religion. (1, 3) It is about accepting Gods word. (8) About worship and glorifying God. (4) An aspect of a firm believer. (1, 4) One who surrenders everything to God. (6) One who believes in God. (1) Being spiritual is being faithful to God. (1) Someone who reads the Bible. (8) Being able to practice Christ's teachings. (5)
b. Religious obligations [sees religiosity in terms of the person's religious obligations] (7)	**b. Religious obligations** [sees spirituality in terms of obligatory requirements] (6)
1. Religious persons are those who go to Church. 2. A religious person is a person of prayer. 3. I observe religious traditions (e.g., devotions) in the Church. 4. Religiosity is measured in personal spiritual habits that I do. 5. It is about religious acts and devotions. 6. Passing by the church I do the sign of the cross. 7. I am active in church activities. (* eliminated items) I think I am not religious because I don't have time for the church. (1) I have stopped visiting the church now. (1) I take active part in Church assemblies. (1) I think religious persons perform religious rituals in church everyday. (1, 3, 5) Being religious is about showing one's beliefs in one's daily life. (3, 4)	1. I respect those who perform clerical (priestly) function in Church. 2. I don't go to Church but only during Simbang Gabi Masses. 3. I put into action the Lord's teachings. 4. I can still pray even without going to Church. 5. It is important that I dedicate a time for God. 6. I remember the souls or spirits of people who have died. (* eliminated items) Its about living out one's devotion to God. (2, 3) Spirituality is about being religious. (1, 2, 3) Following God's laws. (1, 2, 3) It reminds me of the Church. (1) It is an aspect of being religious. (1) One who believes without belonging to a church. (2)
c. Divine Affiliation [sees religiosity in terms of identification with the divine] (4)	**c. Divine Affiliation** [looks at spirituality as a means to build relationship with God] (5)
1. I believe a religious person is God-centered. 2. For me, religiosity promotes blind faith. 3. I feel that I need to have a relationship with God. 4. Religiosity means having a blessed life with God. (* eliminated items) The life I live reflects Jesus' teachings. (3, 4) I practice Christ's teachings in my life. (3) Being religious involves a personal acceptance of Jesus. (3, 4) A religious person is someone faithful to God. (3) A religious person is someone who lives his/her life for God. (3) I show utmost respect for God. (3, 4) One who is religious is God-fearing. (1) I love God above all. (3)	1. In my life, I try to do God's will. 2. In every decision I make, I put God first. 3. I feel that spiritual persons are enlightened by God. 4. Salvation for me is essential for religion. 5. I believe that God is merciful. (* eliminated items) None

Table 1. Cont.

RELIGIOSITY	SPIRITUALITY
HUMAN Dimension	HUMAN Dimension
a. Interior traits and dispositions [sees religiosity in terms of interior dispositions] (7)	a. Interior traits and dispositions [describes inner dispositions/spirituality as being induced by religious and institutional engagements] (20)
1. A religious person is someone who realizes their faults. 2. A religious person is someone who is well disciplined. 3. Religious persons are concerned about doing good deeds. 4. I think those who are religious have strong values and morals. 5. A religious person lives a stress-free life. 6. Religious persons are quite conservative. 7. Religiosity is associated with being hypocritical.	1. Those who are religious are compassionate. 2. He/she is a loving and trusting person. 3. Religious people have a sincere heart. 4. I feel that a religious person is very reflective. 5. I feel the love of God in my life. 6. I feel that God is beside me when I'm down. 7. I'm always happy because God is in me. 8. I'm willing to do everything to please God. 9. I feel safe because of God. 10. Spirituality and religious values go together. 11. Loving someone intimately is a spiritual experience. 12. Serving God wholeheartedly is demanded by spirituality. 13. When I attend Church worship I feel free. 14. When I worship in church I feel holy. 15. A religious individual does not commit mistakes. 16. Religion generates a lifestyle that is founded on God. 17. Religious people possess positive attitudes towards others. 18. I cry with joy as I worship God. 19. My faith makes me feel like a newborn baby. 20. I only pray when I have a problem.
Social commitment [being religious is demonstrated in significant help given to others/world]	b. Social commitment [sees spirituality in terms of the human role as advocate for social transformation] (7)
(* eliminated upon merging with the social commitment component items under "spirituality") It means being open to the world. (1) Someone who serves his neighbor without condition. (4) It is when Christians help their fellow human beings. (4)	1. Spirituality involves concern for the environment. 2. Spirituality demands that I follow my own conscience. 3. Those who reject an immoral social order are religious. 4. Religious persons have the responsibility to improve society. 5. Being religious invites us to help the poor. 6. Lifting our spirit and others is the mark of religion. 7. A religious person is someone who serves neighbour without condition. (* eliminated items) Lifting one's spirit and that of others is the mark of spirituality. (5)
Becoming human [sees religiosity in terms of the desire to promote the well-being of others.]	c. Becoming human [seeing spirituality as a way for human development] (11)
(* eliminated upon merging with the spirituality items due to similarities) It involves getting connected to our emotions and appearance. (2) They possess positive attitudes towards others (2) Someone who is afraid of offending others. (4) One who is reflective about life. (2) It reflects the person's spirit, strength, freedom and faith. (3) A mark of complete dedication. (6) Has self-respect and respect for others. (7) It is shown in acts arising from one's pure intentions. (1, 5)	1. Spirituality involves looking at our lives with purpose. 2. Those that I know to be religious are in touch with themselves. 3. Faith essentially completes me as a person. 4. Spirituality involves inner peace of mind. 5. Religious persons possess a clean heart and mind. 6. Spirituality is a reflection of my beliefs and decisions. 7. Holy persons are those who value life. 8. Religion taught me to face life's problems without questioning God. 9. Religion reminds me that God created me. 10. A religious person is a role model. 11. Religiosity involves getting connected to our emotions and appearance. (* eliminated items) The spiritual life show our inner self. (1) A spiritual person is a model. (10)

Needed permissions were secured from the universities to conduct the survey using the 80-item self-report measure (FSAR). Students 18 years old and above participated in the survey after the instrument was explained to them. We first tested the hypothesized model with structural equation modeling. Due to poor fit, we abandoned the proposed model and reverted to traditional scale construction procedures. The data were randomly split into two samples. In the first sample, we performed a principal components analysis to reduce the number of items and examine the latent factor structure. In the second sample, we performed a factor analysis to check for the factorial validity of the measure of students' attitude towards religion.

5. Measures

To understand the underlying factor structure of Filipino students' attitudes towards religion, a self-report Likert scale measure (FSARS) was developed. We observe two levels of item development to cover as much insight as possible. Table 1 shows the first level of item composition with a list of deleted items. The second level presents a revised list of items that were retained earlier in Table 1 now merged with additional items. Since religious constructs are traditionally thought to be multi-dimensional (Brown and Forgas 1980), we framed religiosity and spirituality within the initial pool of the scale. However, upon further examination of the spirituality pool of items, we saw the accommodation of items that equally reflect the human lifestyle and dispositions (Koenig 2010; Voas 2007) vis-à-vis the traditional spiritual articulation (David Elkins et al. 1988). In the process of instrument development, we realized that the inclusion of the spiritual and religious dynamic inevitably remains under the religious factor in the present study. The initial items tapping students' attitudes towards "religion" (cf. Table 1) reflected religious (exterior) and human (interior) factors. The religious factor included items reflecting: institutional affiliation (religious), religious obligation (religious) and divine identification (spiritual). Items constructed to assess the human factor included interior traits and dispositions, social commitment, and becoming human.

Through FGDs and essays, we asked the students about their thoughts, reflections and reactions about religion in terms of spirituality (or being spiritual) and religiosity (or being religious). To identify the items and dimensions of the construct, we manually reviewed the essays and FGD reports. First, we seeped through each essay and agreed which ideas stand out. Many items have to be eliminated in the first level due to duplications and fitness of meaning. The eliminated items (*) are indicated in Table 1. We grouped all items representing student ideas about religiosity and spirituality. We identified the general orientation of ideas on which the items rested. We discerned two general conceptual groups we labeled as conceptual "dimensions" (Religious and Human dimensions). The items under the Religious dimension reflect how students appropriate the senses of religiosity and spirituality interchangeably. We discerned that they are looking at religiosity (and being religious) and spirituality (and being spiritual) in terms of: religious affiliation, religious obligations, and divine identification/affiliation. The conceptual similarities between items representing religiosity and spirituality under the Religious dimension is unexpected. In the beginning of our study, we hinted that a diffused notion of religion by students is likely considering our previous data from two previous local studies (Baring et al. 2016a, 2016b). However, we never expected that the pairing look so closely, as suggested by the two columns in Table 1. Their matching interpretation of human interiority and dispositions, social transformation and human development under the Human dimension with respect to religiosity and spirituality is equally amusing. However, the second and third characterization of spirituality and religiosity (e.g., social transformation and human development) under the Human dimension had duplicated or similar items. Similar items and those that reflect an exclusive reference to Catholicism were eliminated upon merging. Religiosity has a total of 23 items while spirituality has majority of items with 57. After the initial review from the FGDs, free essays and manual elimination of items, the Religious dimension constitute 35 items while the Human dimension have 45 items. A total of 80 items were developed after the review process.

Considering the high concentration of items under social transformation (e.g., 20 items), we revisited the item list to check for any need to move, modify or add items. Table 2 shows the final set of items under each dimension after item analysis, transfer, removal and addition of items. After removing some items, we added new statements thought to represent students' sentiments and behavior about religion. Table 2 shows a revised configuration of items: the Religious dimension has 45 items while the Human dimension has 35 items. Students' attitudes towards religion in this regard is understood in terms of the dynamics of religiosity and spirituality and viewed through Religious and Human dimensions. The religious dimension describes religiosity/spirituality items of institutional engagements, obligations and divine affiliation. The human dimension reflects religiosity/spirituality in terms of interior traits, social commitment and becoming human.

Table 2. The Operational Dimensions of the Construct and Item List (Level 2).

	RELIGIOUS DIMENSION	
INSTITUTIONAL AFFILIATION	**(11 ITEMS)** 1. A religious person follows his/her religion. 7. I love God but I hate religion 26. I remember God when passing by the church 30. My spirituality is a reflection of my beliefs and decisions 34. Religiosity is associated with being hypocritical 37. I respect those who work as priest/pastor/imam. 40. A spiritual person is one who loves religion. 43. Religion reminds me that God created me 52. I am happy to see different religions in my midst 68. I believe in the doctrines of the Church 78. Salvation for me is essential for religion	* * * * * * * *
RELIGIOUS OBLIGATION	**(14 ITEMS)** 2. A religious person is one who goes to Church. 5. For me, religiosity promotes blind faith 8. I observe religious traditions (e.g., devotions) in the Church 14. Religiosity is measured in personal spiritual habits that I do 20. It is about religious acts and devotions 28. A religious person is quite conservative 31. For me spirituality is concerned with religious matters 32. I am active in church activities 38. A religious person is one who is compassionate 55. A religious person knows many things about the Scripture 56. I remember the souls or spirits of people who have died 59. I only go to Church on occasion (ex: Simbang Gabi, fellowship, etc.). 67. When I attend Church worship I feel free 69. When I worship in church I feel holy	* * * * * * * * * * * * * *
DIVINE IDENTIFICATION	**(20 ITEMS)** 9. I feel that I need to have a relationship with God 15. Religiosity means having a blessed life with God 21. In my life, I try to do God's will 25. Spirituality is about believing in God 27. In every decision I make, I put God first 33. I feel that a spiritual person is enlightened by God 41. I believe that God is merciful 45. I put into action the Lord's teachings. 48. I leave everything to God 49. I can still pray even without going to Church 53. It is important that I dedicate a time for God 54. I feel the love of God in my life 57. I feel that God is beside me when I'm down 58. I'm always happy because God is in me 60. I'm willing to do everything to please God 61. I feel safe because of God 66. Serving God wholeheartedly is demanded by faith 73. Religion generates a lifestyle that is founded on God. 74. I believe a religious person is God-centered 77. I cry with joy as I worship God.	* * * * * * * * * * * *
HUMAN DIMENSION		
INTERIOR TRAITS/DISPOSITION	**(12 ITEMS)** 3. A religious person is someone who realizes his/her faults. 6. A religious person is someone who is well-disciplined 13. A religious person is easily persuaded to believe in something 16. I think a religious person is one who has strong values and morals 18. My faith provides me inner peace of mind 22. A religious person lives a stress-free life. 50. I think that a religious person is very reflective. 62. Spirituality and religious values go together 65. A religious person is a person of prayer 72. My faith demands that I follow my own conscience. 75. A religious person possesses positive attitudes towards others 80. I only pray when I have a problem.	 * * * * * * * * *

Table 2. The Operational Dimensions of the Construct and Item List (Level 2).

HUMAN DIMENSION	RELIGIOUS DIMENSION	
SOCIAL COMMITMENT	**(6 ITEMS)** 10. A religious person is concerned about doing good deeds 11. A religious person is one who rejects an immoral social order 17. A religious person has the responsibility to improve the society 23. Being religious invites us to help the poor. 35. A religious person is someone who serves neighbor without condition 76. Religion involves concern for the environment	 * * *
BECOMING HUMAN	**(17 ITEMS)** 4. Believing in faith involves looking at our lives with purpose. 12. Faith essentially completes me as a person 19. I think religion keeps us blinded from the truths. 24. A religious person possesses a clean heart and mind 29. Lifting our spirit and others is the mark of religion. 36. Spirituality is beyond any religion. 39. Religion taught me to face life's problems without questioning God 42. A person of faith is one who is loving and trusting. 44. Spirituality indicates how one's beliefs are practiced in daily life 46. A religious person has a sincere heart 47. A religious person is a role model 51. Religiosity involves getting connected to our emotions and physical appearance 63. A holy person is one who values life 64. Loving someone intimately is a spiritual experience. 70. Those that I know to be religious are in touch with themselves 71. A religious individual does not commit mistakes 79. My faith makes me feel like a newborn baby **TOTAL ITEMS—80**	 * * * * * * * * * * * * * *

The numbers correspond to the item's actual placement in the final pre-survey scale. The (*) indicates that the item is not included in the three-factor model (Model 3) which had the best fit.

This conceptual definition was formulated after literature review of relevant local and foreign studies, students' free essays and FGDs conducted in two schools. The orientation of their perspectives is distinctly different from previous scales of religion (Francis et al. 1995) or of theistic faith (Astley et al. 2012). The items were rated on a 5-point Likert-type response scale, from 1 = *strongly disagree* to 5 = *strongly agree*. We considered that our measure (FSAR scale) reflect students' articulated ideas while carefully weighing scholarly discussions on the matter to address some of the cultural peculiarities of the measure (Hill and Maltby 2009).

6. Results

6.1. Test of Hypothesized Model

To test the proposed model, we conducted structural equation modeling (with Amos 19, bootstrapping with 5000 iterations). In the first model, we examined the six proposed dimensions without higher order factors. As shown in Table 3 (Model 1), the fit was poor. Next, we tested the model with the six dimensions falling under two higher order factors (i.e., Religious and Human). As shown in Table 3 (Model 2), the fit for this model was also poor. As the hypothesized model failed to fit the data appropriately, we moved to construct a measure using the initial items.

Table 3. Model Fit Statistics.

	Model Fit Statistics					
	$\chi^2(\delta\phi)$	CFI	NFI	RMSEA {90% CI}	AIC	ECVI {90% CI}
Model 1	30,425.43 (3065)	0.698	0.676	0.057 {0.057, 0.058}	30,775.43	11.27 {11.06, 11.47}
Model 2	30,656.50 (3073)	0.696	0.673	0.057 {0.057, 0.058}	30,990.5	11.34 {11.14, 11.55}
Model 3	856.80 (149)	0.93	0.916	0.059 {0.055, 0.063}	938.8	0.688 {0.623, 0.758}

6.2. Scale Construction

To explore possible underlying factors in attitudes toward religion items, we first split the dataset randomly in half creating two samples (cf. Table 4). In the first sample (*n* = 1367), we conducted principal components analyses to reduce the number of items. In the second sample (*n* = 1366), we conducted a factor analysis (principal axis factoring). Because we expected the factors to be related, we used oblimin rotation for the analyses. After removing items with low loadings, singletons, doubletons, and items loading on multiple factors (see Table 1 for eliminated items), we arrived at a final scale containing three factors as suggested by eigenvalues and scree plot (see Table 4 for items and pattern matrix factor loadings, and see Table 5 for structure matrix loadings). Factor 1 contained items reflecting perceptions of religious belief (eight items). Institutional affiliation is the norm for Factor 1. Factor 2 contained items reflecting affective responses towards religion (six items). Factor 2 refers to students' identification with the divine through affective responses. Cognitive and behavioral items under divine identification did not perform well after oblimin rotation. Factor 3 contained items reflecting behavioral responses towards religion (five items). In contrast to Factor 2, Factor 3 assesses items of religiosity reflecting interiority, social commitment, and well-being. In the second sample, the factor structure was replicated (see Tables 4 and 5). Congruence coefficients between the two samples, with factor analysis and oblimin rotation for both samples, were adequate: Factor 1 = 0.99; Factor 2 = 0.99; and Factor 3 = 0.97. Additionally, we tested the model as separate factors with structural equation modeling using the second sample and found good fit with the data (Table 3, Model 3). The three-factor structure was retained. We examined the correlations between the factors and found them all positively correlated with one another in both samples (see Table 4).

Table 4. Factor Loadings for Religion Attitudes Measure, Pattern Matrix.

Item	Sample 1 F1	Sample 1 F2	Sample 1 F3	Sample 2 F1	Sample 2 F2	Sample 2 F3
1. Religion generates a lifestyle that is founded on God.	**0.741**	0.015	0.025	**0.679**	−0.07	0.007
2. A spiritual person is one who loves religion.	**0.727**	0.08	−0.096	**0.686**	0.123	−0.041
3. A religious person possesses positive attitudes towards others.	**0.724**	0.064	0.149	**0.634**	−0.056	0.155
4. I believe a religious person is God-centered.	**0.703**	−0.011	0.116	**0.685**	−0.111	−0.001
5. Religion involves concern for the environment.	**0.676**	−0.069	0.017	**0.55**	−0.009	0.176
6. Religion reminds me that God created me.	**0.606**	−0.125	−0.015	**0.546**	−0.103	0.021
7. Salvation for me is essential for religion.	**0.582**	−0.198	−0.04	**0.467**	−0.117	0.048
8. Religion taught me to face life's problems without questioning God.	**0.528**	−0.058	0.139	**0.475**	−0.106	0.044
9. I feel the love of God in my life.	−0.052	**−0.838**	0.051	−0.018	**−0.802**	0.012
10. I feel that God is beside me when I'm down.	0.011	**−0.835**	−0.005	0.003	**−0.808**	0.01
11. I feel safe because of God.	0.018	**−0.823**	0.018	0.082	**−0.805**	−0.068
12. I'm always happy because God is in me.	0.032	**−0.796**	−0.061	−0.013	**−0.763**	−0.013
13. It is important that I dedicate a time for God.	0.017	**−0.774**	0.057	0.064	**−0.606**	0.132
14. I'm willing to do everything to please God.	0.148	**−0.59**	−0.001	0.18	**−0.468**	0.033
15. A religious person is someone who realizes his/her faults.	0.075	0.049	**0.718**	0.099	0.045	**0.54**
16. A religious person is one who rejects an immoral social order.	0.026	0.057	**0.684**	0.067	−0.005	**0.449**
17. A religious person is someone who is well-disciplined.	0.084	0.063	**0.68**	0.065	0.065	**0.546**
18. Believing in faith involves looking at our lives with purpose.	−0.143	−0.209	**0.656**	−0.163	−0.148	**0.568**
19. A religious person is concerned about doing good deeds concerned about doing good deeds.	0.087	−0.052	**0.647**	0.144	0.009	**0.56**
Eigenvalue	6.82	2.11	1.37	6.85	1.96	1.34
Variance	35.91	11.08	7.21	36.06	10.33	7.05
α	0.85	0.88	0.73	0.85	0.88	0.69
Mean	4.09	4.48	4.18	4.11	4.49	4.18
Standard Deviation	0.63	0.6	0.59	0.61	0.57	0.56
Correlation with F1	–	0.51	0.54	–	0.53	0.53
Correlation with F2	–	–	0.39	–	–	0.41

Note. Sample 1 principle components analysis, Sample 2 factor analysis (both using oblimin rotation). All correlations significant at $p < 0.01$.

Table 5. Factor Loadings for Religion Attitudes Measure, Structure Matrix.

	Sample 1			Sample 2		
Item	F1	F2	F3	F1	F2	F3
Item 1	**0.746**	−0.32	0.362	**0.716**	−0.402	0.429
Item 2	**0.648**	−0.208	0.212	**0.603**	−0.19	0.296
Item 3	**0.764**	−0.305	0.46	**0.75**	−0.435	0.545
Item 4	**0.762**	−0.36	0.444	**0.738**	−0.442	0.444
Item 5	**0.714**	−0.373	0.352	**0.656**	−0.357	0.497
Item 6	**0.655**	−0.388	0.308	**0.608**	−0.377	0.382
Item 7	**0.651**	−0.441	0.296	**0.551**	−0.365	0.37
Item 8	**0.618**	−0.338	0.402	**0.551**	−0.356	0.366
Item 9	0.341	**−0.833**	0.314	0.377	**−0.799**	0.373
Item 10	0.376	**−0.838**	0.286	0.4	**−0.814**	0.387
Item 11	0.389	**−0.838**	0.308	0.433	**−0.813**	0.353
Item 12	0.354	**−0.789**	0.226	0.349	**−0.751**	0.334
Item 13	0.384	**−0.801**	0.33	0.433	**−0.698**	0.45
Item 14	0.407	**−0.654**	0.269	0.425	**−0.571**	0.354
Item 15	0.384	−0.23	**0.736**	0.388	−0.254	**0.576**
Item 16	0.316	−0.189	**0.677**	0.328	−0.246	**0.49**
Item 17	0.37	−0.207	**0.689**	0.347	−0.22	**0.553**
Item 18	0.252	−0.371	**0.662**	0.236	−0.333	**0.544**
Item 19	0.408	−0.312	**0.705**	0.461	−0.321	**0.638**

Note. Sample 1 principle components analysis, Sample 2 factor analysis (both using oblimin rotation).

6.3. Age, Sex, and Academic Program

Having constructed the measure, we next examined correlations with age and mean responses by participant sex and academic program using the full dataset (i.e., both samples combined). Zero-order correlations showed that participants' age was significantly negatively related to religious beliefs ($r = -0.07$, $p = 0.001$) and affective responses towards religion ($r = -0.06$, $p = 0.003$), and non-significantly related to behavioral responses towards religion ($r = -0.04$, $p = 0.067$). However, the size of the sample likely contributed to the significance of the correlations between age and the first two factors. To examine possible differences depending on sex of participants we conducted a MANOVA with sex of participant as the independent variable and religious dimensions as dependent variables. The omnibus test was not significant: Wilks' $\Lambda = 0.99$, $F(3, 2729) = 0.79$, $p = 0.498$, $\eta_p^2 = 0.001$. No significant differences were observed between male and female participants on the three religious dimensions. Lastly, we conducted a MANOVA with participants academic program as the independent variable and religious dimensions as the dependent variables. The four academic programs reflected sciences (e.g., nursing), social sciences (e.g., psychology), business (e.g., accounting), and education. The omnibus test was significant: Wilks' $\Lambda = 0.99$, $F(3, 2634) = 0.79$, $p < 0.001$, $\eta_p^2 = 0.004$. As shown in Table 6, students in business and social sciences rated their religious beliefs significantly higher than science students. Business students rated their degree of affective responses towards religion significantly higher than science students. Business and education students rated their degree of behavioral responses towards religion significantly higher than science students. However, we should note that the effect sizes are very small.

Table 6. Means (Standard Deviation) by Participants' Academic Program.

Variable	Sciences	Social Sciences	Business	Education	F(3, 2636)	p-Value	η_p^2
Religious Beliefs	4.02 (0.63) a	4.13 (0.62) b	4.15 (0.60) b	4.10 (0.63) ab	5.69	0.001	0.006
Affective Responses	4.44 (0.57) a	4.47 (0.59) ab	4.55 (0.56) b	4.52 (0.59) ab	4.08	0.007	0.005
Behavioral Responses	4.12 (0.60) a	4.17 (0.59) ab	4.22 (0.57) b	4.22 (0.52) b	4.06	0.007	0.005

Note. Means with different subscripts are significantly different at $p < 0.05$.

7. Discussion

From the analyses performed earlier, we gathered very favorable results for the underlying factor structure and corresponding reliability scores. The overall internal consistency score for the FSAR scale is $\alpha = 0.82$, indicating higher incidences of shared co-variances and suggests that the FSAR scale is a consistent measure of students' attitudes towards religion. The FSARS is a reliable measure to assess Filipino student attitudes towards religion in this context. From an initial 80-item self-report measure, FSARS was reduced to 19 items after a series of principal components analyses. The sub-scales identified from the item pool were found to be positively correlated to one another. The correlations affirm the presence of significant relationships between each distinct sub-scale.

Construct validity of the new model was supported with factor analysis. A unique configuration constituting three underlying factors is confirmed. The scale describes students' cognitive, affective, and behavioral appreciations of religion. Factor 1 is a configuration of religious beliefs (institutional affiliation). Factor 2 represents students' emotional dispositions towards God (divine identification). Factor 3 refers to the behavioral dimension (religious lifestyle). Factor 3 assesses religiosity covering interior disposition, social commitment and well-being. FSARS assesses institutional affiliation, divine identification and religiosity. Note that the notion "religion" in this context is not restricted to institutional meanings appended to the Christian faith. Given that the retained items reflect students' personal meaning-making patterns, the three factors articulate personal appropriations of belief, the divine, and religious practice. Brown and Forgas (1980) three-factor model from an earlier study suggested a contrast between the institutional and personal components. Instead of a conceptual contrast, however, the three-factor structure from our data manifests the interaction between the personal (Factors 2 and 3) and institutional (Factor 1) orientations.

Recent studies on religious attitudes that utilize the religiosity-spirituality framework also cite the personal-religious dynamics. Tsang and McCullough (2003) proposed two-level hierarchical model of religiosity and spirituality reflects aspects of our appreciation prior to the survey. Their model underscored "dispositional" and "operational" levels which refer to personal-religious viewpoints. The three factors (religious belief, affective response, and religious behavior towards religion) in this study also imply personal-religious perspectives. Other related scales describe similar affective dimensions (Astley et al. 2012). The identification of affective perceptions among the latent factors points to the fundamental role that emotions play in their appreciation of religion. Davies (2011) succinctly identified the role of emotions in the formation of religious identity. Among the young, the influence of the affective disposition remains an essential point to understand religious belief.

Consistent with previous data (Baring et al. 2016b), the factors underscore the place of the sacred in student perceptions towards religion. Previous studies (Hill et al. 2000; Tsang and McCullough 2003) highlight the broad sense in which the sacred is understood in empirical studies: "a divine being, divine object, Ultimate Reality, or Ultimate Truth as perceived by the individual" (Hill et al. 2000, p. 66). Despite recent deviations from institutional identification in recent youth studies on belief, "religion" from these data remains nested in discourses of the sacred. This steadfast association with the sacred, in its new articulations (Baring et al. 2017; Baring 2012) appear peculiar to the Southeast Asian (ASEAN) experience while the Western data have demonstrated evident separation from traditional notions of the sacred. Factors 1 (religious belief) and 2 (affective response) reaffirm the youth's appropriation of religion as a sacred affiliated construct. Lynch (2007) discussion of new spiritualities in the West also provides some grounding about how notions of the divine are reinterpreted in peculiar articulations not devoid of institutional underpinnings. These contemporary interpretations describe atypical characterizations of the sacred in fine distinctions of what Lynch calls "progressive spirituality."

The strong association between religious perspectives and social life in the third sub-scale underscores students' beliefs towards ethical and moral issues. The strong undercurrent linking students' ethical mindset with religious perspectives appears to negate an earlier rejection of the relationship between religion and one's ethical view (Parboteeah et al. 2008). The significant relationship given to religious development and moral development among students had been acknowledged in prior literature (King and Boyatzis 2004; Van Someren 2000). This moral position is also affirmed in a previous study (Baring et al. 2016b) that showed the affinity of students' attitudes towards ethical and moral perspectives (Baring et al. 2017). This significant connection counters previous views which see students' worldview as something that excludes moral or ethical considerations. The third factor presents a counter position to perceptions that regard students' apparent indifference to social issues. If anything, the firmness of the moral stance articulated in Factor 3 complements students' openness towards pro-social values and behaviors (Lee et al. 2016) while studying. Such disposition suggests how students' religious perspectives relate with their prosocial behavior (Batara 2015).

8. Conclusions

While most empirical studies on youth inquire religiosity in relation to other variables, the present study has ventured to know the underlying constitution of student attitudes towards "religion" from an unlikely mix of religious and human aspects of belief. Unexpectedly, the results brought us into underlying factors fraught with traditional attitude components towards religion: Belief towards the institution, Affective response to God, and Behavioral aspects of belief. The a priori definition we worked out about their attitudes came out very different from the results. However, shadows of student spirituality/religiosity (Baring et al. 2016a) are gleaned from the results. In our desire to see the contours of the student spiritual and religious mindset, we ended up mining specific conceptual connections between the sacred, moral and institutional dynamics beneath their perspectives. This view can be better appreciated in the bigger context of the ASEAN experience which is tied up with cultural and religious diversity (Baring 2012). On a specific note, the results bespeak of the significant undercurrent of diverse religious experiences (Baring 2011) influencing the young generation.

Overall, the FSAR Scale can provide meaningful profile assessments for educational settings with multi-faith conditions. However, the sample used for the validation of FSARS represented a specific geographic location in northern Philippines within an educational setting for the tertiary level. The present measure did not include students who did not profess some form of religious belief or those that explicitly dissociate themselves from structured belief systems for lack of data. The FSARS measure's analysis for validation did not include religious affiliation since we considered that the sampled population had dominant Catholic populations. Instead, we considered how the measure interacted with gender, age and academic programs. Further enrichment of the scale might be considered to include respondents from other geographic locations. We recommend that FSARS be further examined with respect to religious affiliation in settings where a significant presence of other religious denominations is notable.

Acknowledgments: This research is the fruit of the collaborative efforts of the research team. It is not funded by any external agency or funding institution. The team did not receive funds relating to the cost of publishing in open access. We wish to acknowledge the support of the administrations of Holy Angel University and Don Honorio Ventura Technological State University for allowing us to conduct the survey.

Author Contributions: The team members agreed to divide work for the completion of this research through the following: Rito Baring, Philip Sarmiento, Nestor Sibug, Paolo Lumanlan, Benita Bonus and Cristina Samia conceived and designed the study, developed the instrument draft, performed the survey and did post-survey work; Baring and Stephen Reysen pursued and wrote analysis and interpretation of data/results until its completion with editing.

Conflicts of Interest: The authors declare no conflict of interest.

References

Abad, R. 2001. Religion in the Philippines. *Philippine Studies* 49: 337–67.
Alexander, Hanan, and Terence McLaughlin. 2003. Education in religion and spirituality. In *The Blackwell Guide to the Philosophy of Education*. Edited by Nigel Blake, Paul Smeyers, Richard Smith and Paul Standish. Malden: Blackwell Publishing.

Astley, Jeff, Leslie Francis, and Mandy Robbins. 2012. Assessing attitude towards religion: The Astley–Francis Scale of attitude towards theistic faith. *British Journal of Religious Education* 34: 183–93. [CrossRef]
Baring, Rito. 2011. Plurality in unity: Challenges towards religious education in the Philippines. *Religious Education* 106: 459–75.
Baring, Rito. 2012. Children's Image of God and their parents: explorations in children's Spirituality. *International Journal of Children's Spirituality* 17: 277–89. [CrossRef]
Baring, Rito, and Rebecca Cacho. 2015. Contemporary engagements and challenges for Catholic religious education in Southeast Asia. In *Global Perspectives on Catholic Religious Education in Schools*. Edited by Michael Buchanan and Adrian Gellel. Basel: Springer Publishing, pp. 143–53.
Baring, Rito, Romeo Lee, Madelene Sta. Maria, and Yan Liu. 2016a. Configurations of student spirituality/religiosity: Evidence from a Philippine university. *International Journal of Children's Spirituality* 21: 163–76. [CrossRef]
Baring, Rito, Dennis Erasga, Elenita Garcia, Jeane Peracullo, and Lars Ubaldo. 2016b. The Young and the sacred: an analysis of empirical evidence from the Philippines. *Young* 25: 26–44. [CrossRef]
Baring, Rito, Romeo Lee, Madelene Sta. Maria, and Yan Liu. 2017. Exploring the Characteristics of Filipino University Students as Concurrent Smokers and Drinkers. *Asia Pacific Social Science Review* 17: 80–87.
Batara, Jame Bryan. 2015. Overlap of religiosity and spirituality among Filipinos and its implications towards religious prosociality. *International Journal of Research Studies in Psychology* 4: 3–21. [CrossRef]
Brown, Laurence, and Joseph Forgas. 1980. The structure of religion: A multi-dimensional scaling of informal elements. *Journal for the Scientific Study of Religion* 19: 423–31. [CrossRef]
Büssing, Arndt. 2017. Measures of Spirituality/Religiosity: Description of Concepts and Validation of Instruments. *Religions* 8: 11. [CrossRef]
Catholic Bishops Conference of the Philippines-Episcopal Commission on Youth (CBCP-ECY) and Catholic Educational Association of the Philippines (CEAP). 2014. *The National Filipino Catholic Youth Study 2014*. Manila: CBCP-ECY and CEAP.
Davies, Douglas. 2011. *Emotion, Identity, and Religion: Hope, Reciprocity, and Otherness*. Oxford: Oxford University Press.
Dy-Liacco, Gabriel, Ralph Piedmont, Nichole Murray-Swank, Thomas Rodgerson, and Martin Sherman. 2009. Spirituality and religiosity as cross-cultural aspects of human experience. *Psychology of Religion and Spirituality* 1: 35–52. [CrossRef]
David Elkins, James Hedstrom, Lorie Hughes, Andrew Leaf, and Cheryl Saunders. 1988. Toward a humanistic-phenomenological spirituality: Definition, description, and measurement. *Journal of Humanist Psychology* 28: 5–18. [CrossRef]
Francis, Leslie. 1993. Reliability and validity of a short scale of attitude towards Christianity among adults. *Psychological Reports* 72: 615–18. [CrossRef]
Francis, Leslie, John Lewis, Ronald Philipchalk, Laurence Brown, and David Lester. 1995. The internal consistency reliability and construct validity of the Francis scale of attitude toward Christianity (adult) among undergraduate students in the U.K., U.S.A., Australia and Canada. *Personality and Individual Differences* 19: 949–53. [CrossRef]
Giordan, Giuseppe, and William Swatos Jr., eds. 2012. *Religion, Spirituality and Everyday Practice*. New York: Springer.
Good, Marie, and Teena Willoughby. 2014. Institutional and Personal Spirituality/Religiosity and Psychosocial adjustment in adolescence: Concurrent and Longitudinal associations. *Journal of Youth and Adolescence* 43: 757–74. [CrossRef] [PubMed]
Hambleton, Ronald. 2005. Issues, Designs and technical guidelines for adapting tests into multiple languages and cultures. In *Adapting Educational and Psychological Tests for Cross-Cultural Assessment*. Edited by Ronald K. Hambleton, Peter Merenda and Charles Spielberger. Mahwah: Lawrence Erlbaum, pp. 3–18.
Hernandez, Brittany. 2011. The Religiosity and Spirituality Scale for Youth: Development and Initial Validation. Doctoral dissertation, Louisiana State University, Baton Rouge, LA, USA. Available online: http://etd.lsu.edu/docs/available/etd-10142011-115001/unrestricted/hernandez_diss.pdf (accessed on 20 February 2017).

Hill, Peter, and Lauren Maltby. 2009. Measuring religiousness and spirituality: Issues, existing measures, and the implications for education and well-being. In *International Handbook of Education for Spirituality, Care and Wellbeing*. Edited by Marian de Souza, Leslie Francis, James O'Higgins-Norman and Daniel Scott. New York: Springer.

Hill, Peter, Kenneth Pargament, Ralph Hood Jr., Michael McCullough, James Swyers, David Larson, and Brian Zinnbauer. 2000. Conceptualizing religion and spirituality: Points of communality, points of departure. *Journal for the Theory of Social Behavior* 30: 51–77. [CrossRef]

King, Pamela Ebstyne, and Chris Boyatzis. 2004. Exploring adolescent spiritual and religious development: Current and future theoretical and empirical perspectives. *Applied Developmental Science* 8: 2–6. [CrossRef]

Koenig, Harold. 2009. Research on religion, spirituality, and mental health: A review. *The Canadian Journal of Psychiatry* 54: 283–92. [CrossRef] [PubMed]

Koenig, Harold. 2010. Spirituality and mental health. *International Journal of Applied Psychoanalytic Studies* 7: 116–22. [CrossRef]

Lee, Romeo, Rito Baring, Madelene Sta. Maria, and Stephen Reysen. 2016. Attitude towards technology, social media usage and grade point average as predictors of global citizenship identification in Filipino university students. *International Journal of Psychology* 52: 213–19. [CrossRef] [PubMed]

Lynch, Gordon. 2007. *The New Spirituality: An Introduction to Progressive Belief in the Twenty-First Century*. London: I.B. Taurus.

MacDonald, Douglas, Friedman Harris, Brewczynski Jacek, Holland Daniel, Salagame Kiran Kumar, Mohan Krishna, Gubrij Zuzana Ondriasova, and Cheong Hye Wook. 2015. Spirituality as a Scientific Construct: Testing Its Universality across Cultures and Languages. *PLoS ONE* 10: e0117701. [CrossRef] [PubMed]

Mangahas, Mahar, and Linda Guerrero. 1992. *Religion in the Philippines: The 1991 ISSP Survey*. Manila: SWS Occasional Paper, May.

Mansukhani, Roseann, and Ron Resurreccion. 2009. Spirituality and the development of positive character among Filipino adolescents. *Philippine Journal of Psychology* 42: 271–90.

McQuillan, P. 2006. Youth spirituality: A reality in search of expression. *Australian eJournal of Theology* 6: 1–13. [CrossRef]

Ocampo, Anna Carmella, Roseann Mansukhani, Bernadette Mangrobang, and Alexandra Mae Juan. 2013. Influences and perceived impact of spirituality on Filipino adolescents. *Philippine Journal of Psychology* 46: 89–113.

Parboteeah, Praveen, Martin Hoegl, and John Cullen. 2008. Ethics and religion: An empirical test of a multidimensional model. *Journal of Business Ethics* 80: 387–98. [CrossRef]

Prasad, Hari Mohan, and Rajnish Mohan. 2009. *Group Discussion and Interview*, 2nd ed. Victoria: Abe Books.

Tan, Charlene. 2009. Reflection for spiritual development in Adolescents. In *International Handbook of Education for Spirituality, Care and Wellbeing*. Edited by Marian de Souza, Leslie Francis, James O'Higgins-Norman and Daniel Scott. Dordrecht: Springer.

Tsang, Jo-Ann, and Michael McCullough. 2003. Measuring religious constructs: A hierarchical approach to construct organization and scale selection. In *Handbook of Positive Psychological Assessment*. Edited by Shane Lopez and Charles Snyder. Washington: American Psychological Association.

Van Someren, David. 2000. The Relationship between Religiousness and Moral Development: A Critique and Refinement of the Sociomoral Reflection Measure Short-Form of Gibbs, Basinger, and Fuller (John C. Gibbs, Karen S. Basinger, Dick Fuller). Ed.D. thesis, Clark University, Worcester, MA, USA. Available online: http://youthandreligion.nd.edu/related-resources/bibliography-on-youth-and-religion/faith-and-moral-development/ (accessed on 5 February 2017).

Voas, David. 2007. Does Religion Belong in Population Studies? *Environment and Planning* 39: 1166–80. [CrossRef]

Zwingmann, Christian, Klein Constantin, and Büssing Arndt. 2011. Measuring Religiosity/Spirituality: Theoretical Differentiations and Categorization of Instruments. *Religions* 2: 345–57. [CrossRef]

© 2018 by the authors. Licensee MDPI, Basel, Switzerland. This article is an open access article distributed under the terms and conditions of the Creative Commons Attribution (CC BY) license (http://creativecommons.org/licenses/by/4.0/).

Article

Validation of the SpREUK—Religious Practices Questionnaire as a Measure of Christian Religious Practices in a General Population and in Religious Persons

Arndt Büssing [1,2,*]**, Daniela R. Recchia** [1]**, Mareike Gerundt** [2]**, Markus Warode** [2] **and Thomas Dienberg** [2]

[1] Institute for Integrative Medicine, Faculty of Health, Witten/Herdecke University, 58239 Herdecke, Germany; Daniela.RodriguesRecchia@uni-wh.de
[2] IUNCTUS—Competence Center for Christian Spirituality, PTH/School of Theology Münster, 48149 Münster, Germany; gerundt.iunctus@pth-muenster.de (M.G.); warode.iunctus@pth-muenster.de (M.W.); th.dienberg@web.de (T.D.)
* Correspondence: arndt.buessing@uni-wh.de

Received: 28 November 2017; Accepted: 8 December 2017; Published: 9 December 2017

Abstract: Measures of spirituality should be multidimensional and inclusive and as such be applicable to persons with different worldviews and spiritual-religious beliefs and attitudes. Nevertheless, for distinct research purposes it may be relevant to more accurately differentiate specific religious practices, rituals and behaviors. It was thus the aim of this study to validate a variant version of the SpREUK-P questionnaire (which measures frequency of engagement in a large spectrum of organized and private religious, spiritual, existential and philosophical practices). This variant version was enriched with items addressing specific rituals and practices of Catholic religiosity, by further differentiating items of praying and meditation. The instrument was then tested in a sample of Catholics (inclusively nuns and monks), Protestants, and in non-religious persons. This 23-item SpREUK-RP (Religious Practices) questionnaire has four factors (i.e., *Prosocial-Humanistic practices; General religious practices; Catholic religious practices; Existentialistic practices/Gratitude and Awe*) and good internal consistency (Cronbach's alpha ranging from 0.84 to 0.94). An advantage of this instrument is that it is not generally contaminated with items related to persons' well-being, and it is not intermixed with specific religious attitudes and convictions.

Keywords: Christian religious practices; Catholics; engagement frequency; validation; questionnaire

1. Introduction

Our societies are becoming more and more diverse (i.e., culturally, ethnically, philosophically, politically), and thus a person's spiritual attitude may become more diverse, ranging from disinterest or strict a-religiosity to explicit dedicated religiosity or individualized patchwork spirituality (whatever the specific faith tradition is). Spirituality is a changing concept which is related to religiosity, but may also overlap with secular concepts such as humanism, existentialism, and probably also with specific esoteric views (Zwingmann et al. 2011). Therefore, measures of spirituality should be multidimensional not only in terms of the variety of topics, but also in terms of the related behaviors (Büssing 2012)—but not that exclusive that they are valid only for specific religious groups. To finally compare data from different societies and spiritual-religious orientation groups, inclusive instruments are preferred that account for this diversity.

Apart from this diversity, one also has to consider different 'layers' of spirituality that could be exemplified by *Faith/Experience* as the influencing core dimension, by *Attitudes* formed and shaped from this core dimension, and by subsequent *Behaviors* related to these attitudes and convictions (Table 1). It might be appropriate to use different valid measures related to these layers simultaneously instead of using instruments that condense all of these topics into one rather unsatisfying and less differentiated scale. Conceptually one has to clearly differentiate the 'core' dimensions (the faith/experience component) and the related 'outcomes' (i.e., attitudes, behaviors and rituals) (Table 1). Therefore, one may use different validated instruments to address the topics of these layers. A clear focus on common dimensions of spirituality which may be shared by specific religious groups and secular persons might be useful, but also on those dimensions which differ between religious and non-religious groups.

Table 1. Schematic levels of representation of different 'layers' aspects of spirituality (modified according to Büssing 2017).

Faith/Experience		
tradition		spiritual experience
Attitudes		
Cognition: beliefs, afterlife convictions, ideals etc.		Emotion: unconditional trust, hope, etc.
Behaviors		
Ethics: charity, etc.	Rituals: prayer, meditation, etc.	Altruism: charity, etc.

One of those instruments, which measures the frequency of spiritual-religious practices (overview in Zwingmann et al. 2011) is the SpREUK-P questionnaire (SpREUK is the German language acronym for "Spiritual and Religiosity as a Resource to cope with Illness; P = practices). It was originally designed as a generic instrument to measure the engagement frequencies of a large spectrum of organized and private religious, spiritual, existential and philosophical practices (Büssing et al. 2005). In its shortened 17-item version (SpREUK-P SF17) it differentiates five factors (Büssing et al. 2012), e.g., Religious practices, Prosocial-humanistic practices, Existentialistic practices, Gratitude/Awe, and Spiritual (mind body) practices. Because of this diversity of spiritual-religious practices and engagements, the instrument is suited for both secular and also religious persons. The sub-scale "Religious practices" has a clear focus on mono-theistic religions, while the sub-scale "Spiritual (mind body) practices" refers more to Eastern religious practices. This latter (non-Christian) sub-scale does not make any demands to represent Eastern forms of spirituality/religiosity thoroughly, but to be a contrast to Christian religious practices.

Nevertheless, for specific research purposes it may be relevant to more accurately differentiate Christian practices, rituals and behaviors. In Catholic pastoral workers from Germany for example, private praying and also praying the Liturgy of Hours were to some extent related to life satisfaction and lower depression, while participating or celebrating the Holy Eucharist or partaking in Sacramental Confession were rather not related (Büssing et al. 2016). Further, in Italian Catholics working as volunteers for handicapped persons, praying the Rosary was moderately related to their perception of the Sacred in their lives, but not private prayers or attending the Sunday service (Büssing and Baiocco, unpublished data). Thus, further differentiating items may be of relevance to elucidate the underlying motives, intentions and perceptions.

1.1. Aim of the Study

The aim of this study was to validate a variant version of the SpREUK-P questionnaire that was enriched with items addressing specific Catholic rituals and practices, and with more differentiated praying and meditation items. This variant version was tested in a sample of Catholics (inclusively nuns and monks, Protestants, and in non-religious persons as a reference group.

2. Material and Methods

2.1. Enrolled Persons

To test the new instrument, a heterogeneous sample of participants was recruited, among them religious persons from Franciscan but also from other religious congregations. Participation calls were sent to the German Congregation Superiors ("Ordens-Oberen-Konferenz"), to local Caritas societies, to university students (i.e., Alpen-Adria Universität Salzburg and Witten/Herdecke university), to a course on Christian Spirituality (University Zürich), to various social and management associations as well as to the private networks of the study team ('snowball sampling'). The sample should be regarded as a convenience sample.

All participants were informed about the purpose of the study on the first page of the questionnaire (which did not ask for names, initials or location), and confidentiality and anonymity were guaranteed. With filling in the German language questionnaire and sending it back to the study team, participants agreed that their data would be anonymously evaluated. As most of the local Religious communities were small, we provided the opportunity to fill in the questionnaire either online (used by 25% of religious participants) or as a printout (used by 75% of the religious participants).

2.2. Measures

2.2.1. Engagement in Religious Practices (SpREUK-P)

The generic SpREUK-P (P—practices module) questionnaire was designed to measure the engagement frequencies of a large spectrum of organized and private religious, spiritual, existential and philosophical practices particularly in secular societies (Büssing et al. 2005). These practices and forms of engagement refer to the level of behaviors as described in Table 1. The shortened 17-item SpREUK-P differentiates 5 sub-constructs (Büssing et al. 2012), i.e.,

- Religious practices (alpha = 0.82), i.e., praying, church attendance, religious events, religious symbols
- Existentialistic practices (alpha = 0.77), i.e., self-realization, reflections upon the meaning of life, trying to gain insight (also into myself)
- Prosocial-humanistic practices (alpha = 0.79), i.e., helping others, considering their needs, doing good, thoughts to those in need
- Gratitude/Awe (alpha = 0.77), i.e., feeling of gratitude, reverence, experiencing the beauty in life
- Spiritual (mind body) practices (alpha = 0.72), i.e., meditation (Eastern style), rituals ("from other religious traditions than mine"), reading spiritual/religious books.

To make more accurate statements about religious practices of Catholics and derived a 'religious practices' module of the SpREUK-P (SpREUK-RP), we added 6 new items and more clearly differentiated the praying and meditation items (p1 and p4). Catholic items were PC1 (partaking Sacramental Confession), PC2 (receive the Holy Communion), PC3 (worship of the 'Sacrament'), PC4 (ask the 'Mother of God' for help and support), PC5 (praying the Rosary) and PC6 (strong relation to special saints). Praying was differentiated as p1a (private praying, for myself, for others), p1b (praying the Liturgy of Hours) and p1c (intercessory prayer), while meditation was differentiated as p4a (meditation, Christian style) and p4b (meditation, Eastern styles). We also added items from the primary version of the SpREUK 1.1 (Büssing et al. 2005) which were not used in its 17-item short version (i.e., p26 feeling connected with others, p27 volunteer work for others, p6 reading religious/spiritual books, p9 turn to nature, p17 being aware of how I treat the world around, and p21 belief in (my) guardian angel).

The items are scored on a 4-point scale (0—*never*; 1—*seldom*; 2—*often*; 3—*regularly*). The scores were referred to a 100% level (transformed scale score), which reflect the degree of an engagement in the distinct forms of a spiritual/religious practice ("engagement scores"). Scores > 50% would indicate higher engagement, while scores < 50 indicate rare engagement.

2.2.2. Transcendence Perception (DESES-6)

To refer to an experiential dimension as described in Table 1, we used the *Daily Spiritual Experience Scale* (DSES). This instrument was developed as a measure of a person's perception of the transcendent in daily life, and thus the items measure experience rather than particular beliefs or behaviors (Underwood 2002; 2011). Here we used the 6-item version (DSES-6; Cronbach's alpha = 0.91) which uses specific items such as feeling God's presence, God's love, desire to be closer to God (union), finding strength/comfort in God, being touched by beauty of creation (Underwood 2002). The response categories from 1 to 6 are *many times a day, every day, most days, some days, once in a while* and *never/almost never*. Item scores were finally summed up.

2.2.3. Franciscan-Inspired Spirituality Questionnaire (FraSpir)

To measure whether or not a person's spirituality/religiosity is based on an attitude of searching for the Spirit of the Lord as a fundamental source, and living from the Gospel as a matter of religious dedication, we used a 13-item subscale from the *Franciscan-inspired Spirituality Questionnaire* (FraSpir) (Büssing et al. 2017). This "Live from the Faith/Search for God" scale (Cronbach's alpha = 0.97) refers to the attitudes layer as described in Table 1. The scale uses items such as "My faith is my orientation in life", "My faith/spirituality gives meaning to my life", "I try to live in accordance with my religious beliefs", "I feel a longing for nearness to God", "I keep times of silence before God", etc.. For Christians, living from the Gospel and searching the Sacred is the core principle which would have an influence on their attitudes and behaviors (Table 1).

The 13 items were scored on a 5-point scale from disagreement to agreement (0—does not apply at all; 1—does not truly apply; 2—half and half (neither yes nor no); 3—applies quite a bit; 4—applies very much).

2.2.4. Life Satisfaction (SWLS)

To measure life satisfaction, as a construct that is conceptually not directly related to spiritual practices and engagement, we relied on the German version of Diener's *Satisfaction with Life Scale* (SWLS) (Diener et al. 1985). This 5-item scale (alpha = 0.92) uses general phrasings such as "In most ways my life is close to my ideal", "The conditions of my life are excellent", "I am satisfied with my life", "So far I have gotten the important things I want in my life", and "If I could live my life over, I would change almost nothing". Although this instrument does not differentiate the fields of satisfaction, it is nevertheless a good measure of a person's global satisfaction in life as it also addresses the self-assessed balance between the ideal and the given life situation. A benefit of the SWLS is the fact that it is not contaminated with positive affect variables, vitality, health function, etc. It can thus be used to analyze which other dimensions of spiritual engagement and experience would contribute to pastoral workers' overall life satisfaction. The extent of respondents' agreement or disagreement is indicated on a 7-point Likert scale ranging from *strongly agree* to *strongly disagree*.

2.2.5. Well-Being Index (WHO-5)

To assess participants' well-being, which is conceptually also not directly related to spiritual practices and engagement, we used the *WHO-Five Well-being Index* (WHO-5). This short scale avoids symptom-related or negative phrasings and measures well-being instead of absence of distress (Bech et al. 2013). Representative items are "I have felt cheerful and in good spirits" or "My daily life has been filled with things that interest me". Respondents assess how often they had the respective feelings within the last two weeks, ranging from 0 (*at no time*) to 5 (*all of the times*).

2.3. Statistical Analyses

Descriptive statistics, internal consistency (Cronbach's coefficient α) and factor analyses (principal component analysis using Varimax rotation with Kaiser's normalization) as well as analyses of variance (ANOVA), first order correlations and stepwise regression analyses were computed with SPSS 23.0.

To confirm the structure found by exploratory factor analysis, we performed a structured equation model (SEM) using the Lavaan packages of software R. This methodology involves many techniques such as multiple regression models, analysis of variance, confirmatory factor analysis, correlation analysis etc. With SEM one could determine the meaningful relationships between variables since the parameter estimates deliver the best scenario for the covariance matrix, and the better the model goodness of fit, the better the matrix is. The goodness of fit statistics used to evaluate the model are the root mean square error (RMSEA) which should be ≤0.05; the root mean square residual (RMSR) which should be ≤0.06; the comparative fit index (CFI) which should be ≥0.95 and the Tucker-Lewis index (TLI) which should be ≥0.95.

Given the exploratory character of this study, the significance level of ANOVA and correlation analyses were set at $p < 0.01$. With respect to classifying the strength of the observed correlations, we regarded r > 0.5 as a strong correlation, an r between 0.3 and 0.5 as a moderate correlation, an r between 0.2 and 0.3 as a weak correlation, and r < 0.2 as negligible or no correlation.

3. Results

3.1. Participants

Among the 420 enrolled persons, men were predominant (62.5%); most had a high school education (70.0%) and were Catholics (65.1%). Participants from a religious congregation constituted 20.6% of the sample, 22.1% were university students, and the other participants were from the fields of pedagogy, medicine, psychology, theology, and others professions (Table 2). Among the religious, 72% were from Franciscan congregations, and 28% were from other religious congregations. All further sociodemographic data are depicted in Table 1.

Participants' life satisfaction was in the upper range, well-being scores in the upper mid-range, and transcendence perception in the mid-range (Table 2).

Table 2. Description of the sample (N = 420).

	Scores	Range
Age (years) (Mean ± SD)	44.0 ± 18.8	18–88
Gender (%)		
Women	37.5	
Men	62.5	
Educational level (%)		
Secondary school (Haupt-/Realschule)	14.1	
High school (Gymnasium)	70.0	
other	15.9	
Religious denomination (%)		
Catholic	65.1	
Protestant	20.0	
Other	4.1	
None	10.8	

Table 2. Cont.

	Scores	Range
Profession (%)		
Students	22.1	
Medicine/psychology	14.6	
Pedagogy	13.8	
Theology	8.8	
Other	21.1	
Religious community	20.6	
Life satisfaction (SWLS) (Mean ± SD)	27.7 ± 4.7	4–35
Well-being (WHO-5) (Mean ± SD)	60.7 ± 17.3	12–100
Transcendence perception (DSES-6) (Mean ± SD)	21.4 ± 7.8	6–36

3.2. Reliability and Factor Analysis of the SpREUK-P in Its Variant Version

Factor analysis revealed a Kaiser-Mayer-Olkin value of 0.93, which was a measure for the degree of common variance, indicating its suitability for statistical investigation by means of principal component factor analysis. Due to low item to scale correlations, six items were eliminated from the item pool prior to exploratory factor analysis (mainly from the previous scale "Spiritual (Mind-Body) practices"). During the process of factor analyses, one item was eliminated because of too low factor loading (p27 volunteer work for others), and three items because of strong side loadings (p4a meditation (Christian style), p6 reading religious/spiritual books, PC3 worship of Sacrament). Exploratory factor analysis of the resulting 23 items pointed to four main factors which accounted for 72% of variance (Table 3):

- The 8-item factor *Prosocial-Humanistic practices* (40% explained variance; Cronbach's alpha = 0.91) is comprised of five items from the primary "Prosocial-humanistic practices" scale, and items from other scales which all share the topic of conscious dealing with the world around and with others. The item p31 addressing the perception and the value of beauty in the world load on this factor, too.
- The 6-item factor *General religious practices* (22% explained variance; Cronbach's alpha = 0.94) uses four items from the primary "Religious practices" scale and two new items.
- The 5-item factor *Catholic religious practices* (5% explained variance; Cronbach's alpha = 0.90) is comprised of five 'Catholic' items.
- The 4-item factor *Existentialistic practices/Gratitude and Awe* (4% explained variance; Cronbach's alpha = 0.84) combines two existentialistic items and two items from the primary "Gratitude/Awe scale".

The Difficulty Index (mean value 1.59/3) of these items is 0.53; all but one item (PC5) was in the acceptable range from 0.2 to 0.8 (Table 3).

Table 3. Reliability and factorial structure.

Primary Scale		Mean ± SD (Range 0–3)	Difficulty Index (1.59/3 = 0.53)	Corrected Item-Scale Correlation	α if Item Deleted (α = 0.931)	Prosocial-HUMANISTIC Practices	General Religious Practices	Catholic Religious Practices	Existentialistic Practices/Gratitude and Awe
	Cronbach's alpha Eigenvalue					0.906 90.2	0.940 50.0	0.896 10.1	0.838 10.0
PHP	p25 try to do good	2.25 ± 0.72	0.75	0.496	0.927	0.840			
PHP	p23 consider the needs of others	2.27 ± 0.70	0.76	0.488	0.927	0.827			
PHP	p22 try to actively help others	2.14 ± 0.79	0.71	0.495	0.927	0.819			
PHP	p26 feel connected with others	2.14 ± 0.87	0.71	0.588	0.926	0.728			
/	p17 be aware of how I treat the world around	2.27 ± 0.79	0.76	0.379	0.929	0.654			0.338
GA	p31 have learned to experience and value beauty	2.30 ± 0.80	0.77	0.468	0.928	0.646			0.490
PHP	p24 thoughts are with those in need	1.82 ± 0.84	0.61	0.636	0.925	0.640	0.382		
ExP	p16 convey positive values and convictions to others	2.07 ± 0.82	0.69	0.469	0.928	0.640			0.421
RP	p20 participate in religious events (regardless of obligations)	1.33 ± 1.10	0.44	0.744	0.923		0.796		
RP	p2 celebrating the Eucharist	1.22 ± 1.25	0.41	0.751	0.923		0.796	0.405	
new	p1c intercessory prayer	1.30 ± 1.17	0.43	0.769	0.922		0.790	0.334	
RP	p1a private praying (for myself, for others)	1.55 ± 1.17	0.52	0.773	0.922		0.779		
new	PC2 receive the Holy Communion	1.29 ± 1.28	0.43	0.725	0.923		0.763	0.400	
RP	p19 In my private area, religious symbols are important to me	1.27 ± 1.14	0.42	0.772	0.922		0.715	0.354	
new	PC5 praying the Rosary	0.56 ± 0.91	0.19	0.413	0.928			0.873	
new	PC1 Sacramental Confession	0.59 ± 0.94	0.20	0.481	0.927			0.828	
new	PC4 ask the "Mother of God" for help and support	0.90 ± 1.04	0.30	0.524	0.927			0.793	
new	PC6 strong relation to special saints	0.71 ± 1.00	0.24	0.449	0.928			0.727	

122

Table 3. Cont.

Primary Scale		Mean ± SD (Range 0–3)	Difficulty Index (1.59/3 = 0.53)	Corrected Item–Scale Correlation	α if Item Deleted (α = 0.931)	Factor Loading			
						Prosocial-HUMANISTIC Practices	General Religious Practices	Catholic Religious Practices	Existentialistic Practices/Gratitude and Awe
	Cronbach's alpha Eigenvalue					0.906 90.2	0.940 50.0	0.896 10.1	0.838 10.0
new	p1b praying the Liturgy of Hours	0.65 ± 1.13	0.22	0.568	0.926			0.708	
ExP	p11 try to get insight (also into myself)	2.17 ± 0.88	0.72	0.476	0.927	0.433	0.419		0.714
ExP	p10 reflect upon the meaning of life	2.16 ± 0.87	0.72	0.465	0.928	0.416			0.704
GA	p30 feeling of wondering awe	1.61 ± 1.01	0.54	0.642	0.925		0.400		0.690
GA	p29 feeling of great gratitude	1.96 ± 0.93	0.65	0.640	0.925	0.487	0.303		0.573
Excluded items									
new	PC3 Sacrament worship	0.76 ± 1.05							
SpP	p4a meditation (Christian style)	0.89 ± 1.09							
SpP	p4b meditation (Eastern style)	0.56 ± 0.94							
SpP	p6 reading religious/spiritual books	1.34 ± 1.10							
SpP	p7 work on a mind-body discipline (i.e., yoga, qigong, mindfulness etc.)	1.17 ± 1.08							
SpP	p8 perform distinct rituals (originated in other religious/spiritual traditions than mine)	0.60 ± 0.94							
ExP	p13 work on my self-realization	1.96 ± 0.88							
/	p21 believe in (my) guardian angel	1.61 ± 1.14							
/	p9 turn to nature	1.81 ± 0.97							
/	p27 volunteer work for others	1.61 ± 1.01							

Main component analysis (Variamax rotation with Kaiser normalization; rotation converged in 8 iterations); only factor loadings are depicted < 0.03; *Abbreviations*: ExP—Existentialistic practices; GA—Gratitude/Awe; PHP—Prosocial-humanistic practices; RP—religious practices; SpP—Spiritual (Mind-Body) practices; /—not related to a specific scale in the primary version; new—new item. Items with loading > 0.5 were highlighted (bold)

3.3. Structured Equation Model

After exploratory factor analysis (EFA) to identify correlative structure between the variables to get specific factors, we intended to validate the suggested structure by structured equation modelling (SEM). This method is a comprehensive methodology which involves techniques such as multiple regression models, analyses of variance, confirmatory factor analysis, correlation analysis etc. Investigation of the model structure using Exploratory Factor Analysis (EFA) involving four factors, showed that the model could not be validated through structured equation modelling (SEM: CFI = 0.860, TLI = 0.842, RMSEA = 0.105, SRMR = 0.082).

With SEM we could determine the meaningful relationships between variables since the parameter estimates deliver the best scenario for the covariance matrix. This means, that the better the model goodness of fit, the better the matrix. The following factorial structures could be identified (Figures 1–4):

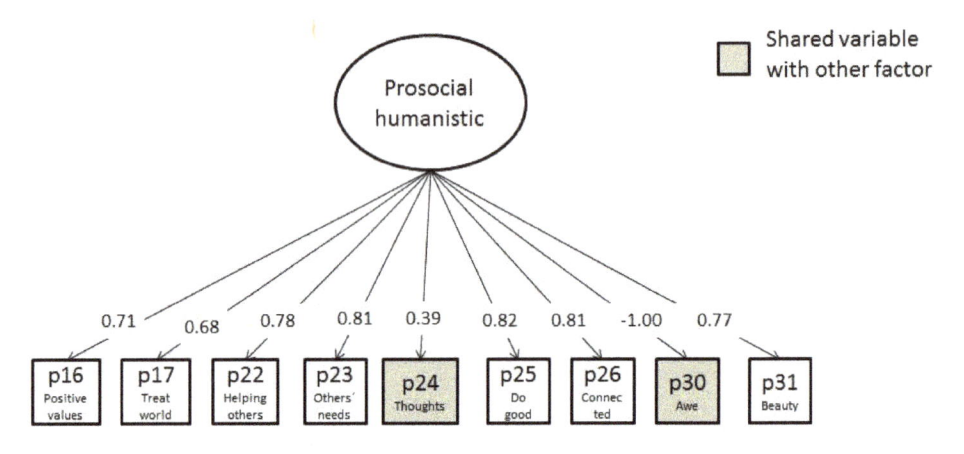

Figure 1. Factor Prosocial-humanistic practices from SEM.

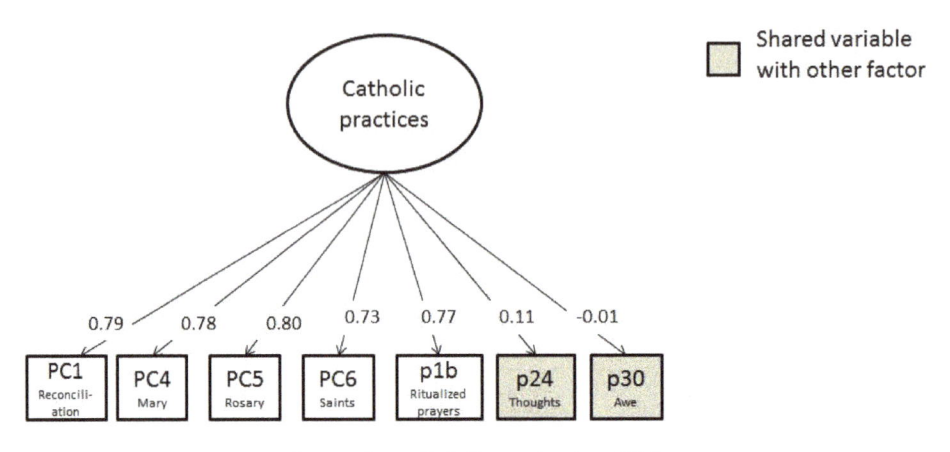

Figure 2. Factor Catholic practices from SEM.

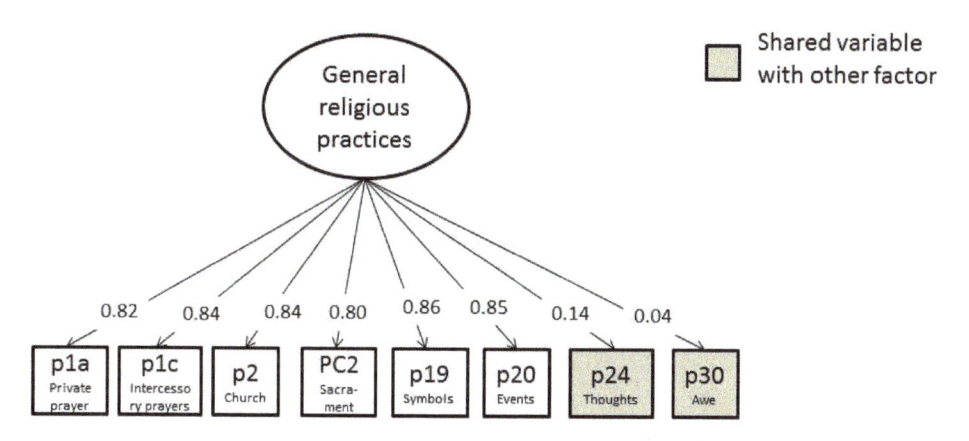

Figure 3. Factor General religious practices from SEM.

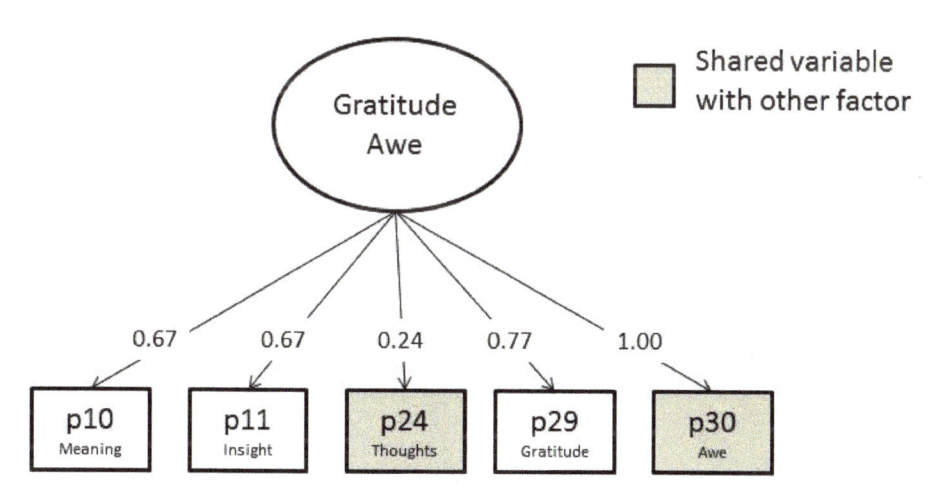

Figure 4. Factor Gratitude/Awe from SEM.

The new paths found through SEM provide a better representation of the relationship between the variables better (CFI = 0.96, TLI = 0.96, RMSEA = 0.05, SRMR = 0.06). Two items (p24—thoughts are with those in need; p30—feeling of wondering awe) are shared by other factors, and both load with variable strength to all four factors. Such cross-loadings are common in more complex statistical models where less restrictions are made in order to allow the variables and its correlations to move free between the latent constructs (Asparouhov and Muthén 2009). This new model with the new paths between factors and variables, as well as the correlation, now has a (very) good reliability: Prosocial-humanistic α = 0.91, Catholic practices α = 0.84 General religious practices α = 0.93 and Gratitude Awe α = 0.85.

These four factors are moderately to strongly interconnected, particularly Prosocial-humanistic practices and Gratitude/Awe (r = 0.90), Catholic practices and General religious practices (r = 0.73), (Figure 5), as well as a strong interconnection between the variables p2 (celebrating the Eucharist) and pc2 (receive the Holy Communion) (r = 0.75) (Figure 6). Regression analyses indicate that General religious practices account for 43% of the variance found in Catholic practices (as depending variable).

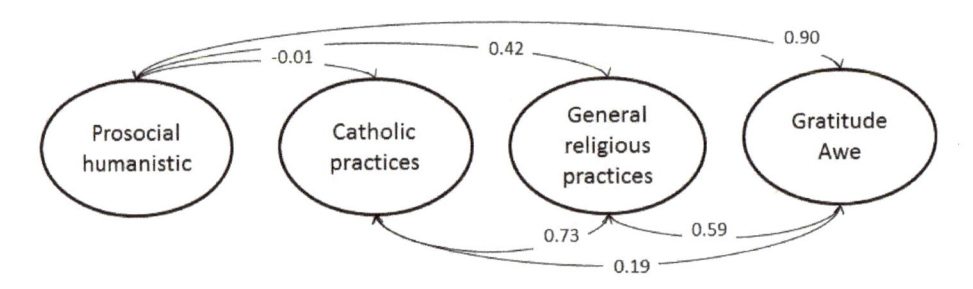

Figure 5. Correlations between factors.

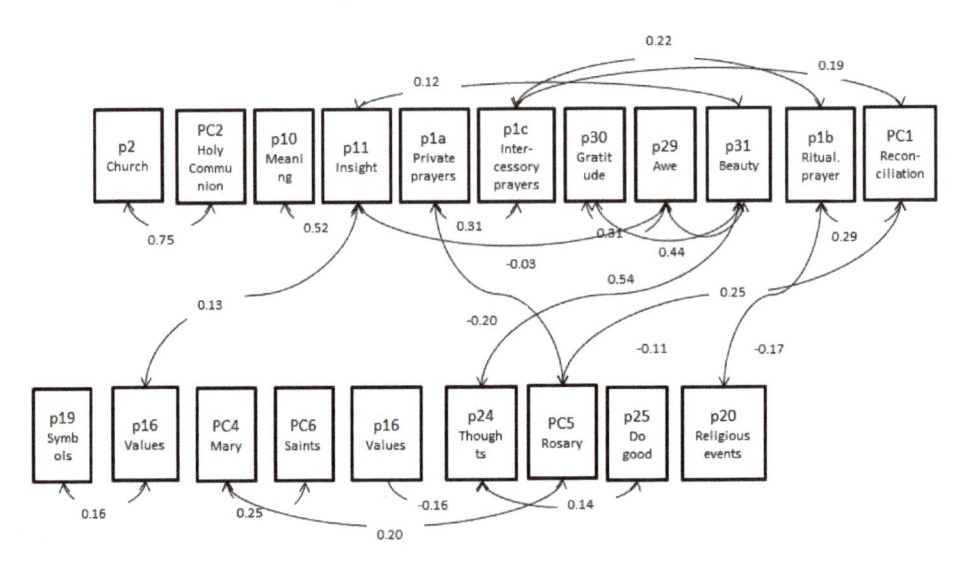

Figure 6. Correlations between variables.

3.4. Correlations with Life Satisfaction, Well-Being and Transcendence Perception

General religious practices (GRP) were strongly interrelated with Catholic religious practices (CRP), and Existentialistic practices/Gratitude and Awe (ExGA) with Prosocial-humanistic practices (PHP) (Table 4). However, CRP was only marginally related to PHP and weakly to ExGA.

The new scales correlated very strongly with the respective scales of the primary instrument (SpREUK-P SF17) (Table 4). The primary scale "Existentialistic practices" (SpREUK-P SF17) correlated strongly with PHP and ExGA, but only weakly with GRP, and not with CRP. Spiritual Mind-Body-practices (SpREUK-P SF17) correlated only weakly with ExGA, marginally with PHP and CRP, but not with GRP.

With respect to convergent validity, the new scales correlated moderately to strongly with Transcendence perception (DESE-6), and with "Live from the Faith/Search for God" (FraSpir) (Table 4). The subscales PHP and ExGA were moderately related to both measures of spiritual-religious perceptions and attitudes. With respect to discriminant validity, neither CRP nor GRP correlated significantly with life satisfaction or well-being. However, PHP was moderately related to life satisfaction and weakly to well-being, and ExGA marginally to life satisfaction and well-being.

Table 4. Correlation analyses.

	Religious Practices (SpREUK-RP)			
	Prosocial-Humanistic Practices	General Religious Practices	Catholic Religious Practices	Existentialistic Practices/Gratitude and Awe
Spiritual-religious practices (SpREUK-P SF17)				
Religious practices	0.491 **	**0.988 **	**0.689 **	0.505 **
Prosocial-humanistic practices	**0.887 **	0.448 **	0.189 **	0.596 **
Existentialistic practices	0.589 **	0.201 **	−0.015	**0.794 **
Gratitude/Awe	**0.804 **	0.524 **	0.247 **	**0.891 **
Spiritual Mind-Body practices	0.119	0.030	0.181 **	0.254 **
Spiritual-religious Attitudes and Perceptions				
Transcendence Perception (DSES-6)	0.392 **	**0.542 **	0.496 **	0.417 **
Live from the Faith/Search for God (FraSpir)	0.366 **	**0.693 **	**0.658 **	0.454 **
Life satisfaction/Well-being				
Satisfaction with Life Scale (SWLS)	0.307 **	0.073	−0.024	0.168 **
Well-being (WHO-5)	0.248 **	0.007	−0.051	0.124

** $p < 0.01$ (Spearman rho); strong correlations were highlighted (bold).

3.5. Expression of SpREUK-RP Scores in the Sample

In this sample, *Prosocial-humanistic practices* (PHP: 70.7 ± 21.2) and *Existentialistic practices/Gratitude and Awe* (ExGA: 65.8 ± 25.3) scored highest, *General religious practices* scored in the lower mid-range (GRP: 44.3 ± 36.7) and *Catholic religious practices* (CRP: 22.9 ± 28.4) lowest (Table 5). All factors except GRP showed skewness (CRP with 39% stating "never"); positive kurtosis was found for PHP and negative kurtosis for GRP (Table 5).

Younger persons scored significantly lower for GRP, CRP and ExGA, which were highest in older persons. For PHP, there were no significant age-related differences. A lower educational level was associated with higher CRP and GRP scores, while there were no significant differences for ExGA or PHP. There were no relevant gender-related differences.

Table 5. Mean values in the sample.

		Prosocial-Humanistic Practices	General Religious Practices	Catholic Religious Practices	Existentialistic Practices/Gratitude and Awe
	n	411	412	412	410
All	Mean	70.74	44.27	22.89	65.75
	SD	21.19	34.65	28.35	25.34
	Skewness	−1.14	0.19	1.22	−0.64
	SE to Skewness	0.12	0.12	0.12	0.12
	Kurtosis	1.47	−1.44	0.41	−0.21
	SE to Kurtosis	0.24	0.24	0.24	0.24
All	z-Mean	0.00	0.00	0.00	0.00
	z-SD	1.00	1.00	1.00	1.00
	Gender				
Women (n = 150)	z-Mean	−0.13	0.03	0.07	−0.11
	z-SD	0.92	1.07	1.08	0.98
Men (n = 261)	z-Mean	0.07	−0.02	−0.04	0.06
	z-SD	1.04	0.96	0.95	1.01
F-value		3.97	0.22	1.19	2.53
p-value		0.047	n.s.	n.s.	n.s.

Table 5. Cont.

		Prosocial-Humanistic Practices	General Religious Practices	Catholic Religious Practices	Existentialistic Practices/Gratitude and Awe
		Educational level			
Secondary school (n = 58)	z-Mean	0.04	0.40	0.47	0.11
	z-SD	0.98	1.02	1.19	1.05
High school (n = 279)	z-Mean	−0.02	−0.09	−0.11	−0.04
	z-SD	1.01	0.98	0.92	1.00
Others (n=65)	z-Mean	−0.03	−0.02	−0.02	−0.06
	z-SD	0.98	0.99	0.92	0.92
F-value		0.09	5.93	8.84	0.56
p-value		n.s.	0.003	<0.0001	n.s.
		Age groups			
<30 years (n = 131)	z-Mean	−0.05	**−0.72**	**−0.59**	−0.23
	z-SD	0.85	**0.64**	**0.55**	0.92
30–40 years (n = 44)	z-Mean	−0.11	−0.19	−0.07	−0.09
	z-SD	0.89	1.02	0.98	1.01
40–50 years (n = 55)	z-Mean	0.08	0.15	−0.08	0.23
	z-SD	0.96	0.87	0.69	0.99
50–60 years (n = 87)	z-Mean	−0.08	0.44	0.26	0.05
	z-SD	1.23	0.91	0.97	1.01
>60 years (n = 80)	z-Mean	0.15	**0.59**	**0.72**	0.17
	z-SD	1.01	**0.88**	**1.19**	1.04
F-value		0.93	41.39	30.47	3.30
p-value		n.s.	<0.0001	<0.0001	0.011
		Religious congregation			
No (n = 324)	z-Mean	0.08	−0.18	**−0.36**	0.03
	z-SD	0.83	0.93	**0.67**	0.95
Yes (n = 85)	z-Mean	**−0.31**	**0.69**	**1.38**	−0.14
	z-SD	**1.47**	**0.97**	**0.85**	1.17
F-value		10.43	58.07	402.34	2.12
p-value		0.001	<0.0001	<0.0001	n.s.
		Religious denomination			
Catholics (n = 262)	z-Mean	−0.02	0.35	0.36	0.03
	z-SD	1.09	0.98	1.06	1.02
Protestants (n = 83)	z-Mean	0.11	−0.48	**−0.64**	−0.08
	z-SD	0.78	0.74	**0.45**	0.95
Other (n = 17)	z-Mean	0.46	−0.12	−0.46	**0.71**
	z-SD	0.84	0.70	0.49	**0.71**
None (n = 45)	z-Mean	**−0.36**	**−1.05**	**−0.70**	**−0.37**
	z-SD	**0.79**	**0.38**	**0.32**	**0.92**
F-value		3.53	43.72	39.95	5.26
p-value		0.015	<0.0001	<0.0001	0.001

[1] z-means and standard deviations (SD) are standardized z factor values; strong deviations from the standardized mean are highlighted (bold).

Catholics had the highest CRP and GRP scores compared to all other enrolled persons. Nuns and monks scored significantly higher on CRP and GRP compared to other respondents, but significantly lower on PHP; with respect to ExGA there were no significant differences. While it is in line with the expectations that persons without any religious denomination score low on GRP and CRP, they also had low scores on PHP and ExGA (Table 5).

4. Discussion

Our intention was to develop a variant version of the already established SpREUK-P questionnaire. This new version focused more clearly on Christian religious practices, and included items specific for Catholic rituals and practices. Adding the respective items resulted in an elimination of the primary items referring to the "Spiritual (Mind-Body) practices" scale of the original instrument. Two of the new items (p1c intercessory prayer, PC2 receive the Holy Communion) load to the primary scale "Religious practices" which is now relabeled *General religious practices*, while the other new ('Catholic') items would build a discrete new factor labeled *Catholic religious practices*.

The primary scale "Prosocial-humanistic practices" was enriched by two items of primary SpREUK-P (p17 be aware of how I treat the world around; p26 feel connected with others), and by one item from the primary "Existentialistic practices" scale (p16 convey positive values and convictions to others) and one from the SpREUK-P SF17's scale "Gratitude/Awe" scale (p31 have learned to experience and value beauty). The two items of the SpREUK-P SF17's scale "Gratitude/Awe" (p30 wondering awe; p29 great gratitude) and two items from the primary scale "Existentialistic practices" (p11 try to get insight; p10 reflect upon the meaning of life) together form the new scale *Existentialistic practices/Gratitude and Awe*. Both of these short version scales have lost one item to the *Prosocial-humanistic practices* scale, and thus it is not a surprise that these scales are strongly interrelated.

While *Prosocial-humanistic practices* score highest in the sample (which means that socially desired activities are of high relevance for all participants), *General religious practices* were moderately related to these engagements and behaviors, while *Catholic religious practices* were only marginally related. It might be that these practices and rituals associated with Catholic religiosity focus more on transcendent sources (i.e., specific saints, mother Mary, praying the Rosary and the Liturgy of Hours) rather than sources related to concrete persons. This is interesting because from a theological point of view Christ can be experienced by others in need (Duncan 1998). In line with this observation, nuns and monks in particular, scored lower on *Prosocial-humanistic practices*, while Catholics as a more general group did not. This observation has to be interpreted with caution, because nuns and monks score high and in in the upper range for these religious rituals and practices (GRP: 68.1 ± 33.8; CRP: 62.0 ± 24.0), moreover their other engagement scores are in the upper range (ExGA: 62.0 ± 29.7; PHP: 64.1 ± 31.0). Nevertheless, persons not participating in religious congregations score much higher on *Prosocial-humanistic practices* (PHP: 72.5 ± 17.5) and highly in *Existentialistic practices/Gratitude and Awe* (ExGA: 66.6 ± 24.2). Whether they have more chances to meet and care for others or whether their religion is more focused on their encounter with God in their prayer life, remains a matter of further analyses. In fact, non-congregational persons score in the lower range of *General religious practices* and very low on *Catholic religious practices*, and a-religious persons scored lowest on all sub-scales. These effects cannot be explained by gender-related effects, because gender showed no relation to the engagement frequency of these practices. Apart from these observations we found significant difference on engagement in religious rituals and practices related to the educational level, an effect that has been observed in other studies (Büssing et al. 2005).

With respect to convergent validity, the new scales correlated moderately to strongly with spiritual-religious attitudes and perceptions (i.e., Transcendence perception, and "Live from the Faith/Search for God"). These measures refer to the Faith/Experience level of the representation of different aspects of the spirituality model (Table 1) which will influence the levels of attitudes on the one hand and behaviors (rituals and practices) on the other hand.

With respect to discriminant validity, neither "Catholic religious practices" nor "General religious practices" were significantly related to a person's life satisfaction or well-being. These findings would indicate that the religious scales of the SpREUK-RP are not *per se* contaminated with perceptions of general well-being. However, PHP were moderately related to life satisfaction and weakly to well-being. Detail analyses revealed that life satisfaction correlated strongest with the experience of beauty (p31: $r = 0.29$) and with trying to actively help others (p22: $r = 0.24$). These perceptions and behaviors may result in feelings of ease and thus satisfaction in life.

Limitations

A limitation of this study is the imbalance of Christian denominations with a dominance of Catholics. Further, women and persons with lower educational level are underrepresented. For the validation process this is not of major relevance, but for future studies more balanced samples are needed. Sensitivity-to-change analyses are for spiritual-religious engagement practices less relevant; nevertheless, future studies should address the development of these engagements during different phases of life.

5. Conclusions

We can confirm the 23-item variant version (SpREUK-RP), which more specifically addresses Christian religious practices as compared to the SpREUK-P, as a valid and reliable multidimensional instrument to be used in future studies. A benefit of the instrument is that it is not generally contaminated with items related to persons' well-being, and is not intermixed with specific religious attitudes and convictions. Compared to the primary SpREUK-P, which was designed to address not only religious but also secular forms of spiritual practices, the SpREUK-RP is intended to be used in education programs that refer to value-based attitudes and behaviors derived from specific Christian contexts.

Acknowledgments: There was no external funding for this study. We are grateful to all participants who filled in the questionnaire.

Author Contributions: A.B. has designed the questionnaire; A.B. and D.R.R. have analyzed the data; A.B., M.G., M.W. and T.D. have written and finally approved the manuscript.

Conflicts of Interest: The authors declare no conflict of interest. As a Capuchin, T.D. belongs to a Franciscan congregation; but this has not inappropriately influenced the data analysis, representation or interpretation of reported research results.

References

Asparouhov, Tihomir, and Bengt Muthén. 2009. Exploratory structural equation modeling. *Structural Equation Modeling* 16: 397–438. [CrossRef]

Bech, Per, Lis Raabaek Olsen, Mette Kjoller, and Niels Kristian Rasmussen. 2013. Measuring well-being rather than the absence of distress symptoms: A comparison of the SF-36 mental health subscale and the WHO-Five well-being scale. *International Journal of Methods in Psychiatric Research* 12: 85–91. [CrossRef]

Büssing, Arndt, Peter F. Matthiessen, and Thomas Ostermann. 2005. Engagement of patients in religious and spiritual practices: Confirmatory results with the SpREUK-P 1.1 questionnaire as a tool of quality of life research. *Health and Quality of Life Outcomes* 3: 53. Available online: https://www.ncbi.nlm.nih.gov/pubmed/16144546 (accessed on 26 September 2005).

Büssing, Arndt, Franz Reiser, Andreas Michalsen, and Klaus Baumann. 2012. Engagement of patients with chronic diseases in spiritual and secular forms of practice: Results with the shortened SpREUK-P SF17 Questionnaire. *Integrative Medicine: A Clinician's Journal* 11: 28–38.

Büssing, Arndt. 2012. Measures of Spirituality in Health Care. In *Oxford Textbook of Spirituality in Healthcare*. Edited by Mark Cobb, Christina M. Puchalski and Bruce Rumbold. New York: Oxford University Press, pp. 323–31.

Büssing, Arndt, Eckhard Frick, Christoph Jacobs, and Klaus Baumann. 2016. Health and Life Satisfaction of Roman Catholic Pastoral Workers: Private Prayer Has a Greater Impact Than Public Prayer. *Pastoral Psychology* 65: 89–102. [CrossRef]

Büssing, Arndt. 2017. Messung spezifischer Aspekte der Spiritualität/Religiosität. In *Spiritualität. Auf der Suche nach ihrem Ort in der Theologie*. Edited by Thomas Möllenbeck and Ludger Schulte. Münster: Aschendorf-Verlag, pp. 138–64.

Büssing, Arndt, Markus Warode, Mareike Gerundt, and Thomas Dienberg. 2017. Validation of a novel instrument to measure elements of Franciscan inspired Spirituality in a general population and in religious persons. *Religions* 8: 197. [CrossRef]

Diener, Ed, Robert A. Emmons, Randy J. Larsen, and Sharon Griffin. 1985. The Satisfaction with Life Scale. *Journal of Personal Assessment* 49: 71–75. [CrossRef] [PubMed]

Duncan, Geoffrey. 1998. *Seeing Christ in Others. An Anthology of Worship, Meditation and Mission*. Norwich: Canterbury Press.

Underwood, Lynn G. 2002. The Daily Spiritual Experience Scale: Development, Theoretical Description, Reliability, Exploratory Factor Analysis, and Preliminary Construct Validity Using Health-Related Data. *Annals of Behavioral Medicine* 24: 22–33. [CrossRef] [PubMed]

Underwood, Lynn G. 2011. The Daily Spiritual Experience Scale: Overview and Results. *Religions* 2: 29–50. [CrossRef]

Zwingmann, Christian, Constantin Klein, and Arndt Büssing. 2011. Measuring Religiosity/Spirituality: Theoretical Differentiations and Characterizations of Instruments. *Religions* 2: 345–57. [CrossRef]

© 2017 by the authors. Licensee MDPI, Basel, Switzerland. This article is an open access article distributed under the terms and conditions of the Creative Commons Attribution (CC BY) license (http://creativecommons.org/licenses/by/4.0/).

religions

Article

Validation of a Novel Instrument to Measure Elements of Franciscan-Inspired Spirituality in a General Population and in Religious Persons

Arndt Büssing [1,2,*], Markus Warode [2], Mareike Gerundt [2] and Thomas Dienberg [2]

[1] Professorship Quality of Life, Spirituality and Coping, Faculty of Heath, Witten/Herdecke University, 58313 Herdecke, Germany
[2] IUNCTUS—Competence Center for Christian Spirituality, Philosophical-Theological Academy, 48148 Münster, Germany; warode.iunctus@pth-muenster.de (M.W.); gerundt.iunctus@pth-muenster.de (M.G.); th.dienberg@web.de (T.D.)
* Correspondence: Arndt.Buessing@uni-wh.de; Tel.: +49-2330-623246

Received: 3 August 2017; Accepted: 15 September 2017; Published: 19 September 2017

Abstract: Today there are several approaches for bringing mindfulness, which conceptually refers to the Buddhist Vipassana tradition, into organizations. Programs referring to value-based attitudes and behaviors derived from specific Christian contexts are rarely evaluated. A prerequisite are reliable instruments for measuring the respective outcomes. We therefore performed a cross-sectional study among 418 participants to validate an instrument measuring specific aspects of Franciscan-inspired spirituality (FraSpir), particularly the core dimensions and transformative outcomes. Exploratory factor analysis of this FraSpir questionnaire with 26 items pointed to four main factors (i.e., "Live from Faith/Search for God"; "Peaceful attitude/Respectful Treatment"; "Commitment to Disadvantaged and Creation"; "Attitude of Poverty"). Their internal consistency (Cronbach's alpha) ranged from 0.79 to 0.97. With respect to convergent validity, there were sound correlations with engagement in religious practices, gratitude and awe, and prosocial-humanistic practices. The 26-item instrument was found to be a reliable and valid instrument for use in training and education programs. Interestingly, nuns and monks scored significantly higher on the Faith and Poverty subscales than others, but similarly on the two subscales addressing considerate action in the world. These attitudes and behaviors are not exclusively valued by those of religious faith, but by all.

Keywords: spirituality; Franciscan; validation; questionnaire

1. Introduction

Today there are several approaches for bringing mindfulness into organizations (i.e., Apple, Google, Deutsche Bank etc.), to teach stressed managers and personnel how to meditate in order to reduce stress, increase well-being and performance, improve (more conscious) interaction with staff, and so forth (Vogus and Sutcliffe 2012; Dane and Brummel 2013; Reb and Choi 2015). These approaches refer to meditation techniques derived from a Buddhist Vipassana tradition, yet often without this specific context. Trained attitudes are foremost experiential awareness (attention) and non-judgmental acceptance (non-reaction) of the situation as it is. These behaviors can be learned by all, whatever their religious or spiritual orientation.

However, there are also other approaches which refer to value-based attitudes and behaviors derived from specific Christian contexts (Fernando 2007; Dienberg et al. 2007; Rohrhirsch 2013; Benke 2008; Naughton and Specht [1985] 2011; Bouckaert and Zsolnai 2011; Zindel 2012). One of these refers to Franciscan spirituality. This specific school of spirituality has its foundation in the life of medieval friar S. Francis of Assisi (1181/82-1226), founder of Franciscan orders.

The later S. Francis was born as Giovanni di Pietro di Bernardone, a son of a prosperous merchant, and lived the carefree life of a wealthy young man and powered by ambitious career dreams. Confronted with a serious illness he experienced a significant spiritual crisis which was the start of his spiritual conversion, aiming to find a deeper sense and for the ultimate in life.

During a pilgrimage to Rome he lived the life of a beggar, which further changed his attitudes. Giovanni started to live as a poor person and to imitate the life of Jesus Christ. Because he regarded the whole experiential creation as a reflection of God, he thus regarded everything (all creatures, the elements, sun and moon, and even death and his chronic illness) as his brothers and sisters. This long way of spiritual transformation which started with inner conflicts, lost perspectives, and break with his previous life resulted in an experience of God's presence in all suffering others and the whole of creation. Thereby he won a new view of world and society, person and church (Kuster 2016).

This lifestyle attracted many followers who were later organized as "Friars Minor". They were obliged to assume personal and corporate poverty as an attitude of humility. Still today, S. Francis is recognized for his patronage of the sick and the poor and the natural environment. Aspects of Franciscan-inspired spirituality are fundamental training concepts for organizations (Blastic 1993; Dienberg 2009, 2013; Warode and Gerundt 2015; Warode 2016), which, to date, have not been evaluated. A first step for such an evaluation is an operationalization of circumscribed aspects of Franciscan-inspired spirituality, so that they can be measured and quantified in a standardized way. Here it was the intention to analyze the prevalence of the respective ideals and attitudes referring to Franciscan spirituality in today's society.

1.1. Franciscan Spirituality

In the Christian tradition, there are many different schools of spirituality that tried and try to live the *Imitatio Christi* in different ways. In all of these schools an "inner transformation" plays an essential role, and refers to an individual "source experience" (Waaijman 2002). This experience has changed peoples' life towards a more consequent and often radical *Imitatio Christi*. Others wanted to share the respective experience or to simply follow these role models on their radical way of life, and these followers were often organized as movements or religious communities with distinct structures and rules and unique forms of spirituality (i.e., Franciscans, Benedictines, Jesuits, etc.). Particularly the Franciscans as a non-monastic order have a clear focus on living from the Gospel with subsequent consequences for their life in the 'outside' world, living with and for others in need and respectful engagement for God's creation.

For our approach, we focus on essential elements of Franciscan spirituality. Its center is the Gospel (Dienberg 2016), and the development of specific attitudes and virtues as a process of 'inner transformation'. This transformation includes a basic new orientation towards the Gospel and its expression in today's concrete life. Closely related is an attitude of searching the Spirit of the Lord. For S. Francis, this search was expressed by a life in poverty, humility and fraternity, by attitudes of reverence and respect for the creation and all living beings, resulting in a peace-making mindset. Material and immaterial poverty—along with humility—is probably the most difficult and, at the same time, crucial attitude to be developed. Both values are seen as the central characteristics of a Franciscan way of following Christ (Peters 1995).

Poverty means to renounce material goods, not to cling to property or home. S. Francis intended to live in accordance with the Gospel, referring to Jesus who had no place to "lay his head" (Matthew 8:20). Poverty understood in this way means to avoid egoistic and self-centered attitudes and behaviors, to accept oneself as dependent. A consequence is to experience life as a gift, to search for God in the simple things in one's daily life, and in the poor and the suffering. Because of this attitude of being lesser, serving is the consequent reaction to the call of the world. It includes the attitudes of obedience, attentiveness and mindfulness towards the world, towards life and others. These aspects are crucial for an inner transformation for the sake of others, and also a service for a social and economic organization. S. Francis's intention was to find God and God's traces everywhere in the world and in everything that lives and exists. This is not meant as romanticized enthusiasm for the beauty of nature, but as taking responsibility for the creation, a command that was given by God. In line with this, being related is a further aspect of the intended process of personal transformation. This can be through direct encounter with the creation around and with people, through attentive listening to the call of the world, and thus by taking responsibility for the protection and preservation of the environment and compassionate care for others.

Within the last years, several of these spiritual core competences (attitudes and behaviors based on Franciscan spirituality) were introduced in management and organizational development programs to combine theoretical and practice-oriented contents (Gerundt 2012; Warode and Gerundt 2015; Dienberg 2016; Dienberg and Warode 2015; Warode and Gerundt 2014). The relevance of these competences is theoretically described with respect to people's attitudes and behavior. In order to evaluate the transformative component of Franciscan spirituality in today's society, an instrument for measuring these has to address both the core component of Franciscan spirituality (faith) and the transformative components (outcomes).

1.2. Aim of the Study

We therefore intended to operationalize and make measurable specific aspects of Franciscan Spirituality, particularly the core dimension and the transformative outcomes. It was not aim to identify perfect Franciscans, but to analyze the prevalence of the respective ideals and attitudes in today's society, either as intentions or concrete behaviors. Therefore, a new instrument was developed (the Franciscan-inspired Spirituality questionnaire) and tested with participants either with or without a Christian background, in religious (nuns and monks) or lay persons, young adults and older adults, women and men.

2. Material and Methods

2.1. Enrollment of Participants

A heterogeneous sample of participants from a general population and, as a reference group, religious persons from Franciscan but also from other religious congregations was recruited. Calls for participation were sent to the German Superiors Congregation (Ordens-Oberen-Konferenz), to local Caritas societies, university students (i.e., Alpen-Adria Universität Salzburg and Witten/Herdecke University), a course on Christian Spirituality (University Zürich), and various social and management associations, but also to the private networks of the study team (snowball sampling). The sample should thus be regarded as a convenience sample.

All participants were informed about the purpose of the study on the first page of the questionnaire (which does not ask for names, initials or location), and were guaranteed confidentiality and anonymity. In completing this German-language questionnaire and sending it back to the study team, participants agreed that their data were anonymously evaluated. Because most of the local religious communities are small, we provided the opportunity to fill the questionnaire either online (used by 25% of nuns and monks) or as a print-out (used by 75% of the nuns and monks).

2.2. Measures

2.2.1. Franciscan-inspired Spirituality Questionnaire (FraSpir)

Referring to core concepts of Franciscan spirituality (Warode and Gerundt 2014, 2015), we conceptually started with six theoretically derived main topics (ideals). These were intended to represent attitudes and behaviors which could be principally found in all persons, not only in nuns and monks, namely:

- Living from the Gospel.
- Searching for the Spirit of the Lord.

- Attitude of (material and immaterial) Poverty.
- Awe and respect for the Creation.
- Considerate action in the World: Fraternal encounter and support of disadvantaged persons.
- Considerate action in the World: Sustainable and peace-bearing values.

The group regarded Living from the Gospel and Searching for the Sacred as core principles which would have an influence on a person's attitudes and behaviors. With these conceptual considerations in mind, we formulated 30 items which could fit to these topics (between four to seven items for each topic), and discussed their putative relevance in terms of face validity.

The items were scored on a five-point scale from disagreement to agreement (0—does not apply at all; 1—does not truly apply; 2—half and half (neither yes nor no); 3—applies quite a bit; 4—applies very much).

The resulting item pool was then submitted to empirical investigation as the Franciscan-inspired Spirituality (FraSpir) questionnaire, and tested for its psychometric properties

2.2.2. Transcendence Perception (DESES-6)

The Daily Spiritual Experience Scale was developed as a measure of a person's perception of the transcendent in daily life, and thus the items measure experience rather than particular beliefs or behaviors (Underwood 2006, 2011). Here we used the six-item version (DSES-6; Cronbach's alpha = 0.91), which uses specific items such as feeling God's presence, God's love, desire to be closer to God (union), finding strength/comfort in God, being touched by beauty of creation (Underwood and Teresi 2002). The response categories from 1 to 6 are: never/almost never; once in a while; some days; most days; every day; many times a day. Item scores were finally summed up.

2.2.3. Engagement in Spiritual Practices (SpREUK-P)

The generic SpREUK-P (P—practices module) questionnaire was designed to measure the engagement frequencies of a large spectrum of organized and private religious, spiritual, existential and philosophical practices (Büssing et al. 2005). The shortened 17-item instrument (SpREUK-P SF17) differentiates five sub-constructs (Büssing et al. 2012), namely:

- *Religious practices* (alpha = 0.82), i.e., praying, church attendance, religious events, religious symbols.
- *Existentialistic practices* (alpha = 0.77), i.e., self-realization, spiritual development, meaning in life, turn to nature.
- *Prosocial-humanistic practices* (alpha = 0.79), i.e., help others, consider their needs, do good, connectedness.
- *Gratitude/Awe* (alpha – 0.77), i.e., feeling of gratitude, reverence, experience beauty in life.
- *Spiritual (mind body) practices* (alpha = 0.72), i.e., meditation (Eastern style), rituals ("from other religious traditions than mine"), reading spiritual/religious book.

The items of the SpREUK-P are scored on a four-point scale (0—never; 1—seldom; 2—often; 3—regularly). The scores can be referred to a 100% level (transformed scale score), which reflect the degree of engagement in the distinct forms of a spiritual/religious practice (engagement scores). Scores > 50% indicate higher engagement, while scores <50 indicate rare engagement

2.2.4. Life Satisfaction (SWLS)

To measure life satisfaction, we relied on the German version of Diener's Satisfaction with Life Scale (SWLS) (Diener et al. 1985). This five-item scale (alpha = 0.92) uses general phrasings such as "In most ways my life is close to my ideal", "The conditions of my life are excellent", "I am satisfied with my life", "So far I have gotten the important things I want in my life", and "If I could live my life over, I would change almost nothing". Although this instrument does not differentiate the fields of satisfaction, it is nevertheless a good measure of a person's global satisfaction in life, as it also addresses the self-assessed balance between the ideal and the given life situation. A benefit of the SWLS is the fact that it not contaminated with positive affect variables, vitality, health function, and so forth. It can thus be used to analyze which other dimensions of spiritual engagement and experience would contribute to a person´s overall life satisfaction. The extent of respondents' agreement or disagreement is indicated on a seven-point Likert scale ranging from "strongly agree" to "strongly disagree".

2.2.5. Well-being (WHO5)

To assess participants' well-being, we used the WHO-Five Well-being Index (WHO-5). This short scale avoids symptom-related or negative phrasings and measures well-being instead of absence of distress (Bech et al. 2013). Representative items are "I have felt cheerful and in good spirits" or "My daily life has been filled with things that interest me". Respondents assess how often they had the respective feelings within the last two weeks, ranging from 0 (at no time) to 5 (all of the time).

2.3. Statistical Analyses

Descriptive statistics, internal consistency (Cronbach's coefficient α) and factor analyses (principal component analysis using Varimax rotation with Kaiser's normalization), as well as first order correlations (Spearman rho), were computed with SPSS 23.0. Given the exploratory character of this study, significance level was set at $p < 0.01$. With respect to classifying the strength of the observed correlations, we regarded $r > 0.5$ as a strong correlation, an r between 0.3 and 0.5 as a moderate correlation, an r between 0.2 and 0.3 as a weak correlation, and $r < 0.2$ as negligible or no correlation.

3. Results

3.1. Participants

Among the 418 enrolled participants, men were predominant (62%); most had a high school education (70%) and were Catholics (65%). Twenty-two percent of participants were from a religious congregation, and 22% were university students; the other participants were from the fields of pedagogy, medicine, psychology, theology, and others professions (Table 1). Among the Religious (nuns and monks), 73% were from Franciscan congregations, and 27% from other religious congregations. All further sociodemographic data are depicted in Table 1.

Participants' life satisfaction was in the upper range, well-being scores in the upper mid-range, and Transcendence perception in the mid-range (Table 1).

Table 1. Description of the sample (N = 418).

	Scores	Range
Age (years) (Mean ± SD)	43.9 ± 18.7	18–88
Gender (%)		
Women	37.6	
Men	62.4	
Educational level (%)		
Secondary school (Haupt-/Realschule)	13.9	
High school (Gymnasium)	70.1	
other	15.9	
Religious denomination (%)		
Catholic	64.9	
Protestant	20.1	
Other	4.1	
None	10.9	

Table 1. Description of the sample (N = 418).

	Scores	Range
Profession (%)		
Students	22.2	
Medicine/psychology	14.4	
Pedagogy	13.9	
Theology	7.8	
Other	21.2	
Religious community	20.5	
Life satisfaction (SWLS) (Mean ± SD)	28.8 ± 4.6	6–35
Well-being (WHO5) (Mean ± SD)	60.7 ± 17.3	12–100
Transcendence perception (DSES-6) (Mean ± SD)	21.4 ± 7.8	6–36

3.2. Reliability and Factor Analysis of the FraSpir Questionnaire

Factor analysis revealed a Kaiser-Mayer-Olkin value of 0.94, which is a measure for the degree of common variance, indicating its suitability for statistical investigation by means of principal component factor analysis. From the primary item pool we eliminated four items with either factor loadings <0.5 or strong side loadings. Exploratory factor analysis of the resulting 26 items pointed to four main factors, which accounted for 67% of variance (Table 2). Internal consistency (Cronbach's alpha) of these four sub-scales ranged from 0.79 to 0.97.

The Difficulty Index of these items (mean value 2.55/4) is 0.64; all but three items are in the acceptable range from 0.2 to 0.8 (Table 2). The response to the items 21–23 indicate ceiling effects, which are due to desired behaviors.

With 13 items, factor 1 was the strongest (43% explained variance), followed by factor 2 with six items (13% explained variance), factor 3 with four items (6% explained variance), and factor 4 with three items (5% explained variance). Factor 1 can be labeled "Live from the Faith/Search for God" and is comprised of 10 items referring to the theoretical topics "Living from the Gospel" and "Searching for the Spirit of the Lord", two items referring to "Awe and respect for the Creation" and one from the topic "Attitude of Poverty". Factor 2 can be labelled "Peaceful attitude/Respectful treatment" and uses six items referring to "Considerate action in the world: Lasting and peace-bearing values". Factor 3 can be labelled "Commitment to the Disadvantaged and Creation" and is comprised of two items each from the topics "Awe and respect for the Creation" and "Considerate action in the world: Fraternal encounter and support of disadvantaged people". Factor 4 can be labelled "Attitude of Poverty" and uses three items referring to the topic "Attitude of Poverty".

Table 2. Reliability and factorial structure.

Theoretical Topics		Mean ± SD	Difficulty Index (2.55/4 = 0.64)	Corrected Item-Scale Correlation	α if Item Deleted (α = 0.95)	Live from the Faith/Search for God	Peaceful Attitude /Respectful Treatment	Commitment to the Disadvantaged and Creation	Attitude of Poverty
	Cronbach's Alpha					0.967	0.811	0.842	0.785
	Eigenvalue					11.1	3.3	1.5	1.4
Living from the Gospel	f1 My faith is my orientation in life.	2.5 ± 1.5	0.63	0.81	0.92	0.892			
Searching for the Spirit of the Lord	f7 I listen to God's word in me.	1.9 ± 1.4	0.48	0.84	0.94	0.891			
Searching for the Spirit of the Lord	f5 I try to track down the divine in the world.	2.3 ± 1.5	0.58	0.84	0.94	0.874			
Living from the Gospel	f4 My faith/spirituality gives meaning to my life.	2.5 ± 1.5	0.63	0.83	0.94	0.871			
Searching for the Spirit of the Lord	f11 I feel a longing for nearness to God.	2.0 ± 1.6	0.50	0.81	0.94	0.862			
Living from the Gospel	f2 I try to live in accordance with my religious beliefs.	2.5 ± 1.4	0.63	0.77	0.94	0.858			
Searching for the Spirit of the Lord	f8 I keep times of silence before God.	2.0 ± 1.5	0.50	0.82	0.94	0.852			
Searching for the Spirit of the Lord	f6 I have a sense of the sacred in my life.	2.2 ± 1.4	0.55	0.81	0.94	0.842			
Searching for the Spirit of the Lord	f9 Before important decisions I seek advice in prayer.	2.0 ± 1.5	0.50	0.77	0.94	0.805			
Searching for the Spirit of the Lord	f10 I always try to remain a seeker.	2.5 ± 1.4	0.63	0.71	0.94	0.746			
Awe and respect for the Creation	f14 Again and again I am awed by the beauty of God's creation.	2.9 ± 1.3	0.73	0.70	0.94	0.689			
Awe and respect for the Creation	f17 I feel a great gratitude that I want to share with others.	2.6 ± 1.2	0.65	0.74	0.94	0.610	0.305		
Attitude of Poverty	f12 I maintain a humble deal with the resources entrusted to me.	2.5 ± 1.1	0.63	0.55	0.95	0.524			
Lasting and peace-bearing values	f23 It is important to me to understand the positions and opinions of other people and to accept them internally (although I do not necessarily share them).	3.3 ± 0.8	0.83	0.31	0.95		0.812		
Lasting and peace-bearing values	f22 I always try to put myself into others and wonder how I would feel in their situation.	3.3 ± 0.7	0.83	0.27	0.95		0.775		
Lasting and peace-bearing values	f24 I always check my attitudes and views, because the others might be right.	3.1 ± 0.8	0.78	0.33	0.95		0.724		
Lasting and peace-bearing values	f21 I am conscious of the fact that I deal with others well and respectfully.	3.5 ± 0.6	0.88	0.27	0.95		0.693	0.347	

Table 2. Reliability and factorial structure.

		Mean ± SD	Difficulty Index (2.55/4 = 0.64)	Corrected Item-Scale Correlation	α if Item Deleted (α = 0.95)	Live from the Faith/Search for God	Peaceful Attitude/Respectful Treatment	Commitment to the Disadvantaged and Creation	Attitude of Poverty
							Factor Loading		
Lasting and peace-bearing values	F25 I actively go to people who are not so good with me, and try to clarify the causes.	2.2 ± 0.9	0.55	0.38	0.95		0.602		
Lasting and peace-bearing values	F26 In conflicts I always try to find ways of reconciliation.	2.7 ± 0.8	0.68	0.29	0.95		0.571		
Awe and respect for the Creation	f15 I actively engage for the well-being of disadvantaged people.	2.5 ± 1.1	0.63	0.56	0.95			0.839	
Fraternal encounter and support of disadvantaged	f20 I actively engage in the social field.	2.6 ± 1.3	0.65	0.47	0.95			0.784	
Fraternal encounter and support of disadvantaged	f18 I am trying to find ways to help people in need.	2.7 ± 1.0	0.68	0.50	0.95			0.746	
Awe and respect for the Creation	f16 I am actively involved in the protection and maintenance of creation	2.1 ± 1.1	0.53	0.57	0.95	0.349		0.629	
Attitude of Poverty	f29 I can well imagine relinquishing material possessions.	2.2 ± 1.1	0.55	0.51	0.95				0.823
Attitude of Poverty	f30 Not clinging to material possessions gives me a sense of serenity and freedom.	2.4 ± 1.2	0.60	0.57	0.95	0.375			0.775
Attitude of Poverty	f28 Professional advancement and career are not a decisive motivator in my life.	2.5 ± 1.2	0.63	0.48	0.95				0.660
Excluded items									
Fraternal encounter and support of disadvantaged	f19 With all I do (also professionally), I try to help others get better.	3.3 ± 0.9							
Living from the Gospel	f3 My ethical and religious beliefs shape my actions (even in my professional life).	2.8 ± 1.4							
Lasting and peace-bearing values:	f27 In conversations with others it is important to me not to teach.	2.6 ± 0.9							
Attitude of Poverty	f13 My life, my talents and abilities are a gift for me.	3.3 ± 1.0							

3.3. Expression of FraSpir Scores in the Sample

The participants scored highest on "Peaceful attitude/Respectful treatment", while all other sub-scales scored in the mid-range (Table 3). To clarify which sociodemographic variables were related to the expression of the FraSpir scores, we performed analyses of variance (Table 3).

With respect to gender there were some small but significant differences for "Peaceful attitude/Respectful treatment" and "Commitment to Disadvantaged and Creation", but none for the other sub-scales. All but one sub-scale ("Peaceful attitude/Respectful Treatment") showed significant differences for age. Here, the highest scores were found in the oldest and the lowest in the youngest cohort (Table 4). Education level showed significant differences only for "Attitudes of poverty", which scored highest in participants with secondary school education (data not shown).

Participants with a religious affiliation scored significantly higher on all sub-scales compared to those without a religious affiliation (data not shown). Religious (nuns or monks) scored significantly higher on "Live from the Faith/Search for God" and on "Attitude of Poverty", but not on the other sub-scales (Table 3). There were no significant differences between participants from Franciscan congregations or other religious congregations (F < 1.0; n.s.). However, monks had significantly higher subscale scores than nuns, particularly for "Live from the Faith/Search for God" (F = 22.8; $p < 0.0001$) and "Commitment to Disadvantaged and Creation" (F = 12.6; $p = 0.001$), and less pronounced for "Peaceful attitude/Respectful treatment" (F = 9.2; $p = 0.003$) and "Attitude of Poverty" (F = 7.1; $p = 0.009$).

Table 3. Mean score values of Franciscan-inspired spirituality (FraSpir) subscales.

		Live from the Faith/Search for God	Peaceful Attitude/Respectful Treatment	Commitment to the Disadvantaged and Creation	Attitude of Poverty
All	Mean	2.34	3.03	2.47	2.34
	SD	1.18	0.56	0.95	0.98
All	z-Mean [1]	0.00	0.00	0.00	0.00
	z-SD	1.00	1.00	1.00	1.00
Gender					
Women	z-Mean	−0.09	−0.19	−0.20	−0.05
	z-SD	1.04	1.06	1.02	0.96
Men	z-Mean	0.06	0.12	0.12	0.03
	z-SD	0.98	0.95	0.97	1.03
F-value		2.22	9.44	10.29	0.57
p-value		n.s.	0.002	0.001	n.s.
Religious Community					
No	z-Mean	−0.23	0.00	−0.04	−0.19
	z-SD	0.97	0.97	1.03	0.95
Yes	z-Mean	**0.88**	0.02	0.16	**0.74**
	z-SD	**0.49**	1.12	0.89	**0.84**
F-value		102.72	0.06	2.82	67.34
p-value		<0.0001	n.s.	n.s.	<0.0001
Age Groups					
<30 y	z-Mean	**−0.82**	0.07	**−0.34**	**−0.61**
	z-SD	**0.81**	0.93	1.09	**0.99**
30–40 y	z-Mean	−0.14	−0.08	−0.20	0.00
	z-SD	0.91	0.91	1.00	0.82
40–50 y	z-Mean	0.25	−0.10	0.02	0.17
	z-SD	0.89	1.11	0.92	0.76
50–60 y	z-Mean	**0.62**	−0.05	0.41	0.33
	z-SD	**0.57**	0.98	0.75	0.88
>60 y	z-Mean	**0.59**	−0.04	0.23	**0.51**
	z-SD	**0.72**	1.11	0.90	**0.87**
F-value		65.94	0.46	10.01	25.61
p-value		<0.0001	n.s.	<0.0001	<0.0001

Notes: [1] z-means and standard deviations (SD) are standardized z factor values; strong deviations from the standardized mean are highlighted (bold).

3.4. Correlations between FraSpir Scores and Other Measures of Spirituality

The FraSpir items were moderately to strongly interrelated (particularly the sub-scale "Live from the Faith/Search for God", which correlated strongly with "Attitude of Poverty"), while "Live from the Faith/Search for God" was only weakly related to "Peaceful attitude/Respectful treatment" (Table 4).

With respect to convergent validity, "Live from the Faith/Search for God" correlated strongly with Transcendence perception (DESE-6), with the frequency of Religious practices (SpREUK-P), and moderately with Gratitude/Awe (SpREUK-P) and with Prosocial-humanistic practices (SpREUK-P) (Table 4). "Commitment to Disadvantaged and the Creation" correlated strongly with "Prosocial-humanistic practices", which is plausible from a conceptual point of view, too. Similarly, "Peaceful attitude/Respectful Treatment", as a non-religious attitude and behavior, was moderately related to Prosocial-humanistic practices, but not to Religious practices. The scale "Attitude of Poverty" was weakly related to Religious practices and Transcendence perception.

With respect to discriminant validity, the FraSpir subscales correlated either marginally or only weakly with life satisfaction or well-being (Table 4). Because "Commitment to Disadvantaged and the Creation" was moderately related to life satisfaction, the underling four variables were tested independently. It was found that item f20 ("I actively engage in the social field") correlated best with life satisfaction ($r = 2.8$; $p < 0.0001$).

Table 4. Correlation analyses.

	Live from the Faith/Search for God	Peaceful Attitude /Respectful treatment	Commitment to the Disadvantaged and Creation	Attitude of Poverty
Live from the Faith/Search for God	1.000			
Peaceful attitude/Respectful treatment	0.292 **	1.000		
Commitment to Disadvantaged and Creation	0.496 **	0.439 **	1.000	
Attitude of Poverty	0.577 **	0.305 **	0.384 **	1.000
Transcendence Perception (DSES-6)	0.816 **	0.305 **	0.413 **	0.488 **
Spiritual-Religious Practices (SpEUK-P SF17)				
Religious practices	0.700 **	0.075	0.348 **	0.359 **
Prosocial-humanistic practices	0.305 **	0.414 **	0.509 **	0.235 **
Existentialistic practices	0.185 **	0.222 **	0.175 **	0.039
Gratitude/Awe	0.456 **	0.218 **	0.307 **	0.228 **
Spiritual Mind-Body practices	0.285 **	0.138 **	0.172 **	0.232 **
Life satisfaction/Well-being				
Life satisfaction (SWLS)	0.185 **	0.267 **	0.304 **	0.122
Well-being (WHO5)	0.127 **	0.227 **	0.199 **	0.061

** $p < 0.01$ (Spearman rho); moderate to strong correlations are highlighted (bold).

4. Discussion

The FraSpir questionnaire was not intended to be a specific measure for identifying good Franciscans, but to operationalize and make measurable relevant values and behaviors related to Franciscan Spirituality in a general population. Particularly the core dimensions ("Living from the Gospel" and "Searching for the Spirit of the Lord") and the transformative outcomes, specifically an "Attitude of poverty", "Awe and respect for the Creation" and "Considerate acting in the world" were in the forefront of interest.

The tested 26 items of the FraSpir questionnaire had a very good internal consistence (Cronbach's alpha = 0.95) and clustered in four main factors, which accounted for 67% of variance (Cronbach's alpha of these four factors ranged from 0.79 to 0.97).

The first factor ("Live from the Faith/Search for God") represents the intended core dimensions, and includes also three items referring to feelings of gratitude and awe in terms of the creation and of maintaining a humble relationship to entrusted resources. This connection between the underlying dimensions of Search (for God), Trust (in the Gospel) and Respect (of Creation) is interesting from a conceptual and theological point of view.

Factor 2 ("Peaceful attitude/Respectful treatment") is represented exclusively by items of the theoretically derived topic "Considerate action in the world: Lasting and peace-bearing values". It refers to the intentions to change perspectives and to understand the positions and opinions of others, and thus represents the intention to deal with others in respectful ways. Moreover, it also includes the intention to actively solve conflicts, to clarify the causes and to find ways of reconciliation. This topic refers to good interaction with others.

Factor 3 ("Commitment to Disadvantaged and Creation") consists of two items each from the theoretically derived topics "Considerate action in the world: Fraternal encounter and support of the disadvantaged" and "Awe and respect for the Creation". It combines intentions and concrete behavioral aspects of prosocial engagement for persons in need on the one hand, but also an active engagement for the "protection and maintenance of creation". This topic refers to taking responsibility for others and the environment.

Factor 4 ("Attitude of Poverty") is represented by three items of the respective theoretical topic, specifically on an intentional ability not to cling to material possessions or to strive for successful career as the main motivator in life; both as an inner act of "serenity and freedom" from material and immaterial possessions.

With respect to convergent validity, the correlations with external measures are sound and plausible. Specifically, factor 1 ("Live from the Faith/Search for God") correlate strongly with respondents' Transcendence perception and their engagement in religious practices. Factor 3 ("Commitment to Disadvantaged and Creation") correlated strongly with the frequency of Prosocial-humanistic practices, while factor 2 ("Peaceful attitude/Respectful treatment") was moderately related to Prosocial-humanistic practices. Factor 4 ("Attitude of Poverty") showed only some weak correlations with Religious practices and Transcendence perception; it is thus not per se a specific spiritual attitude, but might be the consequence of a distinct life style.

With respect to discriminant validity, the FraSpir factors were either not, or only marginally, related to respondents' life satisfaction or well-being. This would indicate that the items are not contaminated with these feelings and perceptions. However, "Commitment to the Disadvantaged and Creation" was moderately related to life satisfaction, which is not plausible at first glance. Detailed analyses revealed that the best correlating variable was f20 ("I actively engage in the social field"), which would indicate that being engaged socially might result in good feelings and contribute to life satisfaction.

When "Live from the Faith/Search for God", "Commitment to Disadvantaged and Creation" and "Attitudes of Poverty" are moderately to strongly related to religious engagement of participants, but not "Peaceful attitude/Respectful treatment" (which could be regarded as a socially desired behavior), then one would expect that these attitudes and behaviors score high particularly in Religious (nuns and monks). This is in fact true for the factor "Live from the Faith/Search for God" and for "Attitudes of Poverty", but not for "Commitment to the Disadvantaged and Creation" or "Peaceful attitude/Respectful treatment". This means that a person's "Considerate action in the world" is not exclusively a matter of being religious but relevant for all participants. A respectful and peaceful relational behavior may have been shaped by previous religious demands and imperatives, but today it seems to be more an ethical issue than a religious imperative.

Interestingly, particularly "Commitment to the Disadvantaged and Creation" scored significantly lower in women than in the male participants recruited in this sample, and also lower in nuns compared to monks. The reason for this gender-associated commitment differences is unclear. Further, "Commitment to Disadvantaged and Creation" was significantly lower in younger participants compared to older ones. For age, one may assume a shift of priorities or meaning-in-life constructs with increasing age. Data from Fegg et al. (2007) would underline age-related differences in meaning-in-life dimensions with priorities for altruism and spirituality, particularly in older participants.

It is important to note that "Peaceful attitude/Respectful treatment" scored highest for all the respondents. This indicates that it is a generally accepted and socially desired behavior. In contrast, "Commitment to the Disadvantaged and Creation" scored much lower (but nevertheless in the higher range). Both are from the theoretically defined factor "Considerate action in the world", and thus the associations are plausible from a conceptual point of view. Particularly, the slightly lower scoring Commitment scale was much more related to the Faith and Gratitude component than the factor addressing respectful treatment of others. The latter might be more an intention (which thus would score higher), while the first is more an active and difficult to convert behavior (which thus would score lower).

Conceptually it is interesting that two gratitude and awe items (i.e., "awed by the beauty of God's creation" and "great gratitude that I want to share with others") load on factor 1, which covers the core topics "Living from the Gospel" and "Searching for the Spirit of the Lord", while the other two items of the intended topic "Awe and respect for Creation" (i.e., "actively engaged for the well-being of disadvantaged people" and "actively involved in the protection and maintenance of creation") would load with two other items, addressing active engagement in the social field, make up an independent factor labelled "Commitment to the Disadvantaged and Creation". Gratitude and awe seem to be related to a longing for the Sacred in life. Detail analyses showed that both items, Awe (f14) and Gratitude (f17), were in fact related best, and strongly so ($r > 0.60$), with faith, which gives meaning to life (f4), to having a sense of the Sacred in life (f6), to listening to God's word (f7), and to the intention to search for the divine in the world (f5).

Limitations

A limitation of this study is the dominance of participants with a high school education, of men and of Catholics. For the validation process this is not of major relevance, but for future studies a more balanced sample is needed. Further, the instrument's sensitivity to change has to be analyzed in faith and value-based education programs which focus on a person's transformation of attitudes and behaviors. These analyses are currently in preparation.

5. Conclusions

The 26-item FraSpir questionnaire was found to be a reliable and valid instrument, which might be useful in training and education programs that refer to value based attitudes and behaviors derived from specific Christian contexts. Particularly the transformative aspects of Franciscan spirituality seem to be of relevance also for non-religious participants, because a considerate action in the world with a focus on a peace-bearing respectful treatment of others (especially in the context of organizations) on the one hand, and a commitment to disadvantaged participants and the environment on the other, might be shared by most people.

Acknowledgments: There was no external funding for this study. We are grateful to all who have completed the questionnaire. Thanks a lot to David Martin for his support as a native speaker.

Author Contributions: A.B. and M.W. initiated this study and designed the questionnaire; A.B. has analyzed the data; A.B., M.G., M.W. and T.D. wrote and finally approved the manuscript.

Conflicts of Interest: The authors declare no conflict of interest. As a Capuchin, T.D. belongs to a Franciscan congregation; but this has not inappropriately influenced the data analysis, representation or interpretation of reported research results.

References

Bech, Per, Lis Raabaek Olsen, Mette Kjoller, and Niels Kristian Rasmussen. 2013. Measuring well-being rather than the absence of distress symptoms: A comparison of the SF-36 mental health subscale and the WHO-Five well-being scale. *International Journal of Methods in Psychiatric Research* 12: 85–91. [CrossRef]

Benke, Christoph. 2008. Spiritualität und Leitungskultur. *Geist und Leben. Zeitschrift für Christliche Spiritualität* 3: 161–73.

Blastic, Michael. 1993. Franciscan Spirituality. In *The New Dictionary of Catholic Spirituality*. Edited by Michael Downey. Collegeville: The Liturgical Press, pp. 408–18. ISBN 978-0-814-65525-2.

Bouckaert, Luk, and Laszlo Zsolnai. 2011. *The Palgrave Handbook of Spirituality and Business*. London: Palgrave Macmillan. ISBN 978-0-230-32145-8.

Büssing, Arndt, Peter F. Matthiessen, and Thomas Ostermann. 2005. Engagement of patients in religious and spiritual practices: Confirmatory results with the SpREUK-P 1.1 questionnaire as a tool of quality of life research. *Health and Quality of Life Outcomes* 3: 53. [CrossRef] [PubMed]

Büssing, Arndt, Franz Reiser, Andreas Michalsen, and Klaus Baumann. 2012. Engagement of patients with chronic diseases in spiritual and secular forms of practice: Results with the shortened SpREUK-P SF17 Questionnaire. *Integrative Medicine: A Clinician's Journal* 11: 28–38.

Dane, Erik, and Bradley J. Brummel. 2013. Examining workplace mindfulness and its relations to job performance and turnover intention. *Human Relations* 67: 105–28. [CrossRef]

Dienberg, Thomas. 2009. Das Leben nach dem Evangelium. Modernes Management und die Regel des heiligen Franziskus. In *Wissenschaft und Weisheit 71*. Münster: Aschendorff-Verlag, pp. 196–227. ISSN 0043-678.

Dienberg, Thomas. 2013. *Economia e Spiritualità. Regola Francescana e Cultura D'impresa*. Bologna: Edizioni Dehoniane.

Dienberg, Thomas. 2016. *Leiten—Von der Kunst des Dienens. Franziskanische Akzente*. Würzburg: Echter-Verlag. ISBN 978-3429039356.

Dienberg, Thomas, and Markus Warode. 2015. Evangelical Poverty and the "Fraternal Franciscan Economy"—New aspects for a reflected business education. In *Prosperity, Poverty and the Purpose of Business. Rediscovering Integral Human Development in the Catholic Social Tradition. Handbook of the 9th International Conference on Catholic Social thought and Business Education, Manila, Philippines, February 26–28*. Manila: De La Salle-College of Saint Benilde, pp. 142–46.

Dienberg, Thomas, Gregor Fasel, and Michael Fischer. 2007. *Spiritualität & Management*. Berlin: LIT Verlag. ISBN 978-3825809089.

Diener, Ed, Robert A. Emmons, Randy J. Larsen, and Sharon Griffin. 1985. The Satisfaction with Life Scale. *Journal of Personal Assessment* 49: 71–75. [CrossRef] [PubMed]

Fegg, Martin J., Mechtild Kramer, Claudia Bausewein, and Gian D. Borasio. 2007. Meaning in life in the Federal Republic of Germany: Results of a representative survey with the Schedule for Meaning in Life Evaluation (SMiLE). *Health Qual Life Outcomes* 5: 59. [CrossRef] [PubMed]

Fernando, Mario. 2007. *Spiritual Leadership in the Entrepreneurial Business: A Multifaith Study*. Northhampton: Edward Elgar Publishing. ISBN 978-1-84720-350-2.

Gerundt, Mareike. 2012. Die Ordensregeln des Franziskus von Assisi als Schatzkammer für moderne Personalführung. In *Wissenschaft und Weisheit. Franziskanische Studien zu Theologie, Philosophie und Geschichte*. Edited by Baumeister Theofried, Thomas Dienberg and Johannes Baptist Freyer. Münster: Aschendorff Verlag, vol. 75, pp. 102–60. ISSN 0043-678X.

Kuster, Niklaus. 2016. *Franziskus. Rebell und Heiliger*. Freiburg: Herder. ISBN 978-3-451-30153-7.

Naughton, Michael, and David Specht. 2011. *Leading Wisely in Difficult Times. Three Cases of Faith and Business*. New York: Paulist Press. First published 1985. ISBN 13-978-0809147380.

Peters, Frank. 1995. *Aus Liebe zur Liebe. Der Glaubensweg des Menschen als Nachfolge Christi in der Spiritualität des hl. Franziskus von Assis*. Kevelaer: Butzon & Bercker. ISBN 978-3-7666-9947-3.

Reb, Jochen, and Ellen Choi. 2015. *Mindfulness in Organizations. Foundations, Research, and Applications*. Cambridge: Cambridge University Press.

Rohrhirsch, Ferdinand. 2013. *Christliche Führung—Anspruch und Wirklichkeit: Führen Mit Persönlichkeit und Ethik*. Wiesbaden: Springer Gabler. ISBN 978-3658021535.

Underwood, Lynn G. 2006. Ordinary Spiritual Experience: Qualitative Research, Interpretive Guidelines, and Population Distribution for the Daily Spiritual Experience Scale. *Archive for the Psychology of Religion* 28: 181–218. [CrossRef]

Underwood, Lynn G. 2011. The Daily Spiritual Experience Scale: Overview and Results. *Religions* 2: 29–50. [CrossRef]

Vogus, Timothy J., and Kathleen M. Sutcliffe. 2012. Organizational Mindfulness and Mindful Organizing: A Reconciliation and Path Forward. *Academy of Management Learning & Education* 11: 722–35.

Waaijman, Kees. 2002. *Spirituality. Forms, Foundations, Methods*. Leuven: Peeters Publisher. ISBN 978-90-429-1183-3.

Warode, Markus. 2016. Das Franziskanische Führungskonzept. In *Führen und Führen Lassen in der Praxis: Fallbeispiele*. Edited by Blessin Bernd and Alexander Wick. München: UTB GmbH, pp. 353–65. ISBN 978-3825286576.

Warode, Markus, and Mareike Gerundt. 2014. Franziskanische Werte—Inspiration und Interpretation. Was Leitungsverantwortliche vom heiligen Franz von Assisi lernen können. *Pax et Bonum, Magazin der Franziskanerbrüder vom Heiligen Kreuz* 3: 10–14.

Warode, Markus, and Mareike Gerundt. 2015. Führungskräfte profitieren von Franziskus von Assisi. *Ordenskorrespondenz, Zeitschrift für Fragen des Ordenslebens* 2: 217–24.

Zindel, Daniel. 2012. *Geistesgegenwärtig Führen. Spiritualität und Management*. Cuxhaven: Neufeld-Verlag. ISBN 978-3-937896-72-4.

© 2017 by the authors. Licensee MDPI, Basel, Switzerland. This article is an open access article distributed under the terms and conditions of the Creative Commons Attribution (CC BY) license (http://creativecommons.org/licenses/by/4.0/).

Article

Validation of the Gratitude/Awe Questionnaire and Its Association with Disposition of Gratefulness

Arndt Büssing [1,2,*], Daniela R. Recchia [1] and Klaus Baumann [2,3]

[1] Professorship Quality of Life, Spirituality and Coping, Faculty of Heath, Witten/Herdecke University, 583131 Herdecke, Germany; Daniela.RodriguesRecchia@uni-wh.de
[2] IUNCTUS—Competence Center for Christian Spirituality, Philosophical-Theological Academy, 48149 Münster, Germany; klaus.baumann@theol.uni-freiburg.de
[3] Caritas Science and Christian Social Work, Faculty of Theology, Albert-Ludwig University, Freiburg, 79085 Freiburg im Breisgau, Germany
* Correspondence: Arndt.Buessing@uni-wh.de; Tel.: +49-2330-623246

Received: 13 March 2018; Accepted: 3 April 2018; Published: 8 April 2018

Abstract: Self-transcendent feelings such as gratitude, compassion, and awe are highly relevant for human societies. So far, empirical research has focused more on the relational aspects of these feelings (concrete persons), and less on the spiritual aspects referring to the Sacred in a person's life. We intended to validate an extended version of the former three-item Gratitude/Awe scale. This extended scale was designed with a focus on the experiential aspects of being moved and touched by certain moments and places/nature, on related reactions of pausing with daily activities, and on the subsequent feelings of awe and gratitude. Enrolling 183 test persons (67% women; 59% with a Christian confession) in a cross-sectional study, we can confirm that the seven-item Gratitude/Awe scale (GrAw-7) has good psychometric properties (Cronbach's alpha = 0.82) and moderate correlation (r = 0.42) with grateful disposition (GQ-6 questionnaire). Structured equation modeling (SEM) confirmed that both constructs, although moderately related, are different. While Gratitude/Awe was best predicted by the frequency of meditation practice, a grateful disposition was best predicted by the frequency of praying and by general life satisfaction. The GrAw-7 scale is not contaminated with specific religious topics or quality of life issues, and can be easily implemented in larger studies.

Keywords: awe; gratitude; spirituality; validation; questionnaire

1. Introduction

Self-transcendent feelings such as gratitude, compassion, and awe (Stellar et al. 2017) may have an influence on the social behavior of individuals and social groups. In their review, Stellar et al. (2017) argued that "self-transcendent emotions help individuals form enduring commitments to kin, nonkin, and social collectives". This perspective emphasizes that they are highly relevant for human societies, and empirical research so far focuses much more on the relational aspects than on the 'self-transcendent' (spiritual) aspects referring to the Sacred in a person's life.

There is currently a debate in philosophical literature as to what exactly constitutes an emotion, and whether or not feelings and emotions are different (Whiting 2011). The terms feelings and emotions are often used interchangeably, but—from a psychological point of view—they are different (Pettinelli 2014) and they arise in different areas of the brain. Feelings can be seen as the mind's interpretations of bodily perceptions and emotions (which arise in the amygdala). Thus, it is difficult to differentiate whether gratitude and awe are emotional perceptions or feelings.

Emmons and Crumpler stated that gratitude is regarded as an "emotional state and an attitude toward life that is a source of human strength in enhancing one's personal and relational wellbeing"

(Emmons and Crumpler 2000) and is thus an essential dimension of a person's subjective quality of life (Hill and Allemand 2011). Gratefulness as a trait or disposition can be the result of positive experiences (in the past and in the present) and is thus associated with pleasant feelings. Moreover, it can enable the perception of positive experiences in the future and may thus be related to confidence and hope. In this sense, it is a basic human attitude that one's existence (one's coming, being, and remaining in existence) is not a result of one's achievements, but rather "thanks to" others or one other. Such an attitude of gratitude strengthens the conviction that hope, with regard to an uncertain future and trust for the present, is not illusory (Häußling 1988). Gratitude may also arise as the result of the kindness a person receives from a donor and thus requires an interpersonal context (Algoe and Haidt 2009), and is in this case a positive feeling. McCullough et al. (2002) found that a 'grateful disposition' (as measured with the 6-item form of the Gratitude Questionnaire [GQ-6]) is strongly related to life satisfaction, happiness, hope, and optimism. With respect to indicators of spirituality, there were only some weak correlations between a gratitude disposition with spiritual transcendence, self-transcendence, personal relationship with God, etc. (McCullough et al. 2002). Among personality traits, self-rated agreeableness was related best.

In contrast to gratitude, feelings of awe may occur in specific situations of wondering astonishment and admiration when facing breathtaking landscapes, experiencing mystical experiences, etc. (Keltner and Haidt 2003; Pearsall 2007). Because they are already the mind's 'interpretations' of these perceptions, one could argue that awe is not an emotion but a feeling. Nevertheless, Shiota et al. (2007) defined awe as an "emotional response to perceptually vast stimuli that overwhelm current mental structures, yet facilitate attempts at accommodation". Fagley (2012) argued that awe is an aspect of appreciation which refers to "feeling a deep emotional, spiritual, or transcendental connection to something". It is more than, and different from, a trembling feeling and fascinated astonishment (in the sense of Otto's "*mysterium tremendum et fascinosum*"). Rather, it implies being attracted to, and shying away from the sublime; both loving trust and humble dread (Wisse 1988). There is not necessarily a specific interpersonal context, but "situational appraisals that facilitate gratitude", as Algoe and Stanton (2012) suggested. These perceptions make persons stop in their activities, and they may assume that time 'stands still' in these moments. Feelings of awe can be matter of a spiritual experience and/or the subjective perception of the transcendent, and may therefore result in feelings of gratitude towards life in general, distinct persons, and towards the numinous. In fact, awe is a perception which is strongly associated with feelings of gratitude ($r = 0.59$), but only weakly associated with the general experience of beauty in life ($r = 0.30$), whilein contrast gratitude was strongly related to the experience of beauty in life ($r = 0.51$) (Büssing et al. 2014). This indicates that these feelings are related, but their underlying processes and directions may be distinct.

These perceptions of awe and gratitude can be measured in a standardized way with the three-item subscale on "Gratitude/Awe" (Cronbach's alpha = 0.77) of the SpREUK-P questionnaire (which addresses the frequency of spiritual/religious, existential, and prosocial-humanistic practices) (Büssing et al. 2005, 2012). In persons with multiple sclerosis and psychiatric disorders, this scale was found to be best related to engagement in religious practices ($r = 0.48$) and prosocial-humanistic practices ($r = 0.41$) (Büssing et al. 2014). It was concluded that "Gratitude/Awe could be regarded as a life orientation towards noticing and appreciating the positive in life—despite the symptoms of disease" (Büssing et al. 2014). In Catholic priests, the 3-item scale "Gratitude/Awe" was best related to the perception of the Sacred in their life (Daily Spiritual Experience Scale, DSES-6: $r = 0.43$), with prosocial-humanistic practices ($r = 0.41$), and with life satisfaction (Satisfaction with Life Scale, SWLS: $r = 0.36$), while in non-ordained Catholic pastoral workers the correlations between "Gratitude/Awe" and transcendence perception ($r = 0.36$), prosocial-humanistic practices ($r = 0.39$), and life satisfaction ($r = 0.24$) were less pronounced (Büssing et al. 2017). The association with the perception of the Sacred in life is of particular relevance as it indicates that these feelings of awe and gratitude may arise because a person has a distinct state of mindful awareness or a disposition of openness towards the Sacred in the daily life concerns rather than being a matter of wellbeing or satisfaction with different aspects of life.

To clarify this, we decided to extend the conceptual framework of SpREUK-P's "Gratitude/Awe" subscale and develop a discrete scale with a clear focus on the experiential aspects of being moved and touched by certain moments and places/nature, on related reactions of pausing with daily activities, and on the subsequent feelings of awe and gratitude. The intention was to operationalize the reality when individuals give room for the experience of such spiritual moments of pausing for a moment, moments of reflection, and encounters with the Sacred wherever it is. These perceptions operationalized in the extended "Gratitude/Awe" questionnaire are thus suggested to represent states of mindful awareness rather than the direct reactions of gratefulness in response to the kindness of concrete persons. Therefore, these feelings are assumed not to be strongly related with wellbeing or general satisfaction with life. When these feelings are in fact influenced by a person's spirituality, then one would expect a positive association with indicators of spirituality such as praying or meditation. In contrast, health behaviors such as smoking, alcohol consumption, or sporting activities are suggested to be unrelated to perceptions of gratitude and awe. Further, these feelings of gratitude and awe are assumed to be related to a 'grateful disposition', but nevertheless as conceptually distinct.

Therefore, we intended (1) to validate an extended version of the "Gratitude/Awe" scale with respect to its factorial structure and internal consistency; (2) to analyze correlations with 'grateful disposition'; and (3) to analyze correlations with wellbeing and life satisfaction on the one hand, and praying/meditation and health behaviors on the other.

2. Material and Methods

2.1. Enrolled Persons

For the process of validation, we enrolled a heterogeneous sample of participants among students, pastoral professionals, Caritas workers, medical professionals, etc. acquired via snowball sampling in research and private networks. The resulting sample should be regarded as a convenience sample.

The first page of the questionnaire holds information about the purpose of the study (which did not ask for names, initials, or location), and an assertion that confidentiality and anonymity is guaranteed. By filling in the German language questionnaire and sending it back to the study team, participants agreed that their data would be treated anonymously.

2.2. Measures

2.2.1. Gratitude and Awe (GrAw-7)

The generic SpREUK-P (P—practices module) questionnaire contains the three-item subscale on "Gratitude/Awe" (Cronbach's alpha = 0.77) addressing feelings of gratitude, reverence/awe, and experiencing the beauty in life (Büssing et al. 2005, 2012). These items were supplemented by four additional items, i.e., "I stop and then think of so many things for which I'm really grateful", "I stop and am captivated by the beauty of nature", "I pause and stay spellbound at the moment", and "In certain places, I become very quiet and devout". Thus, gratitude and awe operationalized in this way are matter of an 'emotional' reaction towards an immediate and 'captive' experience, and not a reaction in response to a person's benevolence, and further not necessarily a matter of a 'grateful disposition'. All items were scored on a four-point scale (0—never; 1—seldom; 2—often; 3—regularly). The resulting scores were sum scores ranging from 0 to 21.

2.2.2. Dispositional Gratitude (GQ-6)

To measure gratitude in daily life, we used the Gratitude Questionnaire-Six Item Form (GQ-6) (McCullough et al. 2002). This instrument addresses an affective trait in terms of a 'disposition toward gratitude' rather than a mood state or an emotion. This disposition is defined "as a generalized tendency to recognize and respond with grateful emotion to the roles of other people's benevolence in the positive experiences and outcomes that one obtains" (McCullough et al. 2002, p. 112). Representative items are "I have so much in life for which to be thankful" or "I am grateful to a wide variety of people". Internal consistency of the GQ-6 is good with Cronbach's alpha = 0.82 (McCullough et al. 2002). The six items are scored on a seven-point scale from strong disagreement (1) to strong agreement (7); two items had a reverse coding.

2.2.3. Life Satisfaction (BMLSS-10)

Life satisfaction was measured using the Brief Multidimensional Life Satisfaction Scale (BMLSS; alpha = 0.87) (Büssing et al. 2009). The items address intrinsic (myself, life in general), social (friendships, family life), external (work situation, where I live), and prospective (financial situation, future prospects) dimensions of life satisfaction, as well as satisfaction with the individual's abilities to manage daily life concerns and satisfaction with their health. Each of these 10 items was introduced by the sentence 'I would describe my level of satisfaction as ... ', and they were scored on a seven-point scale ranging from dissatisfaction (0) to satisfaction (6). The mean scores were referred to a 100% level.

2.2.4. Wellbeing (WHO-5)

The WHO-Five Wellbeing Index (WHO-5) measures wellbeing instead of the absence of distress (Bech et al. 2003). Representative items are "I have felt cheerful and in good spirits" or "My daily life has been filled with things that interest me". Respondents assess how often they had the respective feelings within the last two weeks, ranging from at never (0) to all of the time (5). Here we report the sum scores.

2.2.5. Health Behaviors and Indicators of Spirituality

We measured the frequency of health behaviors such as smoking (never, 1–10 per day, 10–20 per day, >20 per day), alcohol consumption (never, 1× per month, 2–3× per month, 1–2× per week, several times per week), sporting activities (never, 1× per month, 2–3× per month, 1–2× per week, several times per week), and indicators of spirituality such as meditation (never, at least once per month, at least once per week, several times per week) and praying (never, at least once per month, at least once per week, several times per week) using single items.

2.3. Statistical Analyses

Descriptive statistics, internal consistency (Cronbach's coefficient α), and factor analyses (principal component analysis using Varimax rotation with Kaiser's normalization) as well as analyses of variance (ANOVA) and first order correlations analyses were computed with SPSS 23.0.

To confirm the structure found by exploratory factor analysis, we performed a structured equation model (SEM) using the Lavaan packages of software R. This methodology involves many techniques such as multiple regression models, analysis of variance, confirmatory factor analysis, correlation analysis, etc. With SEM one could determine the meaningful relationships between variables, since the parameter estimates deliver the best scenario for the covariance matrix; the better the model goodness of fit, the better the matrix is. The goodness of fit statistics used to evaluate the model included the root mean square error (RMSEA), which should be ≤ 0.05; the root mean square residual (RMSR), which should be ≤ 0.06; the comparative fit index (CFI), which should be ≥ 0.95; and the Tucker-Lewis index (TLI), which should be ≥ 0.95.

Given the exploratory character of this study, the significance level of ANOVA and correlation analyses were set at $p < 0.01$. With respect to classifying the strength of the observed correlations, we regarded $r > 0.5$ as a strong correlation, an r between 0.3 and 0.5 as a moderate correlation, an r between 0.2 and 0.3 as a weak correlation, and $r < 0.2$ as negligible or no correlation.

3. Results

3.1. Participants

As shown in Table 1, among the 183 enrolled persons, women were predominant (67%). Also, most participants had a high school education (77%). Christian confessions were predominant (59%); 17% identified with other religious denominations, and 24% stated that they had no religious affiliation.

Table 1. Description of the sample (N = 183).

	Scores
Age (years) (Mean ± SD)	51.8 ± 15.5
Gender (%)	
Women	67.5
Men	33.0
Educational level (%)	
Secondary school (Haupt-/Realschule)	21.5
High school (Gymnasium)	77.3
other	1.1
Religious denomination (%)	
Catholic	39.8
Protestant	19.3
Other	16.6
None	24.3

3.2. Reliability and Factor Analysis of the Gratitude/Awe Questionnaire

Explorative Factor analysis of the seven items revealed a Kaiser-Mayer-Olkin value of 0.83, which, as a measure for the degree of common variance, indicating the item pool's suitability for statistical investigation by means of principal component factor analysis. Exploratory factor analysis pointed to one single main factor (eigenvalue 3.4) which accounted for 48% of variance (Table 2). Internal consistency of the seven-item scale (GrAw-7) was good (Cronbach's alpha = 0.82).

Table 2. Reliability and factorial structure.

Items	No Response (n)	Mean	SD	Difficulty Index (2.04/3 = 0.68)	Item to Scale Correlation	Alpha If Item Deleted (alpha = 0.824)	Factor Loading
ED7: I stop and then think of so many things for which I am really grateful	5	1.84	0.79	0.61	0.693	0.778	0.802
ED5: I pause and stay spellbound at the moment	3	1.73	0.73	0.58	0.661	0.784	0.783
ED1 I have a feeling of great gratitude	0	2.17	0.66	0.72	0.585	0.798	0.725
ED2: I have a feeling of wondering awe	2	1.85	0.74	0.62	0.586	0.798	0.707
ED6: In certain places, I become very quiet and devout	3	2.02	0.76	0.67	0.530	0.808	0.661
ED4: I stop and am captivated by the beauty of nature	1	2.26	0.71	0.75	0.486	0.814	0.594
ED3: I have learned to experience and value beauty	2	2.44	0.56	0.81	0.433	0.820	0.545

Main component analysis (Variamax rotation with Kaiser normalization).

The difficulty index (mean value 2.04/3) of these items was 0.68; all items were in the acceptable range from 0.2 to 0.8 (Table 2). This means that there were no ceiling or bottom effects in the responses. While all responded to item ED1, a maximum of 3% of participants did not respond to item ED7 (Table 2).

The statement that one has "learned to experience and value beauty" scored highest, followed by "I stop and am captivated by the beauty of nature"; the lowest scores were found for staying "spellbound at the moment" (Table 2).

3.3. Structured Equation Model

To validate the instrument's structure found by exploratory factor analysis, we performed structured equation modeling (SEM). This method is a comprehensive methodology which involves techniques such as multiple regression models, analyses of variance, confirmatory factor analysis, correlation analysis, etc.

SEM was adjusted as a validation of the previous factor structure with the GrAw-7 items. This model presented good fit statistics and a Cronbach's alpha of 0.82 (Figure 1).

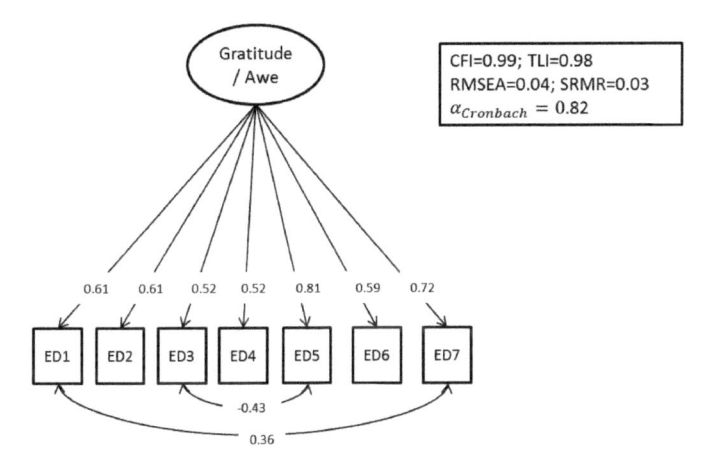

Figure 1. SEM for Gratitude/Awe (GrAw-7).

We also tested a model that includes the both the GrAw-7 and GQ-6 constructs (Figure 2). Here we found some weak correlations between the single items. Although all four fit measures were very good, the total Cronbach's alpha was at the minimum accepted value (=0.59). This would underline that both instruments should be seen as independent measures.

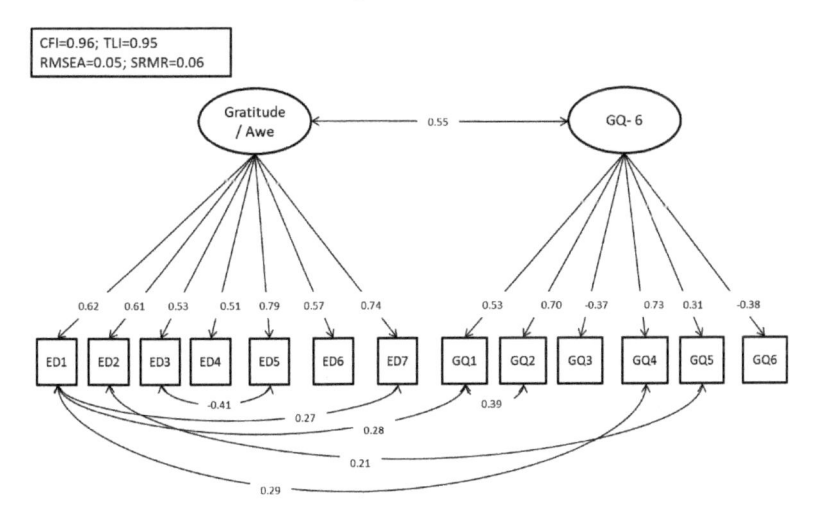

Figure 2. SEM for Gratitude/Awe (GrAw-7) and gratitude disposition (GQ-6). Values on arrows between items (in boxes) and factors (in circles) represent loadings, while items between boxes and circles, respectively, represent correlations.

3.4. Expression of Gratitude/Awe Scores in the Sample

The mean GrAw-7 sum score was 14.1 ± 3.5 (range: 5 to 21; 25% quartile 12.0; 75% quartile 16). The scores showed nearly normal distribution (Skewness 0.09 with standard error 0.18, Kurtosis −0.24 with standard error 0.36); 7% of persons reached the maximal score of 21.

There were no significant gender-related differences for GrAw-7 (F = 1.95) and GQ-6 (F = 0.76) scores in the sample (data not shown). However, age showed a weak positive association with GrAw-7 but not with GQ-6 (Table 3). Further, the scores of both scales did not differ significantly between Christians and nonreligious persons (GrAw-7: F = 1.66, p = 0.178; GQ-6: F = 2.23; p = 0.086).

Table 3. Correlations between gratitude, wellbeing, and health behavior.

	Gratitude/Awe (GrAw-7 Sum)	Gratitude (GQ-6 Sum)
Gratitude/Awe (GrAw-7)	1.000	0.418 **
Gratitude/Awe (SpREUK-P)	0.833 **	0.478 **
Life satisfaction (BMLSS-10)	0.148	0.332 **
Wellbeing (WHO-5)	0.293 **	0.247 **
Frequency smoking	−0.083	−0.079
Frequency alcohol consumption	−0.152	−0.103
Frequency sporting activities	0.147	0.141
Frequency meditation	0.407 **	0.332 **
Frequency praying	0.341 **	0.442 **
Age	0.205 **	−0.038

** p < 0.01 (Spearman rho); moderate to strong correlations are highlighted (bold).

3.5. Correlations between Gratitude/Awe and External Indicators

The GrAw-7 was strongly related with SpREUK-P´s 3-item Gratitude/Awe scale (r = 0.83), and moderately correlated with the GQ-6 scale (r = 0.42). In contrast to the GQ-6, which addresses a person's grateful disposition and is moderately related to life satisfaction (BMLSS) and weakly related to wellbeing (WHO-5), the Gratitude/Awe scale is not significantly related to life satisfaction and only weakly associated with wellbeing as well (Table 3).

Neither smoking nor alcohol consumption nor sporting activities were found to be significantly related to both scales, while frequency of meditation and praying were moderately related to the GrAw-7 and the GQ-6 (Table 3).

3.6. Predictors of Gratitude/Awe and Dispositional Gratefulness

To analyze predictors of Gratitude/Awe (GrAw-7) and dispositional gratefulness (GQ-6), we performed regression analyses and included only those variables which were found to have some significant influences (i.e., life satisfaction, wellbeing, meditation, and praying).

As shown in Table 4, Gratitude/Awe was predicted best by meditation, with a further effect of praying, while wellbeing had a small correlation, and life satisfaction was not at all associated with Gratitude/Awe. The included variables explain 26% of variance.

In contrast, a grateful disposition was explained best by praying, followed by life satisfaction and meditation, while wellbeing had no significant effect. The included variables explain 29% of variance.

Table 4. Regression models.

	R^2	Beta	T	P
Dependent variable: GrAw-7	0.26			
(constant)			7.237	<0.0001
Life satisfaction (BMLSS-10)		0.010	0.127	0.899
Wellbeing (WHO-5)		0.174	2.206	0.029
Meditation		0.323	4.614	<0.0001
Praying		0.201	2.815	0.005
Dependent variable: GQ-6	0.29			
(constant)			14.619	<0.0001
Life satisfaction (BMLSS-10)		0.278	3.724	<0.0001
Wellbeing (WHO-5)		−0.032	−0.417	0.678
Meditation		0.184	2.688	0.008
Praying		0.345	4.923	<0.0001

4. Discussion

This study confirms that the extended version of the Gratitude/Awe scale (GrAw-7) has good psychometric properties (Cronbach's alpha = 0.82) and sound correlation with external measures, particularly with grateful disposition. Although both measures, Gratitude/Awe (GrAw-7) and grateful disposition (GQ-6), were moderately related, they are conceptually different, as confirmed by SEM. Also, their pattern of predictors is different. While Gratitude/Awe was best predicted by meditation practice, a grateful disposition was best predicted by praying, general life satisfaction, and meditation practice as well. Although wellbeing was weakly correlated with both variables, it was not found to be a significant predictor. The extended GrAw-7 scale focused on feelings of awe, which may be accompanied by subsequent feelings of gratefulness. These feelings of gratitude are suggested to be states of a mindful awareness rather than reciprocal gratefulness in response to the kindness of concrete persons.

Wood et al. (2008) suggested that the conceptualization of gratitude (in terms of gratitude to others) should be extended with the inclusion of having an awareness of the present moment, feelings of wondering awe, compassion, and other variables, resulting in the more general concept of 'appreciation'. This is of importance from a conceptual point of view when it is the intention to clarify the complex interplay of influencing variables resulting in 'gratitude'. However, our intention was to develop a short and circumscribed measure of wondering awe in distinct moments which may result in feelings of gratitude for life, persons, nature, etc., rather gratitude towards a concrete person providing benefits. In this sense, we understand it as a state, not as a trait. It thus does not cover the whole range of meanings implied by the term 'gratitude', but rather a specific dimension or experience which is not specifically directed to some circumscribed event or human other. It seems to be closely related to the biblical Hebrew term of "berakah", by which the Jewish faithful express that they are struck or touched here and now by God, or by God's word, act, silence, absence (Häußling 1988, p. 207). "Gratitude" in this sense permeates the religious emotivity of biblical belief. It is nourished by the amazement about God or what became an experience of God (Schimanowski et al. 1997), by numinous awe in front of God or what are considered moments of theophany (Neumann 2006). In this understanding, gratitude and awe are intrinsically connected in front of the Sacred, which can be experienced as the depth dimension (P. Tillich) of all reality (Wisse 1988). Referring to John 1,1-3, which states that God's word originated "all things", one may assume that this living "word" is still speaking through all things and beings to those who stop and listen. Experiencing this ubiquitous presence, gratitude becomes a pervasive, non-directed gratefulness.

There are two relevant other instruments which hold specific subscales addressing awe: the "Appreciation Scale" by Adler and Fagley (2005) and the "Dispositional Positive Emotions Scale" (DPES) by Shiota et al. (2006). The 57-item "Appreciation Scale" is conceptually close to our instrument, as it also includes subscales addressing awe, gratitude, and present moment. Fagley (2012) found that the subscales on gratitude (r = 0.70), present moment (r = 0.48), and awe (r = 0.38) were moderately to strongly associated with grateful disposition (GQ-6). In our study, we found that Gratitude/Awe (GrAw-7) was moderately related to grateful disposition (GQ-6: r = 0.42), but that Gratitude/Awe was not significantly related to general and multidimensional life satisfaction, while a grateful disposition exhibited a moderate relation. Nevertheless, in our study both scales were only weakly related to wellbeing. Also, SEM confirmed that these concepts are distinct, despite some weak correlations.

The six-item awe subscale on "Dispositional Positive Emotions Scale" (DPES) addresses feelings of awe, feelings of wonder, seeing beauty all around, having many opportunities to see the beauty of nature, looking for patterns in objects, and seeking out experiences that challenge the individual's understanding of the world (Shiota et al. 2006). With the DPES's awe subscale, Piff et al. (2015) found awe to be associated with increased generosity and prosociality. The authors suggested that awe may "trigger an almost metaphorical sense of smallness of the self" which may be perceived when one is confronted with something "larger", i.e., a starry sky, landscapes, etc. In contrast to the DPES awe subscale, which addresses feelings of admiration of nature's beauty, the GrAw-7 scale refers more to attentional and open experiences ('mindful awareness') evoked by distinct places, nature, or specific moments, and these feelings of 'wonder' that may make a person stop and pause for a moment.

Limitations

We do not assume that the study population is representative of a 'normal' population; the snowball sampling strategy obviously resulted in a dominance of persons with a high school education. For the validation process this is not of major relevance, but for future studies a more balanced sample would be required.

5. Conclusions

The seven-item Gratitude/Awe (GrAw-7) scale was confirmed as a short, reliable, and valid measure with good psychometric properties (Cronbach's alpha = 0.82) and a sound correlation with grateful disposition. The scale is not contaminated with specific religious topics or quality of life issues. Because of its brevity, it can be easily implemented in larger studies to measure different aspects of spirituality also in secular societies. This attitude can probably also be found in a-religious persons and could be seen as a measure of 'mindful awareness' in terms of nonreligious (secular) spirituality.

Acknowledgments: There was no external funding for this study. We are grateful to all who have filled the questionnaire.

Author Contributions: AB has designed the questionnaire, has analyzed the data and written the manuscript. DRR has performed the SEM analyzed and contributed to write the manuscript. KB contributed in writing the manuscript. All authors approved the final version of the manuscript.

Conflicts of Interest: The authors declare no conflict of interest.

References

Adler, Mitchel G., and Nancy S. Fagley. 2005. Appreciation: Individual Differences in Finding Value and Meaning as a Unique Predictor of Subjective Well-Being. *Journal of Personality* 73: 79–114. [CrossRef] [PubMed]

Algoe, Sara B., and Jonathan Haidt. 2009. Witnessing excellence in action: The "other-praising" emotions of elevation, gratitude, and admiration. *Journal of Positive Psychology* 4: 105–27. [CrossRef] [PubMed]

Algoe, Sara B., and Annette L. Stanton. 2012. Gratitude When It Is Needed Most: Social Functions of Gratitude in Women with Metastatic Breast Cancer. *Emotion* 12: 163–68. [CrossRef] [PubMed]

Bech, Per, Lis Raabaek Olsen, Mette Kjoller, and Niels Kristian Rasmussen. 2003. Measuring well-being rather than the absence of distress symptoms: A comparison of the SF-36 mental health subscale and the WHO-Five well-being scale. *International Journal of Methods in Psychiatric Research* 12: 85–91. [CrossRef] [PubMed]

Büssing, Arndt, Peter F. Matthiessen, and Thomas Ostermann. 2005. Engagement of patients in religious and spiritual practices: Confirmatory results with the SpREUK-P 1.1 questionnaire as a tool of quality of life research. *Health and Quality of Life Outcomes* 3: 53. [CrossRef] [PubMed]

Büssing, Arndt, Julia Fischer, Almut Haller, Thomas Ostermann, and Peter F. Matthiessen. 2009. Validation of the Brief Multidimensional Life Satisfaction Scale in patients with chronic diseases. *European Journal of Medical Research* 14: 171–77. [CrossRef] [PubMed]

Büssing, Arndt, Franz Reiser, Andreas Michalsen, and Klaus Baumann. 2012. Engagement of patients with chronic diseases in spiritual and secular forms of practice: Results with the shortened SpREUK-P SF17 Questionnaire. *Integrative Medicine: A Clinician's Journal* 11: 28–38.

Büssing, Arndt, Ane-Gritli Wirth, Franz Reiser, Anne Zahn, Knut Humbroich, Kathrin Gerbershagen, Sebastian Schimrigk, Michael Haupts, Niels Christian Hvidt, and Klaus Baumann. 2014. Experience of gratitude, awe and beauty in life among patients with multiple sclerosis and psychiatric disorders. *Health and Quality of Life Outcomes* 12: 63. [CrossRef] [PubMed]

Büssing, Arndt, Eckhard Frick, Christoph Jacobs, and Klaus Baumann. 2017. Self-Attributed Importance of Spiritual Practices in Catholic Pastoral Workers and their Association with Life Satisfaction. *Pastoral Psychology* 66: 295–310. [CrossRef]

Emmons, Robert A., and Cheryl A. Crumpler. 2000. Gratitude as a human strength: Appraising the evidence. *Journal of Social and Clinical Psychology* 19: 56–69. [CrossRef]

Fagley, Nancy S. 2012. Appreciation uniquely predicts life satisfaction above demographics, the Big 5 personality factors, and gratitude. *Personality and Individual Differences* 53: 59–63. [CrossRef]

Häußling, Angelus. 1988. Dank/Dankbarkeit. In *Praktisches Lexikon der Spiritualität*. Edited by Christian Schütz. Freiburg: Herder, pp. 205–8.

Hill, Patrick L., and Mathias Allemand. 2011. Gratitude, Forgiveness, and Well-Being in Adulthood: Tests of Moderation and Incremental Prediction. *The Journal of Positive Psychology* 5: 397–407. [CrossRef]

Keltner, Dacher, and Jonathan Haidt. 2003. Approaching awe, a moral, spiritual, and aesthetic emotion. *Cognition and Emotion* 17: 297–314. [CrossRef]

McCullough, Michael E., Robert A. Emmons, and Jo-Ann Tsang. 2002. The grateful disposition: A conceptual and empirical topography. *Journal of Personality and Social Psychology* 82: 112–27. [CrossRef] [PubMed]

Neumann, Klaus. 2006. Ehrfurcht. In *Handbuch Theologischer Grundbegriffe zum Alten und Neuen Testament*. Edited by Angelika Berlejung and Christian Frevel. Darmstadt: Wissenschaftliche Buchgesellschaft, pp. 140–41.

Pearsall, Paul. 2007. *Awe: The Delights and Dangers of Our Eleventh Emotion*. Deerfield Beach: Health Communications Inc., ISBN 978-0-7573-0585-6.

Pettinelli, Mark. 2014. The Psychology of Emotions, Feelings and Thoughts. OpenStax-CNX Module: m14358. Available online: https://cnx.org/contents/vsCCnNdd@130/The-Psychology-Of-Emotions-Fee (accessed on 20 February 2018).

Piff, Paul K., Pia Dietze, Matthew Feinberg, Daniel M. Stancato, and Dacher Keltner. 2015. Sublime sociality: How awe promotes prosocial behavior through the small self. *Journal of Personality and Social Psychology* 108: 883–99. [CrossRef] [PubMed]

Schimanowski, Gottfried, Helmut Schultz, Hans Helmut Eßer, Karl Heinz Bartels, and Jürgen Fangmeier. 1997. Dank/Lob. In *Theologisches Begriffslexikon zum Neuen Testament*. Edited by Lothar Coenen and Klaus Haacker. Wuppertal: R. Brockhaus Verlag, pp. 239–51.

Shiota, Michelle N., Dacher Keltner, and Oliver P. John. 2006. Positive emotion dispositions differentially associated with Big Five personality and attachment style. *Journal of Positive Psychology* 1: 61–71. [CrossRef]

Shiota, Michelle N., Dacher Keltner, and Amanda Mossman. 2007. The nature of awe: Elicitors, appraisals, and effects on self-concept. *Cognition and Emotion* 21: 944–63. [CrossRef]

Stellar, Jennifer E., Amie M. Gordon, Paul K. Piff, Daniel Cordaro, Craig L. Anderson, Yang Bai, Laura A. Maruskin, and Dacher Keltner. 2017. Self-Transcendent Emotions and Their Social Functions: Compassion, Gratitude, and Awe Bind Us to Others through Prosociality. *Emotion Review* 9: 200–7. [CrossRef]

Whiting, Demian. 2011. The Feeling Theory of Emotion and the Object-Directed Emotions. *European Journal of Philosophy* 19: 281–303. [CrossRef]

Wisse, Stephan. 1988. Ehrfurcht. In *Praktisches Lexikon der Spiritualität*. Edited by Christian Schütz. Freiburg: Herder, pp. 267–69.

Wood, Alex M., John Maltby, Neil Stewart, and Stephen Joseph. 2008. Conceptualizing gratitude and appreciation as a unitary personality trait. *Personality and Individual Differences* 44: 619–30. [CrossRef]

© 2018 by the authors. Licensee MDPI, Basel, Switzerland. This article is an open access article distributed under the terms and conditions of the Creative Commons Attribution (CC BY) license (http://creativecommons.org/licenses/by/4.0/).

![religions logo] *religions* [MDPI]

Review

Measuring Symptoms of Moral Injury in Veterans and Active Duty Military with PTSD

Harold G. Koenig, M.D.

1. Departments of Psychiatry and Medicine, Duke University Medical Center, Durham, NC 27710, USA; Harold.Koenig@duke.edu
2. Department of Medicine, King Abdulaziz University, Jeddah, Saudi Arabia

Received: 13 December 2017; Accepted: 14 March 2018; Published: 17 March 2018

Abstract: The Moral Injury Symptom Scale-Military Version (MISS-M) is a 45-item measure of moral injury (MI) symptoms designed to use in Veterans and Active Duty Military with PTSD. This paper reviews the psychometric properties of the MISS-M identified in a previous report, discusses the rationale for the development of the scale, and explores its possible clinical and research applications. The MISS-M consists of 10 theoretically grounded subscales that assess the psychological and spiritual/religious symptoms of MI: guilt, shame, betrayal, moral concerns, loss of meaning/purpose, difficulty forgiving, loss of trust, self-condemnation, spiritual/religious struggles, and loss of religious faith/hope. The scale has high internal reliability, high test-retest reliability, and a factor structure that can be replicated. The MISS-M correlates strongly with PTSD severity, depressive symptoms, and anxiety symptoms, indicating convergent validity, and is relatively weakly correlated with social, spiritual, and physical health constructs, suggesting discriminant validity. The MISS-M is the first multidimensional scale that measures both the psychological and spiritual/religious symptoms of MI and is a reliable and valid measure for assessing symptom severity in clinical practice and in conducting research that examines the efficacy of treatments for MI in Veterans and Active Duty Military personnel.

Keywords: moral injury; internal conflict; post-traumatic stress disorder; veterans; active duty military

1. Introduction

Veterans and individuals currently serving in the military often have traumatic experiences while participating in combat operations that place them at risk for post-traumatic stress disorder (PTSD). This is evident from research showing that PTSD is one of the most common mental disorders suffered by Veterans seen in the U.S. Veterans Administration Health System (Hoge and Warner 2014; Fulton et al. 2015), and this is also true for Active Duty Military personnel (Lane et al. 2012). PTSD in military settings, especially when it becomes chronic, is notoriously difficult to treat, with only about 20–30% of persons with this disorder achieving anything close to a full remission of symptoms (Steenkamp et al. 2015; Steinert et al. 2015). PTSD is also often accompanied by extensive psychiatric comorbidity including depression, anxiety, substance abuse, and relationship problems (Ginzburg et al. 2010; Pietrzak et al. 2011). PTSD carries with it a significant risk of suicide in both Active Duty Military (Ramsawh et al. 2014) and Veterans in particular (McKinney et al. 2017; Elbogen et al. 2017).

Moral injury (MI) is a separate syndrome that often accompanies military-related PTSD (Figure 1), and if not addressed, may interfere with treatment response leading to poor outcomes in those with PTSD. The diagnosis of PTSD according to the Diagnostic and Statistical Manual of Mental Disorders, 5th edition (DSM-5) (American Psychiatric Association 2013) is based on four major fear/trauma-based symptom clusters that cause functional disability: hyperarousal/irritability, avoidance, emotional negativity/numbing, and intrusive nightmares/flashbacks. PTSD is established as a diagnosis based on (1) extensive research identifying the psychological and physiological changes that characterize this condition and cause functional disability; (2) review by experts of this evidence and agreement by consensus that PTSD warrants an independent separate diagnosis (with specific diagnostic criteria as indicated in the DSM-5 and ICD-10); and (3) research showing that this disorder responds (although often only partially) to a range of psychological and pharmacological treatments designed specifically to target it.

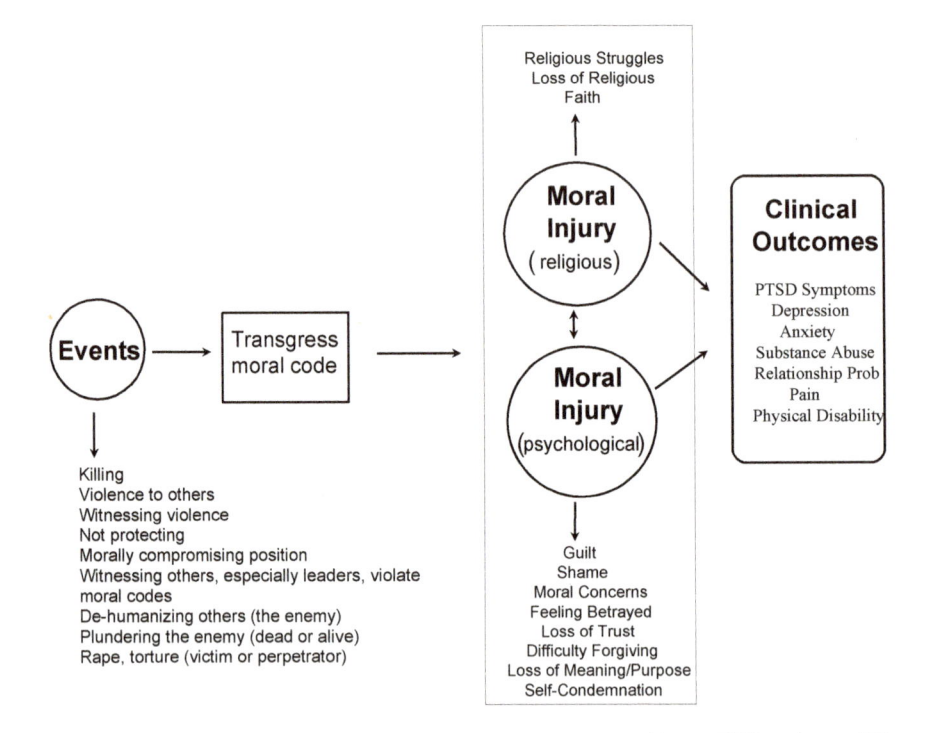

Figure 1. Illustration of the relationship between traumatic events, moral injury, PTSD and comorbid psychological, social, behavioral, and physical outcomes (adapted from Koenig et al. (2017), used with permission).

In contrast, the symptoms of MI according to trauma experts, result from "perpetrating, failing to prevent, bearing witness to, or learning about acts that transgress deeply held moral beliefs" (Litz et al. 2009, p. 695); "a betrayal of what's right, by someone who holds legitimate authority, in a high-stakes situation" (Shay 1994; Shay 2014, p. 183); or "a deep sense of transgression including feelings of shame, grief, meaninglessness, and remorse from having violated core moral beliefs" (Brock and Lettini 2012, p. xiv). Thus, MI involves a compilation of symptoms that often accompanies PTSD, but has not yet been subject to the kind of research and consensus among experts in the field that is necessary to call it a separate disorder or diagnosis deserving inclusion in the DSM or ICD diagnostic nomenclature. MI, then, is a "syndrome" in need of further study in order to distinguish it from PTSD and other psychiatric conditions, to examine its effects on psychological, social, and occupational functioning, and to determine treatment response. In this respect, then, MI is not yet an established and billable diagnosis like PTSD.

The moral dilemmas, ethical questions, and guilt caused by actions and experiences during wartime have been the subject of academic discussion since the early 1980's (Friedman 1981), although researchers did not begin to define and truly study this construct until nearly 30 years later when MI was highlighted in a seminal article published by Brett Litz and colleagues (Litz et al. 2009).

2. Measurement

During the ensuing years, two measures of MI were developed and psychometrically validated. The first one, a 9-item scale, was developed by military psychiatrist William P. Nash and colleagues (Nash et al. 2013) in active duty U.S. marines and was called the Moral Injury Events Scale (MIES). The second measure of MI, a 19-item scale, was developed by psychologist Joseph M. Currier and colleagues (Currier et al. 2015b) and called the Moral Injury Questionnaire-Military Version (MIQ-M). Both of these scales measured the actual occurrence of traumatic experiences (e.g., "I acted in ways that violated my own moral code or values" or "I was involved in the death of an innocent in the war") and the severity of current symptoms caused by those events (i.e., "I am troubled by having acted in ways that violated my own morals or values"). Because of this combination of events and symptoms, such measures while useful for diagnostic purposes, are less helpful for following changes in response to treatment. Effective interventions are likely to change the symptoms of MI, but will not change the fact that the traumatic event occurred. Furthermore, neither of the scales above assess religious or spiritual struggles or changes in religious faith, factors known to adversely affect those with PTSD. As a result, we developed a new multi-dimensional measure of MI symptoms, the Moral Injury Symptom Scale-Military Version (MISS-M) that takes both of these concerns into account (Koenig et al. 2018a).

Objectives

The purpose of this paper is to (1) discuss the development of the MISS-M, (2) review the psychometric properties of the scale reported previously (Koenig et al. 2018a), (3) explore the clinical and research applications of this scale, and (4) provide a copy of the instrument in the Appendix A of this article.

3. Development of the Moral Injury Symptom Scale-Military Version (MISS-M)

In reviewing the literature on MI, our interdisciplinary team of mental health and religious professionals came up with 10 theoretically-grounded dimensions that characterize this syndrome based on the writings and research of trauma experts (Litz et al. 2009; Shay 1994; Shay 2014; Brock and Lettini 2012; Nash et al. 2013; Currier et al. 2015b; Drescher et al. 2011). We identified eight psychological dimensions of MI (guilt, shame, betrayal by others, moral concerns, loss of meaning/purpose, difficulty forgiving, loss of trust, and self-condemnation) and two spiritual/religious dimensions (spiritual/religious struggles and loss of religious faith/hope). We then populated these dimensions with 54 items that were derived from existing scales and from additional items developed by our team based on the strong face validity of item content. The rationale for including each of the 10 dimensions and the items included in them are reviewed below.

3.1. Guilt

Veterans are frequently plagued by feelings of guilt over actions perpetrated during combat or over failing to protect one's comrades or innocent civilians. It doesn't matter whether such actions result from simply doing one's duty as a soldier, being ordered to do so by those in command, or losing control and doing things out of rage or vengeance. These actions inevitably leave moral scars—and one of those scars is guilt. Feelings of guilt have long been associated with PTSD resulting from combat experiences (Hendin and Haas 1991; Lee et al. 2001), have been specifically labeled as a form of MI (Litz et al. 2009), and have been assessed in both existing MI measures (Nash et al. 2013; Currier et al. 2015b) prior to the development of the MISS-M. This dimension, then, was considered essential for inclusion in the MISS-M. Five questions were initially used to assess guilt, two from the MIQ-M (Currier et al. 2015b) and three items from the Combat Guilt Scale (CGS)—a 15-item multi-dimensional measure of guilt developed in combat Veterans (Henning and Frueh 1997). These questions focus on feeling guilty over failing to save a life, surviving when others didn't, and feeling bad over enjoying the hurting or killing others.

3.2. Shame

While often used interchangeably, shame and guilt are two quite different constructs. In the psychoanalytic literature, shame and guilt are both functions of the superego (Lewis 1971). Shame involves greater self-consciousness and self-imaging; i.e., it is more about personal identity. Shame is a feeling about the self that arises from the consciousness of having done something dishonorable or improper (it is about *ourselves*), whereas guilt is the remorse that one feels for having committed a crime or wrongful act affecting others (it is about *others*). Depending on the particular personality of the individual, one may experience either shame or guilt or both as a result of actions during wartime—for example, shame over having deserted one's comrades during the heat of battle to save oneself, or guilt over having killed innocents during a fit of rage. Shame is a form of injury to a person's self-identity. As with guilt, shame is extensively referred to in both the psychological and theological literature on MI (Litz et al. 2009; Drescher et al. 2011; Worthington and Langberg 2012). Therefore, two questions were used to assess shame in the MISS-M, one from the CGS and one from the work of Andrews and colleagues (Andrews et al. 2009) studying shame in Veterans. Both focus on measuring feelings of shame towards oneself for what was done or not done during combat operations.

3.3. Betrayal

In the classic text by military psychiatrist Jonathan Shay, *Achilles in Vietnam*, he emphasized the central role that feelings of betrayal play in the construct of MI (Shay 1994). Achilles is betrayed by his commander, Agamemnon, leading to rage towards his commander and feelings of care for only a small group of companion fighters. As noted earlier, Shay defined moral injury as "a betrayal of what's right, by someone who holds legitimate authority, in a high-stakes situation" (Shay 2014). These feelings of betrayal during wartime usually involve betrayal by others in authority (e.g., those who gave the order to kill), but also may involve a betrayal by oneself or one's moral standards, or after returning back to civilian life, betrayal by a community that one fought for (as was often experienced by Vietnam Veterans returning home). The dimension of betrayal in the MISS-M was assessed by the 3-item betrayal subscale of Nash and colleagues' MIES (Nash et al. 2013) that focuses on feeling betrayed by leaders, fellow service members, and those outside the military.

3.4. Violation of Moral Values

At the heart of MI is the violation of moral values. Such violation involves perceived transgressions of deeply held moral or ethical beliefs that are perpetrated by either oneself or others. Besides assessing betrayal (as noted above), the MIES also measures the violation of moral values. This dimension of MI was measured by Nash and colleagues using six questions, three assessing commission and three assessing omission. These questions were arrived at by a literature review, the generation of a pool of items by trauma experts, a selection of items by consensus, and ultimately a factor analysis to identify those items that best measured this dimension (Nash et al. 2013). These questions focused on witnessing, perpetrating, and distress related to such transgressions; three of the six involve events and three involve feelings. Therefore, given its focus on symptoms, the MISS-M included the three questions from the MIES that assess feelings in order to measure concerns related to (1) witnessing others' immoral acts, (2) perpetrating immoral acts themselves, and (3) failing to act when feeling morally obliged to do so.

3.5. Loss of Meaning

Loss of meaning and related existential concerns were one of the key aspects of MI identified by Drescher and colleagues during interviews with 23 seasoned mental health and religious professionals who had years of experience providing care to Active Duty Military personnel and Veterans (Drescher et al. 2011, p. 11). Loss of meaning was also the central focus of a report by Fontana and Rosenheck (Fontana and Rosenheck 2005) in a study of 1,168 Vietnam era Veterans struggling with PTSD symptoms. These investigators found that Veterans who had difficulty coping with combat trauma often experienced a loss of meaning in their lives, and frequently sought help from mental health professionals and clergy (in particular) when dealing with such issues. This prompted investigators to recommend that greater consideration be given to addressing existential issues in the treatment of PTSD. This dimension of MI, then, seemed essential to include. Consequently, loss of meaning was assessed in the MISS-M by six questions, five taken from a subscale of the 10-item Meaning in Life Questionnaire (Steger et al. 2006) that measures the extent to which a person feels his/her life has meaning. In addition, one item was taken from the MIQ-M (Currier et al. 2015b) that asks how exposure to death during war has changed the person.

3.6. Difficulty Forgiving

Nearly 15 years ago, Witvliet and colleagues (Witvliet et al. 2004) reported that difficulty forgiving was strongly linked to PTSD symptoms in Vietnam Veterans. Litz and colleagues (Litz et al. 2009) emphasized the difficulty that many military personnel have in forgiving themselves for what some believe are unforgiveable things they did during the heat of battle. Litz and colleagues go on to emphasize that both self-forgiveness and forgiveness of others are key to overcoming the moral injuries that involve guilt, shame, and self-condemnation for actions perpetrated during war, and letting go of anger towards those in authority whom they believe betrayed them. Likewise, Worthington and Langberg (Worthington and Langberg 2012) stressed the devastating effects of harboring resentments and unforgiveness towards self and others, describing secular and religiously tailored programs to help such individuals forgive themselves and others. The need to forgive God has also been described in studies of morally injured Veterans (Currier et al. 2014; Johnson 2014).

For the MISS-M, ten questions were initially chosen to assess difficulties forgiving others, self, and God as a result of wartime experiences. Six of these items came from the Heartland Forgiveness Scale (HFS) (Thompson et al. 2005). The HFS has been used in Veteran populations and the overall score is inversely correlated with PTSD symptoms, a relationship that is mediated by anger and negative affect (Karairmak and Guloglu 2014). In addition, four questions were developed by our research team to assess feeling forgiven by God, forgiving God, forgiving self, and the need to seek forgiveness in the first place.

3.7. Loss of Trust

Drescher and colleagues emphasized that the loss of trust resulting from feelings of betrayal often haunts those with MI and interferes with their ability to maintain family relationships and friendship networks (Drescher et al. 2011). Likewise, in a qualitative study of Vietnam and non-Vietnam Veterans, Flipse Vargas and colleagues (Flipse Vargas et al. 2013) found that loss of trust in the government and people in general was a recurrent theme identified as a problem these Veterans struggled with as a result of wartime experiences. Similarly, Kopacz and colleagues (Kopacz et al. 2016) emphasized the lack of trust that many morally injured veterans experienced as a result of what was done to them during wartime, and may use as an excuse to continue hurting others after returning home. Thus, in order to capture this dimension, six questions were taken from the General Trust Scale (Yamagishi and Yamagishi 1994) to assess the extent to which the person believes that other people are honest and trustworthy, basically good and kind, respond similarly if trusted, and also, to what extent the person feels he or she can be trusted by others.

3.8. Self-Condemnation

Self-condemnation and low sense of self-esteem have been repeatedly emphasized by trauma experts as a key dimension of MI (Litz et al. 2009; Worthington and Langberg 2012; Maguen and Litz 2012; Litz et al. 2017). Unresolved guilt, shame, and difficulty forgiving oneself drive this negative moral emotion that often leads to depression and in some cases even suicide (Worthington and Langberg 2012; Kopacz et al. 2016; Bryan et al. 2016). In order to capture this dimension, ten items from the Rosenberg Self-Esteem Scale (SES) (Rosenberg 1965) were used to assess self-condemnation and self-deprecation. The SES is a standard measure of global self-worth that measures both positive and negative feelings about the self.

3.9. Spiritual/Religious Struggles

There is growing evidence that spiritual/religious struggles are strongly correlated with PTSD symptoms in military populations (particularly Veterans) and appear to impede recovery and adversely affect physical health. Spiritual struggles related to trauma during wartime include feeling punished by God for actions done (violence/killing) or not done (protection of innocents); questioning God's power and control for not having protected oneself or one's comrades from assault, injury, or death; feeling deserted by one's faith community after returning home from military service; and internal struggles over whether God is loving, caring or concerned about people, if allowing horrific events to take place. The presence of religious struggles of this type were found to predict a slower recovery from PTSD among 532 Veterans admitted to a 60–90 day residential PTSD treatment program (Currier et al. 2015a). Based on these findings and other research documenting strong positive associations between religious struggles and PTSD symptoms (Currier et al. 2015b; Witvliet et al. 2004; Currier et al. 2014), seven items from the negative religious coping subscale of the Brief RCOPE (Pargament et al. 1998) were used in the MISS-M to assess spiritual/religious struggles. This 7-item subscale has been shown to predict greater mortality in Veterans (Pargament et al. 2001) and has been associated with higher pro-inflammatory cytokine levels (interleukin-6) in medically ill populations (Ai et al. 2009).

3.10. Loss of Religious Faith/Hope

Research shows that loss of religious faith is present in 30% of Veterans and is associated with prolonged use of VA mental health services among those with PTSD (Fontana and Rosenheck 2004). In that study of 1385 Veterans being treated for PTSD symptoms (95% serving in Vietnam), participants were asked "How much was/is religion a source of strength and comfort to you?" This question was asked for two periods—at the time they entered the military and currently. The difference in religious comfort between the two periods was calculated, with 29% reporting that religion had become less of a source of comfort. Loss of religious faith in that study was found to be a stronger predictor of number of outpatient mental health treatment sessions than was social support (number of persons they felt close to), previous experiences of violence encountered, or ability to hold down a full-time job. There is also an extensive literature showing a strong association between religious faith and the spiritual concept of hope, suggesting a close link between these two separate but related constructs (Clarke 2003; Koenig et al. 2012, p. 302). Thus, a dimension of MI that assessed loss of religious faith and hope seemed appropriate, and its inclusion in the MISS-M is supported by work of theologians and mental health professionals in the trauma literature (Litz et al. 2009; Drescher et al. 2011; Worthington and Langberg 2012). Two items make up this subscale of the MISS-M, one that was adapted from the study of Vietnam Veterans above that asks about loss of religious faith as a result of wartime experiences (Fontana and Rosenheck 2004). The second question, developed by study authors based on its strong face validity, asks about loss of hope in the future.

Thus, the MISS-M is composed of 10 subscales that comprehensively assess the construct of MI, are theoretically grounded on how trauma experts define MI, and are made up of items from both established scales and from items crafted by our study team to best capture the psychological and spiritual/religious conflicts that are the core of MI.

4. Psychometric Properties of the MISS-M

The 54 items above were administered to 427 Veterans and Active Duty Military with PTSD symptoms resulting from serving in a combat zone (Koenig et al. 2018a). Participants were recruited from the Veterans Administration Medical Center (VAMC) in Durham, North Carolina; the Charlie Norwood VAMC in Augusta, Georgia; the Veterans Administration Greater Los Angeles Healthcare System; the Michael E. DeBakey VAMC in Houston, Texas; the South Texas Veterans Health Care System; and Liberty University in Lynchburg, Virginia. Over 86% of participants scored 33 or higher on the PTSD Checklist-DSM-5 Military Version (PCL-5) (Weathers et al. 2013) indicating relatively severe PTSD symptoms (unpublished data). All questionnaires were filled out in-person except at the Liberty University site (Active Duty Military only) where the questionnaire was completed online. Each of the 54 items on the MISS-M was rated on a scale from 1 to 10 in terms of agreement or disagreement, reverse scoring items as necessary so that higher scores indicate greater MI.

4.1. Factor Analysis

The overall sample was randomly split into two groups. In the first group (n = 214), exploratory factor analysis (EFA) was performed on the original 54 items. In the second group (n = 213), those items that met the cutoff criterion (factor loadings $\geq$ 0.45 on EFA) were subject to confirmatory factor analysis (CFA). As noted above, each one of the 10 dimensions of MI chosen has a strong theoretical rationale that justifies its inclusion in the MISS-M. Therefore, to ensure that items with strong face validity for a particular dimension ended up on the subscale assessing that dimension, EFA and CFA were conducted at the subscale level.

EFA revealed a single factor for each dimension/subscale of the MISS-M except for the difficulty forgiving and self-condemnation subscales, for which two factors were identified (based entirely on whether a question was stated in a positive or a negative direction). Of the 54 items assessed, 9 failed to meet the factor loading cut-off criterion, resulting in the final 45-item MISS-M. These 45 items were then subjected to CFA again at the subscale level in the second sample. The resulting factor loadings were 0.41–0.76 for the 4-item guilt subscale, 0.78 for the 2-item shame subscale, 0.56–0.91 for the 3-item betrayal subscale, 0.66–0.89 for the 3-item moral concerns subscale, 0.73–0.90 for the 4-item loss of meaning subscale, 0.42–0.78 for factor 1 and 0.60–0.77 for factor 2 of the 7-item difficulty forgiving subscale, 0.73–0.93 for the 4-item loss of trust subscale, 0.65–0.81 for factor 1 and 0.74–0.84 for factor 2 of the 10-item self-condemnation subscale, 0.52–0.87 for the 6-item spiritual/religious struggles subscale, and 0.58 for the 2-item loss of religious faith/hope subscale. With the exception of the loss of religious faith/hope subscale, eigenvalues for all factors making up the subscales were equal to or exceeded 1.0 (range 1.55 to 10.94) (based on the Kaiser-Guttman rule) (Kaiser 1991). Thus, overall, CFA replicated the factor structure of subscales making up the 45-item MISS-M.

4.2. Reliability

In the overall sample (n = 427), the internal consistency (Cronbach's alpha) of the 45-item MISS-M was acceptable (α = 0.92, 95% CI = 0.91–0.93), as was the reliability of most of the individual subscales (α range 0.56–0.91). Internal consistency α's of 0.70 or higher are considered adequate (Cronbach 1951). The test-retest reliability of the overall 45-item MISS-M was assessed in 64 Veterans after an average of 10 days. The intra-class correlation coefficient (ICC) demonstrated high test-retest reliability for the overall MISS-M (ICC = 0.91, 95% CI = 0.85–0.95) and ICC's of 0.78 to 0.90 for individual subscales. ICC's of 0.70 or higher are considered adequate (Shrout and Fleiss 1979).

4.3. Validity

In addition to the factor analytic validity demonstrated by the CFA above, construct validity of the 45-item MISS-M was indicated by high correlations between the 10 subscales and the total MISS-M score (Pearson r's ranging from 0.45 to 0.78). Discriminant validity was suggested by relatively weak correlations between the total MISS-M score and other social, religious and physical health constructs such as involvement in community activities (r = −0.33), importance of religion (r = −0.23) or spirituality (−0.18), severity of physical pain (r = 0.21), and impairment of physical functioning (r = 0.27). Finally, convergent validity was indirectly demonstrated by relatively strong correlations with other psychiatric symptoms that one might hypothesize would accompany MI, such as PTSD symptoms (assessed by the 20-item PCL-5) (r = 0.56), depressive symptoms (assessed by the 14-item Hospital Anxiety and Depression Scale; HADS (Zigmond and Snaith 1983) (r = 0.62), and anxiety symptoms (also assessed by the HADS) (r = 0.59). Convergent validity could not be tested directly because the MISS-M is the first multi-dimensional measure of MI symptom severity (severity of symptoms alone, not including MI events) (published online on December 1, 2017), and there were no other pure MI symptom severity measures to compare it with at the time the study was conducted (September 17, 2015, through August 1, 2017).

5. Prevalence of Moral Injury Symptoms

Scores on individual items of the MISS-M provided an indication of the prevalence of significant MI symptoms in this sample of Veterans and Active Duty Military. The average score on the 45-item MISS-M was 223.6 (SD = 61.6, with a range of 86 to 403). Nearly 90% of participants indicated a 9 or 10 on a 1 to 10 severity scale for at least one MI symptom and half (50%) gave this rating for more than five of the 45 MI symptoms. Dimensions with the highest scores (indicating greater MI) were the loss of trust and moral concerns subscales, with items on these subscales averaging 5.8 on the 1 to 10 response range.

Thus, MI as assessed by the MISS-M was widespread and strongly correlated with severity of PTSD and comorbid depression and anxiety among these Veterans and Active Duty Military, most of whom had relatively severe PTSD symptoms from serving in combat.

6. Limitations

The MISS-M was designed specifically to cover the dimensions of MI that experts in the field have indicated are part of the MI construct. As such, we conducted the factor analysis at the subscale level to ensure that each of these dimensions were included in the final scale. Not all psychometricians may agree with this approach, but our team felt that being comprehensive in our assessment of this construct took first priority. Another concern about the MISS-M is that the loss of religious faith/hope dimension had a relatively low alpha (0.56), which is below the threshold of 0.70. Nevertheless, given the strong face validity of these items, we felt that this subscale should be included—particularly given the evidence that this dimension might interfere with treatment response in PTSD (Fontana and Rosenheck 2004). Finally, given the small number of Active Duty Military personnel in our validation study (n = 54), further research is needed to replicate the psychometric properties of the MISS-M in this population, as well as in other populations of Veterans from different regions of the U.S. and from other countries.

7. Clinical and Research Applications of the MISS-M

As a symptom measure of MI severity, the MISS-M has at least two potential applications: (1) in clinical settings to screen for MI symptoms and (2) in research settings to examine relationships between MI, mental health, and physical health outcomes, and to assess change over time in response to interventions that target MI symptoms.

7.1. Clinical Applications

The MISS-M may be used to screen Veterans and Active Duty Military with PTSD symptoms in order to identify those who are also suffering from MI (which may be preventing the successful treatment of PTSD). While no cutoff on the MISS-M has yet been determined that indicates significant MI that requires intervention (see below), scores on the individual subscales may give some indication of where problems exist that require clinical attention from mental health professionals and/or trained clergy (chaplains or pastoral counselors). Interventions have been developed (or are being developed) to treat the psychological symptoms of MI (Litz et al. 2017; Steenkamp et al. 2011; Maguen and Burkman 2013; Paul et al. 2014) and to treat *both* the psychological and the spiritual/religious symptoms (Harris et al. 2011; Koenig et al. 2017; Pearce et al. 2018). Many of these interventions, with some exceptions (Litz et al. 2017; Koenig et al. 2017; Pearce et al. 2018), were not designed specifically to target MI but rather to treat specific MI symptoms like guilt or shame, or PTSD symptoms more generally (given that until the MISS-M was developed there was no multi-dimensional measure that only assessed MI symptom severity). Nevertheless, be aware that there are interventions out there that may help to relieve MI whether that occurs in Veterans, Active Duty Military personnel, or even those not in the military who are disabled with PTSD (from rape or others forms of trauma).

7.2. Research Applications

Researchers may find the MISS-M useful for both observational and experimental studies in current or former military personnel. The MISS-M may be used in studies that examine the relationship between MI symptoms and mental health outcomes such as PTSD, depression, anxiety, substance use, relationship problems, occupational difficulties, chronic pain, and impairments in physical functioning. These may be either cross-sectional studies that establish an association or longitudinal studies that examine the effects of MI on these outcomes over time. The MISS-M may also be used in randomized clinical trials that seek to examine the effects of interventions on relieving the symptoms of MI. As suggested above, research examining the effects of interventions on MI has been lacking because a pure MI symptom measure that could be assessed over time in clinical trials until now has not been available. The existence of the MISS-M helps to fill that gap and may now be used to assess the effects of treatments directed specifically at reducing MI symptoms. To assist in this regard, future research is needed to identify a cutoff point on the MISS-M that indicates clinically significant symptoms with functional impairment (or is sufficient to block successful treatment of PTSD) that require intervention. In addition, research is needed to determine if scores on the MISS-M are sensitive to change over time (and to identify a clinically significant change score). Such studies are forthcoming, along with the development of a 10-item short form of the MISS-M (the MISS-M-SF), which as with the long version described in this article, may be used as either a screening tool for clinical applications or as an outcome measure or predictor of health outcomes in research studies (Koenig et al. 2018b).

8. Conclusions

Moral injury is widespread among Veterans and Active Duty Military personnel with PTSD symptoms resulting from experiences in combat. Unless addressed, MI may interfere with the successful treatment (both psychological and pharmacological) of PTSD. Until now, there was no pure MI symptom scale that could be used as an outcome measure to test the efficacy of various interventions directed specifically at reducing MI. The Moral Injury Symptom Scale-Military Version is a reliable and valid measure for assessing symptoms of MI. The MISS-M may be used to screen Veterans and Active Duty Military for MI, and may be utilized in clinical trials to determine the efficacy of treatments for this common and widespread syndrome that often accompanies PTSD.

Conflicts of Interest: The author declares no conflict of interest.

Appendix A

The Moral Injury Symptom Scale—Military Version (long-form)

Introduction: *The following statements/questions may be difficult, but they are common experiences of combat Veterans or Active Duty Military returning from battle.* They concern your experiences while in a combat or war zone and how you are feeling now. Just do the best you can, and try to answer every question. Circle a *single* number between 1 and 10 for each ("strongly disagree" to "strongly agree"):

Guilt
1. I feel guilt for surviving when others didn't.
2. I feel guilt over failing to save the life of someone in war.
3. Some of the things I did during the war out of anger or frustration continue to bother me.
4. It bothers me sometimes that I enjoyed hurting/killing people during the war.

Shame
5. If people knew more about the things I did during the war they would think less of me.
6. I feel ashamed about what I did or did not do during this time.

Betrayal
7. I feel betrayed by leaders who I once trusted.
8. I feel betrayed by fellow service members who I once trusted.
9. I feel betrayed by others outside the US military who I once trusted.

Violation of Moral Values
10. I am troubled by having witnessed others' immoral acts.
11. I am troubled by having acted in ways that violated my own morals or values.
12. I am troubled because I violated my morals by failing to do something that I felt I should've done.

Loss of Meaning
Introduction: Circle a *single* number between 1 and 10 that describes how true each statement is for you ("absolutely untrue" to "absolutely true"):

13. I understand my life's meaning.
14. My life has a clear sense of purpose.
15. I have a good sense of what makes my life meaningful.
16. I have discovered a satisfying life purpose.

Difficulty Forgiving
Introduction: Circle a *single* number between 1 and 10 that describes how true or false each statement is for you ("almost always false of me" to "almost always true of me"):

17. Although I feel bad at first when I mess up, over time I can give myself some slack.
18. I hold grudges against myself for negative things I've done.
19. It is really hard for me to accept myself once I've messed up.
20. I don't stop criticizing myself for negative things I've felt, thought, said, or done.
21. I believe that God has forgiven me for what I did during combat.
22. I have forgiven God for what happened to me or others during combat.
23. I have forgiven myself for what happened to me or others during combat.

Loss of Trust
Introduction: Circle a *single* number between 1 and 10 that describes how much you agree or disagree with each statement ("strongly disagree" to "strongly agree"):

24. Most people are basically honest.
25. Most people are trustworthy.
26. Most people are basically good and kind.

27. Most people are trustful of others.

Self-Condemnation

Introduction: Circle a *single* number between 1 and 10 for each statement ("strongly disagree" to "strongly agree"):

28. On the whole, I am satisfied with myself.
29. At times I think I am no good at all.
30. I feel that I have a number of good qualities.
31. I am able to do things as well as most other people.
32. I feel I do not have much to be proud of.
33. I certainly feel useless at times.
34. I feel that I'm a person of worth, at least on an equal plane with others.
35. I wish I could have more respect for myself.
36. All in all, I am inclined to feel that I am a failure.
37. I take a positive attitude toward myself.

Introduction: Below are feelings that combat Veterans often have due to combat experiences. How much have you? Circle a *single* number between 1 and 10 for each statement ("a great deal" or "very true" to "not at all" or "very untrue"):

Spiritual/Religious Struggles

38. I wonder whether God had abandoned me.
39. I felt punished by God for my lack of devotion.
40. I wondered what I did for God to punish me.
41. I questioned God's love for me.
42. I questioned the power of God.
43. I wondered whether my church had abandoned me.

Loss of Religious Faith/Hope

44. *Compared to when you first went into the military* has your religious faith since then ... ("weakened a lot," "weakened a little," "strengthened a little," "strengthened a lot")
45. How hopeful are you about the future? ("not at all" to "very hopeful")

Scoring: First, reverse score items 13–16, 17, 21–28, 30–31, 34, 37, and 44–45, and then sum all items together (or those of individual subscales if subscale scores are desired). Possible score range is 45 to 450, with higher scores indicating more severe moral injury. For a fully formatted version of the 45-item MISS-M (and the 10-item MISS-M-SF), contact the author: Harold.Koenig@duke.edu.

References

Ai, Amy L., E. Mitchell Seymour, Terrence N. Tice, Ziad Kronfol, and Steven F. Bolling. 2009. Spiritual struggle related to plasma interleukin-6 prior to cardiac surgery. *Psychology of Religion and Spirituality* 1: 112–28. [CrossRef]

American Psychiatric Association. 2013. *Diagnostic and Statistical Manual of Mental Disorders (DSM-5®)*. Arlington: American Psychiatric Association Publishing.

Andrews, Bernice, Chris R. Brewin, Lorna Stewart, Rosanna Philpott, and Jennie Hejdenberg. 2009. Comparison of immediate-onset and delayed-onset posttraumatic stress disorder in military veterans. *Journal of Abnormal Psychology* 118: 767–77. [CrossRef] [PubMed]

Brock, Rita Nakashima, and Gabriella Lettini. 2012. *Soul Repair: Recovering from Moral Injury after War*. Boston: Beacon Press.

Bryan, Craig J., AnnaBelle O. Bryan, Michael D. Anestis, Joye C. Anestis, Bradley A. Green, Neysa Etienne, Chad E. Morrow, and Bobbie Ray-Sannerud. 2016. Measuring moral injury: Psychometric properties of the Moral Injury Events Scale in two military samples. *Assessment* 23: 557–70. [CrossRef] [PubMed]

Clarke, David. 2003. Faith and hope. *Australasian Psychiatry* 11: 164–68. [CrossRef]

Cronbach, Lee J. 1951. Coefficient alpha and the internal structure of tests. *Psychometrika* 16: 297–334. [CrossRef]

Currier, Joseph M., Kent D. Drescher, and J. Irene Harris. 2014. Spiritual functioning among veterans seeking residential treatment for PTSD: A matched control group study. *Spirituality in Clinical Practice* 1: 3–15. [CrossRef]

Currier, Joseph M., Jason M. Holland, and Kent D. Drescher. 2015a. Spirituality factors in the prediction of outcomes of PTSD treatment for U.S. military veterans. *Journal of Traumatic Stress* 28: 57–64. [CrossRef] [PubMed]

Currier, Joseph M., Jason M. Holland, Kent Drescher, and David Foy. 2015b. Initial psychometric evaluation of the moral injury questionnaire—Military Version. *Clinical Psychology & Psychotherapy* 22: 54–63.

Drescher, Kent D., David W. Foy, Caroline Kelly, Anna Leshner, Kerrie Schutz, and Brett Litz. 2011. An exploration of the viability and usefulness of the construct of moral injury in war veterans. *Traumatology* 17: 8–13. [CrossRef]

Elbogen, Eric B., H. Ryan Wagner, Nathan A. Kimbrel, Mira Brancu, Jennifer Naylor, Robert Graziano, and Eric Crawford. 2017. Risk factors for concurrent suicidal ideation and violent impulses in military veterans. *Psychological Assessment*. [CrossRef] [PubMed]

Flipse Vargas, Alison, Thomas Hanson, Douglas Kraus, Kent Drescher, and David Foy. 2013. Moral injury themes in combat veterans' narrative responses from the National Vietnam Veterans' Readjustment Study. *Traumatology* 19: 243–50. [CrossRef]

Fontana, Alan, and Robert Rosenheck. 2004. Trauma, change in strength of religious faith, and mental health service use among veterans treated for PTSD. *Journal of Nervous and Mental Disease* 192: 579–84. [CrossRef] [PubMed]

Fontana, Alan, and Robert Rosenheck. 2005. The role of loss of meaning in the pursuit of treatment for posttraumatic stress disorder. *Journal of Traumatic Stress* 18: 133–36. [CrossRef] [PubMed]

Friedman, Matthew J. 1981. Post-Vietnam syndrome: Recognition and management. *Psychosomatics* 22: 931–43. [CrossRef]

Fulton, Jessica J., Patrick S. Calhoun, H. Ryan Wagner, Amie R. Schry, Lauren P. Hair, Nicole Feeling, Eric Elbogen, and Jean C. Beckham. 2015. The prevalence of posttraumatic stress disorder in Operation Enduring Freedom/Operation Iraqi Freedom (OEF/OIF) Veterans: A meta-analysis. *Journal of Anxiety Disorders* 31: 98–107. [CrossRef] [PubMed]

Ginzburg, Karni, Tsachi Ein-Dor, and Zahava Solomon. 2010. Comorbidity of posttraumatic stress disorder, anxiety and depression: A 20-year longitudinal study of war veterans. *Journal of Affective Disorders* 123: 249–57. [CrossRef] [PubMed]

Harris, J. Irene, Christopher R. Erbes, Brian E. Engdahl, Paul Thuras, Nichole Murray-Swank, Dixie Grace, and Henry Ogden. 2011. The effectiveness of a trauma focused spiritually integrated intervention for veterans exposed to trauma. *Journal of Clinical Psychology* 67: 425–38. [CrossRef] [PubMed]

Hendin, Herbert, and Ann Pollinger Haas. 1991. Suicide and guilt as manifestations of PTSD in Vietnam combat veterans. *American Journal of Psychiatry* 148: 586–91. [PubMed]

Henning, Kris R., and B. Christopher Frueh. 1997. Combat guilt and its relationship to PTSD symptoms. *Journal of Clinical Psychology* 53: 801–8. [CrossRef]

Hoge, Charles W., and Christopher H. Warner. 2014. Estimating PTSD prevalence in US veterans: Considering combat exposure, PTSD checklist cutpoints, and DSM-5. *Journal of Clinical Psychiatry* 75: 1439–41. [CrossRef] [PubMed]

Johnson, W. Brad. 2014. The morally-injured veteran: Some ethical considerations. *Spirituality in Clinical Practice* 1: 16–17. [CrossRef]

Kaiser, Henry F. 1991. Coefficient alpha for a principal component and the Kaiser-Guttman Rule. *Psychological Reports* 68: 855–58. [CrossRef]

Karairmak, Ozlem, and Berna Guloglu. 2014. Forgiveness and PTSD among veterans: The mediating role of anger and negative affect. *Psychiatry Research* 219: 536–42. [CrossRef] [PubMed]

Koenig, Harold George, Dana King, and Verna B. Carson. 2012. *Handbook of Religion and Health*, 2nd ed. New York: Oxford University Press.

Koenig, Harold G., Nathan A. Boucher, Rev John P. Oliver, Nagy Youssef, Scott R. Mooney, Joseph M. Currier, and Michelle Pearce. 2017. Rationale for spiritually oriented cognitive processing therapy for moral injury in active duty military and veterans with posttraumatic stress disorder. *Journal of Nervous and Mental Disease* 205: 147–53. [PubMed]

Koenig, Harold G., Donna Ames, Nagy A. Youssef, John P. Oliver, Fred Volk, Ellen J. Teng, Kerry Haynes, Zachary D. Erickson, Irina Arnold, Keisha O'Garo, and Michelle Pearce. 2018a. The Moral Injury Symptom Scale—Military Version. *Journal of Religion and Health* 57: 249–265. [CrossRef] [PubMed]

Koenig, Harold G., Donna Ames, Nagy A. Youssef, John P. Oliver, Fred Volk, Ellen J. Teng, Kerry Haynes, Zachary D. Erickson, Irina Arnold, Keisha O'Garo, and Michelle Pearce. 2018b. Screening for moral injury: The Moral Injury Symptom Scale – Military Version Short Form. *Military Medicine*. in press.

Kopacz, Marek S., April L. Connery, Todd M. Bishop, Craig J. Bryan, Kent D. Drescher, Joseph M. Currier, and Wilfred R. Pigeon. 2016. Moral injury: A new challenge for complementary and alternative medicine. *Complementary Therapies in Medicine* 24: 29–33. [CrossRef] [PubMed]

Lane, Marian E., Laurel L. Hourani, Robert M. Bray, and Jason Williams. 2012. Prevalence of perceived stress and mental health indicators among reserve-component and active-duty military personnel. *American Journal of Public Health* 102: 1213–20. [CrossRef] [PubMed]

Lee, Deborah A., Peter Scragg, and Stuart Turner. 2001. The role of shame and guilt in traumatic events: A clinical model of shame-based and guilt-based PTSD. *Psychology and Psychotherapy: Theory, Research and Practice* 74: 451–66. [CrossRef]

Lewis, Helen B. 1971. Shame and guilt in neurosis. *Psychoanalytic Review* 58: 419–38. [PubMed]

Litz, Brett T., Nathan Stein, Eileen Delaney, Leslie Lebowitz, William P. Nash, Caroline Silva, and Shira Maguen. 2009. Moral injury and moral repair in war veterans: A preliminary model and intervention strategy. *Clinical Psychology Reviews* 29: 695–706. [CrossRef] [PubMed]

Litz, Brett T., Leslie Lebowitz, Matt J. Gray, and William P. Nash. 2017. *Adaptive Disclosure: A New Treatment for Military Trauma, Loss, and Moral Injury*. New York: Guilford Publications.

Maguen, Shira, and Kristine Burkman. 2013. Combat-related killing: Expanding evidence-based treatments for PTSD. *Cognive and Behavioral Practice* 20: 476–79. [CrossRef]

Maguen, S., and Brett Litz. 2012. Moral injury in veterans of war. *PTSD Research Quarterly* 23: 1–6.

McKinney, Jessica M., Jameson K. Hirsch, and Peter C. Britton. 2017. PTSD symptoms and suicide risk in veterans: Serial indirect effects via depression and anger. *Journal of Affective Disorders* 214: 100–7. [CrossRef] [PubMed]

Nash, William P., Teresa L. Marino Carper, Mary Alice Mills, Teresa Au, Abigail Goldsmith, and Brett T. Litz. 2013. Psychometric evaluation of the Moral Injury Events Scale. *Military Medicine* 178: 646–52. [CrossRef] [PubMed]

Pargament, Kenneth I., Bruce W. Smith, Harold G. Koenig, and Lisa Perez. 1998. Patterns of positive and negative religious coping with major life stressors. *Journal for the Scientific Study of Religion* 37: 710–24. [CrossRef]

Pargament, Kenneth I., Harold G. Koenig, Nalini Tarakeshwar, and June Hahn. 2001. Religious struggle as a predictor of mortality among medically ill elderly patients: A two-year longitudinal study. *Archives of Internal Medicine* 161: 1881–85. [CrossRef] [PubMed]

Paul, Lisa A., Daniel F. Gros, Martha Strachan, Glenna Worsham, Edna B. Foa, and Ron Acierno. 2014. Prolonged exposure for guilt and shame in a veteran of Operation Iraqi Freedom. *American Journal of Psychotherapy* 68: 277–86. [PubMed]

Pearce, Michelle, Kerry Haynes, Natalia R. Rivera, and Harold G. Koenig. 2018. Spiritually-integrated cognitive processing therapy: A new treatment for moral injury in the setting of PTSD. *Global Advances in Health and Medicine* 7: 1–7. [CrossRef] [PubMed]

Pietrzak, Robert H., Risë B. Goldstein, Steven M. Southwick, and Bridget F. Grant. 2011. Prevalence and Axis I comorbidity of full and partial posttraumatic stress disorder in the United States: Results from Wave 2 of the National Epidemiologic Survey on Alcohol and Related Conditions. *Journal of Anxiety Disorders* 25: 456–65. [CrossRef] [PubMed]

Ramsawh, Holly J., Carol S. Fullerton, Holly B. Herberman Mash, Tsz Hin H. Ng, Ronald C. Kessler, Murray B. Stein, and Robert J. Ursano. 2014. Risk for suicidal behaviors associated with PTSD, depression, and their comorbidity in the US Army. *Journal of Affective Disorders* 161: 116–22. [CrossRef] [PubMed]

Rosenberg, Morris. 1965. *Society and the Adolescent Self-Image*. Princeton: Princeton University Press.

Shay, Jonathan. 1994. *Achilles in Vietnam: Combat Trauma and the Undoing of Character*. New York: Scribner.

Shay, Jonathan. 2014. Moral injury. *Psychoanalytic Psychology* 31: 182–91. [CrossRef]

Shrout, Patrick E., and Joseph L. Fleiss. 1979. Intraclass correlations: Uses in assessing rater reliability. *Psychological Bulletin* 86: 420–28. [CrossRef] [PubMed]

Steenkamp, Maria M., Brett T. Litz, Matt J. Gray, Leslie Lebowitz, William Nash, Lauren Conoscenti, Amy Amidon, and Ariel Lang. 2011. A brief exposure-based intervention for service members with PTSD. *Cognitive and Behavioral Practice* 18: 98–107. [CrossRef]

Steenkamp, Maria M., Brett T. Litz, Charles W. Hoge, and Charles R. Marmar. 2015. Psychotherapy for military-related PTSD: A review of randomized clinical trials. *JAMA* 314: 489–500. [CrossRef] [PubMed]

Steger, Michael F., Patricia Frazier, Shigehiro Oishi, and Matthew Kaler. 2006. The Meaning in Life Questionnaire: Assessing the presence of and search for meaning in life. *Journal of Counseling Psychology* 53: 80–93. [CrossRef]

Steinert, Christiane, Mareike Hofmann, Falk Leichsenring, and Johannes Kruse. 2015. The course of PTSD in naturalistic long-term studies: High variability of outcomes. A systematic review. *Nordic Journal of Psychiatry* 69: 483–96. [CrossRef] [PubMed]

Thompson, Laura Yamhure, Charles R. Snyder, Lesa Hoffman, Scott T. Michael, Heather N. Rasmussen, Laura S. Billings, Laura Heinze, Jason E. Neufeld, Hal S. Shorey, Jessica C. Roberts, and et al. 2005. Dispositional forgiveness of self, others, and situations. *Journal of Personality* 73: 313–59. [CrossRef] [PubMed]

Weathers, Frank W., Brett T. Litz, Terence M. Keane, Patrick A. Palmieri, Brian P. Marx, and Paula P. Schnurr. 2013. The PTSD Checklist for DSM-5 (PCL-5) (2013). Scale Available from the National Center for PTSD. Available online: www.ptsd.va.gov (accessed on 14 June 2017).

Witvliet, Charlotte V. O., Karl A. Phipps, M. E. Feldman, and Jean C. Beckham. 2004. Posttraumatic mental and physical health correlates of forgiveness and religious coping in military veterans. *Journal of Traumatic Stress* 17: 269–73. [CrossRef] [PubMed]

Worthington, Everett L., Jr., and Diane Langberg. 2012. Religious considerations and self-forgiveness in treating complex trauma and moral injury in present and former soldiers. *Journal of Psychology and Theology* 40: 274–88. [CrossRef]

Yamagishi, Toshio, and Midori Yamagishi. 1994. Trust and commitment in the United States and Japan. *Motivation and Emotion* 18: 129–66. [CrossRef]

Zigmond, Anthony S., and R. Philip Snaith. 1983. The hospital anxiety and depression scale. *Acta Psychiatrica Scandinavica* 67: 361–70. [CrossRef] [PubMed]

© 2018 by the author. Licensee MDPI, Basel, Switzerland. This article is an open access article distributed under the terms and conditions of the Creative Commons Attribution (CC BY) license (http://creativecommons.org/licenses/by/4.0/).

MDPI
St. Alban-Anlage 66
4052 Basel
Switzerland
Tel. +41 61 683 77 34
Fax +41 61 302 89 18
www.mdpi.com

Religions Editorial Office
E-mail: religions@mdpi.com
www.mdpi.com/journal/religions

CPSIA information can be obtained
at www.ICGtesting.com
Printed in the USA
LVHW071336100619
620724LV00031B/639/P

9 783038 979326